# GLOBAL PHILANTHROPY

Editors
Norine MacDonald QC + Luc Tayart de Borms
With a foreword by Stephan Schmidheiny

Published by: MF Publishing

Copyright © 2010 MF Publishing


MF Publishing
35 Grosvenor Gardens
London SW1W 0BS
United Kingdom

A catologue record for this book can be found from the British Library.

Editors: Norine MacDonald QC + Luc Tayart de Borms
Editorial Coordinators: Jane Francis + Alexander Jackson
Design by: Chris Freeman
Printed and bound in France by: Actuacolor


ISBN: 978 0 9564422 0 8

*The focus of this book is philanthropists and philanthopic organisations, but we want to take this opportunity to dedicate it to the many "unsung heroes" in these stories - the hardworking and dedicated staff of our own organisations and the organisations written about in these pages.*

*Without them neither this book nor the work which we all care about so much would exist. On our own behalf and on behalf of the other authors here, we send them our heartfelt thanks for all they do, and do so well, in the name of philanthropy around the world.*

# Contents

# FOREWORD

My two decades of involvement in philanthropy attest to my desire to use the success of my business ventures to encourage positive social change and innovative solutions to pressing global issues.

In the course of my philanthropy I have often observed that, across the globe there are individuals and organisations that in their own unique way are all doing the same thing – harnessing their human, organisational and financial resources to improve the societies in which they live.

Although as philanthropists we are often aware of each others' presence, perhaps we sometimes fail to truly understand and learn from the challenges and the opportunities which have arisen in the work of our colleagues around the world.

The present volume is a welcome amendment to this knowledge gap. Building on the previous work by the same editors, *European Philanthropy: A rich past, a promising future*, it lifts the exploration of philanthropic action, to look at philanthropy across the globe.

The papers presented in this volume enable us to take a first look at the common themes, and goals of philanthropy around the world – some, like mine, born out of a desire to use accumulated wealth from business to enhance society – others more traditional forms of giving, engrained in cultures for thousands of years, others part of a wider community desire to assist those in need.

The twenty-seven contributions by different authors – all active philanthropic players – on their work and experiences enable us to understand the deep-rooted common human desire to help people less fortunate than ourselves, but also allow us to see the diversity of philanthropic forms in different cultures. On each continent social entrepreneurs, businesses, and foundations are active in developing new approaches to social issues in their own unique cultural and historical context.

*Global Philanthropy* presents inspiring stories from across the globe, travelling from New Zealand through Australia, across Asia to Turkey, Russia and Europe and then on to Africa and Brazil, reaching its final destination in North America. This journey, although not exhaustive, ensures that a rich diversity of philanthropic voices is heard.

By documenting the similarities and yet the diversity of philanthropy across the world, *Global Philanthropy* will help those interested in philanthropy the world over understand their counterparts in different countries and cultures, encouraging them to learn from each other's experiences and to enrich their own practice.

The various chapters not only shed light on the different backgrounds and visions of philanthropists, they also provide insights into the different forms of philanthropic structures. These range from community trusts in New Zealand; Eastern European civil society groups; family-based foundations in the Gulf; European or North American networks of philanthropists to Chinese or Russian government-operated non-governmental organisations.

There is, in other words, no single template for a philanthropic structure, and there is no single spark which inspires a philanthropist. My own philanthropy has been inspired by, and closely aligned with, my activities as a businessman, seeking to create economic and social value for the societies in which I work. As the chapters in *Global Philanthropy* make clear, others have been motivated by religious impulses; by a cultural context which prioritises giving; or by their own personal, individual experiences.

As well as helping us to understand what inspires and shapes philanthropy, the book raises important questions for the reader. How *should* foundations or other philanthropic organisations operate? How can philanthropists leverage their resources most effectively? How can we build sustainable partnerships between countries or regions? How can we work best with the people that our philanthropy is aiming to help?

This volume cannot of course answer all of these questions, but by providing a snapshot of global philanthropy, it enables us all to draw inspiration and ideas from around the world and begin improving, and strengthening, our own philanthropic efforts.

Stephan Schmidheiny
16 February 2010

NORINE MACDONALD QC

# 1 Global Philanthropy
## THE EVOLVING MOSAIC OF GLOBAL PHILANTHROPY: "A PHILANTHROPIC THRILLER"

Editing *Global Philanthropy* has been an inspiring, thought-provoking journey of discovery.

The insights of our authors into their own experiences have revealed a deep-rooted and evolving mosaic of global philanthropy. Each philanthropic actor – whether an individual or a foundation – represents a "tile" in this evolving mosaic, with its own separate and unique character. Together they make up a rich and interconnected whole: the global community of philanthropists.

This book is intended to provide readers with inspiring accounts of global giving, but we also hope that it will provoke thoughts on the essence of philanthropy and the challenges it faces: what is the future of philanthropy? Can we expand the limits of our aspirations for the impact our work has on the world both today and in the future?

It does not claim to provide a comprehensive picture of all of the elements of global philanthropy today – there is always more to learn, for all of us. We are, however, confident that it can be viewed as a "philanthropic thriller" that will make readers eager to discover the history and future, and the challenges and opportunities of global philanthropy.

The chapters in this book were selected to illustrate the diversity of philanthropic approaches, following the sweep of the sun from the East to the West of the planet that we all share.

We hope that by sharing the knowledge that around the world there are others facing similar challenges and aiming for similar goals, we can help to strengthen the global community of philanthropists, and inspire them in their work. The narratives we present in this book illustrate that all of today's philanthropists have a common goal: to make the world a better place and to improve the lives of their fellow human beings.

There are many ways of describing this goal. In the course of editing *Global Philanthropy*, we have found a multitude of different terms for philanthropy, ranging from corporate social investment to the Indonesian practice of *gotong royong* (mutual aid), and from the Islamic almsgiving of *sadaqa* to capacity-building and social change.

Globalisation is making us all more inter-connected but this has not had as much impact on philanthropy as one might expect. We hope that this book will interest philanthropic actors in what is going on in other countries and regions and encourage collaboration between philanthropists, enabling them to pool their experience and knowledge. By doing so, we can unlock even greater potential for each of our own philanthropic initiatives.

## Philanthropy's three legged stool

To understand questions about the impact and the future of philanthropy we can visualise each philanthropic actor or institution as shaped and influenced by three pillars: cultural background, the administrative model it works within, and the social and political context in which it operates.

Firstly, different philanthropists and foundations are a product of their own **cultural framework**. Religious and cultural traditions have been a driving force behind charitable giving for thousands of years and these traditions survive and flourish today. As Rory Francisco-Tolentino explains, in the Asia-Pacific region, close family structures fuse with a wide variety of religions – Islam, Buddhism, Hinduism, and Christianity – to place philanthropy firmly in social life.

In traditional Maori culture, philanthropy is a way of being, forming part of the tight bonds which make up the community. Recognising this fact, and recognising the growing political and social visibility of Maori communities, philanthropists in New Zealand have begun to build bridges with indigenous non-profit organisations, enriching the evolution of the nation's philanthropic culture, as Jennifer Gill and Trevor Gray observe.

Philanthropy is not always so integrated into the bedrock of culture and society. Denis Tracey suggests, for instance, that Australia's history as a tightly controlled colony encouraged a dynamic that the government, not individuals, is responsible for solving social problems and as a result has created an environment that is not conducive to philanthropic giving.

Secondly, philanthropies are constructed within **various administrative approaches**. The US model of philanthropy, that sees foundations structured around the American tax code provisions, often relies on an endowment model – a structure often assumed in Western philanthropic literature to be the only or dominant form of structuring philanthropy.

However, philanthropy's rich history has created many different administrative models. The US model itself has come under pressure in recent years, with increasing calls for transparency and accountability, as Michael Seltzer and Karen Menichelli point out in their chapter. Vincent McGee recounts his rich experience in the diverse and innovative ways in which foundations can approach their giving, highlighting that there is no one single model.

China's state-driven push towards modernisation has strongly influenced the relatively recent development of the Chinese philanthropic sector. Although government presence is strong in the sector, the underlying aim remains to encourage and improve social and economic development.

Europe has its own rich and complex system of philanthropy, the product of a long tradition of privately funded foundations and strong systems of private social welfare. As Gerry Salole and Luc Tayart de Borms report, the European philanthropic sector is actually larger than that of the US, and is phenomenally diverse in its approach with many models based in centuries-old national traditions.[1]

One of the earliest models of giving - in Europe and elsewhere - was that of the religious foundation. Fernando Rossetti notes that in Brazil, from the arrival of European Christianity in the early sixteenth century, most philanthropy was driven and delivered by the Catholic Church, which operated schools, hospitals and other social services, funded by the aristocracy and royalty.

Islam, too, has driven the shape and structure of giving institutions. Shamsh Kassim-Lakha, Chair of the Board of the Pakistan Centre for Philanthropy highlights the Quranic influence behind many Islamic philanthropic structures, but also the strong social and community networks that exist in many Muslim societies. These structures have evolved from religious organisations, and many still rely on private donations to fund their humanitarian and social work.

The rich complexities of the Islamic world have led to many different administrative forms. As Namık Ceylanoğlu and Zeynep Meydanoğlu describe, foundations also have a long history in Turkey, playing an integral role in providing many public and social services including administering

---

1 In this publication, the decision was taken not to write about European philanthropy in detail, as it has already been extensively covered in the co-editors' 2008 book, *Philanthropy in Europe: A rich past, a promising future*. In *Global Philanthropy*, the European region is represented by two chapters: a glimpse into the challenges facing countries in Central and Eastern Europe in Rayna Gavrilova's chapter and a general overview of European philanthropy and an update on progress towards a European Foundation Statute in Gerry Salole and Luc Tayart de Borms' chapter.

property holdings during the Ottoman Empire, rapidly adapting to change during the Republican era, to finally emerge unscathed in the present day, ready to step up to the challenge of the new millennium and "experimenting like never before".

Thirdly, each philanthropist's priorities are determined by their own social and political context. Often this context can be profoundly personal. Australian philanthropist Steve Killelea often travels to conflict zones around the globe as part of his work with his own philanthropic organisation, The Charitable Foundation. In the course of his travels he began to think about the drivers of those conflicts and the potential solutions. The result was his Global Peace Index, which seeks to measure and support peace around the world.

In a similar way, Jim Balsillie, Co-CEO of Research in Motion - the inventors of the "BlackBerry" - used his business skills and experience to support institutes that aim to build Canada's strength in the field of international affairs, having noticed the weakness of private sector institutions which supported Canada's role in the world.

Likewise in Brazil, Maria Alice Setubal was inspired by her mother, Tide Setubal. Since 2005 she has worked with communities in São Paulo to contribute to local development and the empowerment of the community, encouraging social change and civic participation.

Laura Silber reveals that George Soros' experience of growing up as a European Jew during the Second World War inspired his Open Society Institute. He was determined to ensure that the post-communist states of Central and Eastern Europe would have the pluralism and democracy that was lacking from his own youth. And in Africa, TrustAfrica's Bhekinkosi Moyo underlines that his philanthropic work is influenced in a very personal way by his own life experiences moving from a recipient of philanthropy to a philanthropic actor himself.

These three pillars help us to frame the work of each philanthropic actor. For example Peter Cleaves' discussion of the Emirates Foundation shows that the specific cultural context in which the Foundation was created has resulted in work programmes which are national in focus but global in importance –education, social development, and environmental awareness.

## Many voices in the philanthropic choir

We can place the work of each philanthropist into an astonishingly broad range of different categories. These include **humanitarian philanthropy**, the provision of emergency relief to the needy in times of crisis. Such giving plays a strong role in many cultures, but particularly in Muslim philanthropy as Tariq Cheema observes in his chapter on the subject. The principle of *zakat*, or alms-giving, is one of the five pillars of the Islamic faith: it is both a profoundly spiritual and a social act.

Humanitarian philanthropy has a long history. In many societies, the tradition of giving stretches back thousands of years. Buddhist societies follow the practice of *thamtaan*, giving to those in need, and the Nepalese undertake the age-old custom of *muthi daan*, the provision of food – drawn from the family's own meal – to the poor and needy. Atallah Kuttab and Dina Sherif highlight the deep roots of the Arab region's culture of giving, inspired by the three monotheistic religions – Judaism, Christianity, and Islam – which emerged there.

Humanitarian philanthropy has deep roots in many societies, where it has evolved out of local charitable organisations. Ailing Zhuang's chapter on Chinese philanthropy illustrates the role that community and religious organisations played in traditional China in strengthening local networks of clan, family and hometown.

Olga Alexeeva sees Russian philanthropy as an "old new" phenomenon: integral to Russian society, where monasteries and churches were vital humanitarian instruments, it was declared "obsolete" by the communists but has since re-emerged, often dedicated once more to alleviating suffering.

In both China and Russia, philanthropy survived decades of major social and political change, in which philanthropists' motives were often questioned by the state. This only serves to highlight the continuing relevance of humanitarian philanthropy. Such philanthropy has provided an essential lifeline to many who are starving, destitute, and suffering. In an age of conflicts and severe social, economic, ecological and demographic change, humanitarian philanthropy remains vital.

**Cultural philanthropy**, like humanitarian philanthropy, has deep roots. Patronising the arts goes back to the classical era, and has been supported by rulers, governments and citizens ever since. Namık Ceylanoğlu and Zeynep Meydanoğlu note that in the Ottoman Empire, for instance, traditional foundations financially supported monuments, public baths, palaces and mosques, all as part of the rich tapestry of Ottoman social life.

We have recently seen the growth of socially conscious cultural philanthropy. This holds that art is itself a tool of social development, of reconciliation and of peace.

**Investment philanthropy** is an emerging strand of giving. It allows philanthropists to secure a "return" on their investment while doing "good" at the same time through investing in worthy causes. This radical new model has formed a bridge between the private and philanthropic sectors, and helped to erode the belief that capitalism or entrepreneurship and charity are incompatible.

Tamzin Ractliffe, in her discussion of the Global Federation of Social Investment Exchanges, explores the way the federation has applied business and investment principles to the philanthropic field. The aim is "creating wealth in ways that maximise social transformation and economic empowerment of all members of society while minimising environmental impacts". This has helped to harness the power of South Africa's thriving financial sector to its under-developed social welfare system.

Fernando Rossetti illuminates a similar experience in Brazil. The country's foundation and business leaders began meeting to establish ways in which both sectors could be more effective and more supportive of social development. In 1995, they created the Group of Institutes, Foundations and Enterprises (GIFE), which aims to strengthen the role which private social investment plays in addressing Brazil's social and economic challenges.

As part of this move towards cooperation between the private and philanthropic sectors, we have seen a growth in **corporate philanthropy**: philanthropic organisations which act as the charitable arm of large companies.

Driven by the understanding that companies have a responsibility to give something back, these foundations harness the resources and the reach of their corporate parents to make a real impact in the philanthropic world. In Japan, as Sujin Kwon relates, the Toyota Motor Corporation decided to set up a foundation in the 1970s to strengthen its links with society and to give something back.

Although corporate philanthropy is seen as new, in many parts of the world the link between private companies and charitable giving have deep roots. The Sir Ratan Tata Trust, for instance, was founded in 1919, as a way for the Indian industrialist to pass on his fortune "for the advancement of Education, Learning and Industry in all its branches" in his native country.

## Policy philanthropy: "Reorganising the fishing production chain"

Globalisation has created new opportunities and new challenges: it has linked the world together in unprecedented ways and created some areas of collateral damage.

Conflicts, poverty and migration remain issues of concern, but sit alongside newer issues such as the environment, climate change, mega-cities, and social and economic crises. Philanthropy's challenge is to find ways to address these problems, which are political in nature and global in scope, and require immediate responses and significant new thinking.

One way of facing today's challenges is through what we can call **"policy philanthropy"**. This seeks to encourage and advocate for change in the policies of governments, as well as international organisations. Unlike the public and private sectors, philanthropy can address policy issues which are controversial, political or seen as "untouchable" by others.

By virtue of this "neutral space" which it occupies, as well as its reputation for integrity and altruism, philanthropy can and should encourage and support change in the policies of governmental actors at all levels and those other sectors, such as business and regulatory authorities, that impact approaches to the issues of the day.

Policy philanthropy's unique value is that it encourages societies to make changes rather than philanthropy itself solving the problems. It is based on the concept found in the old Chinese proverb – "Give a man a fish and you feed him for a day. Teach a man to fish and you feed him for a lifetime" – and taking it to the next stage. As Fernando Rossetti observes in the Brazilian context, the evolution of philanthropy can be seen as having three stages: giving fish, then teaching to fish, and finally moving on to reorganising the fishing production chain.

Policy philanthropy aims to generate sustainable solutions. For instance, it seeks to address insurgencies in conflict zones not through short-term military measures but through strengthening social actors who can tackle the root causes of these insurgencies. Empowering civil society organisations, educators, and businessmen to change and develop their societies can help to create long-term peace and stability.

At the heart of this approach is a recognition that importing outside solutions may not always be the most effective way to address today's challenges. Policy philanthropy must be appropriate to the context which it aims to change. To do so, collaboration with philanthropic actors from different cultures can be key to identifying the right strategies and approaches.

## Fast tracking philanthropic collaboration

Today's challenges require coordinated, global action. Today's governments are unable or unwilling to provide the necessary leadership to tackle them, within the necessary time frames. At Copenhagen in December 2009, for instance, national governments were meant to overcome national interests to address climate change. But they did not. Where governments lead, the private sector often follows. Neither is living up to its full potential as drivers of the requisite policy changes.

The philanthropic sector has an essential role to play in pressurising governments and businesses. Before we can partner effectively with these sectors, we need to increase collaboration within our own community. Recognising the diversity of the mosaic of global philanthropy, and drawing on each others' experiences and traditions will help us to do that. In her chapter, Jane Wales recounts that the Global Philanthropy Forum was set up to provide a unique opportunity for philanthropists to network, share information with each other, and establish enduring partnerships, which is so critical when we look at the diverse and complex issues facing our world today.

Rayna Gavrilova outlines the real social change that such partnerships have helped to create in Central and Eastern Europe. The Trust for Civil Society in Central and Eastern Europe, although funded by six large international foundations (which may seem distant to the people on the ground), seeks to support the development of non-governmental organisations in these states, bridging the gap between foundations and grassroots actors.

Of course, partnerships with the private and public sectors are taking place already, although they have not always been as fruitful as they are now. The late 1990s and early 2000s were like the "Wild West" for public-private sector partnerships: there were few rules, few previous experiences to be guided by, and many "rough and tough" experiences. Public-private partnerships have evolved since then. Although they are often still challenging, they can be very rewarding.

Pooling resources and knowledge from all three sectors has led to institutions like the Global Fund to Fight AIDS, Tuberculosis and Malaria. Michael Madnick, who has worked with the Fund's Board, highlights just how innovative the Fund has been. Its actions to bring together actors from the private, public and philanthropic sectors were, as he remarks, "groundbreaking in their importance but also their complexity".

Collaboration – between sectors but also between philanthropists themselves - is only possible in the wake of the great tide of globalisation. The globalised world, which has contributed to so many problems and challenges, has also been a source of great opportunity. The philanthropic sector can take advantage of the possibilities for greater cooperation and information-sharing across borders that globalisation has created.

At the moment, collaboration between philanthropists in different parts of the world is still limited. Some regions which are united by a common language have taken advantage of this fact to strengthen their bonds, as Emílio Rui Vilar and Rui Hermenegildo Gonçalves tell us in their chapter on Portuguese-speaking Africa.

However, in most regions the mosaic has not yet been fully put together. Partly philanthropic cooperation is held back by the restrictions of national governments. The legal and regulatory frameworks which govern transnational philanthropy are ill matched. Establishing a European Foundation Statute, as Gerry Salole and Luc Tayart de Borms recommend, is an essential next step for Europe, and such work to ease global giving is needed urgently to maximise the sector's global impact.

The number and diversity of philanthropic cultures and priorities can also make cooperation difficult. It may be easier to work with others who share our culture and traditions, but it often lacks the spirit of enrichment and the increase in impact which cross-cultural partnerships can bring. Our differences should not be seen as obstacles to cooperation but as reasons for it. And these differences should be discussed, openly and frankly: we must be honest with ourselves and each other if we are to fulfil our role.

## A leadership role for philanthropy: "Generosity, creativity and bravery"

A leadership role for philanthropic actors on the issues of the day is critical: these are challenging times, and philanthropy must rise to the occasion. We must consistently pressurise all levels of government, business, and international agencies to do away with moribund approaches, and to wade out of their bureaucratic swamps. We must make the most of the fact that we have the ability to be innovative and flexible and to speak our minds.

The philanthropic sector must also recognise its duty to convene open debate. Philanthropists have the unique ability to bring together actors from all sectors and all walks of life, to discuss controversial and challenging issues that the public and the private sectors – for their own reasons – cannot, or will not, address.

By creating a space for discussion, the philanthropic sector can coordinate and be at the forefront of devising new responses to today's problems. It cannot simply follow the lead of governments and businesses, and it cannot blindly support the status quo. It must take on a leadership role of its own, and it must carry with it an agenda for deep-rooted inter-generational change.

This will unsettle some. Governments and businesses, and even other philanthropists, might be unwilling to support dramatic change, even when it is urgently required. Philanthropists support change but some may baulk at radical change.

But change is fundamental to our task; the guiding aim – improving society, reducing suffering – must always be kept in our minds. I am not criticising philanthropists here: I am urging them on. Olga Alexeeva depicts modern Russian philanthropy as "*an incredible mix of generosity and distrust, creativity and stereotypes, bravery and complacency*", and I would argue that this can be applied to all parts of the evolving mosaic of philanthropy.

In this regard, we should always remember that it is our responsibility, our duty, to work for the people at the bottom of societies. We have to use our privileged positions and our resources to provide them with a much-needed voice and to advocate for policies that address the issues they face in their daily lives.

At the outset I argued that the philanthropic community is a mosaic –

each beautiful tile coming together to form a global "picture from space" of generosity and commitment to others. We hope the stories contained in this volume will trigger an aspiration to strengthen and expand this intriguing mosaic, and to create an inter-generational kaleidoscope of philanthropic leadership committed to these three ideals of "generosity, creativity and bravery".

JENNIFER GILL AND TREVOR GRAY

# 2 Aotearoa New Zealand

## INNOVATION IN PHILANTHROPY DOWNUNDER

This chapter reflects a discussion on the uniqueness of philanthropy and its role in Aotearoa/New Zealand. The discussion took place between Jennifer Gill, chief executive officer of the ASB Community Trust, and Trevor Gray, manager of the Tindall Foundation. Both organisations are based in Auckland, New Zealand. Seeing ourselves as a pragmatic and practical people, the definition of "innovation" most appropriate to New Zealand philanthropy would probably best be that expressed by recent visitor Geoff Mulgan, from the Young Foundation in Great Britain:

*"Innovation is often given complex definitions.*
*We prefer the simple one: 'new ideas that work.'"*[1]

### Background of philanthropy in New Zealand

New Zealand, or Aotearoa as it is known in Māori, with a population of just over four million people, has a history of government-led social innovation and of a relatively small private philanthropic sector. New Zealand was one of the last countries to be colonised by the British, and with the signing of the Treaty of Waitangi in 1840 by representatives of Queen Victoria and the indigenous people, the Māori, the foundations of the modern state were established.

---

1   Mulgan, G (2006) *Social Silicon Valleys: A Manifesto for Social Innovation,* Young Foundation. Cited in Kasper, G and Clohesy, S (2008) *Intentional Innovation,* W.K. Kellogg Foundation

New Zealand has an unusual philanthropic profile. The sector comprises a small but strategic group of family foundations with a history of supporting social innovation; an indigenous population, the Māori, who are increasingly players in the philanthropic world; and a significant and unique group of community and energy trusts established two decades ago from the sale of state-owned energy assets and the trustee savings banks that were established by the early Scottish settlers over 160 years ago.

This discussion of philanthropy in this chapter must be set in the context of a small, remote, relatively young democracy with a significant history of social innovation. In 1893 New Zealand was the first country to enfranchise all women, having enfranchised Māori men in 1867.[2] In 1938 the then Labour Prime Minister Michael Joseph Savage introduced the welfare state "for the first time to provide, as generously as possible, for all persons who have been deprived of the power to obtain a reasonable livelihood through age, illness, unemployment, widowhood or other misfortune".[3]

While these are but a few examples of a steady stream of New Zealand's government-led social reforms, what is less well documented and understood is the role of "philanthropy" in the history of social innovation in this country.

From the earliest days of the colony, trusts and foundations were established as early settlers accumulated wealth and property. Sir John Logan Campbell, the "undisputed father of the city (Auckland)",[4] Thomas John Macarthy in Wellington and others settled significant endowed trusts which endure today. However, New Zealand's early post-European settlement history was not generally conducive to the growth of significant private philanthropy. Unlike other colonies, such as Australia and the United States (US), New Zealand did not experience an industrial boom in the late nineteenth century and therefore did not benefit from a consequent growth of a wealthy industrial elite amassing personal fortune, who in turn could have created grant-making foundations.[5]

Historian James Belich in his book Making Peoples[6] tells us that "New Zealand was settled by British immigrants eager to begin life in a "better Britain", one that was not bounded by traditional British concepts of class. A society where one could own land and with hard work, prosper.

Margaret Tennant in *Paupers and Providers* explores the rise of

---

2  This compares with Australia when Aboriginal people were enfranchised in 1967

3  Quoted in Gustafson, B (1986) From *the Cradle to the Grave: A Biography of Michael Joseph Savage*, Auckland: Reed Methuen

4  Reidy, J (2008) *Te Kaitiaki o te Putea, The History of the ASB Community Trust 1998-2008*, Auckland: ASB Community Trust

5  Gill, J and McMains, T (2007) "Funding Community Development" in Chile, L (ed) *Community Development Practice in New Zealand*, Auckland: AUT University (pp 285-312)

6  Belich, J (1996) *Making Peoples*, Auckland: Allen Lane (pp 298-312)

the welfare state in New Zealand from the 1860s when most provincial governments were providing "relief" in the form of short term financial assistance to impoverished migrants. Government assistance or "charitable aid" as it came to be called was distinguished from private and religious philanthropy, which was often called "benevolence".[7]

By the late nineteenth century New Zealand was seen as a "social laboratory". Settlers had hopes of a "new society free from poverty and want, public forms of welfare made an early appearance in the colony." Tennant describes charitable aid as "a distinctive colonial euphemism, drawing on the prestige of voluntary charity while avoiding mention of the Poor Law". The early colonial governments of both Australia and New Zealand "wanted to avoid a welfare system that would reflect badly on the new colony". Right from the beginning in New Zealand, a central government subsidy was added to funds raised locally through the rating system and these were combined with voluntary donations in a "way not envisaged in the 'old country'".[8]

The establishment of the welfare state in New Zealand early in the twentieth century meant, therefore, that the provision of health, education and welfare services was perceived by both the government and the people as a government responsibility right through the twentieth and into the twenty-first century, and the citizenry were taxed accordingly.

## Current size and forms of philanthropy in New Zealand[9]

Philanthropy and non-government funding continues to be an important component of this socially-experimental milieu.

Research commissioned from Business and Economic Research Ltd (BERL)[10] by Philanthropy New Zealand in 2006 estimated that individual New Zealanders and non-government organisations gave 1.27 billion New Zealand dollars (NZD) to charities and other community purposes in 2006, which equates to 0.81 percent of gross domestic product (GDP). This compares with Australia at 0.68 percent and the United States at 1.6 percent. Total giving by trusts and foundations in New Zealand in 2006 was estimated by BERL at 742.1 million NZD. Unless otherwise stated, this 2006 research has provided the data on giving included in this chapter.

---

7   Tennant, M (1989) *Paupers and Providers,* Wellington: Allen and Unwin (p1)

8   Ibid (p2)

9   Under their definition of "philanthropy" the authors have determined not to include the significant gaming and national lottery funding that is distributed to charities and community causes in New Zealand.

10   Business and Economic Research Ltd (2007) *Giving New Zealand, Philanthropic Funding 2006,* Wellington: Philanthropy New Zealand

Prior to 1990 and the establishment of the New Zealand Association of Philanthropic Trusts (now known as Philanthropy New Zealand) as a national coordinating body, trusts and foundations in New Zealand were small and operated largely independently of each other. The sector was dominated by trusts and foundations administered by trustee companies, and by a few well-established family trusts such as the J R McKenzie Trust, the Todd Foundation and the Sutherland Self Help Trust.

By 2009 the original twenty members of Philanthropy New Zealand (PNZ) had grown to one hundred. PNZ members now include corporate trusts and foundations, statutory grant-making trusts created through the sale of community banks and energy utilities, and a few new and innovative family foundations including the Tindall Foundation and the Wayne Francis Charitable Trust. Annual distributions by family trusts and foundations had risen from the 28 million NZD estimated by PNZ[11] in 1991 to the 353.7 million NZD recorded by BERL in 2006.[12]

In 2002 PNZ commissioned a study on funding flows to the non-profit, non-government sector. This study estimated total giving at 1.63 billion NZD[13] including philanthropic, government and corporate funding. The importance of this research was its identification of the large contribution that continues to be made by the state to the provision of welfare and social services in contemporary New Zealand.

In its 2006 report to PNZ, BERL reported that the New Zealand Government spent the equivalent of 22.5 percent of GDP on health, welfare and education. This contrasts with other nations where philanthropy may play a greater role in the funding of such services.

The oldest form of philanthropy in New Zealand consists of a group of family trusts and foundations, some established in the late nineteenth century. These have been joined more recently by statutory trusts established from the sale of trustee savings banks and energy companies, a small number of community foundations, growth in corporate philanthropy, some venture philanthropy and a growing number of Māori-funded philanthropic initiatives.

---

11  Gray, A (1991) *The Philanthropic Sector in New Zealand,* Wellington: New Zealand Association of Philanthropic Trusts

12  Sources of Giving (in New Zealand dollars) as outlined by BERL; Family Trusts 115,505,000 / Higher Education Institutions 9,207,000 / Community Trusts 111,832,000 / Energy Trusts 116,304,000 / Licensing Trusts 6,360,000 / Gaming Machine Societies 272,000,000, Lottery Grants Board 110,937,000. Total 742,145,000. All figures are in NZD, at the time of writing (27 July 2009), NZD = 0.4535 euros

13  Robinson, D and Hanley, P (2002) *Funding New Zealand*, Wellington: Philanthropy New Zealand

## Family trusts and foundations

Family trusts and foundations, not directly established by specific statute, are the earliest and most enduring form of philanthropy in New Zealand.

A majority of family trusts in New Zealand were established in the first half of the twentieth century, many based on wealth acquired in the retail sector. The life stories of these early New Zealand philanthropists are classic "rags to riches" stories. Families often experienced poverty and hardship in their early lives and they decided, later in life, to share their wealth with those they perceived as being less fortunate than themselves.

Sir John McKenzie, for example, was New Zealand's richest man in 1950 when he established the J R McKenzie Trust. McKenzie was a retailer who had started his life in business with a single haberdashery shop in Melbourne, Australia, in 1905.

At the time of McKenzie's death in 1955, the company had over seventy stores throughout New Zealand and was both importing and manufacturing goods in New Zealand. He had established a number of trusts in his lifetime, the largest of which, the J R McKenzie Trust,[14] was established in 1940 with an initial capital base of 300,000 pounds (the pound was currency until 1967 before being replaced by the dollar). It was later expanded to one million New Zealand pounds, making it the largest trust in Australasia at that time.[15]

McKenzie's son, Roy, continued the family tradition, expanding holdings in the family company Rangatira Ltd, to include hotels, fishing, food production and manufacturing. Roy (later Sir Roy) also applied his entrepreneurial talents to the community by providing financial backing for social movements from both his personal fortune and a number of trusts and foundations that he and his father had established. He supported the establishment of the Hospice movement, Outward Bound, the Women's Refuge movement and a range of innovative services for children with disabilities and special needs.

The newest and currently most significant family trust in New Zealand is the Tindall Foundation established by Sir Stephen Tindall, founder of The Warehouse chain of retail discount stores. These "big red sheds" have also, in a reverse of the McKenzie story, had a period of operating in Australia. As well as being very large, by New Zealand standards, the Tindall Foundation is proving to be the most innovative and pro-active foundation in New Zealand at present, with an estimated 10 million NZD

---

14   J R McKenzie Trust [online] [accessed 11 February 2010]. Available from the World Wide Web: http://www.jrmckenzie.org.nz/

15   Gill, "J M McKenzie, John Robert Hugh 1876 - 1955" *Dictionary of New Zealand Biography,* [online], available from the World Wide Web: http://www.dnzb.govt.nz/

per annum set aside for both charitable and innovative programmes in the community. This makes the Tindall Foundation[16] one of the largest family foundations in Australasia.

Other more recent private foundations include those established separately by TradeMe (New Zealand's EBay) founder Sam Morgan and his father Gareth, both of which continue the innovation focus and the link to trading as the source of initial wealth.

Half of all non-statutory trusts in New Zealand are administered through trustee companies such as the Public Trust, Tower, Perpetual Trustees and the New Zealand Guardian Trust. These companies are responsible for managing significant assets held in various forms of trusts, including philanthropic trusts. These companies manage some very large bequests such as the Sir John Logan Campbell Residuary Estate in Auckland and the T G Macarthy Trust in Wellington.

## Corporate philanthropy

Corporate or company trusts are recent arrivals on the New Zealand philanthropic scene and BERL estimated that they distribute 89 million NZD or 7 percent of the total philanthropic funding in New Zealand annually. Although relatively small-scale, some of New Zealand's more innovative philanthropy is being conducted by the Vodafone New Zealand Foundation, through empowering youth to address the issues that they face.

The Foundation manages two core programmes on an annual basis: the Grant Making Programme and the World of Difference Programme. The aim of both programmes is to encourage positive and healthy outcomes for New Zealanders aged twelve to twenty-four. In 2008 the Foundation's World of Difference programme won the Prime Minister's Social Heroes Award.[17]

## Community foundations

Community foundations are growing rapidly in the US, Europe, Australia and elsewhere. While the movement is very much in its fledgling stages, the Acorn Foundation[18] has proven this concept can work in New Zealand. It is currently building a capital base while successfully complementing the work of longer established grant-makers in its Bay of Plenty community.

---

16  *Tindall Foundation* [online] [accessed 11 February 2010]. Available from the World Wide Web: http://www.tindall.org.nz/

17  *Vodafone New Zealand Foundation* [online] [accessed 22 July 2009]. Available from the World Wide Web: http://foundation.vodafone.co.nz

18  *Acorn Foundation* [online] [accessed 11 February 2010]. Available from the World Wide Web: http://www.acornfoundation.co.nz/

## Statutory trusts

According to academic Peter McKinlay, who has written extensively on the period of major structural reform in New Zealand in the 1980s and 1990s, over 5 billion NZD is currently held on behalf of New Zealand consumers and communities in a series of regionally based community trusts. Shortly after establishment in 1998 this represented 1,400 NZD for each New Zealand resident.[19] These distributive statutory trusts are the result of the restructuring of New Zealand's trustee savings banks and electricity distributors. They effectively distribute income generated from "community capital", (assets held in perpetuity, for designated communities or groups of consumers). Total distribution by the community and energy trusts was recorded by BERL as 228.1 million NZD in 2006.

Continuing a tradition of government-led social reform, these trusts have their genesis in the restructuring of the New Zealand economy that began with the election of a Labour government in 1984. The government began a programme of broad social and economic reform that has transformed the country.

*Traditionally, successive New Zealand Governments accepted as responsibility not just to redistribute income and opportunities as between individuals but also to underwrite the prosperity of different regions, industry sectors or institutions. One of the main drivers for the reform process which began in 1984 was the recognition that government interventions, intended to ensure equity of outcomes, quite frequently had the opposite effect and collectively had played major role in New Zealand's relatively poor economic performance.[20]*

## Community trusts

The New Zealand system of regional trustee savings banks, first established by the Scottish settlers in 1847, had a long-established history of returning profits to their local community through grants to charitable organisations.

The purpose of the Wellington Savings Bank was said by the President of the Bank's Board of Trustees in 1964 to be "to encourage thrift in its area and to distribute its profits to local charitable, cultural and educational organisations".[21] These banks had no shareholders or "owners" and no independent capital. They operated instead under a government guarantee on deposits and were subject to regulation on the nature of their investments.

19   McKinlay, P (1999) *Public Ownership and the Community*, Wellington: Institute of Policy Studies, Victoria University of Wellington (p1)

20   Ibid

21   Manson, K and Manson, H (2001) *Making a Difference a History of the Community Trust of Wellington*, Wellington: The Community Trust of Wellington

The reforms of the late 1980s saw the government divesting itself of the ownership of a number of publicly owned enterprises: Air New Zealand, the New Zealand Post Office and New Zealand Railways to name a few. It was inevitable that the regional trustee savings banks would also come under scrutiny. The Government's objective was to put an end to the government guarantee, which it saw as presenting a significant financial risk, and to encourage the restructuring of what was seen to be a group of relatively weak and potentially non-viable banks. The immediate means of dealing with this problem was thought to be restructuring the banks as limited liability companies. Following the passage of The Community Trust Act 1998, twelve community trusts were established. These trusts were deemed to be the "owners" of the Banks and were instructed by the government of the day to sell them.

Three banks emerged from this process: the ASB Bank (a member of the Commonwealth Bank of Australia Group), Westpac Trust (an amalgamation of the Australian bank Westpac and the remaining trustee savings banks) and the TSB, which remains in the sole ownership of the TSB Community Trust. As the sole shareholder of TSB Bank, each year the Trust receives a dividend from the bank that it can distribute towards "charitable, cultural, philanthropic, recreational and other purposes beneficial to the community, principally in Taranaki". TSB continues to operate as a strongly performing regional bank.

McKinlay identified the following as the distinctive aspects of the community trusts:

- The trust deed for each trust followed a standard format provided by the government and each initial trust deed required the approval of the Minister of Finance.
- Each trust was to hold its income and capital on trust to be applied for charitable, cultural, philanthropic, recreational and other activities that are beneficial to the community, principally in the geographic area defined for each trust.
- Each trust is a perpetual trust.
- Trustees are appointed by the Minister of Finance.
- Public accountability was to be by way of: the publication of annual audited accounts in local newspapers, the publication of a list of donations, and the holding of a meeting every year open to members of the public, at which the public has the opportunity to put questions to the trustees, but no right to pass any resolutions binding on them .
- There is no formal requirement on either the trusts or the Minister of Finance, when appointing trustees or to consult with the public either about the appointment of trustees or for the trusts to consult with community about the areas of activity that they fund.

New Zealand and Italy are the only two countries in world with trusts of this nature. An analysis of the history and role of these trusts can be found in Community Trusts in New Zealand, a report produced in April 2002 by the former Secretary of the New Zealand Treasury, Graham Scott.[22]

The largest grant-making trusts in New Zealand currently fall into this category. The statutory trusts vary in size from region to region, the initial size of the capital of each regional trust being determined by the size of the trust bank in the region before the sale of the bank. At 31 March 2008 the ASB Community Trust had a corpus of 1.1 billion NZD and an annual distribution of 43.6 million NZD in a region with a population of 1.4 million. By comparison the Wellington Community Trust had assets of 42.6 million NZD and an annual distribution of 1.3 million NZD for a population of 410,000.

In 2006 BERL calculated giving by the twelve combined community trusts at 111.8 million NZD, slightly less than giving by the fourteen family trusts and foundations who participated in the study, at 115.5 million NZD and the nine energy trusts at 116.3 million NZD.

## Energy trusts

Twenty-eight energy trusts resulted from the restructuring of the distribution sector of the New Zealand electricity industry. Prior to 1990 the sector comprised twenty-one municipal electricity departments that were owned and operated by local authorities, thirty-eight electric power boards and one government operated electricity supply authority.

> The Central Lakes Trust was established to grant funds for community charitable purposes. The fund was created in November 2000 when the Otago Central Electric Power Board bestowed the Central Lakes Trust with assets valued at 155 million dollars. The Trust has had a significant impact on many community groups in the Otago Southland area since its inception, having approved grants totalling almost 39 million dollars in the seven years to 31 March 2008
>
> Although the Trust now has a diversified portfolio, Central Lakes Trust[23] retains full ownership of Pioneer Generation Limited who own, operate and maintain twelve power stations throughout Central Otago and Southland.

---

22  Scott, G (2002) *Community Trusts in New Zealand*, Wellington: Southern Cross International

23  *Central Lakes Trust* [online] [accessed 11 February 2010] Available from the World Wide Web: http://www.centrallakestrust.org.nz/

The 1984-1990 Labour government passed legislation modelled on the trustee savings bank legislation, which would have seen the creation of another group of community trusts. In 1990 the Labour government lost office and the incoming national government opted instead to put in place a process under which each individual supply authority would determine its future ownership structure. This resulted in some parts of the country in the sale of shares in the company, in some to a "share give away" to local consumers, and in some to the creation of locally focussed grant-making trusts.

Consequently there is great variety between the models that have developed at a local level. A majority of the energy trusts have opted to apply all or part of their income in the form of a rebate to each household in their region. Some, however, have launched significant grant-making programs, or decided to form non-charitable trusts with a focus on regional economic development, promotion of energy efficiency and conservation and projects related to the energy industry rather than the community or not-for-profit sector.

The trustees of the energy trusts have found themselves the guardians of substantial assets held in the name of the community. Not only do the majority of trusts have to ensure that their community is provided with energy in the form of gas and/or electricity, but they also have complex investment and profit distribution decisions to make. In contrast with the community trusts derived from banking, the energy trusts do not have a common set of powers of investment and distribution because the establishing authorities were given significant autonomy in determining the future ownership structure for the new energy companies.

Energy trusts' granting policies vary significantly, in part because unlike the community (bank) trusts they are not standardised in terms of their potential beneficiaries.

The differences between the energy trusts and the community trusts are significant as the trustees of the community trusts are appointed by the government of the day with no community input. Local energy consumers elect trustees every three years. The trustees of the energy trusts are running multi-million dollar energy supply industries with their performance measured through the ballot box every three years.

## Māori and philanthropy

A number of Māori have argued recently that philanthropy is inherent in *Māoritanga* (the Māori way of living). Historically in Māori society there is an understanding of the existence of a special relationship between a giver and a receiver: giving is an expression of love or *aroha* and it is also one of *māna* or prestige. The giver and the receiver are then tied into a relationship bound by *utu* or reciprocity where the giver will have enhanced his or her *māna* by giving.

New Zealand journalist, Carol Archie, explored Māori concepts of philanthropy in an article in Philanthropy New Zealand's Newsletter in 2001. She wrote:

*"After a successful day's fishing or hunting in traditional Māori society the bounty was shared around with everyone. Stories abound of the fisherman or hunter who drops off so much of his catch to his whanau (family) on the way home that he has none left for himself. Such behaviour is admired because it is an expression of aroha — and by giving, one increases one's māna ... In the communal life of whanau and hapu, Māori had highly developed customs for giving and sharing with others. However the communal responsibility would appear to be very different from the Western tradition of an individual philanthropist giving money or goods with disinterest (and usually to strangers), preferably anonymously, for the wider public benefit ... In traditional Māori society utu, or reciprocity, was a ruling principle. Life was based on a continual shift of debt and obligation ... Sometimes a debt might be repaid generations later ... for Māori, a special relationship was understood between the giver and the receiver. Giving was an expression, not just of aroha or love but of māna. Māna is the spiritual power and authority held by individuals and groups which can be increased by giving ..."[24]*

Māori are an increasingly important political force in New Zealand. The 2006 Census recorded 565,329 Māori, representing 15 percent of the population. In formal representation in the New Zealand Parliament, Māori comprise 15.9 percent of MPs. Informally, in community organisations, government departments and as holders of significant assets as a result of treaty settlements, Māori are major participants in all aspects of New Zealand society, including a significant number appointed by the government as trustees of community trusts.

In recognition of the significant loss of land that occurred during European settlement and in recognition of the Treaty of Waitangi, signed by Māori and representatives of the British Crown in 1840, recent settlements have seen significant tracts of publicly owned land returned to Māori tribes along with cash settlements amounting to billions of dollars.

---

24  Archie, C (2001) "Maori Concepts of Philanthropy" *New Zealand Philanthropy*, Volume 2 Number 25, October 2001

In 1998 after one hundred and fifty years of negotiation the Ngāi Tahu, the people of Te Waipounamu, (the South Island), received a cash settlement of 170 million NZD and significant landholdings. This tribal group of thirty thousand now manages assets of 368 million NZD and is developing enterprises in property, fisheries, tourism and philanthropy. The Ngāi Tahu Fund is a key part of Ngāi Tahu's 2025 Strategy to revitalise culture and give rūnanga (tribal authority) and whānau (family) greater opportunities. The fund has allocated over 3.2 million NZD since its inception in October 2005, aiming to "Strengthen Ngāi Tahu cultural excellence through sustainability, innovation and tenacity".[25]

## Philanthropic innovation in New Zealand

Worldwide philanthropy is often associated with funding the innovative edge of social, cultural and environmental opportunities. In fact philanthropists have been charged with ensuring this is the only space they occupy. Partly to justify the tax diverted from the public purse, but also because they have a responsibility to do so, given the relative freedom from constraints they enjoy in comparison with public and other forms of funding. Indeed Fleishman,[26] Porter and Kramer[27] and many others exhort philanthropy to only engage in "strategic", "effective" "systems-change" and more recently "venture" philanthropy which tackles the cause rather than the symptoms of issues, in innovative and sometimes risky ways.

Limiting the definition of innovation to those that seek to change whole systems as a way of dealing with the causes of social, educational, health and environmental issues narrows down even further the opportunities for philanthropy, as indicated by Michael Learner in a powerful article published in Alliance in 2006:

> "Paul Ylvisaker, one of the most eminent thinkers in American philanthropy, once acutely suggested that there were three types of philanthropy: charity, patronage, and systems-change philanthropy. Most sophisticated funders eschew charity completely. They accept as reasonable, to varying degrees, patronage of the arts and education and

25 *Ngāi Tahu Fund Allocations* [online] [Accessed on 27 July 2009]. Available from the World Wide Web: http://www.ngaitahu.iwi.nz/Ngai-Tahu-Whanui/Ngai-Tahu-Fund/FundingAllocations.php

26 Fleishman, J.L (2007) *The Foundation: A Great American Secret – How Private Wealth is Changing the World,* New York: Public Affairs Books

27 Porter, M and Kramer, M (1999) "Philanthropy's New Agenda – Creating Value", *Harvard Business Review,* November-December 1999

*awards of various kinds. But their metier is systems-change philanthropy – philanthropy designed to change the way social systems work."[28]*

Learner's following exposition of the "shadow" of US philanthropy in general, and systems-change philanthropy and its practitioners in particular, makes sobering reading as he deconstructs the issues and outcomes he associates with this very focused form of giving.

However, systems-change innovations still appeal as the holy grail of philanthropy. Especially to those from worlds other than where the problems lie, those impatient for solutions to chronic issues, or those fatigued by providing constant support to charitable initiatives only to see symptoms remain static or increase.

This is no different in New Zealand. But, because of the unique assemblage of philanthropic players here, who becomes involved in supporting systems-change innovation and how it is implemented by funders most definitely is. While similarities are more with the European than the US philanthropic environment (strong social contract with government, history of egalitarianism, a welfare state, some government-initiated innovation), the dominance of distributive philanthropy (i.e. distributors of community capital as opposed to private capital) in New Zealand compared to genuine private philanthropy appears to distort this picture in interesting ways.

While the small size of the country's population and relatively simple governance structures make it somewhat easier to generate social innovations compared to larger countries with federal arrangements, the level of social innovation may not be as great as the relatively high per capita availability of funding broadly defined here as "philanthropic" might indicate.

## Who funds innovation in New Zealand?

Despite the apparent abundance of philanthropic funding available in New Zealand, support for truly innovative practice is available from relatively few sources. This pool of funding is always under strain and limits the amount of innovation that can be sustained when compared to other countries with larger and less risk-averse philanthropic sectors.

With New Zealand's unusual mix of dominant distributive funders, an interesting challenge exists regarding the ability and appetite of each type of funder to support innovative initiatives.

***Family Foundations*** generally can and do display what would be seen internationally as a moderate interest in supporting innovation and some

---

28   Learner, M (2006) "Light and shadow in organized philanthropy", *Alliance*, December 2006 [online] [Accessed 27 July 2009]. Available from the World Wide Web: http://www. alliancemagazine.org/en/content/light-and-shadow-organized-philanthropy

tolerance for risk, but they have limited resources. The Tindall, McKenzie, Todd and Wayne Francis trusts are increasingly working collaboratively to address some of the fundamental issues facing our society such as climate change and have historically had some success in influencing public policy in the fields of waste management, education and healthcare. Newer entrants to this grouping like the Morgan Family Charitable Foundation[29] also favour a strong venture philanthropy approach to their giving.

*Community Trusts* in some regions are major funders but they are primarily distributive, with a very broad focus but a limited amount of support for truly systems-change innovation. The Southland Zero Fees Scheme and the ASB Community Trust Maori and Pasifika Education Initiative discussed below are two examples of innovative and risky projects, but these are the exception rather than the rule for community trusts.

*Energy Trusts* are even more diverse and generally less engaged with innovative, systems-change initiatives. A few have supported education-based programmes (e.g. Top Energy and Northpower support for Education for Enterprise programmes in Northland),[30] while others have supported innovative work in research into the health benefits of retrofitting older housing stock and energy conservation. Given that many simply distribute their profits as annual consumer rebates, the ability of this group to make major contributions to the innovation funding pool is limited.

## Recent developments in innovative philanthropy

New Zealand trusts and foundations have supported a range of innovations in the fields of education, affordable housing, waste management and climate change, capacity building and social entrepreneurship. The provision of early funding for a passionate individual, or group, with a novel idea or way of dealing with a cause of disadvantage has often been the hallmark of this approach, as the following case studies of recently funded innovative initiatives demonstrate.

### The zero fees scheme

Each community trust has its own unique regional response to local issues. In 2000 the Community Trust of Southland,[31] established from the sale of the Southland Savings Bank, was approached by the local polytechnic

---

29  *Morgan Family Foundation* [online] [accessed 11 February 2010]. Available from the World Wide Web:http://www.morgancharity.com/

30  Top Energy *Sponsorship* [online] [accessed 27 July 2009]. Available from the World Wide Web: http://www.topenergy.co.nz/sponsorship/index.htm

31  *Community Trust of Southland* [online] [accessed 11 February 2010]. Available from the World Wide Web: http://www.ctos.org.nz/

with a proposal to provide free higher education in the region. The Trust, in partnership with local licensing trusts, local authorities and local businesses established a fund totalling 7.25 million NZD. This was then committed to the Southland Institute of Technology (SIT) over a three-year period to pay course fees for any student, from anywhere in New Zealand, enrolling in an approved course at SIT. This initiative increased student numbers at SIT by 55 percent in the first year of the programme.

After eighteen months, enrolments at SIT passed the three thousand student enrolment threshold required to make the scheme self-funding. Nine years later the scheme continues to be self-sustaining. SIT is no longer reliant on philanthropic funding, but is able to generate its own income from central government student fee subsidies. New Zealand economists Infometrics Ltd have estimated that the local Southland economy has grown by approximately 25 million NZD since the inception of the scheme.[32]

## Māori and Pasifika educational initiative

In 2006 the Trustees of another savings bank trust, the ASB Community Trust, identified and agreed to address a major national issue: the low educational achievement of young Māori and Pacific Island (Pasifika) students in the New Zealand education system.

The Trust then set about using a community consultation model to contextualise and define the issue and to look for culturally appropriate, community-based,[33] innovative responses. Trustees agreed to allocate 20 million NZD to support a process of problem identification with the aim of supporting a limited number of evidence based interventions over five years. Trustees recognised that there is a high level of risk in this and have to date identified seven community organisations with whom they are working very closely, developing governance and management capacity in preparation for programme delivery.

The project began in 2005 with a *hui* or meeting called by the Trust's chair, himself an eminent Māori leader. A group of some thirty Māori academics, community leaders and educators were invited to assist the Trust to work in a culturally appropriate way to both define and agree upon the issues and work towards solutions. A parallel consultation process was initiated with a group of Pasifika community leaders.

After about eighteen months the two groups began meeting and together developed an agreed process for both calling for and selecting the final projects. Those projects were finally recommended to the board of the ASB Community Trust for funding early in 2009.

---

32  Prendergast, J (2009) "Hair Brained Philanthropy Turns Around Ailing New Zealand Region", *Fundraising and Philanthropy Australasia*, Issue 18 April 2009

33  *ASB Community Trust* [online] [accessed 11 February 2010]. Available from the World Wide Web: http://www.asbcommunitytrust.org.nz/

More than three hundred expressions of interest were received for this project and over eighteen months these were whittled down to seven that will receive full funding over the next five years.

The project has been fully resourced by the Trust and there is a commitment to fully funding all aspects of the successful projects, including documentation and evaluation. The ultimate aim is to take the results to government, the educational and academic community and policy makers and to discuss with them ways in which educational policies and practices could be addressed to improve educational outcomes for Māori and Pasifika in Aotearoa/New Zealand.

Projects approved for funding to date have included: a leadership academy for Māori boys drawing on Tikanga Māori (Māori custom) and the values of the Māori Battalion; a mentoring programme for Pasifika boys initiated by the steel industry; governance and management training for Pasifika providers of early childhood education services to Pasifika children; and working with the local school in developing a support programme for Māori *whanau* (families) in a low income neighbourhood.[34]

## New Zealand Housing Foundation (NZHF) affordable housing

As with most developed countries, New Zealand has a group of people who fall just below the threshold of being able to purchase their first home through mainstream means. These are not sub-prime borrowers, but rather those who are able to pay weekly rent not quite equivalent to what would be required to service a mortgage and thus purchase a home, and/or who have not been able to save enough for a loan deposit. Without some tweaking of the system, this group are consigned to be permanent renters, which is not the preferred state for families in New Zealand. Home ownership enhances their ability to develop an asset base, reduces their transience and overall improves the life chances for themselves and their children. This is the group the New Zealand Housing Foundation (NZHF)[35] seeks to help become homeowners through innovative financing arrangements. Initial support for NZHF was primarily from the Tindall Foundation innovation donations pool, with additional funding from the ASB Community Trust, Housing New Zealand and mainstream banks.

The mix of shared equity, shared ownership, rent-to-buy, social housing and capital-gain-as-deposit have been successfully piloted by the NZHF over the last five years. Despite the recent dramatic changes in the housing market, these instruments have stood the test of time in both rising and falling markets. NZHF is now working on a major scale-up of three

---

34  *Maori and Pasifika Education Initiative* [online] [Accessed 27 July 2009]. Available from the World Wide Web: http://www.initiative.org.nz/about-asb-community-trust

35  *New Zealand Housing Foundation* [online] [Accessed 27 July 2009]. Available from the World Wide Web: http://www.housingfoundation.co.nz

affordable housing packages that utilise both donations and programme-related social loans, as a platform to attract local and central government partners, and private and institutional investors.

## Building Pacific organisations

The Pasifika peoples of New Zealand are diverse and rapidly growing population. This group of 266,000 people comprises 8 percent of the New Zealand population and is expected to rise to 12 percent of the population by 2021. The Pasifika population is predominantly young, urbanised and New Zealand-born, but has historically been over-represented among the unemployed, lower skilled workers and low-income earners.

This capacity-building project set out to help Pasifika organisations in New Zealand enhance their capacity to operate effectively for their people. It was established in response to a recognition by the J R McKenzie Trust that they received relatively few applications from Pasifika groups and that those applications that were received were "light in the core skills of governance, management and administration".[36] Most applicants to the J R McKenzie Trust aspired to provide community services in culturally-appropriate ways.

This population covers seven main ethnic groups[37] — many at much greater risk of disadvantage than the mainstream — and with limited experience and capacity in operating effective organisations. This was seen by some as part of the cause of the chronic issues that presented themselves in Pasifika groups and communities.

Led by the J R McKenzie Trust and co-funded by the Tindall Foundation, this initiative was created and delivered with extensive Pasifika community input. Over a four-year period, Pasifika organisations could apply for capacity-building help from a range of certified consultants. The programme was regularly reviewed by a Pasifika and funder reference group and changes were made along the way. The history and final evaluation of the project indicate it was very innovative in its approach and that it achieved its aims. For both trusts there were a number of learning opportunities about their own philanthropic practice when building constructive, ongoing relationships with minority groups and disadvantaged populations.[38] A participant in the project reported:

*When we started it was a family affair and it wasn't until we had been going for about three years that we all went on a retreat ...we were*

---

36  Uta'i, S (2006) *Final History and Evaluation of the Building Pacific Organisations Programme*, Wellington: J R McKenzie Trust

37  The Pacific nations are: Samoa, Cook Islands, Tonga, Niue, Tokelau and Tuvalu.

38  Utai, op cit.

*able to distinguish between governance and management and also
realise how important each of those roles were. This was quite hard
as the management were mainly young and our Board are mainly
elders.*

## Hikurangi Foundation climate change initiative

Climate change has emerged as a serious issue for philanthropy as
the science has become more incontrovertible, but the forms of effective
engagement available to philanthropic funders seem harder to identify. In
particular, the complexity of the issues involved – which increasingly span
the broader environmental, social, political and economic landscapes with
a plethora of emerging and conflicting opinions and information – make it
very difficult for funders to be as definitive in decisions as seems possible
in other areas of interest.

The same is true in New Zealand, which has the added factors of an
unusual greenhouse gases profile distorted by agricultural emissions, plus a
trading need to be genuine about the "clean green 100 percent" image that
provides a key economic premium to the country.[39] Very few philanthropic
funders have supported climate change initiatives, in fact the BERL report
indicated that only 3 percent of philanthropic funding is directed at even
broader "environmental" projects. This limits the independent voices
available to inform objective public discourse and engagement. This
became particularly evident in the public discourse when the previous
Labour government introduced a very comprehensive Emissions Trading
Scheme (ETS)[40] which is currently under review by the present national
government.

Following a scoping study of issues and opportunities, the Todd and
Tindall Foundations agreed to co-fund a specialist body with multi-sector
governance to seek ways to leverage public understanding, engagement
and change around sustainable living, with a particular focus on climate
change. The Hikurangi Foundation[41] has quickly established itself as an
active, thoughtful player and a neutral, respected voice and convenor
in this space, far more so than the foundations themselves or other
special-interest groups could be. A parallel organisation also set up by

---

39  Ministry for Environment, *Valuing New Zealand's Clean Green Image* [online] [Accessed
27 July 2009]. Available from the World Wide Web: http://www.mfe.govt.nz/publications/sus-
dev/clean-green-image-value-aug01/

40  Ministry for Environment, *Factsheet Emissions Trading Scheme* [online] [Accessed
27 July 2009]. Available from the World Wide Web: http://www.mfe.govt.nz/publications/
climate/emissions-factsheets/

41  *Hikurangi* [online] [Accessed 27 July 2009]. Available from the World Wide Web: http://
www.hikurangi.org.nz

the Tindall Foundation – the Carbon Farming Group[42] – has a similar but narrower role to cover land-based and agricultural information and issues.

## Future trends

New Zealand has an unusual philanthropic "matrix" which has not yet been researched in detail. However, it appears that in relation to the funding of innovation – especially systems-change innovation – the predominance of distributive and relatively more risk-averse funders may have impacted on the proportion of such initiatives supported by the New Zealand philanthropic sector compared to countries such as the US and Canada.

While the authors do not see evidence of significant growth in overall New Zealand philanthropy in the near future, there have been a number of recent legislative changes designed to increase philanthropic giving. These include a significant liberalisation of the income tax regime for donations, including the establishment of trust and foundations, and systems to encourage payroll giving, all of which may increase the total pool of philanthropic funding, and hence the size of the fraction available to fund innovation.

As part of the global trend, there is some evidence that a number of newly wealthy business people, some returning from overseas, are looking at alternate philanthropic models such as venture philanthropy and programme-related investment, rather than the more traditional grant-making trust model that their parents or grandparents might have established a generation earlier.

For example the innovative and intensive "I Have A Dream"[43] programme, which supports students from disadvantaged communities through school and university was introduced into New Zealand by an information technology entrepreneur who returned to the country from the US. Scott Gilmour is actively and personally involved in the programme as well as being its dominant and committed long term funder.

The Wayne Francis Trust – set up by a successful property developer – does not receive applications but seeks ways it can engage with organisations and initiatives "to bring about systemic change for improved education, community and health outcomes and the lifelong well being of young people".[44]

---

42 *Carbon Farming Group* [online] [Accessed 27 July 2009]. Available from the World Wide Web: http://www.carbonfarming.org.nz

43 *I Have a Dream* [online] [Accessed 27 July 2009]. Available from the World Wide Web: http://www.ihaveadream.org.nz/index.html

44 *Wayne Francis Charitable Trust* [online] [Accessed 27 July 2009]. Available from the World Wide Web: http://www.wfct.org.nz/

This list is by no means exhaustive or complete, but gives some idea of the increasing attraction of newer philanthropists to more narrowly focused, engaged and outcome-based ways of supporting systems-change innovations, through models, pilots, convening, research, advocacy or combinations of all.

In the decade preceding the collapse of the world investment markets in late 2008 there had been a significant growth in individual wealth in New Zealand. The impact of the crash on these individuals and their philanthropic intent and capacity has yet to be understood.

The recent crash in world investment markets has also impacted severely on the value of many endowments held in trustee companies and by family and community trusts. This has resulted in some cases in staff lay-offs and in many (but not all) in cuts to grants programmes.

## Conclusions

New Zealand is well known for innovation. It is endemic in the culture and unlikely to change.

Looking at the history of this country, we suggest that both the government and the established philanthropic sector will continue to propose and support innovative responses to social problems, supported by corporate and venture philanthropists.

Despite the fact there are fewer and smaller innovation-compatible funding sources than in other countries, in the opinion of the authors this should only limit the amount and speed of social innovation in the future, rather than the range, depth, and degree of risk taken.

DENIS TRACEY

# Australia
# GROWING PHILANTHROPY IN AUSTRALIA: AN ALUMNI-BASED INITIATIVE

## Background to Australian philanthropy

The opening sentences of Michael Liffman's 2004 book, *A Tradition of Giving: Seventy-five Years of Myer Family Philanthropy*,[1] give useful context to Australian philanthropy:

> *Australia has little tradition of significant philanthropic giving. Compared with the United States, private donated wealth has played a minor part in the building of Australia's major civic, welfare, and cultural institutions. Australia still has no real counterparts to the Carnegies, Rockefellers, Fords or their more recent manifestations: Bill Gates, George Soros or the Packard family. Australia's wealthy families have neither their mythic quality, their power, their reputation for beneficence, nor, perhaps, their notoriety. Nor are the small number of philanthropic foundations established by some of Australia's philanthropic families perceived as fundamental to the fabric of Australian society, and even to its international identity, as it the case, for example, with the Ford Foundation…*

The practice of philanthropy in Australia in the nineteenth and twentieth centuries was basically similar to that in comparable countries – the

---

1 Liffman, M (2004) *A Tradition of Giving: Seventy-five years of Myer Family Philanthropy*, Melbourne: MUP, (p. 1)

United States (US), Britain, Canada and other western societies: similar, but mostly smaller. In colonial times (1788-1900) benevolent institutions and other charitable bodies were commonplace and active. Also during this time many bequests were made to universities, art galleries and other institutions. Some of these are still in operation.

Any discussion of philanthropy in Australia needs to include the achievements of Sidney Myer who, during the 1920s and early 1930s, established himself as the doyen of Australian philanthropists. Originally named Simcha Baevski, Myer was born in Russia in 1878. He migrated to Melbourne in 1899 and, after first working as a hawker (selling goods from door to door), opened a shop in Bendigo, a prosperous country town about 150 kilometres from Melbourne. This business thrived and ten years later he opened the Myer Emporium, a large store in the heart of Melbourne which, by the 1920s was said to be the largest store in the Southern Hemisphere.

With his business success, Myer's philanthropic genius bloomed. Having already established himself as an unusually benevolent employer, he began making large gifts to the university, hospitals and other public institutions. On Christmas Day 1930, as the Great Depression was beginning to bite, Myer hosted a dinner for over eleven thousand citizens of Melbourne. Not surprisingly, this received huge press coverage and established Myer's standing as one of Melbourne's leading citizens.

Sidney Myer died suddenly in 1934. It is said that over one hundred thousand mourners attended his funeral. He bequeathed one tenth of his estate to establish a foundation that remains one of Australia's largest and best-known. Both during his life and after, Sidney Myer's philanthropy was probably modelled on that of overseas counterparts such as Carnegie, Rockefeller and Rowntree. He is Australian philanthropy's most influential pioneer.

Notwithstanding this model, Australia does not have the sort of strong philanthropic culture that is such an established part of civic life in the US or in Europe. Australians generally believe that physical infrastructure (roads, utilities, etc.) and basic services (education, health and welfare) should be provided by government. They also believe that governments have a role in supporting sporting and cultural activities at both the grass-roots and fully professional levels. As Michael Liffman observes, philanthropy has never been a central pillar of Australian society.

True, Australians have always given to charity, to welfare (including animal welfare), to education, to the arts and to religious organisations; but more often than not, this has been regarded as a top-up, rather than basic core funding. Commentators have often speculated on the differences between Australian and US philanthropy. In *Giving it Away: in Praise of Philanthropy*,[2] I expressed a fairly common explanation.

---

2 Tracey, D (2003) *Giving it Away: in Praise of Philanthropy,* Melbourne: Scribe, (p. 14)

*Australia was established largely as a division of the British prison system, and from the earliest days the colonial government controlled, or sought to control, virtually all aspects of life. Did this encourage a view that government would always provide basic services and fix problems, a view that continues to influence us today? ...*

*Many of the early immigrants to the USA, on the other hand, were fleeing from government interference. And later, as the covered wagons rolled across the prairies, people knew that they were on their own. If hostile Indians attacked or the horses dropped dead, there was no guarantee that the government would help. Is it possible that this encouraged a stronger commitment to self-help and community co-operation?*

In *Why Rich People Give* Theresa Lloyd offers further useful insights into US philanthropy:[3]

*[I]n the US, philanthropy is an integral and defining element of elite culture ... Philanthropy becomes a mark of class status that contributes to defining and maintaining the culture and organisational boundaries of elite life.*

In Australia this is simply not the case. In the few years since these books were published there have been signs that philanthropy may be embedding itself more securely in Australian culture. There have been several large individual gifts; some outstanding public responses to natural disasters (especially the 2004 Asian Tsunami and the 2009 Victorian bushfires), an increase in the size and sophistication of corporate giving, growing interest in social investment in its various manifestations, and an extensive (though so far unexamined) practice of diaspora philanthropy.

Nevertheless, the idea that governments are and should be responsible for providing infrastructure and basic services is frequently cited in surveys of Australians. It will not be easily shaken.

A lot of information about Australian philanthropy is unknown and probably unknowable. Unlike their counterparts in comparable countries, Australian foundations are not obliged to publish details of their giving, their assets, or indeed their very existence.[4] The most detailed and reliable data on giving is published by the Australian Taxation Office, but this includes only gifts for which a tax deduction has been claimed. Since much

---

3 Lloyd, T (2004) *Why Rich People Give,* Association of Charitable Foundations: London

4 The relatively new Private Ancillary Funds (see below) are listed by the Australian Taxation Office, but not in a way that necessarily leads to useful disclosure.

Australian giving is not tax-deductible (including most gifts to religious bodies), researchers in this country remain relatively frustrated.

## Government initiatives

If, as I suggest, philanthropy is starting to become part of Australia's broader culture, some credit should go to our previous government. During his eleven years (1996-2007) as prime minister, John Howard personally championed several initiatives to encourage more and better giving by Australians. The most important of these was probably the introduction in 2001 of Private Ancillary Funds (PAFs – formerly known as Prescribed Private Funds). These are a form of trust fund designed to encourage private philanthropy by offering businesses, families and individuals greater flexibility in establishing their own philanthropic trust funds. Gifts to PAFs are tax-deductible. Compared to previous structures, they are simple and quite cheap to establish and to operate. By July 2008, 769 PAFs had been established with a total value (at least before the present global financial crisis) of over 1.58 billion Australian dollars (AUD).[5]

During 2009 Kevin Rudd's government introduced a number of changes to the operation of Private Ancillary Funds. Despite some alarm from many in the sector (and probably owing to quite active lobbying by the same individuals and organisations) these changes have amounted to little more than fine-tuning.

The main restriction on the operation of Private Ancillary Funds is that they may donate only to organisations which also have tax-deductible status. This category includes most charities but excludes some groups which, in many other countries, are tax-deductible, including, most notably, religious organisations.

Partly influenced by the fact that Australian charity law remains based on an English statute dating from 1601, the Howard government also set up a number of parliamentary enquiries into various aspects of philanthropy. These attracted some well-researched and perceptive submissions, but few major changes eventuated. As a result, philanthropy in Australia remains comparatively opaque, unaccountable and unregulated. From time to time there are calls for the establishment of an office which might act as a regulator, an ombudsman or an advice bureau – perhaps along similar lines to the Charities Commissioner in the United Kingdom – but neither the Howard government nor, so far, its successor have shown any enthusiasm for this idea.

---

5 According to the Australian Centre for Philanthropy and Nonprofit Studies at Queensland University of Technology [online], available from the World Wide Web: http://www.bus.qut. edu.au/research/cpns/documents/2008_6_PPFs_Final_Web.pdf

From 1999-2007 the Prime Minister's Community Business Partnership advocated, facilitated and celebrated corporate social responsibility, in particular partnerships between companies and non-profit organisations.

In 2005 the government commissioned a report, *Giving Australia*,[6] which has given us the most recent and comprehensive snapshot of Australian philanthropy and volunteering. Its key findings include:

- Total annual giving is about 11 billion AUD; 7.7 billion AUD from individuals and 3.3 billion AUD from businesses
- 87 percent (13.4 million) of adult Australians give. Annual donations average 424A UD
- Since 1997 giving of money by individuals has increased by about 88 percent (or by 58 percent adjusted for inflation)
- Giving in Australia comprises 0.68 percent of gross domestic product. The comparable figure for the US is quoted at 1.68 percent (Note: most other sources cite a larger figure for the US, generally around 2 percent), which is also markedly higher than giving in Europe (for example; 0.84 percent in the United Kingdom, 0.49 percent in the Netherlands and 0.32 percent in France[7]

Though these are not a government initiative, the last ten years or so have also seen the establishment of several community foundations. Community foundations in Australia are based largely on a model developed in the US under which donors set up funds within a larger umbrella foundation. Community foundations' main advantages include flexibility for individual donors in terms of their active involvement with the causes they support, and comparatively low establishment costs and management fees. They tend to operate within a defined locality or among an existing community of people. The most successful community foundation in Australia is the Melbourne Community Foundation which manages about a hundred individual funds and (again, before the global financial crisis), had about 35 million AUD under management.

## Giving by the wealthy

As the quotations at the beginning of this chapter suggest, one of the most striking features of Australian philanthropy is the fact that our wealthiest citizens are not always our most generous.

---

6 Commonwealth of Australia (2005) *Giving Australia: Research on Philanthropy in Australia* [online], available from the World Wide Web: http://www.philanthropy.org.au/ community/transcripts/Giving%20Australia%20Summary.pdf

7 Boettke, Peter J., and Coyne, Christopher J. (2002), *The Political Economy of the Philanthropic Enterprise*, The Mercatus Center: George Mason University [online] [accessed 14 October 2009]. Available from the World Wide Web: http://www.ccoyne.com/The_ Political_Economy_of_the_Philanthropic_Enterprise2.pdf

In 2004 and 2005 the Centre for Philanthropy and Social Investment at Swinburne University of Technology, Melbourne published two papers exploring giving by wealthy Australians.[8] Both were sponsored by Daniel Petre AO, an Australian philanthropist who for several years has been asserting vigorously that wealthy Australians do not give nearly as much as they could or should. I was the lead investigator for both these projects.

In 2008 the Australian Centre for Philanthropy and Nonprofit Studies at Queensland University of Technology published a further report on this topic, also sponsored by Daniel Petre (via the Petre Foundation).[9] The remarks that follow arise from these reports.

As noted, facts and figures for giving in Australia are scarce and limited, and this is particularly the case for wealthy Australians. The Taxation Office (no doubt to its chagrin) mainly collects information on income rather than assets, and in consequence can provide only limited information about the giving practices of the wealthy. From time to time business magazines publish lists purporting to name Australia's most generous citizens. These are usually based on disclosures by recipient organisations, on unattributed sources and on speculation. They are certainly interesting, but seldom possible to verify.

Despite this lack of data, it is estimated that about 40 percent of wealthy Australians give little or nothing. Experienced observers speak of demonstrably wealthy families and individuals who have established no foundation or formalised philanthropic vehicle, and whose giving, if any, is unplanned, reactive, unimaginative and, above all, small.

This view is supported by the fact that since 2001 (as noted above) just 769 Private Ancillary Funds have been established, despite their having been promoted vigorously by the government, by some financial advisers and by potential beneficiaries. Many observers consider that this is not an impressive number, especially since, according to the Capgemini Merrill Lynch *World Wealth Report 2007*,[10] 161,000 Australians personally hold more than 1 million USD in financial assets.

Of course there are exceptions. Several family-based foundations (notably the Myer, Pratt and Vincent Fairfax foundations) practice

8 Asia Pacific Centre for Philanthropy and Social Investment *How the Wealthy Give: comparisons between Australia and comparable countries (USA, Britain and Canada)* (2004) and Encouraging Wealthy Australians to be More Philanthropic (2005) [online], available from the World Wide Web: http://www.petrefoundation.org.au/docs/Wealthy_Aussies_000.pdf and http://www.petrefoundation.org.au/docs/IncreasingPhilanthropy.pdf

9 Australian Centre for Philanthropy and Nonprofit Studies (2008) *Good Times and Philanthropy: Giving by Australia's Affluent* [online], available from the World Wide Web: http://www.bus.qut.edu.au/research/cpns/documents/GoodTimesandPhilanthropyGivingBy AustraliasAffluent_March2008.pdf

10 Capgemini Merrill Lynch *World Wealth Report 2007* [online], available from the World Wide Web: http://www.ml.com/media/79882.pdf (p. 30)

well-researched, sensitive and intelligent grant-making. Dame Elisabeth Murdoch (who recently celebrated her hundredth birthday) is loved and admired for her large and wide-ranging philanthropy. Mining magnate Andrew Forrest finds time and energy to set up imaginative and extensive programmes that will benefit remote parts of Australia and the people who live there. But mentioning these giants simply draws attention to the inactivity of great majority of our rich and famous. It is also true that the largest individual gifts in Australia have come from an American, Chuck Feeney of Atlantic Philanthropies.

Nor does the number of wealthy Australians seem likely to fall. As bankers, financial advisers and fundraisers around the world understand, a gigantic intergenerational transfer of wealth is now gathering momentum as the baby boomers inherit from their parents and, in turn, bequeath to their children. In the US this phenomenon has been widely examined, notably by Paul Schervish of Boston College, whose estimates of the sums involved are truly stupendous. While no research of comparable standard has been undertaken in this country, there seems no reason to doubt that the next fifty or so years will see unprecedented opportunities for philanthropy.

Explanations for wealthy Australians' lack of giving are based on intuition as much as research. The respected social commentator Hugh McKay suggests that newly-rich Australians adopt a sense of entitlement to the privileges of wealth.[11] Once they have achieved material success, he believes, they seem to apply a sort of perverse Darwinism, persuading themselves that it would be inappropriate to share their wealth with people who, because they are poor or disadvantaged, are manifestly less entitled.

No-one has yet explored these speculations through in-depth psychological studies, but in the meantime it is noticeable that when I have asked other Australians why they don't give, their responses have been more often than not "It's the government's job." "Charities are inefficient/corrupt." "No-one has asked me properly." "I need to keep my money in case I get sick," etc.).

From time to time various ideas have been proposed to encourage wealthy Australians to be more generous. They have included both inducements and penalties. These commonly relate in some way to tax; proposing either more and better tax incentives (carrots)[12] or the reintroduction of death duties, which existed as a state-based tax until 1972 (sticks).

Other ideas focus on better recognition for donors. In 1975 the Australian government introduced a new system of civil honours, the Order of Australia, to replace British honours. In consequence knighthoods were

---

11 Private conversation with author

12 Note that in 2007 the Government of Singapore introduced double tax deductions for gifts to Institutions of a Public Character. This is part of a wide-ranging scheme to establish Singapore as a philanthropy hub.

no longer available; a loss regretted by many, including some charities.[13]

Similarly, some have urged the introduction of schemes that appear to have been successful overseas, such as Charitable Gift Annuities or Charitable Remainder Trusts (US), or the Gift Aid Scheme (UK), all of which provide tax incentives for giving, or the Beacon Awards (UK) which award annual prizes to individuals who have made remarkable contributions to charitable causes or to organisations that are of particular benefit to the public. The yearly winners receive cash prizes which must be invested in an innovative way in a charity of their choice. By highlighting the achievements of the prize winners, the awards seek to encourage others.

It is also worth saying that philanthropy in Australia has not generally been well-served by those whose job it is to secure donations. Although the professionalism and skill of Australian fundraisers has improved in recent years – partly due to visits and recruitment of experienced professionals from abroad – there remains a discernable reluctance on the part of some board members, trustees, volunteers and chief executive officers to ask for money. It is also true that a good many non-profit organisations are unable clearly to articulate their vision, strategy and financial plans.

## Australian philanthropy in a global context

As citizens of a comparatively recently-established outpost of western culture, Australians have always been inclined to look overseas for ideas and inspiration. Traditionally we looked to the Old World, first to Britain and later to the US. More recently however we have been paying closer attention to our immediate neighbours, and this is having a profound and mostly beneficial effect on Australian society. Some of the resulting changes are simple, easy and universally welcomed. For example, we think our restaurants, with their fusion of eastern and western cuisine, are now the best in the world, and we are delighted when our sporting success is enhanced by players whose background is in Asia or the Pacific.

Nevertheless, in many respects we remain largely a monocultural society. The names of the individuals who comprise our parliaments, our corporate boardrooms and the senior levels in our professions still come predominantly from the British Isles.

But this is changing very quickly and it should not be long – a generation or two – before other aspects of our society better reflect its contemporary mix. No doubt philanthropy will not be immune from this trend, but I believe it would be premature to speculate on how the structure and practice of our philanthropy will develop.

---

13 "It's such a shame we got rid of knighthoods. I can tell you that during my time here they would have been worth at least another $20 million to the gallery." Edmund Capon, Director of the Art Gallery of New South Wales. (Quoted in Tracey, D., op.cit. (p. 182))

But in at least one respect I think we can predict with confidence. The publication in 2009 of Peter Singer's *The Life You Can Save: Acting Now to End World Poverty*[14] seems to be having a profound effect on Australia's giving. As our remarkable response to the 2004 Tsunami disaster demonstrated, nowadays we feel much more familiar and comfortable with the people who live in Southeast Asia and I think this will be reflected in a growing willingness to contribute to their welfare and development.

Further, over the past twenty years or so Australians have become far more financially literate. This is beginning to be demonstrated by new expressions of philanthropy such as corporate social responsibility, venture philanthropy and social entrepreneurship, and although we remain a comparatively small society, I think our ability and willingness to influence real change in our region of the world will soon be much more apparent.

## Changing Australia's giving culture

It used to be thought that, as a rule, broad cultural change within large and complex societies was not achieved quickly: but no longer. In the past forty or so years western societies have experienced several very large cultural changes: the women's and civil rights movements, concern for the environment, health and fitness. It is easy to overlook the speed and magnitude of these changes. For example, when I was a teenager, my mother worked in the public service and it seemed to me (and, sadly, to her) right and natural that she should earn about ten percent less than her male colleagues. Today such notions would be regarded as eccentric in Australia, just as we nowadays mostly disapprove of killing whales and of discriminating against people on the grounds of their race.

These cultural changes have happened with remarkable speed and it seems to me that this has come about mainly because of strong leadership and careful strategic planning.

In one important respect, changing the culture of giving in Australia should be easier to achieve than those extremely broad changes. The main targets of any campaign will mainly be those who have capacity to give; people who are our leaders in the fields of business, the professions, government, the arts and academia. As it happens, this group corresponds very closely to the lists of alumni of Australian universities.

---

14  Published in Australia by Text Publishing

## Giving to higher education in Australia – the area of expertise of the author

Australians generally regard the provision and support of higher education as a responsibility of government, an impression that is doubtless reinforced by the fact that from 1974-1989 Australian universities did not charge tuition fees for Australian students. This was a federal government initiative introduced by the reforming Whitlam Government (1972-75) but was removed after fifteen years. (It is significant however that it applied at the time that many of today's potential major donors were themselves attending university). These days most Australian university students are obliged to hold part-time jobs to meet the costs of their education.

A further disincentive to educational philanthropy is the fact that compared to most welfare organisations, universities are seen to be large, sophisticated and wealthy. This may be so, but they are also voracious consumers of resources, especially for research purposes. As the competition for government funds grows keener, universities are increasingly drawn to other income sources, such as attracting students from overseas, capitalising more effectively on their intellectual property and becoming more attractive to potential donors. The rest of this chapter will explore this last phenomenon.

Although Australian universities have received gifts and bequests for over a century, the professional and strategic approach to fundraising is a very recent development – probably no more than five years old. In recent years most, if not all, Australian universities have established or expanded the structures and processes through which they seek to attract philanthropic support. This process has generally been uncoordinated, and there is, to some extent, an unhelpful perception that universities are in competition with one another in this area.

The process has also been marked by the recruitment of fundraising professionals from overseas, especially Canada and the US. This has not been without problems. While most of these people have undoubtedly been knowledgeable and experienced in the principles and techniques of fundraising, they have often lacked an understanding of the very different cultural atmosphere that prevails here. This is a pernicious problem, and also a subtle one. While the popular cultures of Australia and North America are certainly similar, there are very deep differences in the way the people of these countries view the world. But these differences are not always obvious, and in an activity as nuanced as fundraising, this can be a serious handicap. It is not surprising if newcomers to Australia sometimes fail to recognise signals and don't know how to ask the right questions in the right way.

During recent months (more or less as I have been writing this chapter) I have been attempting to establish a body whose working title is The Australian Universities Philanthropy and Alumni Alliance (AUPAA). This is envisaged as a forum in which universities can share knowledge and experience, and develop ideas and strategies to approach their alumni in a better-informed and more coordinated way.

As noted above, strategic fundraising in Australian universities is a relatively new activity. Some institutions, especially the larger and older universities, are more advanced than others, and there is an unfortunate and unhelpful perception that this is a competitive field.

Quite recently the Group of Eight (an association of Australia's larger universities) has established forums in which directors of development and alumni services meet to compare knowledge and exchange ideas. This process seems to be making progress, but is not without obstacles. Further, it excludes Australia's other thirty universities.

AUPAA could develop and coordinate education and training in fundraising and development and encourage the growth and professionalism of philanthropy in the tertiary sector.

A good place to start might be in the area of student volunteering. Few students are able to donate money, but many are attracted to the idea of making a positive difference to society, especially in ways that will develop their skills and experience and make them more attractive to employers. AUPAA could develop a pilot project to encourage and enable students to undertake meaningful volunteer work with non-profit organisations. This would contribute to their personal growth and instil notions of social capital and "giving back". It would also look to Europe and the US where such schemes (often called Capstone Projects) are well-established. Crucially the participating students would not just perform unskilled work (a serious weakness in many volunteering programs) but would be introduced to more meaningful tasks, such as mentoring school students or work related to their future profession.

Other activities might include a regular forum to explore ideas and developments, co-ordination of design and delivery of education and training (both formal and executive), producing and disseminating resources, arranging visits by overseas experts, and representing and promoting the interests of philanthropy in the tertiary sector.

At the time this chapter was written the future of the AUPAA idea remained unresolved. Over the coming months it will be developed and, it is hoped, implemented by a group of Australian universities. The next step will be the preparation of a detailed strategic plan.

## The challenges and opportunities ahead for Australian philanthropy

Philanthropic giving in Australia is ready to be developed and expanded. But there are serious obstacles to be overcome. In the first place, Australians, like many others in affluent countries, remain overly preoccupied with material acquisition and disinclined to take realistic steps to alleviate the suffering of people elsewhere. But despite these challenges, the process is eminently worthwhile, first, because of our ability to make a real difference to disadvantage and inequity, and second, because of the very great benefits that it would bring to us.

As many observers have noted through the years, people who give are almost invariable better disposed to themselves and to the world and, in a word, happier.

It seems to me that one of the most promising aspects of the AUPAA idea is its potential to engage the imagination and innate generosity of younger people – students at our universities.

In the meantime, better tax incentives will certainly encourage greater giving, as will better and more imaginative ways of recognising and rewarding people who give. And of course increasing the skills of fundraisers will also have an effect.

But as things stand, the efficacy of these steps will be limited largely to those people who are already disposed to give. We need to go further. Australia needs to develop a renewed culture of giving, one in which it becomes a natural progression from having money to giving it away.

# 4 Australia
## AN EVOLUTION OF PERSONAL GIVING AND THE BUSINESS OF WORLD PEACE

Steve Killelea is one of the most prominent Australian philanthropists, dedicated to peace and to supporting the poor in the developing world. In a time span of ten years, his philanthropy has evolved from setting up a private charity to building an umbrella of related initiatives spanning from development assistance, global peace and economics research, to advocacy and education-influencing systemic global change.

Like many of the world's active and unreservedly enthusiastic entrepreneurs, Steve Killelea has been steadfast and successful in achieving his life's goals: "In my twenties, I came up with three ambitions that I wanted to accomplish in life. First, I wanted to travel and take people on adventure trips around the world – rafting down the Zambezi or trekking through Nepal. My second ambition came from the heart and that was to perform some type of social work. The third aspiration was intuitive and that was to work with computers. I decided initially to act on this third option, but my success in the software industry eventually allowed me to fulfil my other two ambitions. As part of the decision-making process, I quickly realised I couldn't make money out of social work and that travel opportunities would come with success in business. Now, I've been able to accomplish all three."

As Steve's personal and business activities led him to travel the world and visit some of its poorer countries, he gained a keen interest in development assistance and started visiting numerous post-conflict areas. "I developed a global awareness of humanity and came to the conclusion that, while individuals can be faced with very different circumstances, we're basically all the same; we are all part of one humanity. I also realised how small amounts of money can make a really big difference in certain people's lives. I decided then that, if I can substantially change someone's life with my contribution – well, it's a worthy investment."

## A grounded, family-oriented businessman

Steve appreciates the importance of family and considers it a core value for most people in society. "I've been very fortunate. I have a wonderful wife, Debbie, and a very close relationship with my four magnificent children, Jennayah, Rebecca, Louise and Anthony."

"I believe that if relationships are good on the home front, then there's more energy available to focus on external activities. This, in turn, makes for more success. It also builds confidence in one's own character, which makes it that much easier when dealing with difficult business relationships."

"A key factor that has led to my success is having a partner who understands my personal and professional needs – and has allowed me to fulfil them. This has meant living with frequent and often long international business trips and never knowing what time I'll be home for dinner. Many partners would find my lifestyle difficult to cope with and I've been privileged to have found the perfect life partner."

Steve notes that philanthropy has been a catalyst for family bonding; all of his children have visited project sites and his daughter, Jennayah, is on the board of Steve's Foundation: "The charity is not about us, it's about giving. Sharing our charitable involvement among the family has helped us all learn to give – whether it's toward each other, to external family or to friends. Debbie regularly travels into the developing world with me and at times into areas where there's considerable risk. She's always given excellent input into projects and has active involvement in the running of our organisation."

"I also think there's a certain comfort in long-term relationships that nurture the human spirit. It is good to be loved and understood, without having to act in any particular manner."

After his successful software company, Integrated Research Ltd went public in 2000, Steve and his wife Deborah created The Charitable Foundation. They set out to give away half of their wealth to help the poorest of the poor in the developing world, primarily in East and Central Africa and parts of Asia. Since then, the Charitable Foundation has become one of Australia's leading private Foundations specialising in development assistance.

Like many philanthropists of his generation, Steve takes an investment-minded approach to giving, insisting on maximising the impact of each dollar. "One of our main aims is to quantify the benefit we can provide by measuring the dollar cost per beneficiary. We want to know, for example, that we can provide clean water for less than twenty United States dollars per head and to drop the mortality rate for children under five by a quarter."

The Charitable Foundation's preferred programmes focus on delivering clean water, curing blindness, improving health, providing housing, famine relief and agricultural development. At any one time, the Foundation has between twenty to thirty active projects with an expenditure rate of between one hundred thousand and one million US dollars (USD) per annum per project.

## Gulu: A life-changing experience of suffering and great courage

From the hundreds of field experiences Steve could relate there is one highly confronting encounter that will stay with him for the rest of his life: "Debbie and I were in Northern Uganda, visiting a child soldier rehabilitation project we were considering supporting."

"One aspect of this project's rehabilitation process was to find and appoint mentors to counsel the children once they had returned home. These people would encourage the children to tell their horrific stories and then help them understand that this was all in their past. Then they would also help the children find ways to manage their new lives. These counselling roles didn't come without risk. Given the chance, the Lord's Resistance Army (LRA) would target these mentors, which usually meant death if caught. I couldn't help but admire their courage as none of them were paid. They just did it out of compassion for the suffering of the children."

"Our project review included meeting one of these counsellors, so we were taken to a village that over time would be transformed into an "Internally Displaced Persons" camp. These became some of the worst refugee camps in Africa, housing some two million people in Northern Uganda."

"When I first met Matthew, I was struck by his level of intelligence. He was as sharp as any of the research developers working for me at the time. Matthew had been a teacher, but the schools had closed as the war expanded and now he had no work. He had acted as a counsellor for twelve children and had many experiences to share."

"Matthew was in his late forties or early fifties and had two daughters in their twenties to look after. They had no way of making a living and both had lost their husbands. One husband had died of AIDS and they didn't know where the other one was. Apparently, he'd gone in search of work when the local economy collapsed with the war and had never returned. This meant that Matthew was left to support his two daughters and their three children. He did this by growing sugar cane in a vacant allotment next to his hut. The land was full of weeds and small trees with the sugar cane growing in between. As I gazed out over this small parcel of land, barely twenty-five metres by twenty-five metres, I couldn't imagine how he could grow enough cane to feed all of them."

"We talked for about an hour, sitting on low, hand-cut pieces of log, which made-do as stools outside his hut. He suddenly looked up and saw a young woman walking by about twenty metres away and called her over. He said she'd arrived in the camp two weeks ago but he still hadn't heard her story, so he then asked her to share it with us. As I looked into her face, it was like no other face that I had seen. Little did I know that I would come to see these same features a number of times again. In a soft, subdued voice Grace started to retrace the previous eight years of her life."

"At sixteen, Grace had been captured by the LRA and taken into Southern Sudan, where she was given to one of the LRA commanders. During that period she had a child, which died before its first birthday. One day, while the guerrilla group was on a raiding trip into Uganda, they were ambushed by the Ugandan army. While running for her life, Grace was caught in crossfire from the opposing groups and dropped her commander's goods, which it was her job to carry. Her punishment for losing his property was to have her nose and lips cut off. This accounted for her disfigured face."

"After some time, she found an opportunity to escape. It wasn't easy to get away from the LRA as they were constantly on the lookout for defections – and if suspected or caught, painful death was sure to follow. Grace was now somewhere inside Southern Sudan, which was lawless and filled with militias, hundreds of kilometres from home and without any food or money. She struggled for many days finding her way out, but unfortunately was captured and enslaved by a Sudanese man. She was to spend another eighteen months with him, bearing another child who also died within the first year of its life."

"Eventually, Grace managed to escape and this time found her way down into Northern Uganda, where yet again she was captured and enslaved. Now, fortunately for her she was in Uganda, which meant she had some unusual options. After a period of time, she was able to get a letter to her sister, who had some meagre resources and immediately came to find her. The problem was, she didn't know exactly where Grace was, only the area. After three months, she eventually found her sister and was able to arrange for her release."

"Eight years had passed. We realised that at twenty-four, Grace didn't meet the criteria of our programme, which was for children and the age limit was twenty-one. I tentatively asked if there was anything she wanted. Grace immediately responded that she just wanted to go back to school. It suddenly dawned on me that all she really wanted was to go back to the life she had prior to being abducted."

"We were all so moved by Grace's story that we decided to carry out a special intervention and help her out. We arranged for the project manager to look into her situation and see what could be done. Their first action was to check out the state of her health. Sadly, the results showed she had a sexually transmitted disease, tuberculosis, a urinary tract infection and AIDS, which was now well advanced. We cured what diseases we could and gave her living money, but she died some months later from AIDS."

"This interaction would mould my actions for years to come. I realised how great was the suffering of so many people, the courage of some who had nothing to gain and how forgotten and unrecorded the suffering and heroism of so many."

The Comprehensive Community Based Rehabilitation Tanzania (CCBRT) hospital in Dar Es Salaam, partially funded by TCF

## Setting up "The Charitable Foundation" – an intergenerational family charity

In 2001, Steve established The Charitable Foundation, an Australian prescribed private fund, which aims to improve the lives of as many of the poorest of the poor as possible. It does this through the delivery of developmental aid and initiatives toward making a more peaceful world.

The Foundation has been established in perpetuity and has no political, religious, ethnic, age or gender-based criteria for distributing aid.

Jennayah (Steve's daughter) serves on the Foundation's board and

Deborah (Steve's wife) attends board meetings by invitation. The Foundation is therefore very much a family charity with intimate involvement in approving proposals and setting the strategic direction. Most importantly, the family visits the projects. Their hands-on presence and empathy makes a significant difference for the beneficiaries and the people who work with the Foundation.

In partnership with a diverse group of Australian and international NGOs and Foundations, The Charitable Foundation's mission is to implement a broad range of timely, practical and cost-efficient overseas development and peace projects, emergency relief and small-scale assistance to individuals in distress.

"The focus of the Foundation's developmental aid is on the poorest of the poor. Our aim is to take on interventions that are substantially life changing and to reach as many people as we can. Our focus with peace initiatives is on research and proactive on-the-ground projects to either measure peace, build peace through reconciliation or normalisation of economic life in a troubled region. In either situation, the most important metrics of success are significance of impact and post-project sustainability."

## Challenges faced by the Foundation

Maintaining The Charitable Foundation has brought its own unique challenges.

"An early challenge involved legislation changes relating to direct giving. The rules that were in force at the time of establishment allowed the Foundation to directly fund overseas development projects, but legislative changes have restricted this option and we're now mandated to distribute all charitable funds through Australian NGOs. This has added an unnecessary layer of overhead and cost, impacting the amount of money directly reaching the beneficiaries."

"More recently, we've been faced with proposed changes to the prescribed private fund legislation we operate under that could affect the Foundation's annual distribution rate. From the beginning, we aimed to distribute 5 percent of the corpus value at the start of each financial year. However, because of significant unrealised capital gains, the Foundation obtained approval to retain the earnings to allow the total value to grow, with the view to increasing future grant giving and to ensure the Foundation would be viable in perpetuity. The new legislation being proposed could mandate levels of giving per annum higher than what we feel is best practice."

Challenges aside, Steve is rightfully proud of the professionalism he's been able to instil into the operations of the Foundation: "The Charitable

Foundation uses tools and procedures from the business world to measure the effectiveness and impact of the projects and programmes we fund. With this approach, we're hoping to contribute to the professionalization of our partners and the Australian NGO community in general."

One prudent step in this direction has been to entrust the management of the portfolio to a professional fund management firm. This provides a level of separation between the founder and the funds that were originally donated.

## The Charitable Foundation's projects

The Charitable Foundation primarily targets issues of need in Africa and South-East Asia, although other poverty, conflict and disease-stricken areas are included from time to time. To date, the foundation has implemented more than seventy projects spread over nineteen countries, substantially improving the lives of 1.7 million people, predominantly in East Africa and South East Asia.

### Projects currently supported by the foundation include:
- Covering teacher's salaries and running costs of Phaung Daw Oo School in Myanmar.
- Provision of clean water and sanitation for schools in the Kisarawe District of Tanzania.
- The development of a better livelihood in the Savannakhet province of Lao People's Democratic Republic (PDR).
- Scholarships to educate therapists for a prosthetics and orthotics centre in East Timor.
- The improvement of tuberculosis control activities in Papua New Guinea.
- Soil improvement and water conservation in the Tibetan settlement of Doeguling in India.
- A housing and community development project in Siem Reap in Cambodia.
- Expanding agricultural production capacity of the Mulli Children's family farm in Yatta, Kenya for the benefit of two thousand street children.
- Improved vanilla and rice farming techniques in Papua New Guinea.
- Urban housing and community development in Phnom Penh, Cambodia.
- The provision of water and sanitation to communities in Samburu, Kenya and assistance to reduce the prevalence of trachoma.
- Building and renovation of village clinics, a district hospital and a

maternal and child healthcare centre in Luang Prabang province in Lao (PDR).
- Outreach activities of the "Comprehensive Community Based Rehabilitation Tanzania" run disability hospital in Dar Es Salaam, Tanzania.
- Provision of food for vulnerable groups in Chiredzi, Zimbabwe.
- Provision of water and sanitation for the Bac Thong community in Northern Vietnam.
- Provision of clean water, sanitation and environmental sustainability for villages in the Oecusse enclave of East Timor.
- The reduction of poverty in Lao (PDR) through a livelihoods programme in the Mune district.

## Two examples of the Foundation's projects

### Example one: The Samburu project with Christian Blind Mission International (CBMI)

The Samburu District of Northern Kenya is a dry and dusty area characterised by water scarcity throughout the year, plus a lack of infrastructure, inadequate hygiene and high levels of poverty. The Charitable Foundation is implementing a five-year water, sanitation and disease control programme to address endemic levels of trachoma. This programme, implemented through CBM Australia and its local partners, is multifaceted and holistic in its approach.

According to the World Health Organisation (WHO), when more than 10 percent of the population between one to nine years of age have active trachoma infection (TF), there is a significant health risk that requires intervention. In Samburu, the TF prevalence was found to be 35 percent in children of this age bracket. Similarly, WHO suggests that when trichiasis (turned-in eyelids rubbing on the cornea) is present in more than 1 percent of the adult population, urgent intervention is required to prevent blindness. In Samburu, 6 percent of the population over the age of fifteen suffers from trichiasis.

The high rate of trachoma in Samburu is due to multiple factors of limited access to water, a pastoral lifestyle that includes close proximity between cattle and people, poor health and education infrastructure, and poor sanitation practices. Our intervention programme is designed to address all of these factors. For example, to address the extremely limited access to water in the area, which averages fifteen kilometres between homes and the nearest water location, The Charitable Foundation is developing additional water points through a combination of gravity-fed distribution systems, rainwater harvesting and boreholes. The project is also increasing the availability of health services and health-related information through improved medical facilities in the area, including an operating theatre and extensive mobile clinics that will effectively reach the entire project's population. The programme is also providing latrines and is planting trees to help counter the area's encroaching desertification.

## Example two: Soil improvement and water conservation in India

Another example of The Charitable Foundation's work is a project in the Doeguling Tibetan Settlement near Mundgod in India, implemented through the Brisbane (Australia) based Global Development Group.

This settlement had been practicing conventional chemical farming for three decades. Their mono-cropping approach had resulted in degradation and loss of top soil due to wind and water erosion, so crop yields were diminishing from year to year. To encourage the district's farmers to continue and to enjoy a sustainable livelihood, farming had to become profitable. So the community set out to increase the fertility of the land by reverting to organic farming, through erosion control and through water conservation measures, which included replenishing the groundwater aquifer.

Girl washing with fresh water (one of TCF's clean water projects in Cambodia)

The Charitable Foundation's main interventions for the settlement have been the restructuring of their worn out field contour embankments, the establishment of water-harvesting facilities such as valley farm ponds and gabion dams, plus stabilisation and erosion control through gully plugs and the planting of trees on field contour bunds. The soil quality has already shown rapid improvements and the settlement is now hopeful that it will be able to continue to provide a livelihood for themselves and for the younger generation of Tibetans born in the settlements.

## Travel for the Foundation stirs consideration of "what brings about peace?"

As a part of his hands-on approach to philanthropy, Steve regularly travels to the projects The Charitable Foundation supports – many of which are in the world's most dangerous regions.

Throughout his travels, Steve began to notice an ebb and flow to the level of conflict in any given region. "Back in Australia, I began to think more deeply about what conditions created conflict – and, more importantly, what conditions led to peace. I was surprised by how little the world knew about peace and that there wasn't any global ranking of countries by their levels of peacefulness. I thought this could be a powerful instrument to help governments, investors and policy makers promote peace and prosperity. So, I set out to fill this gap by building the 'Global Peace Index'."

"I strongly believe that in order to understand something, you need to measure it and without measurements how can you determine whether your actions help or hinder the achievement of your goals?"

For Steve, peace is at the centre of humanity's ability to survive in the twenty-first century. "Peace is the essential prerequisite for the survival of society as we know it in the twenty-first century. Without peace we will not achieve the levels of cooperation needed to address the global challenges of climate change, overpopulation, lack of freshwater and so on, let alone empower the global institutions needed to regulate these challenges."

## From consideration to creation: The birth of the Global Peace Index

Throughout 2006, Steve's ideas began to take shape into what would become the Global Peace Index, an annual study that would measure the peacefulness of as many countries as possible and uncover the main drivers of peace.

The initial step was to establish a definition of peace that most people would agree on, was measureable and that could be used as a consistent measure over time. The decision was made to define peace as "the absence of violence".

The first edition of the Global Peace Index was published in mid-2007. Now in its third year, the index has received worldwide recognition. Aside from the ranking of countries, which is what attracts most of the public attention, the real value of this work lies in the findings of the research.

Data collection and collation is conducted by the Economist Intelligence Unit, a research organisation affiliated with the Economist Group, publisher of The Economist magazine. Drawing on a global network of 650 analysts, the research team found over twenty thousand data points, which feed into twenty-three qualitative and quantitative indicators of external and internal measures of peace-factors ranging from a nation's level of military expenditure to its relations with neighbouring countries to levels of crime, domestic homicide, and incarceration. Overseeing the research is an international panel of leading peace experts and statisticians who review the methodology, sign off on indicators and set the weightings.

When it was first published, supporters included former US President Jimmy Carter, the Dalai Lama, South African Archbishop Desmond Tutu, British business impresario Sir Richard Branson and Harriet Fulbright of the Fulbright Center who hailed the Index as a breakthrough piece of work. "This index stands to broaden our very definition of what peace is, as well as how to achieve it," Fulbright said. "Peace isn't just the absence of war; it's the absence of violence."

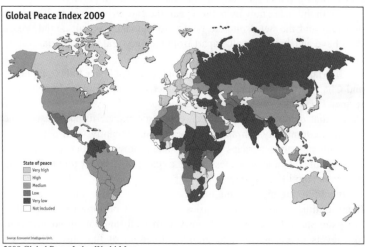

2009 Global Peace Index World Map

The global response was equally significant. Within a month of publication, the index was mentioned in over 500,000 articles on the internet, and the Global Peace Index website had over 250,000 visitors in the weeks following the launch. Since then, the index has enlisted many more endorsers, including the recent Nobel Peace Prize Laureate and former President of Finland Martti Ahtisaari, former United Nations Secretary-General Kofi Annan, as well as Mohammed Yunus, Founder of the Grameen Bank and many other renowned economists.

## The business of world peace

One of the most significant findings of the Global Peace Index has been its special relevance to economics. Businesses can play a decisive role in creating global peace, but there's no real understanding of the impacts of peace on their markets, their costs, and their profits. "As a businessman, I had a keen understanding of the power of numbers. And while I understood intuitively that peace contributed to a company's bottom line – by lowering risk, stabilising markets, and facilitating commerce – I realised there was no set of metrics to measure this."

"One of the key results of the 2009 research relates to the impact of violence on the global economy – the loss to global gross domestic product (GDP) caused by violence was conservatively estimated at 4.8 trillion USD per year." Analysis has confirmed that peace is a significant factor in the creation of wealth.

Research also unveiled that for every ten positions a country moves up in the index, per-capita GDP increases approximately 3,100 USD. "For a lot of countries, that's a pretty significant economic imperative."

"With the index now in its third year, the causes of peace are becoming apparent and the net economic benefit to humanity is substantial. Peace does have an economic value apart from the very real humanitarian values associated with it."

Sir Mark Moody-Stuart, one of the many Global Peace Index supporters and Chair of the Foundation for the United Nations Global Compact and former Chairman of Anglo American stated: "This year's index clearly shows that there are links between economic prosperity and peace. The business community can and does benefit significantly from non-violent environments, but perhaps business must now consider how sound, transparent and ethical business practices can play a larger role in bringing out about stability and peace."

In addition to highlighting this economic imperative, the Global Peace Index outlines what steps countries can take to become more peaceful. For example, it helps to be a country with well-functioning government, low levels of corruption and granting freedom of the press. But even investments in primary and secondary education, in the building of regional relationships and in economic infrastructure can pay handsome dividends in both economic prosperity and peace.

"What's striking is how sensitive the model is. It doesn't require a country to have wholesale changes in its structures or policies in order for it to move up. It doesn't have to completely rebuild itself."

Last year, the Institute for Economics and Peace, a think-tank Steve created to develop the index and support the cause of global peace, published a discussion paper that examined the concept of defining the

Peace Industry. This would be industry sectors that thrive on peace and whose markets and cost structures are adversely affected by violence or war. This year, collaborating with the group "Economists for Peace and Security", the Institute has published research that defines a methodology for calculating not only the cost of violence, but also how to apportion the economic value to different industry sectors within countries.

"The gold ring is really to make the Global Peace Index a tool for business strategy and decision making. With the right data sets, a company could use the index and associated research to look at revenue by nation and correlate revenue to peacefulness. Using the Global Peace Index, you could look at each nation's revenue, the size of their market and then the basket of costs associated with it. This means you can actually put a value on the size of the increase in markets and the reduction in costs, and once you have that, you're able to work out which target markets are likely to be most profitable – and then you have a numerical justification for your investment."

## Parallel between the current economic crisis and running a company

Steve strongly argues that GDP can't be the only measure for a country's success, just as revenue can't be the only measure of a company's success.

"A well-run company is one that considers more than revenue. Likewise, a well-run country should look beyond GDP growth. The wellbeing of a society, their level of peace and the state of the nation's assets, including soft assets such as forests, fish reserves and water, should be as prominent as GDP as this only measures short-term success. Peace, wellbeing and the state of the nation's assets can give a better picture of how the nation will fare in the future."

"Organisations such as the Organisation for Economic Co-operation and Development are now considering how to develop new holistic measures of society's progress and peace is considered an important component of that. In the current economic crisis, this is gaining even more importance."

"In many ways, we get what we measure and if we wish to achieve a higher level of societal progress, our measures have to be much more than achieving strong growth in GDP. As sustainability becomes central to managing our future, we need to develop ways of assessing our success that take it into account along with other factors that are important to a society, such as wellbeing, happiness and peace."

## A vision for the future

Starting with the establishment of a personal charity in 2001, in less than ten years, Steve has been able to realise a global vision and to instigate global systemic change through ongoing initiatives that include:

**Research**: The Institute for Economics and Peace investigates the relationship between economic development and peace, leads research into the structures and drivers of peace and works in partnership with think tanks and academics worldwide.

**Raising awareness**: In 2006, Steve approached the Australian filmmaker, Tim Wise, to start a film company that would promote the cause of peace. "Tim and I have both worked with child soldiers in northern Uganda and we share a belief in the transformative power of film. Tim produced "Child Soldiers", a heartbreaking documentary on children who had become belligerents in numerous war zones around the world. I wanted to reach people with inspiring messages to empower them to act for peace, so we picked film as the medium of communication because of its capacity to convey strong emotional themes." Together, Steve and Tim established One Tree Films, whose mission is to produce world-class documentaries and other forms of media, such as online videos, that have a strong focus on social issues. The first production, Soldiers of Peace, is a documentary film narrated by Michael Douglas, which illustrates the connections between individual acts of heroism and the systematic changes needed if we are to achieve a peaceful world. The film has received international acclaim and won a number of awards, including the Angel Film Award and Best Director (Feature Documentary) at the 2008 Monaco International Film Festival.

**Education of the next generation**: Steve believes that educating the younger generation is absolutely essential. To this aim, he has invested in the development of innovative peace education materials (the Building Blocks of Peace), which are available to schools worldwide free of charge.

**Advocacy**: Through the high visibility of the Global Peace Index, Steve has succeeded in raising the worldwide debate around peace and its importance to sustainability – shifting the focus of many from the lens of conflict to that of peace.

**Local action**: The work of Steve's wife, Deborah, has been focused on local initiatives. For example, after experiencing a lack of support when her family was touched by mental health issues, she decided no other family should ever go through the same frustration. In 2007, Deborah founded the "Be Centre Foundation", a not-for-profit organisation dedicated to supporting children, young people and families impacted by emotional, behavioural, and mental health problems.

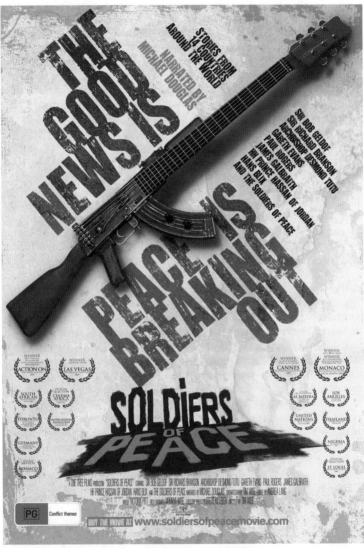

Soldiers of Peace poster

**International action**: Through The Charitable Foundation, Steve and his family will continue to bring their hands-on approach to development in the poorest areas of the world, supporting life-changing interventions to lay the ground for increased development and peacefulness.

## A final word on peace

Despite Steve's tireless and determined drive and the work of The Charitable Foundation, he has never lost sight of the fact that peace ultimately depends on the actions of individuals – whether they are corporate chieftains or Somali warlords. "One of the transforming aspects of my life was understanding how to find my own personal peace. I firmly believe that individuals can transform their societies. I have always been amazed by people who in the worst of conflicts put down their arms and at much personal risk, work for peace."

The Global Peace Index and the work of the Institute for Economics and Peace has received a warm welcome, yet Steve is quick to note there is still much to learn about the economic and political underpinnings of peace. "We don't actually understand much about peace. If you go to any university, you won't find a course in the literature faculty on the literature of peace. You'll find no chairs in the economics departments focusing on the economics of peace, nor will you find any history subjects which are on the history of peace. So the first thing that we need to do is have a much, much better framework to actually understand peace if you want to implement it."

Promoting this understanding is a key role for philanthropists. "Philanthropists who are interested in peace and the study of peace, particularly from an economic perspective, are likely to be highly successful because the area is so new. Funding basic research is a critical first step. Research and innovation have a long history of support from philanthropists and foundations. The Institute for Economics and Peace aims to collaborate with entities worldwide; we believe that by pooling resources so much more can be achieved."

By the same token, Steve sees market opportunities for investors, including foundation endowment managers – an area he has been exploring though his business networks. "We've been working with a couple of fund managers and some different people who have experience in conflict areas, to look at what a Peace Fund would look like. This would be a fund that invests in countries with the highest likely levels of improved peacefulness. Countries with low per capita income but high rankings on the Global Peace Index are likely good targets."

"There's a peace dividend that happens when the level of economic development catches up with the peacefulness of a fast improving society – peace creates opportunities for investment. I love the fact that by investing, business people can help create peace and make money at the same time. That's just excellent."

Sujin Kwon

# 5 Japan

# The Search for the Richness of Human Life: The Toyota Foundation's History in Asia and Future Perspectives

## About the Toyota Foundation

The Toyota Foundation was established in October 1974 by the Toyota Motor Corporation[1] as a grant-making foundation dedicated to contributing to "greater human happiness" and to the "development of the future welfare of society."

Headquartered in Tokyo, the Foundation has a staff of about twenty people.[2] With total assets of 40.1 billion yen, it carries out grant-making activities with a focus on Asia. Each year it distributes around 500 million yen in grants to more than twenty countries; to date it has made approximately seven thousand grants worth a total of some 15 billion yen.

## The road to establishment

In the latter half of the 1960s, car use exploded in Japan as families made automobiles a part of their increasingly convenient lifestyles, and Toyota Motor experienced tremendous growth. This spread of the automobile came at a cost, though, in the form of diverse social problems: traffic

---

1  At the time of its establishment, two companies (the Toyota Motor Company and Toyota Motor Sales Company) provided funding for the new Foundation; these companies merged in 1982 to form the Toyota Motor Corporation.

2  As of July 2009, the Foundation was operated by Chairman Tatsuro Toyoda, President Atsuko Toyama, Managing Director Hiroki Kato, and Secretary General Akihiko Nonomiya, who led a team of thirteen program officers and six staffers in the General Administration Division.

congestion, growing numbers of accidents, noise and air pollution. This was an era during which people began paying attention to the strains caused by Japan's rapid economic development. Criticism of these problems came to be directed not only at automobile manufacturers but at a broad range of companies, and the responsibility of companies to society became a focus of public attention.

In response to this, Toyota Motor recognized that no matter what merits a company might have, its continued growth – and perhaps even its very survival – would be in jeopardy if it lacked the understanding and support of society. The company became convinced of the need to further broaden the social-contributive activities it had been carrying out until then.[3] A group of corporate leaders including Eiji Toyoda,[4] then president of the Toyota Motor Company, decided to carry out a preparatory survey of the philanthropic activities undertaken by Western and Japanese corporations in order to determine methods for contributing to society.[5] As a result of this survey, they decided to opt for the social-contribution method of creating a grant-making foundation. The basic idea behind the establishment of the independent and autonomous foundation was that it would be a "reward to the society".

### The direction of the Toyota Foundation's grants

The Foundation launched its grant-making activities based on the following statement of purpose: "The Toyota Foundation views events from a global perspective as it works to support activities that bring broad, long-term benefits to society. It provides grants for research and projects in areas including human and natural environments, social welfare, and education and culture, in the hope of contributing toward an increase in human happiness and the development of the future welfare of society." In this way, the organization set its course as a private grant-making foundation that did not limit the scope of its activities to the automotive field but sought instead to respond to the increasingly diverse needs of society.

Furthermore, the grant-making process at the Toyota Foundation is managed by the Foundation Secretariat, rather than by national authorities or academic organizations. Playing a vital role in these grant-making activities are the program officers who help determine and develop projects

---

3  In 1968, the Toyota Motor Company and Toyota Motor Sales Company had established the Toyota Transportation Environment Committee and begun research into various traffic issues. The companies had also been involved in traffic safety campaigns and had made contributions in the form of traffic safety facilities, signals, and safety instruction vehicles.

4  Toyoda would go on to become the first chairman of the Toyota Foundation.

5  At this time, the Toyota Transportation Environment Committee mentioned in footnote 3 surveyed organizations including the Toray Science Foundation, Mitsubishi Foundation, Ford Foundation, Rockefeller Foundation, and Lilly Endowment.

to be funded and offer support during the application process. It was Yujiro Hayashi,[6] the Foundation's first Executive Director, who originally took the lead in training these program officers — a position that was almost nonexistent in the foundations operating in Japan at that time. This system, which had already been adopted by the Western grant-making foundations, became one of the defining traits of the Toyota Foundation. At the same time, the Foundation differentiated itself from its counterparts in Western countries by establishing selection committees of external academic specialists to determine which projects would receive funding.

The Toyota Foundation has also aimed through its grant-making activities to support projects both in Japan and in other countries, particularly developing countries. By providing grants focusing on human and natural environments, social welfare, education and culture both domestically and internationally, the Foundation hopes to contribute to the development of Japan and the global community as a whole.

The Foundation has also organized support programs for pioneering research and practical activities that are marked by fresh perspectives and unique creativity, as well as programs targeting young researchers in Japan and overseas. Foundation staff constantly keep their eyes on the future to ensure that the organization's activities contribute to creating greater human happiness.

## International programs

The Toyota Foundation has been providing grants under the Research Grant Program to projects in Japan since 1975. At the time, there were many issues to consider in connection with grant-making overseas, and the organization lacked sufficient foreign connections to begin this work right away. The first step was to interview people affiliated to foundations in other countries. This was followed in 1976 with the provision, on a trial basis, of grants for two projects outside Japan. Thereafter the Foundation launched its international activities focusing on Southeast Asia in earnest from 1979.

Having just started out, the Foundation had neither the funds nor the personnel to provide grants in all the developing nations of the world. With the focus narrowed to Southeast Asia though (a region with deep historical ties and geographical proximity to Japan), the Foundation was confident that it could use its grants in an efficient way.

Southeast Asia in the mid-1970s was the site of frequent boycotts of Japanese products and anti-Japanese public demonstrations. Despite this,

---

6  Previously Hayashi had been a professor in the Tokyo Institute of Technology's Department of Social Engineering; he was asked to become a director four months before the launch of the Toyota Foundation.

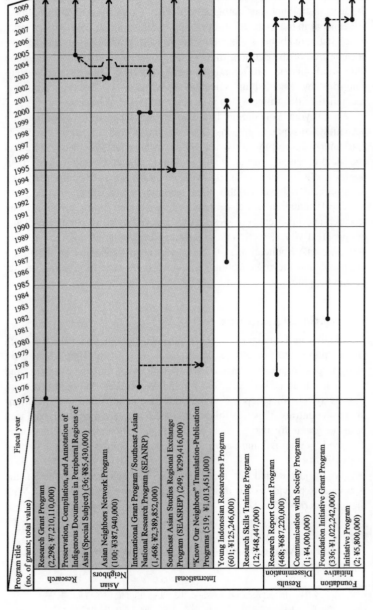

Table 1 The Toyota Foundation's grant programs through the years (1975–2009)

the Foundation believed in its ability to increase mutual understanding between Japan and the region through its grant-making activities, and it moved ahead with its plans accordingly.

Programs referred to in this paper are mainly detailed in table 1. The International Grant Program was first introduced in 1976, followed by the "Know Our Neighbors" Translation-Publication Program which started in 1978. Following this the Southeast Asian Studies Regional Exchange Program (SEASREP) was established in 1995, influenced by the Southeast Asian National Research Program (SEANRP). Then, in 2003, the Asian Neighbors Network Program was developed in order to recognise the importance of regional cooperation. In addition to this, the "Preservation, Compilation, and Annotation of Indigenous Documents in Peripheral Regions of Asia" was organized in 2005, aimed at the preservation of indigenous documents in the region. Some representative international programs will be explained in the following sections of this chapter.

## International Grant Program / SEANRP

The International Grant Program, which afterwards developed into the Southeast Asian National Research Program (SEANRP) in 2000, is the oldest program providing grants outside Japan in the history of the Toyota Foundation.[7] In 1975–1976, the Foundation undertook visits to the United States and Europe to observe how foundations there operated, concluding that the key to international grant-making was to set clear selection criteria for projects, to train program officers, and to develop a network of contacts in the targeted countries and regions.

Kazue Iwamoto,[8] who participated in the visits to the United States and Europe, was then the sole program officer in the Foundation's International Division. When she set off on her first trip to Southeast Asia in April 1977, the region was seething with anti-Japanese sentiment. Equipped with her experience of observing Western foundations, though, she diligently built up a network of contacts, paving the way for the International Grant Program that the Foundation subsequently launched in Southeast Asia.

During the process of providing grants in Southeast Asia on a trial basis, it became clear that there was considerable demand for projects that would consolidate and develop the identities of the various cultures of Southeast Asia. In light of this, the Foundation began to provide grants for projects conceived and implemented by local people on the theme of "Preserving

---

7 The program covered Malaysia, the Philippines, Thailand, and Sri Lanka in 1977 and was extended to Indonesia and Singapore in 1978, to Nepal in 1982, to Vietnam in 1985, to Laos in 1987, and to Cambodia in 1989.

8 Worked for the Toyota Foundation from 1975-85 and 2001-7. Produced the "Know Our Neighbors" Program and the International Grant Program under the theme of the "Preserving and Revitalizing Indigenous Cultures".

and Revitalizing Indigenous Cultures." The Foundation decided that it would be best for such projects to be unearthed by program officers, so the grants were run on the basis of collaboration, from conception to implementation, between local people and program officers.

Let us look at the early days of this grant project. The most successful group of projects were those relating to Tai palm-leaf manuscripts. Palm-leaf manuscripts are ancient documents consisting of palm leaves on which Buddhist sutras, history, customs, literature, or other information is written with a stylus. Before the program began, these documents were in danger of being scattered and lost because their academic value was unrecognized. The first of these projects involved surveying and microfilming palm-leaf documents held in monasteries in northern Thailand. The results attracted interest among other researchers and laid the ground for further projects. At the same time, this marked the beginning of the Foundation's long record of providing grants to maintain the diversity of Southeast Asia by supporting projects aimed at preserving indigenous and regional cultures that had been discarded as countries and societies modernized.[9] As the content of applications from countries in Southeast Asia had been improved following the Foundation's grants over the years, the SEANRP, former International Grant Program, was closed in 2004 and developed into Preservation, Compilation, and Annotation of Indigenous Documents in Peripheral Regions of Asia, as a new subprogram of the Research Grant Program.

These early activities also provided the basis for the Foundation's commitment to respecting the opinions of local people and led to the expansion of international grant-making activities in the form of the "Know Our Neighbors" Translation-Publication Program and the SEASREP.

### Know Our Neighbors Translation-Publication Program

Through direct interaction with people in Southeast Asia, the Foundation realized that many Southeast Asians
   - wanted the Japanese to learn more about their region
   - had a strong desire to learn more about Japan
   - wished to learn about their fellow countries in Southeast Asia

The first of these wishes was motivated by the feeling that Japanese people came to Southeast Asia to sell products without understanding or even trying to understand Southeast Asia and remained ignorant of the effects of Japan's economic aid and its growing corporate presence there. People in Southeast Asia aspired to more Japanese understanding of their cultures. The second point was motivated by the feeling that, although Southeast

---

9  The themes of the program were "Preserving and Revitalizing Indigenous Cultures" (1982-97) and "Cultural Issues in Contemporary Society" (1998-2004).

Asia was overflowing with Japanese goods, Japanese people remained largely invisible; their thoughts and intentions remaining a mystery to local people. There was also, though, interest in learning the secrets of Japan's economic growth. The third desire reflected Southeast Asians' high level of interest in understanding their neighbors, about whom they knew little due to such historical factors as their countries' long periods of separation during colonial rule and the Cold War.

By reflecting on ways in which to satisfy the three points above, the Foundation came up with the idea that publications were an excellent means of deepening mutual understanding between Japan and Southeast Asia and between Southeast Asian countries, because they could accommodate a wide range of information and were readily accessible.

Based on the conviction that translating and publishing Southeast Asian books in Japanese, Japanese books in Southeast Asian languages, and Southeast Asian books in other Southeast Asian languages would help to deepen mutual understanding, the Foundation initiated the "Know Our Neighbors" Translation-Publication Program in 1978 to facilitate the translation and publication of literary works and books on folklore, the humanities, and the social sciences.

To select the Southeast Asian books to be translated into Japanese for Japanese readers, the Foundation formed an expert committee of specialists on Southeast Asia in Japan and advisory groups in four Southeast Asian countries: Indonesia, Malaysia, Singapore, and Thailand.[10] The expert committee and advisory groups compiled lists of recommended books, from which the committee drew up a final list. The Foundation then invited Japanese publishing companies to submit applications for grants with which to translate and publish books on the list. The program owed its success to the presence of three key parties: the talented translators; publishing companies handling books on Southeast Asia, including Imura Cultural Enterprise Co. and Mekong Publishing Co.; and the Foundation, which paid the translators for their work.

Alongside the continued development of the program in Japan, the Foundation commenced the Translation-Publication Program in Southeast Asia in 1982 and the Translation-Publication Program among Southeast Asian Countries in 1983. These subprograms, "for readers in Southeast Asia (afterwards, "for readers among countries in Southeast Asia")", launched after a period of rigorous preparation, answered the needs of Southeast Asian translators and publishing companies.

This program supported the translation and publication of 660 works: 213 in Japan and 447 in other Asian countries. It gave Japanese

---

10  The program subsequently expanded its scope to South Asia, covering a total of eighteen countries.

and Southeast Asians access to diverse works from neighboring countries spanning a range of genres from academic and specialist books to novels and children's stories. One grant that sparked an especially intense reaction was for the translation into Japanese of *Rumah Kaca (House of Glass)*,[11] a novel by the Indonesian author Pramoedya Ananta Toer (1925–2006), who was then a political prisoner. It was even feared that this grant might result in the imposition of restrictions on the Toyota Foundation's activities in Indonesia.

It is hard to overstate the significance of advancing mutual understanding through culture in Southeast Asia, with its multitude of languages and complicated political and economic situation. The translations of Southeast Asian literature undertaken through this program were highly acclaimed for their contribution to deepening Japanese people's understanding of Southeast Asia – inspiring, for example, Japanese literary magazines to carry a special feature on Southeast Asian literature.

The program also provided grants for the production of dictionaries, which are essential for translation, between Southeast Asian languages and Japanese and between different Southeast Asian languages, resulting in the publication of twenty-two such works. Moreover, the program played a significant role in nurturing translators.

## Southeast Asian Studies Regional Exchange Program (SEASREP)

In November 1990 the first International Grant Program Symposium was held in Bangkok, Thailand, as a forum for reporting on research projects conducted under the International Grant Program (renamed the SEANRP), the forerunner of SEASREP. It was also a means of evaluating the program, and provided an opportunity for interaction among grant recipients. Participants in discussions at this event asserted the need for Southeast Asian scholars to transcend spatial and conceptual boundaries that had remained in place since colonial times. For this purpose, they argued, it was necessary to adopt an approach addressing Southeast Asia as a whole; the challenge was to expand Southeast Asian studies at universities in the region in order to cultivate a new generation of thinkers and doers who would not be bound by national borders.

To help meet this challenge, the Toyota Foundation assembled a group (later named a Council) of four Southeast Asian scholars and set out to establish a new program to support the pursuit of Southeast Asian studies from a perspective addressing Southeast Asia as a single region. By 1995 the group had convened three times; SEASREP was launched later that year.

---

11 Translated by Noriaki Oshikawa (1948–), a Japanese scholar of Indonesian literature and then dean of the Faculty of International Relations of Daito Bunka University. His translation of the "Buru quartet" of novels, of which House of Glass is one, earned him the Yomiuri Prize for Literature in 2008.

The program had three principal objectives:
- to cultivate young researchers in the field of Southeast Asian studies
- to encourage research on Southeast Asia
- to facilitate intra-regional interaction among Southeast Asian students.[12]

## Main components of the SEASREP

### Language Training Grants Program
- About thirty applications, ten grants awarded annually
- Annual budget: 51,600 United States dollars (USD)
  (A supplementary budget of 29,000 USD is available for Language Training Grants and Luisa Mallari Fellowships)

### Luisa Mallari Fellowships Program
- About thirty applications, ten grants awarded annually
- Annual budget: 34,000 USD
  (A supplementary budget of 29,000 USD is also available for Language Training Grants and Luisa Mallari Fellowships)

### Comparative and Collaborative Research Grants Program
- About forty applications, fifteen grants awarded annually
- Annual budget: 190,000 USD

### Asian Emporiums Program (formerly the Traveling Classroom Program)
- Offered through various universities in Southeast Asia; enrollment is limited to twenty-five students annually
- Annual budget: 32,000 USD

The Language Training Grants Program enables young scholars to study a Southeast Asian language at universities in the region outside their own countries. Among other outcomes, grant recipients have gone on to write papers and conduct research in the languages they have studied. The program has been praised for playing a major role in raising the quality of Southeast Asian studies and providing a foundation for promoting mutual understanding within the region.

---

12 The program is jointly funded by the Toyota Foundation and the Japan Foundation, which supports SEASREP's objectives.

The Luisa Mallari Fellowships Program is a grant program supporting research by masters and doctoral students; named after Luisa Mallari, who, having studied in Malaysia as a recipient of an Incentive Grant for Young Researchers in Southeast Asian Studies, taught Malay literature at the University of the Philippines until her untimely death in an accident. The program provides students with opportunities to carry out research in another country in the region, with the aim of encouraging them to pursue Southeast Asian studies and comparative research on their own and other countries.

The Comparative and Collaborative Research Grants Program is primarily designed to support two types of activities: collaborative and comparative research on Southeast Asia; and intensive seminars presented by scholars specializing in areas of importance to Southeast Asian studies offered at universities in the region outside the scholar's own country. This program enables scholars from countries within this vast region to collaborate across national borders and promotes deeper exploration of Southeast Asian studies from a variety of perspectives.

The Asian Emporiums Program (formerly the Traveling Classroom Program) is an intensive course, intended for both undergraduate and graduate students, focusing on the societies, cultures, and histories of Southeast Asian nations. The course is offered at a different university each year on a rotating basis. It has so far been held at the University of the Philippines, Thammasat University (Thailand), and Gadjah Mada University (Indonesia). Students in the course, who come from all over Southeast Asia, live together in a dormitory for approximately a month and earn credits that can count toward a degree at their home institutions.

The program also helps to create an environment for cultivating human resources. In some cases, recipients of Language Training Grants have carried out subsequent research with the support of Luisa Mallari Fellowships and have gone on to teach on the Asian Emporiums course.

When SEASREP was first established, not many Southeast Asian scholars pursued Southeast Asian studies outside their home countries.[13] Partly as a result of the Toyota Foundation's grant-making activities, however, researchers of Southeast Asian studies have firmly embraced the idea that the field must be developed through the efforts of scholars who are themselves Southeast Asians. Many of the region's universities now offer "Southeast Asian studies courses by Southeast Asian researchers".[14]

---

13  At the time, the National University of Singapore and Malaya University were the only universities in the region offering undergraduate courses concerned with Southeast Asia.

14  Southeast Asian studies programs have been established at universities including Thammasat University, Chulalongkorn University, Gadjah Mada University, and Vietnam National University. SEASREP Council members and grant recipients have been instrumental in the establishment of these programs.

Through these activities, SEASREP has helped scholars from countries all over this large region to conduct collaborative research across national borders and explore the field more deeply, from a variety of angles. The program has earned widespread acclaim for the prominent role it has played in building the foundations for raising the quality of research and promoting mutual understanding with the region.

The Tokyo Joint Secretariat for SEASREP was originally located on the premises of the Toyota Foundation, but an office was later opened in Manila, in accordance with the Foundation's determination to have Southeast Asians take the lead and the functions of the secretariat have gradually been transferred to the Manila office. In 2005, as SEASREP and the Toyota Foundation marked their tenth and thirtieth anniversaries, respectively, SEASREP took its first steps to becoming an autonomous organization independent of the Foundation. That year all the remaining functions of the secretariat, including the management of the program, were transferred to Manila, and in 2006 the SEASREP Council was renamed the SEASREP Foundation. These developments have enhanced the program's character as an effort led by Southeast Asians.

## Preservation, compilation, and annotation of indigenous documents in peripheral regions of Asia

Within the Toyota Foundation's SEANRP, which traces its roots back to the latter half of the 1970s shortly after the Foundation was established, projects concerned with the preservation of palm-leaf manuscripts and other local indigenous documents[15] stand out for having steadily produced results and helped advance research on regional and local history. The SEANRP ended in fiscal 2004. Beginning in fiscal 2005, "Preservation, Compilation, and Annotation of Indigenous Documents in Peripheral Regions of Asia" (renamed "Preservation, Utilization, and Transmission of Indigenous Documents in Asia" in fiscal 2009) was established for projects concerned with indigenous documents in Asia as a new subprogram (or so-called special subject) of the Research Grant Program.

Amid Asian countries' economic development and political integration, the preservation of indigenous documents is a vital task, as in many countries and regions these documents are in danger of being lost. It is difficult to preserve indigenous documents when economic development is the top priority in politics and regional development, and natural disasters pose

---

15  Indigenous documents are documents that record history, customs, folklore, myths, or endogenous wisdom (knowledge) that are deeply rooted in the respective region, and documents that have the potential to become central to local residents' identity, at the same time contributing to research on the region in question. (Information for Applicants for fiscal 2005).

a constant threat. Even when the value of these documents is recognized, preservation efforts have been stymied by inadequate funding and a lack of personnel with the necessary expertise.

Because these indigenous documents constitute records of the histories and cultures of the respective areas, their preservation has the potential not only to assist academic research but also to help maintain and develop local cultures by providing opportunities for residents to rediscover their local identities. Many participants in grant projects of this type are not academic experts; they include community leaders, former Buddhist monks, private researchers, and others of diverse backgrounds.

Let us take a closer look at one such project, entitled "Preservation, Compilation, and Annotation of Mazar Documents in Ferghana and Xinjiang", led by Jun Sugawara. Conducted in collaboration with local communities, this project is devoted to studying and preserving mazar documents through the publication of facsimile editions.[16] The documents are in the possession of private individuals in Xinjiang, China, and Ferghana, Uzbekistan, two historically related regions situated in the deepest part of inner Asia. In addition to the preservation work, an academic conference was convened in the city of Ürümqi in China's Xinjiang Uighur Autonomous Region, with the assistance of a local organization, for the purpose of determining the cultural and historical significance of the mazar documents. Eventually a collection of papers is expected to be compiled and published, providing a general summary of the project.

One of the major distinguishing features that gives this program such potential is that projects not only yield research results but also involve local people closely in efforts to preserve and pass on the customs and traditions of their communities.

There are countless documents in danger of being lost that should be preserved. The areas targeted by preservation projects are expanding from year to year. In the future the Toyota Foundation will respond to the need for preservation by soliciting projects from all over Asia and supporting the use and passing on of project results, and, with assistance from local residents, endeavor to further strengthen our involvement with the communities involved.

## Asian Neighbors Network Program

The Asian Neighbors Network Program was established in 2003 for the purpose of creating and improving networks for research and practical activities within Asia as a whole.

---

16  Mazar documents are historical records testifying to the religious importance and social functions of the mazar (a type of mausoleum where the remains of an Islamic holy person are interred), which has served as both a religious focal point for the local population and a hub for wide-ranging human interaction.

The launch of the program was prompted largely by the growing trend for interaction and collaboration between nations in East Asia and the surge in international cultural and scholarly exchanges within the region, as well as by the rapid increase in the numbers of grants awarded to Korean and Chinese applicants under the Research Grant Program from 1994 to 2004. The Toyota Foundation was then in the process of expanding its grant-making activities, of which Southeast Asia had previously been the primary focus. Resolving to broaden its geographical scope while continuing to develop its presence in Southeast Asia, the Foundation created a program devoted to facilitating collaboration among people throughout Asia. The new program's theme was "Ties between people will unlock Asia's potential".

Figure 1: written in the Chaghatai Turkic language, is a letter of endowment (*waqf* nameh) issued by the magistrate (hakim) of the city of Kashgar for the mausoleum of a certain Islamic holy man from that city. The document dates from the nineteenth century in 8 Sha'aban, 1278 Annō Hegirae (February 7, 1862), to be exact.

In 2009 the program was renamed the Asian Neighbors Program. Still predicated on the importance of networks, the program has been assigned a new theme – "Toward community formation based on mutual reliance and collaboration" – and continues to provide grant assistance for efforts to build better communities (such as venues for traditional lifestyles and gatherings of people who share a common purpose).

Because this program began as a subprogram of the Research Grant Program, it was originally focused on providing support for scholarly interaction, primarily among researchers. After it became a separate program in the fiscal year of 2005, more emphasis was placed on providing grants for specific problem-solving activities in various parts of Asia, and efforts were made to differentiate the program from the Research Grant Program. Recognizing the difficulty of mounting practical efforts within vertically ordered organizations or the confines of bilateral relationships, this program provides grants for projects devoted to solving problems by forging bonds among diverse people. It is achieving positive results.

Let us take a look at one distinctive project supported by the program. Entitled "A Study of the Creation of Regional and Personal Networks Based on the Legend of Xu Fu: The Possibility of a New Comparative Study on Oral Literature," the project is led by Shiho Tsuji.[17] This project was undertaken with the goal of forging a network for research and interaction, linking people and places connected by the legend of Xu Fu, which has been transmitted across national borders in Japan, China, and Korea. In many of the locations in Japan, China, and Korea where the legend of Xu Fu has enjoyed currency, attempts have been made to exploit the legend in the interest of community revitalization, but such efforts have been disparate and specific to each location. Through this project, Ms Tsuji, the project leader, who has traveled to many of these places and forged links among people at various locations through personal contacts built up over the course of many years, is reinforcing a network for the sharing of information and research findings. The wide-ranging activities of Ms Tsuji and her colleagues and the unusual nature of the material (a legend with currency transcending national borders) have already had an impact: parties in Japan, China, and South Korea are planning to produce a collaborative television series that will mark the first time in the history of television programming in which three countries cooperate together.

The various grant-making activities undertaken by the Toyota Foundation since its establishment have earned the Foundation a certain amount of recognition in Southeast Asia. In the past, however, because the grant support was primarily limited to the domain of academic pursuits, the support framework was largely available only to researchers. Another issue is that relatively few grants have been awarded to projects proposed by applicants from outside Japan. In the fiscal year 2009, therefore, we have made a particular effort to disseminate information on the program to non-governmental organisations and local residents outside Japan (including in South Asia). As a result, we have seen a substantial increase in applications from overseas. We intend to continue to publicize the program and to further expand our network of connections in Asia.

---

17 Xu Fu was a Chinese man who reputedly explored the seas east of China during the reign of Qin Shi Huang, the first Qin emperor, in search of an elixir of life.

## The future of the Foundation's activities

This section presents an overview of the Toyota Foundation's current programs and a look toward the future of its activities, from the perspective of its thirty-five years of grant-making activities to date as shown in figure 2.

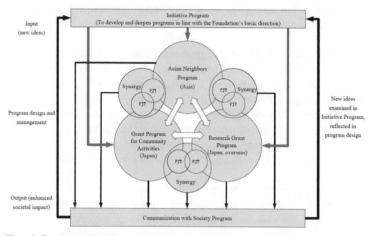

Figure 2: Constitution of the Toyota Foundation programs and interprogram cooperation

### Current programs

*Grant programs for community activities (publicly solicited)*

I have so far focused mainly on the Toyota Foundation's activities in other Asian countries, but since its establishment the Foundation has also been active in making grants within Japan. This program has the basic theme "Forming a Sustainable Framework within the Locality: Toward a New Community of Self-support and Symbiosis." It supports practical projects aimed at restructuring and revitalizing local communities in Japan. Japanese communities face a wide range of challenges, from environmental problems to falling birth rates, the rapid aging of society, depopulation, and education. By supporting the efforts of local residents to develop solutions to these issues, this program seeks to contribute to the revitalization of their communities.

*Research Grant Program (publicly solicited)*

Under the broad concept of "The Search for the Richness of Human Life and Activity," the Research Grant Program is now focusing on "Revitalizing Local Communities under Globalization." It provides support both in and outside Japan for research projects reflecting original thinking and with broad social significance that can show "how, amid the tide of globalization, local communities can harness their latent vitality through flexible restructuring."[18]

*Asian Neighbors Program (publicly solicited; includes Special Subjects)[19]*
A detailed description of this program appeared in the previous section.[20] This program has succeeded in creating opportunities to enhance mutual understanding among Asian nations and to resolve issues in the region.

*Communication with Society Program (not publicly solicited)*
The goal of this program is to share the results of projects funded by the three programs listed above with society at large.[21] The Foundation selects candidate projects through monitoring, and program officers work with grant recipients to ensure that results are transmitted and disseminated to society in an effective manner. Only past grant recipients are eligible for grants under this program. Through this program, the Toyota Foundation performs its role as a hub to connect its grantees with wider society.

*Initiative Program (not publicly solicited)*
This is the program managed with the original concern of the Foundation towards the future of society in order to clarify which subjects are important and how they should be supported. Projects undertaken jointly with other foundations and organizations are also eligible for grants.

**Issues facing the programs and future plans**

I believe that there are five areas in which the Foundation's program management needs to be improved. These areas are as follows:

First, as the individual programs have until now been managed in isolation, there has been little information sharing and cooperation between them.

Second, although the staff members responsible for individual projects have held regular consultations with grant recipients to monitor progress, the mechanisms for feeding the results of these consultations back into program management are inadequate.

Third, as the Foundation's programs have not been reviewed on

18  The Research Grant Program provides grants for research projects in the following areas: "transmission and formation of culture", "society's frameworks", and "individual and interpersonal development."

19  The Special Subject "Preservation, Compilation, and Annotation of Indigenous Documents in Peripheral Regions of Asia," which through fiscal 2008 was part of the Research Grant Program, in fiscal 2009 became the Asian Neighbors Program Special Subject "Preservation, Utilization, and Transmission of Indigenous Documents in Asia."

20  See section "Asian Neighbors Network Program".

21  The methods of dissemination include printed publications, visual media (films, videos, DVDs, etc.), digital media (websites, etc.), symposiums, and workshops.

a continuous basis, insufficient attention has been paid to identifying problems in projects and programs and assessing the extent to which program management has contributed to improvements in Asia.

Fourth, according to the Japanese government's fiscal 2008 white paper on public-interest corporations, there are more than 3,800 grant-making foundations in Japan. While these organizations provide grants in a wide range of fields, the concept of foundations, the roles they play, and the extent of their contributions remain unclear. As a result, foundations have yet to establish a solid position in Japanese society.

Fifth, there is uncertainty regarding the areas in which the Toyota Foundation can contribute to Asia as a private foundation in the future and the approaches it should take in doing so. Below are my proposals for addressing the challenges outlined above.

*Improving interprogram cooperation*

For the Toyota Foundation to continue its activities as an innovative and creative organization, it must ensure that there is organic cooperation between its various programs. To achieve this, the Foundation must make more effective use of the program officer system that is one of its defining characteristics. As well as managing their own programs, program officers should make proactive efforts to achieve greater synergy with the Foundation's other programs by remaining constantly on the lookout for opportunities for cooperation as shown in figure 2.

*The Foundation's role as an interface with society*

The Foundation should function as a network maker – a bridge that transcends national and disciplinary borders to connect grant recipients both with each other and with society. To strengthen the link between society and the results of grant recipients' research, in addition to providing grants the Foundation must increase opportunities for information dissemination, such as workshops and symposiums, and create a forum for interaction where a wide range of people can share information and research results.

*Grants for the future*

One of the purposes of the Foundation is to act as a catalyst in constantly bringing new vitality to society. We live in a dynamic world where people, goods, and information move rapidly from one place to another and competing value systems vie for supremacy. To ensure harmony among diverse groups of people, we need to prepare for the future as well as working to resolve the problems facing us in the present. To this end, I believe the Foundation must develop its ability to discern social trends and use this ability to judge what problems to address through its grant-making activities.

*Consolidating and improving the status of foundations in Japanese society*

We will work to improve society by strengthening our relationships with other grant-making foundations so as to fund projects across a wider range of fields. At the same time, we will strive to disseminate information on the activities of grant-making foundations to the wider community to consolidate and improve the status of foundations.

*Growing with Asia*

In its early years, the Toyota Foundation focused its grant-making activities on Southeast Asia. Today, we are seeking new fields in which we can make a contribution, while widening our focus to include all of Asia. Building on what we have achieved so far, we are striving to improve the planning and implementation of our grant programs to ensure that we distribute our limited resources as efficiently as possible.

## Conclusion

The Toyota Foundation has always set the direction of its grant programs by reconciling the values of these programs with the needs of society. In reconciling these two factors, it has often chosen to support projects even when the ideas behind them were regarded as out of step with the needs of society or the political and economic situation prevailing in Asian countries. Rather than discarding such ideas, the Foundation has aimed to put issues before a wide audience by supporting projects that would be unlikely to receive assistance based on an evaluation of short-term needs. We have always believed that this would lead to new developments.

The Toyota Foundation continues to change through its activities. I would like to highlight two of the changes that have taken place in recent years.

First, we have expanded the disciplinary and geographical scope of our grant-making activities. When the Foundation was set up, the focus of its activities was on Southeast Asia, but now we have widened the region covered by our programs to include the whole of Asia.[22]

Second, in recent years we have been actively striving to engage more closely with society. We believe that introducing the activities of the Toyota Foundation to as many people as possible provides us with excellent opportunities to meet potential future grant recipients.

In contrast to many Japanese foundations, whose grant-making focuses on predefined fields such as social welfare, education and art, the Toyota Foundation makes grants to a wide range of areas, at both the national and international level. These include research (for example the Research Grant Program); collaborative problem-solving (for example the Asian

22  Grants have also been made for projects in Africa and the Americas.

Neighbors Program) and activities aimed at community-building in Japan (for example the Grant Program for Community Activities). In this sense, the foundation is a flexible organization. To maximize this process, the Foundation provides activities such as information sharing and forum building which make the result of each project evolve further and have a wider influence and impact on Japanese society.

Since its inception in 1974, the Toyota Foundation has explored its role of grant-maker overseas, particularly with regards to the needs of its closest Asian neighbours. The programmes mentioned in this chapter such as the "Know Our Neighbors" Translation-Publication program, Asian Neighbors Network Program, and the SEASREP, or Southeast Asian Studies Regional Exchange Program all aim to preserve the distinctive aspects of regional culture and the development of mutual understanding between neighbors.

The Foundation recognises a certain degree of achievement in both of these programs. In the current era of globalization it became clear that there were many common goals shared by many neighbouring countries in Asia and South East Asia, but that often these goals were too complex to be dealt with by individual countries themselves. The programme aims to find ways to reach these common goals and seek effective solutions among people from very different backgrounds.

The Toyota Foundation sits within the wider scope of Japanese philanthropy, with each Foundation taking its own approach and adhering to its own philosophy. Although philanthropy in Japan goes a long way to better the lives of communities, it still needs to work towards the maximization of its potential for making impact. For example, there is a relatively low level of communication between foundations; within Japan, and this could perhaps be resolved through the development of forums through which different philanthropic actors could discuss the role of Japanese grant-making activities as a whole, which is something that younger generations in particular are striving to achieve.

E. H. Carr wrote that "history is an unending dialogue between past and present," and I find that these words come to mind whenever I consider why history is worth studying. Knowledge of the past sheds light on the present and helps us to understand it. In undertaking this review of the Foundation's achievements so far, reading the old documents and talking to people who have been involved with the Foundation for many years, I have rediscovered the history of the Foundation. It has been an extremely valuable experience.

Maintaining the values that have driven the Toyota Foundation since its earliest days and our commitment to opening up new possibilities, we will continue to value the cooperation we enjoy with others as we work to further enrich our grant programs so that they generate greater meaning for even more people.

## Epilogue

I hope that this review will help to deepen further the ties between the Toyota Foundation and the global philanthropic community. I have enjoyed the task of producing it, which has given me an opportunity to re-examine the history of the Toyota Foundation and has convinced me of the indispensable role that social action programs have to play in forging a harmonious, symbiotic society. I am grateful to the NEF-Mercator Fund and to Managing Director Hiroki Kato and Secretary General Akihiko Nonomiya of the Toyota Foundation for giving me this wonderful opportunity.

## Bibliography

- Edward Hallett Carr (1990) *What Is History?*, London: Penguin.
- Seiji Udo and Kenichi Kawaguchi (eds.) (2001) *Tounan Ajia Bungaku Eno Syoutai,* Tokyo: Dandansha
- Takashi Shiraishi (2003) "New Initiatives from Japan", in: Anthony Reid (eds.), *Southeast Asian Studies Pacific Perspectives*, Arizona: Arizona State University, 141-15
- *The Toyota Foundation*, [online] [August 2009]. Available from the World Wide Web: http://www.toyotafound.or.jp
- The Toyota Foundation (1985) *Toyota Zaidan 10 Syuunenn no Ayumi,* Tokyo: Toyo Keizai, Inc.
- The Toyota Foundation (1986) *Korekara no Minkan Josei Zaidan,* Tokyo: Toyo Keizai Inc.
- The Toyota Foundation(2007) *The Toyota Foundation:30 Years of History 1974-2004,* Tokyo: The Toyota Foundation
- Yujiro Hayashi and Yoshinori Yamaoka (1993) *Philanthropy and Society,* Tokyo: DIAMOND Inc.

ASIA PACIFIC PHILANTHROPY CONSORTIUM
RORY FRANCISCO-TOLENTINO

# 6 Asia and the Pacific
## CREATING THE FUTURE THROUGH PHILANTHROPY

## Introduction

Asia is the world's largest and most populous continent – containing 8.6 percent of earth's total surface area or 29.9 percent of its land area, it has approximately four billion people, or 60 percent of the world's current human population.

In recent years, the Asia Pacific region has had one of the fastest growing economies in the world, with countries like China and India growing at rates almost double those of the industrialised west.

In Capgemini's 2009 *World Wealth Report*, it is noted that as a result of the global financial crisis, there was a 19.5 percent drop in high net worth individual (HNWI) wealth to 32.8 trillion United States dollars (USD) in 2008. Of that amount, 9.5 trillion USD, or close to one third, came from HNWI in the Asia Pacific region.[1]

Clearly, it is a region that the world cannot afford to ignore, both for its current, as well as its potential economic strength. It is also a region that faces tremendous challenges brought about by its population and its economic, political and cultural diversity. What role can philanthropy play in helping the region meet its challenges? Can philanthropy help create a brighter future for Asia and the Pacific?

In this chapter, we ask the Board members and friends of the Asia Pacific Philanthropy Consortium (APPC) all fervent advocates, observers

---

1  Capgemini and Merrill Lynch (2009), *World Wealth Report*

or philanthropy practitioners, for their thoughts on philanthropy's impact on their countries, the effect of the current global financial crisis and the role of philanthropy in shaping the future of Asia and the Pacific. APPC is a fifteen year old independent association of philanthropic institutions and organisations dedicated to promoting the flow and effectiveness of philanthropy for Asia and the Pacific. It has fifteen Board members representing thirteen societies in the region.

## A background on Asia Pacific philanthropy

In a 2002 publication, *Investing in Ourselves – Giving and Fundraising in Asia*, undertaken by the Asia Pacific Philanthropy Consortium, and published by the Asian Development Bank, Marianne Quebral and Nina Terol noted: "The history of Asian cultures has contributed much to the growth of philanthropy in the region over the last few centuries. As the continent is home to several of the world's major religions – Islam, Hinduism, Buddhism and Christianity – much of philanthropic giving traces its roots to religious concepts of merit-making, almsgiving and performing charitable acts. Likewise, the close-knit family structure of most traditional Asian communities has made it common for family and neighbours to help one another in times of crises. Giving in this context has thus become an extension of service to one's family, rather than a random charitable act to a stranger."[2]

The publication notes the influence of faith on philanthropy in the region's different cultures:

### Giving in Islam

For Muslims, Islamic teachings mandate that a Muslim who has reached a certain level of income must pay *zakat*, an obligatory social obligation amounting to as much as 2.5 percent of his or her annual net savings. In Indonesia and Pakistan, the government has set up agencies to facilitate *zakat* collection, which is then disbursed to religious and social service organisations. Aside from this mandatory form of giving, Muslims are also encouraged to practice *infaq* and *sadaqah*.

### Giving in Hinduism

Like Muslims, Hindus also express concepts of social contribution: *datra datriva* and *daanam parmrarth*. More than this, however, they are encouraged to perform voluntary service, as *seva* is another Hindu concept.

---

2  Asia Pacific Philanthropy Consortium (2002) *Investing in Ourselves - Giving and Fundraising in Asia*, Manila: Asian Development Bank

## Giving in Buddhism

Buddhism promotes the practice of *thambun*, or giving for merit-making religious purposes, and *thamtaan* or giving to those in need. These concepts are considered the cornerstones of Buddhist philanthropy, as adherence to religious precepts is still a motivating factor for philanthropy among Buddhists.

## Giving in Christianity

Christians practice religious giving through *almsgiving*, *tithing* and contributing to the Church during congregational worship and special occasions (e.g. weddings, baptisms and funerals). This was inspired by the teaching to "Love thy neighbour as thyself." In the Philippines, this was first made operational through the Misericordia, a charitable institution founded by a Jesuit in 1594 for the social elite to give to the needy.

Most traditional Asian societies have developed around small, rural communities and have instilled in members a sense of kinship and willingness to help each other in times of need. In Indonesia, a large portion of the population still lives in rural areas and practices *gotong royong*, a concept of mutual aid. This practice is premised on concepts of man's belonging, interdependence and equality. The first concept is of man being part of community, of his social environment and of the natural and spiritual universe around him. The second concept is that of man being essentially dependent in all aspects of life on his fellows. This being the case, the third concept states man's responsibility to always maintain good relations with other members of his community, these good relations being based on the spirit of equality. The last concept is that of man endeavouring to conform, to do the same, and to be the same as his fellows in the community.

Likewise, the Nepalese have adopted many socio-cultural concepts of giving and volunteering. Among these are the *muthi daan*, *guthi and parma*. *Muthi daan*, literally, "giving a handful", consists mainly of separating a handful of rice or other food grain from the amount taken out for cooking the family meal, and saving it until the quantity reaches a reasonably useful amount. This is then given to the needy in its original form or converted by the donor into money before handing over to the receiving person or organisation. *Guthi*, on the other hand, is the concept of extending support to the members of the clan or community to which one belongs. Lastly, *parma* is the custom of labour exchange among people of mixed age groups or families, similar to the Indonesian *gotong royong*.

Thai society, on the other hand, draws on the relationship between kinsmen for philanthropy in a different way. One finds that even in contemporary Thailand, persons wishing to perform an act of merit-making also solicit the support of family members through co-merit making. This is said to strengthen family ties, as co-merit making is rationalised to be an act that binds families together in "future existence".

These concepts serve to demonstrate how socio-religious culture has influenced the practice and development of philanthropy and volunteerism in the region. However, it should be noted that both religious and communal models of giving may be limiting in that they do not encourage active participation in social and charitable causes outside one's religious belief or community, In Indonesia, for example, it was noted that urbanisation and modernisation have led to the erosion of *gotong royong*, while Indians, on the other hand, lament that "despite a long and distinguished tradition of philanthropy, private giving to promote the public good is still inadequate.

"Likewise, there is a prevalent attitude among the Nepalese that only the government, foreign donors, and affluent philanthropists are responsible for providing for the less fortunate."[3]

New Zealand, a small nation on the outskirts of the Asia Pacific region, has an inherent philanthropy in the culture of the Maori. New Zealand journalist Carol Archie explored Maori concepts of philanthropy in an article in Philanthropy New Zealand's newsletter in 2001. She wrote:

> *"After successful days fishing or hunting in traditional Maori society the bounty was shared around with everyone. Stories abound of the fisherman or hunter who drops off so much of his catch to his whanau (family) on the way home that he has none left for himself. Such behaviour is admired because it is an expression of aroha (love) and by giving, one increases one's mana (prestige) ... In communal life, Maori had highly developed customs for giving and sharing with others. However, the communal responsibility would appear to be very different from the Western tradition of an individual philanthropist giving money or goods with disinterest (and usually to strangers), preferably anonymously, for the wider public benefit ... In traditional Maori society, utu (reciprocity) was the ruling principle. Life was based on a continual shift of debt and obligation ...sometimes a debt might be repaid generations later ...for Maori, a special relationship was understood between the giver and the receiver. Giving was an expression of not just aroha (love) but of māna. Māna is the spiritual power and authority held by individuals and groups which can be increased by giving."[4]*

---

3  Ibid

4  Carol Archie (2001) "Maori Concepts of Philanthropy", *New Zealand Philanthropy*, Vol.2, No.25

## The current state of philanthropy in the region and the impact of the financial crisis

Perhaps one of the biggest weaknesses of the field in the Asia Pacific region is that no philanthropy statistics exist for the region as a whole. While some countries have undertaken relatively recent studies, the studies were undertaken in different years and did not always use the same research methodologies. It is therefore not possible to say with authority what the scale of giving in the region as a whole is, and whether it is unquestionably growing. However, most of the literature on philanthropy in the region would seem to indicate that it has, indeed, been growing, and certainly in the last decade. The studies also indicate a growing awareness of the importance of philanthropy in the individual societies.

The earlier cited publication, *Investing in Ourselves – Giving and Fundraising in Asia*, was a comparative study of individual giving in four countries – India, Indonesia, the Philippines and Thailand. In summarising the major findings of the study, Susan Hockings and Dr Mark Lyons pointed to the common findings across the four countries. They found that in all four countries, almost all high to middle income households made philanthropic gifts in the preceding twelve months before the study. Households in these developing countries appear to be as committed to philanthropy as similar households in northern or developed countries.

There was a uniformly high rate of giving to religious organisations, suggesting that religious traditions are high even among the high and middle income households who were respondents of this study. These groups can be assumed to be the most exposed to the secularising influences of northern culture.

Overall, there was a high rate of support (or philanthropic giving) for individuals in all four countries (from 40 percent to a little over 50 percent). They found that the households' socio-economic status has only a small effect on the giving rate, but a greater effect on the average amount given by givers. It appears that the generosity ratio falls slightly between high-income and middle-income households.

Finally, there was a uniformly high level of importance given to "feelings of compassion" as the motive of giving for all the givers.[5]

A 2005 APPC exploratory study of selected HNWI in six countries in the region (Bangladesh, India, Pakistan, Indonesia, Thailand and the Philippines), noted that: "Almost without exception, the respondents viewed giving as a social and moral responsibility, a way to "give back" to society what they had been blessed, privileged or fortunate to have received. This sense of social and moral responsibility is based to a large extent on

---

5 Asia Pacific Philanthropy Consortium (2002) *Investing in Ourselves - Giving and Fundraising in Asia*, Manila: Asian Development Bank

family values and traditions, as well as on strictures of faith. These Asian philanthropists cited the importance of "seeing" the impact of their giving on the lives of people they help."[6]

Research undertaken in Australia in 2005 showed that the giving of goods, money and services totalled 11 billion Australian dollars, with about 70 percent of that coming from individual Australians and the rest from business. About 87 percent of all adult Australians gave, and about 41 percent volunteered time for good causes. This proportion seems to be on the rise. As a proportion of gross domestic product (GDP) however, Australian giving is 0.68 percent, where it is 1.6 percent in the US and 0.46 percent in Canada.

It appears that those with greater financial capacity in Australia tend to give more. Christine Edwards, chief executive officer (CEO) of The Myer Foundation and The Sidney Myer Fund, and APPC's deputy chair, noted that individual wealth in Australia has been growing rapidly in the last ten years, with philanthropic contributions from the wealthy having tripled in the same time frame. However, philanthropic giving does not appear to have risen in proportion to the rise in their income, with wealthy Australians giving at 0.45 percent of their taxable incomes, compared to 0.68 percent for the rest of the Australian population.

A Philanthropy New Zealand study from 2005-2006 showed philanthropic giving in New Zealand in that period at 1.24 - 1.46 billion New Zealand dollars, estimated at 0.81 percent of the GDP.[7] Jennifer Gill, CEO of ASB Community Trust and APPC Board Member says that of this number, 58 percent came from trusts and foundations, 7 percent from corporations and only 35 percent from individuals. New Zealand has a unique system in the region where regionally-owned savings banks and government-owned energy companies were sold and the proceeds used to set up community trusts mandated to provide income distributions to charitable causes.

China, over the last twenty-five years, has averaged economic growth rates of about 9.37 percent, and its share of global growth from 1995-2002 is estimated at 25 percent, compared to 20 percent for the United States (US). According to Hurun's Rich List, in 2007, China had one hundred and six USD billionaires, up from only fifteen the year before, and none at all in 2002.[8] As individual wealth has increased in China, philanthropy has also grown. An analysis of Hurun's Philanthropy List over five years

---

6 Asia Pacific Philanthropy Consortium (2005) *Philanthropic Leadership and Development: Perspectives from Six Asian Countries,* (unpublished monograph)

7 Business and Economic Research Ltd (BERL) (2007) *Giving New Zealand, Philanthropic Funding 2006,* Wellington: Philanthropy New Zealand

8 Hurun Report, 106 *Billionnaires on China Rich List* [online] [July 2008]. Available from the World Wide Web: http://www.hurun.net/listreleaseen25.aspx

showed that in 2008, the top one hundred philanthropists in China gave 1.8 billion USD.[9] Five years before, the top fifty philanthropists gave 123.9 million USD.[10]

In 2008, charitable donations for China totalled roughly 15 billion USD, with about 11 billion USD going to the Sichuan earthquake relief efforts. The 2008 giving was about 3.5 times the amount of charitable donations in 2007, with 54 percent of 2008 donations coming from individuals.[11] In the first quarter of 2009, only a fraction of the giving was recorded compared to the same period the year before. The Chronicle of Philanthropy attributes this to the economic downturn and perhaps also scepticism about how the earthquake money was spent.[12]

Darwin Chen, honorary chair of Habitat for Humanity China and past chair of APPC, thinks that philanthropy's value is to help maintain social stability. By alleviating poverty, philanthropy minimises feelings against the wealthy. After the Sichuan earthquake, the Chinese central government decreed that every wealthy city give 1 percent of their annual revenues for rehabilitation of Sichuan. "This sent a good message, because in a country as big as China, the government sets the tone for the other sectors".

Ailing Zhuang, executive director of the NPO Development Center Shanghai and APPC Board member agrees that the central government's role in China is critical. When President Hu Jin Tao gave a December 2008 speech expressing the hope that different kinds of charity organisations in China would promote the culture of philanthropy, this was significant, as it was the first time the central government acknowledged the importance of philanthropy in China.

Barnett Baron, executive vice president of The Asia Foundation, APPC founding chair and an East Asian philanthropy scholar, agrees that the Chinese government is indeed encouraging more private philanthropy as a result of the Sichuan earthquake and the significant donations that came from the Chinese themselves, but they would like to carefully control where that philanthropy goes. It should go where the central government determines, not necessarily to building the infrastructure that creates a flourishing civil society. The Chinese government is learning, however, that they should not control everything, so to a certain extent they are

9  Hurun Report, *Top Philanthropists donate $1.8b in five years* [online] [July 2008]. Available from the World Wide Web: http://www.hurun.net/listreleaseen266.aspx

10  Hurun Report, *2004 China Philanthropists List* [online] [July 2008]. Available from the World Wide Web: http://www.hurun.net/listen11.aspx

11  Asian Philanthropy Forum, *China's Evolving Landscape* [online] [15 August 2008]. Available from the World Wide Web: http://www.asianphilanthropyforum.org/2009/08/chinas-evolving-landscape.html

12  Chronicle of Philanthropy, *The State of Chinese Philanthropy A Year After the Killer Quake* [online] [29 May 2009]. Avaiable from the World Wide Web: http://philanthropy.com/giveandtake/index.php?id=1054

able to let some things happen. China has accomplished a lot, especially for such a huge population, and while things are changing in terms of the government's willingness to let private philanthropy play a role, it will change very slowly and very deliberately, with the government always controlling its pace, so that society does not become fragmented.

Won Soon Park, Ramon Magsaysay awardee, and founder of South Korea's The Beautiful Foundation and APPC Board member, noted that although the culture of philanthropy and of helping neighbours has been rooted in Korean culture for a long time, it has never been, until the last decade, defined as such. In addition to the traditional areas of giving, Koreans are beginning to give to such causes as human rights, corporate citizenship and the need to empower public benefit organisations and worker education, something that bodes well for social justice and social transformation.

Dr Joyce Feng, Professor of Social Work and Dean of Student Affairs at the National Taiwan University and APPC Board member, notes that philanthropic giving in Taiwan has enjoyed steady growth in the past decade, with as many as 80 percent of the Taiwanese people giving, especially for natural disasters not only in Taiwan, but across the China Straits to mainland China, especially for the Sichuan earthquake and to Southeast Asia as part of the 2004 tsunami relief and rehabilitation efforts. This has been largely influenced by Taoism's concept of the need to accumulate good deeds to pass on merit to the next generation or for one's next life. She thinks, though, that in modern-day Taiwan, the growth of philanthropy has also been because of a long process of public education by non-profit organisations exhibiting transparency and accountability over funds raised from the public.

Hideko Katsumata, managing director of the Japan Center for International Exchange and APPC Board member, laments a continuing lack of recognition in Japan of the role and importance of civil society organisations in the governance of society. There is reluctance among the government and business sectors to support non-profit activities led by civil society organisations, because of recent fiscal deficits and economic difficulties. After the 1995 Kobe earthquake, when civil society's response was faster and more effective than the government's, incorporation and legal registration for civil society organisations was somewhat eased. The subsequent Public Interest Corporation Reform in 2008 went further in developing a more enabling environment for non-profit work in Japan. It remains an uphill battle for the sector in Japan to gain full-fledged recognition and support.

Eric Teng, CEO of Tan Chin Tuan Foundation and a Board Member of the National Volunteer & Philanthropy Centre (NVPC), shared that in Singapore, there is clear evidence of strong philanthropic giving, with a sharp increase in donation amounts mostly to charities that are accorded "Institutions Of A Public Character" from 341 million Singapore dollars (SGD) in 2006 to 958 million SGD in 2008, or an increase of 180 percent.[13] This is evident, despite a series of controversies involving some charities and despite the financial crisis. Volunteering has risen as well, from 35 million hours in 2006 to 49 million volunteer hours in 2008, a reflection of philanthropy taking root in the Singaporean psyche.

In the Philippines, a report of the League of Corporate Foundations showed that corporate social investment contributions almost doubled between 2007 and 2008, from 2.15 billion pesos (PHP) in 2007 to 4.13 billion PHP in 2008. The report also noted that corporations were focusing on long-term philanthropic investments, such as the environment and sustainable development, rather than on one-off donations.[14]

Surveys conducted by the Public Interest Research and Advocacy organisation in Indonesia showed that close to 100 percent of Indonesians give donations, although the amounts of giving are affected by the country's economic situation, with giving rates dropping when the economy is perceived to be bad.[15]

The significance of philanthropy is highlighted in research undertaken in Pakistan showing that in 1998, individual philanthropy resources (including volunteering and in-kind giving) was at 70 billion Pakistani rupees (PKR) (over 1 billion USD) while government social sector spending in that same year was at 83 billion PKRs.[16] In a Johns Hopkins study, for the 1995-2002 period, total philanthropy (including volunteering) amounted to 0.36 percent of GDP.[17]

Annual corporate giving surveys conducted by the Pakistan Centre on Philanthropy show that corporate giving increased 8 times between 2000 and 2007, from 228 million PKR to 1.87 billion PKR.[18]

The recent global financial crisis affected the whole world. How will it affect the future of philanthropy in the region? While the numbers are not yet in, there is reason for hope, not only in the region, but in the rest of the world.

13 National Volunteer and Philanthropy Centre Singapore, *Individual Giving Survey, 2008* [online] [July 2009]. Available from the World Wide Web: http://www.nvpc.org.sg/pgm/Content/NVPC_F_CMS_SubPage.aspx?PID=4&SID=39&AID=364&IDforEdit=364

14 Linda Atayde (2009) *CSR Report,* [presentation] Manila: League of Corporate Foundations Philippines

15 Public Interest Research and Advocacy Centre (2009) *Sharing for the Nation Patterns and Potentials of Giving Survey in Eleven Cities in Indonesia,* Jakarta: PIRAMEDIA

16 Aga Khan Development Network (2000) *Philanthropy in Pakistan: A Report of The Initiative on Indigenous Philanthropy,* Islamabad: Aga Khan Development Network

17 Aisha Ghaus-Pasha, Haroon Jamad and Muhammad Asif Iqbal, (2002) *Dimensions of the Non-Profit Sector in Pakistan,* Social Policy and Development Centre, Aga Khan Foundation and The Johns Hopkins University Institute of Policy Studies Center for Civil Society Studies

18 Pakistan Centre for Philanthropy (2007) *Corporate Philanthropy in Pakistan,* Islamabad: Pakistan Centre for Philanthropy

In the United States, Rob Buchanan, managing director of International Programs of the Council on Foundations and APPC Board member, commented that in a March 2009 Council survey on the impact of the US economic recession on its members, nearly three quarters of the foundations which responded reported asset declines of 25 percent or more in 2008, and two thirds reported a further 10 percent drop in 2009. As a result, 62 percent of foundation respondents are reducing their 2009 grant-making. However, 32 percent plan to either maintain or increase their giving budgets in response to urgent needs caused by the economic downturn. Most of these foundations have committed their 2009 budgets directly or indirectly to help families, provide human services, assist low-income populations or support economic development. US foundations are also finding other alternatives to stretch their grant making funds. Some are collaborating with other funders, others are assisting their grantees to improve their use of assistance and some are providing operating support for non-profit organisations.

This pattern seems to be true as well in the United Kingdom (UK), where Philanthropy UK reported on April 30, 2009 that "in contrast to the decline in overall wealth, the top one hundred philanthropists on this year's Sunday Times Rich List increased their giving by 8 percent. In total, 2.817 billion British Pounds were given by those in the top one hundred 100 Giving List, 216 million pounds more than last year. This is despite the fact that the overall wealth of the one thousand people on the rich list has fallen by 37 percent in the past year."[19]

Ian Wilhelm, in a *Philanthropy Today* article noted that the economic downturn has indeed affected philanthropy in the region. Asia Pacific foundations have lost, like their American counterparts, between 20-30 percent of their assets and people's wealth has declined. This has affected many non-profits, which used to rely on funding from abroad, and are now forced to tap local funding sources. More severely impacted, however, are smaller non-profit organisations. With the cutbacks, grant makers will more likely give to larger organisations that are better at writing proposals, managing donations and reporting results. An opportunity has opened up, however, in local fundraising. Although often requiring more work, it has also opened the eyes of local fundraisers about its potentials and given them the chance to tell their story.[20]

---

19  Ben Eyre, *Britain's biggest donors give even more despite the recession,* [online] [September 22, 2009]. Available from the World Wide Web: http://www.philanthropyuk.org/ NewsandEvents/Latestnews/Britainsbiggestdonorsgiveevenmoredespitetherecession

20  Ian Wilhelm, *Philanthropy Today: Charities in Asia Work to Keep Donors Engaged During the Recession,* [online] [April 23, 2009]. Available from the World Wide Web: http:// philanthropy.com/free/articles/v21/i13/13001301.htm

In India, the other economic powerhouse in the region, Priya Viswanath, former CEO of Charities Aid Foundation India and APPC Board member, notes the tremendous change in the philanthropy landscape in the last decade. Priya thinks that while Indians have always been a giving people, the last few years have seen a more urbane India practice more organised giving. While no comprehensive research has been undertaken in India to assess the quantum and nature of philanthropic giving in many decades now, there are a few sample surveys, anecdotal accounts and articles on increased giving by individuals in urban cities and towns to community based initiatives and projects.

In a 2004 book on Indian philanthropy written by Viswanath and Noshir Dadrawala, CEO of the Indian Centre for the Advancement of Philanthropy and APPC Board member, it was noted:

"Philanthropy – as traditionally practiced by private trusts, family foundations, corporate donors and intermediary agencies, has had only a limited impact on bridging the equity divide. While a variety of foundations and trusts have made strategic investments in the social space, the inputs and supplements provided by the private sector have been minimal. However, the world is changing rapidly, and so too, the situation in India.

Many trusts established by corporate leaders are increasingly strategic in addressing societal challenges. The information technology revolution has had a significant and positive impact on philanthropic investment trends. Diaspora philanthropy is significant, and has made particularly strategic investments in education and the digital divide. There is the beginning of a philanthropic infrastructure to support and nurture philanthropic engagement. Increasingly, philanthropic and social investment capital in India targets such areas as education, healthcare, population, gender issues, natural resource management, energy and enterprise development; many initiatives are focused on rural areas."[21]

While the global financial crisis has affected India as well, the predictions are that India will grow at 5-6 percent, so from a perceived government standpoint, there is no real recession in India, says Priya.

But is organised philanthropic giving widely practiced and is it addressing issues of poverty and equity? Despite Prime Minister Manmohan Singh's urging corporate leaders to "eschew conspicuous consumption, save more and waste less and care for those who are less privileged and less well-off and be role models for moderation and charity", Shankar Venkateswaran, advisor for Sustainability Limited, thinks India's "HNWI don't make such investments in a country where the distinction between the haves and have-nots is wide, appalling and growing."[22]

21  Noshir Dadrawala and Priya Viswanath (2004) *Philanthropy and Equity: The Case of India,* Massachussetts: Global Equity Initiative, Harvard University

22  Venkateswaran, S (2009) "The Philanthropy Conundrum" *Tehelka Magazine*, Vol. 6, Issue 8

Noshir Dadrawala thinks the government should do much more to encourage philanthropy in times of economic stress, such as providing better tax breaks or deductions. While the non-profit sector is beginning to feel the pinch as grant-making organisations become more selective about their causes and grantees, there is also a sense that in these times of crisis, the non-profit sector has an even bigger and more important role to play. In fact, Dadrawala says, the Finance Minister has just declared the New Income Tax Code that would have the effect of taxing income from the trade, commerce of business of those non-government organisations (NGOs) which are not exclusively engaged in the field of education, medical relief and relief of the poor.

The Bangladeshi government, on the other hand, has announced a stimulus package to deal with the impact of the global economic fallout. The package places emphasis on the agricultural sector, a move that most economists, according to Safi Rahman Khan, executive director of the Bangladesh Freedom Foundation and APPC Board member, think is the right thing to do, considering Bangladesh's high rural population. Safi adds, however, a growing concern about the widening income gap in the country is what philanthropy and the civil society sector can address together with government. It is particularly urgent, since the impact of the global financial crisis will take its toll on the poorest of the population.

It took the United Way of Taiwan, partnering with academia, legislators and the NGO sector, six years to have the Charitable Solicitation Act passed in 2006. However, scepticism over the amount of government control over the affairs of NGOs still exists. While government-NGO relationships are no longer as hostile as before, the NGO sector is beginning to understand that the way to overcome this is to improve the sector's transparency and accountability. Organisations such as the Taiwan NPO Self-Regulation Alliance have become more important in encouraging large scale transparency within the sector – including publishing financial reports of members on the Alliance's website.

The crisis in Thailand, according to Sukich Udindu, currently vice president for corporate social responsibility (CSR) of Minor International Company Ltd and former APPC Board member, is more than just a financial crisis – it is also a social and a political crisis that affects the bigger picture of philanthropy in Thailand. The Thai government has provided an economic stimulus package that will hopefully slow down the economic downturn. Thai businesses, in coping with the crisis, have resorted to reducing working hours in order to not lay off employees immediately. Companies are prioritising their giving commitments and are increasing their giving ability by encouraging increased employee volunteerism. The government has launched a major philanthropy campaign called *Chumchon Porpeng* or Sufficiency Economy Fund, to give resources to the 80,000 communities hardest hit across the country. By providing the funds to the communities themselves, it hopes to promote the community as the centre of development, engaging all the stakeholders in contributing to the solutions. In some ways, Sukich thinks, it is propagating the concept of community foundations in Thailand.

In New Zealand, early in 2009, the government announced a new Community Response Fund, a short-term, limited (two years) fund aimed at immediately addressing both the "cost and the demand pressures the economic downturn is placing on key community-based critical social services for families, children, young and older people". The Community Response Fund assists the providers of critical social services with additional funding to meet the increased demand for their services or to meet their operating costs because of reduced funding. This is in addition to the mid-2008 introduction of significant tax changes encouraging individual and corporate giving, moving the country from being one of the most restrictive in terms of tax credits for philanthropy to one of the most liberal.

Erna Witoelar, APPC chair and former UN Special Ambassador on the Millennium Development Goals for Asia and the Pacific, thinks that Indonesia, having come through the experience of the past Asian financial crisis, was better able to cope with this one. It increased funding for its poverty reduction programmes and expanded temporary employment programmes. Government worked with the private sector to stave off lay-offs because of the crisis. Philanthropy leaders like Erna went on national television to appeal to corporations to maintain their workforce and use their CSR resources for this. Philanthropic giving is not declining as much as they had anticipated, she thinks, and civil society organisations are bringing to the attention of the public the target groups that have been hardest hit.

Natalia Soebagjo of the Centre for Strategic and International Studies Indonesia and APPC Board member, notes that because of the crisis, giving has been directed toward relatively short-term and basic needs. While understandable, the need to be more strategic and longer term in philanthropy has to be addressed when the crisis is over.

As in Thailand and Indonesia, in the Philippines, corporations are redefining their CSR as related to their core business operations. They are looking at more ways to incorporate communities into their supply or market chains, according to Bobby Calingo, former executive director of Team Energy Foundation and APPC treasurer. The crisis has had good effects in that it has propelled businesses to align their programmes to the Millennium Development Goals and to measure performance against those goals. Business is also taking a harder look at the results for the philanthropic resources they are putting in.

# Philanthropy and the future

## Can philanthropy create the future of the region?

Natalia Soebagjo thinks that it is unlikely that philanthropy can play a significant role in preventing the global crisis from happening again. It can, however, help cushion the impact, if and when it does happen. If philanthropists make strategic investments such as in education, it will go a long way to making the country's social capital more stable and therefore more able to weather difficult economic situations.

Christine Edwards suggests that philanthropists can be significant players in change by using their many other resources to influence people. They can do this by acting as convenor, bringing people together who may not otherwise come together, by facilitating intra-philanthropic initiatives that stimulate thinking and debate, and by creating linkages amongst government, academia, the community and business. This influencing role must be harnessed by philanthropists if deep and sustainable change is to occur, especially in difficult economic times.

The role of the philanthropist in changing times is perhaps best exemplified by James Chen, chairman of the Chen Yet Sen Family Foundation. James, a third generation heir to his family's fortune, professionalised the family's philanthropy, helped Chinese yak cheese producers refine their products, improve quality and hygiene levels and establish a marketing entity to help them brand, market and distribute yak cheese. He also developed a social entrepreneurial opportunity with an Oxford University physics professor, who had developed an innovative, fluid-filled variable power lens that could be fitted into frames and adjusted by wearers to achieve enhanced vision. The availability of such a device would be a low-cost solution for vision correction. James Chen and Dr Silver, in developing the enterprise, developed a strategy that would build up parallel applications of the technology into products addressing commercial opportunities in the developed world. The commercial applications, they hope, will sustain the enterprise as they solve the marketing and distribution issues to make affordable vision available in developing countries. His vision to find ways to help others in a financially sustainable way may be a good example of what philanthropy could be moving towards.

Most of the interviews touched on the importance of the role of the state in philanthropy. Barnett Baron thinks that the question of whether philanthropy should be creating the future is part of the debate about the role of government or the state at this juncture in time. Because of what has recently happened, the US is moving toward a government that is intervening in a much stronger way in the provision of social services for its population, rather than allowing the private sector and free markets to handle this, with the government simply providing the regulatory framework. Increasingly, people are cynical about the capacity of deregulated sectors and services to provide the needs of its people, particularly for poor and marginalised populations.

On the other hand, Asia starts with the opposite philosophy – that it is the state's role to provide these services for its citizenry and that philanthropy can enhance and complement, but not reduce the responsibility of the State in this. "In the US, the current movement toward a more dominant state, and in Asia, which is beginning to loosen somewhat its control of philanthropy, there might be a convergence of attitude."

Certainly, there is some reason to think that this "convergence of attitude" is taking place in various countries. In Thailand, as in Singapore, the government has set up the National Center for Giving and Volunteering, to promote the giving culture of the nation. The Stock Market of Thailand, in 2007, established the corporate social responsibility Institute to promote CSR among local and international corporations, large, medium and small. They promote CSR principles such as the Global Compact, and a CSR Club has just been formed for the new movement of CSR and Philanthropy, much like the League of Corporate Foundations in the Philippines, according to Sukich Udindu.

Pakistan is one of the countries where civil society has been able to work effectively with government in creating an enabling regulatory environment for philanthropy, including authorising the Pakistan Centre for Philanthropy to certify non-profit organisations on its behalf. This will hopefully minimise the suspicion and lack of trust towards the sector.

One bright spot in the philanthropy landscape, according to Bobby Calingo, is the interest of the ASEAN Foundation in organising an ASEAN (Association of Southeast Asian Nations) CSR, a movement to promote Corporate Social Responsibility practices among ASEAN nations.

The need for donor education was raised in many of the interviews. In South Korea, believing in the importance of developing a more sustainable and institutionalised culture of giving and sharing, the Beautiful Foundation developed *Na-num-gyo-yuk*, a programme to teach philanthropy in elementary schools. This donor education programme has several themes: definitions and methods of philanthropy, the history and culture of philanthropy, philanthropy and the community and philanthropy and the individual, participation in giving and serving. Aside from classroom lessons, there is a four day summer camp to learn about and experience philanthropy in everyday life. Philanthropy education tools contain animated videos, a children's guidebook and a sharing box – a cardboard piggy bank, with different parts on an image on the top. When put together several sharing boxes form a complete picture.

An impact study made on the programme two years after it began, found that students scored higher in their understanding of others (empathy) and their social commitment. The teachers who were trained to teach philanthropy in the schools noticed that the students who participated in the programme seemed more relaxed, rarely fought each other or picked on peers, and were more generous than other students. Interestingly, the teachers who were trained to teach this module found that their own view of their personal contribution was widened, and they also began volunteering their time and energies outside of school because of what they learned from the programme.

One of the things that has helped philanthropy weather crises is the ability of various sectors to work together to achieve an important goal. In the Philippines, the *57-75 Movement* came about, led by both corporate philanthropy groups and education advocates. The group's name, *57-75*, was inspired by the results of the National Achievement Test at that time. The number *57*, the average test score, symbolised the current state of the Philippine public school system. *75* is the score that the government Education Ministry refers to as the beginning of mastery; the goal of the programme. *57-75* is a reversal in numbers, a good rallying cry to try and turn things around, both in the way the education system is seen and the way issues are addressed. The programme focuses on addressing the three main issues of the Philippine educational system: the school dropout rate, reading proficiency, and improving achievement rates in English, Science and Maths. The programme provides resource holders/philanthropists with the opportunity to pick local areas which have already organised multi-sector education alliances and have formulated education plans to address the issues. The programme implements a series of tested solutions in these local areas, with philanthropic resources that pay for specific interventions, until each area has a complete set of resources to address the needs.

For non-profit organisations in Asia and the Pacific, the global financial crisis is a real opportunity to try new ways to raise funds, especially from within their countries. Because of the crisis, hard questions are being asked about the impact of investments philanthropy has made in the past. Non-profit organisations need to be better governed, more transparent and more accountable, in order to survive the worst of the crisis. Good governance is a competitive advantage, especially in a time of decreasing philanthropic funds. Non-profit organisations need to cast a wider net as well, looking beyond their own borders, to other countries, where increasingly large numbers of Asians live and work. These diaspora populations have great potential for philanthropy and are rooted culturally and emotionally to their homeland. A study of the Pakistani diaspora in the US showed, for instance, that the Pakistani diaspora gave 3.5 percent of their household incomes for philanthropy as compared to 3.1 percent for all other US households.[23] It is yet another opportunity to "tell their story" to an audience that may have more of a desire and a stake in supporting those causes long into the future.

As Shamsh Kassim-Lakha, former Education Minister of Pakistan and currently chair of the Pakistan Centre for Philanthropy said, "The mindset and attitude of developing countries is one of poverty – that they have no resources and it is the industrialised countries that will help them. This is changing. Wealth is being created at a faster pace in developing regions like Asia than in industrialised countries. That wealth, if tapped directly, can be channelled into philanthropy, creating a powerful tool for social transformation."

## Conclusion

It is evident from both the experts quoted in this paper and its background research that philanthropy has grown in Asia and the Pacific in the recent past. And, despite the economic crisis, early signs are showing that philanthropy will continue to move forward. Perhaps because of the economic crisis, the multi-sector partnerships that were previously in their early stages have begun to bloom, as societies struggle to provide for their citizens despite the more limited resources available. However, there remains much scope for improvement.

The sector needs to do more work across the region to advocate with governments to develop a more enabling environment for philanthropy to thrive and develop deeper roots. There has often been tension between states and the non-profit sector in the region regarding the role of philanthropy. Governments have sometimes felt that giving legal and fiscal incentives for philanthropy and non-profit activities will result in their loss of control over both the provision and the quality of social services. Other governments choose to ignore the sector, claiming that compared to government resources, philanthropy resources are miniscule. However, where there is recognition that philanthropic resources can be used effectively to innovate and to test new ways of providing services, it is worth giving recognition and support to the sector. The philanthropy sectors across the region need to develop stronger ties with each other to bring advocacy to the regional, as well as the national levels. There is a need to share information about the impact of the philanthropic sector's work with the general public, so that a proper appreciation of its role is developed.

More cross-country research needs to be done to map the growth of philanthropy in the region in a sustained manner, in order to determine what needs to be done to promote it. Upcoming philanthropy resources,

---

23  Adil Najam (2005) *Pakistani Diaspora in the USA*, Islamabad: Pakistan Centre for Philanthropy

such as diaspora philanthropy and the use of media for philanthropy need to be identified and cases need to be developed that will enable philanthropy support organisations and non-profits to understand the phenomenon and determine how better to encourage it.

The financial crisis has perhaps had a silver lining for the region, in that it has made some governments more receptive to working with other sectors to encourage philanthropy in order to help their communities weather the crisis. Hopefully, the experience of working with each other to solve common problems will be a trust-building experience, and help minimise the distrust the different sectors have held for each other in the past. Realising that it is possible to work together towards a common goal may encourage more sustainable collaborative relationships with each other in the future.

A particular source of optimism for philanthropy for the region has been the growing desire of business, civil society, sometimes the church and academia, to work together to collectively solve what many consider to be intractable problems, such as education, shelter and health care. Given the quantity of the region's population in need of these services, the need for multi-sector partnerships becomes all the more pressing and urgent. As the various sectors bring their different perspectives and skills to the table, making inroads into these intractable problems a seems greater possibility.

Everywhere in the world, helping philanthropists evolve their thinking and strategies to meet real needs, and in more effective ways, is a concern. Asia is no different, in that HNWI express a desire to see their children and grandchildren continue in philanthropic activity but do not quite know how to achieve this. Developing donor education programmes is high on the agenda of organisations such as APPC. However, donor education programmes in Asia may not take the same format or concepts as donor education programmes in western countries. Donor education programmes in Asia have to take into account the particular nuances of Asian cultures and traditions, including the reticence of many wealthy families to become involved in "education" programmes. There is a need for resources to fund the testing of more culturally sensitive donor development programmes.

Donor development programmes must acknowledge the entrepreneurial skills and attitudes that the holders of philanthropic resources often possess – and utilise this to challenge them into thinking about how philanthropy can help bring about more long-lasting solutions to social problems and in the process, help to create a better future for the people of the region.

Organised philanthropy in the Asia Pacific region faces many challenges and a long road ahead if it is to build upon the deep rooted traditions of helping the less fortunate in the region and strengthen its impact on communities and people in need. Despite the challenges of the current economic downturn, Asia Pacific philanthropy is holding its own and shows signs of strengthening rather than caving under the new pressures that the economic crisis has brought. The Asia Pacific Philanthropy Consortium will continue to support the growth and development of philanthropy in the Asia Pacific region by helping to strengthen the institutional infrastructure and improving the operating environment for the philanthropy sector.

AILING ZHUANG

7 China

# PHILANTHROPY IN A TRANSITIONAL CHINA: ITS ROLE, VALUES AND TRENDS

## Part one:  The history of philanthropy in China through to the present day

### The tradition of philanthropy in China

Charity has been an important part of the Chinese traditional culture for thousands of years. The following paragraphs illustrate the predominant forms of benevolent giving in China:

**Giving through the Clan Council (宗亲会):** In traditional China, people were closely connected through paternal family links in the form of Clan Councils. The Clan Councils would provide support to those in need, with education, assistance, health and sustenance being the most widely addressed issues. This tradition is still strong in Chinese communities overseas, where giving to the clan-related families, to the communities where they live and to those in the mother country is based on the concept that "Blood is thicker than water" (血浓于水).

**Giving in one's neighbourhood (邻里捐赠):** The traditional Chinese believe that good neighbours are more accommodating and supportive in times of need than relatives (远亲不如近邻), therefore people often gave to local citizens living in the same disadvantaged conditions as themselves.

**Giving through religious entities** (通过宗教团体进行捐赠): Giving through religious entities was another common means of charity in traditional China, especially at times of natural disaster, when there were many homeless and destitute people with nowhere to go.

**Hometown associations** (同乡会): The Chinese place high value on the links to their roots, and often provide assistance to those in need hailing from the same place. Hometown associations still play a significant role connecting people either living overseas or in China. For example, in the early period of immigration from China to the United States, many of the new immigrants from Hokian (Fujian Province) benefited from the help of the Hokian Home-Town Association (福建同乡会).

**Career associations** (行业协会): An example of a career association can be found in the 1930s, when actors and actresses were low-ranking in Chinese society; their children were not admitted to good schools in Shanghai. The actors and actresses formed the Shanghai Actors and Actresses Association and raised funds among themselves to build a school for their children.

**Alumni associations** (同学会): Alumni associations were another way of offering assistance to those in distressing situations such as poor housing, low standard tuition, and lack of food amongst many other of the concerns in traditional China.

The philosophy of giving was deeply rooted in the Chinese tradition: "Care for what others care for, and be happy with what others are happy with" (忧天下之忧而忧，乐天下之乐而乐). This motto bore deep influence on the intellectuals in traditional China and resulted in the intellectuals giving regularly to charity through education, health and other means of relief.

## The emergence of new forms of philanthropy

Modern philanthropy in today's China is a result of the Chinese government's implementation of a nation-wide policy to reduce poverty and realise national modernisation in agriculture, industry, national defence, science and technology. Its main purpose is to raise additional funding to respond to social issues such as education, health and welfare, and to work towards poverty reduction, and deliver other humanitarian aid.

In order to enhance the productivity of the State Owned Enterprises (SOEs), the welfare actions carried out by SOEs were shared by other social entities. The Chinese government was the primary driving force in the creation of these new social entities: non-government and non-profit organisations. Most of the foundations founded in China between the early

1980s and the mid-1990s were founded or initiated by the government. The China Children and Youth Foundation was the first foundation to be created, and was followed by other social forces and individuals who hoped to make a difference. The Amity Foundation, created in 1985, was the earliest foundation founded by a non-state entity, the China Christian Council.

By 2008, the formally registered non-profit organisations (NPOs) in China amounted to about 420,000, including 1,500 foundations, 225,000 social associations (membership organisations) and 189,000 non-profit organisations, not including unregistered voluntary groups, NPOs registered in the Industry and Trade Bureau, NPOs under the umbrella of other organisations, and branches of international non-governmental organisations (INGOs) based in China.

Education, health, welfare, poverty reduction, disaster relief and reconstruction, environment, legal aid, and community services are the main areas to which people give either through direct giving, or through methods such as corporate giving, or giving through foundations.

Chinese philanthropy has transformed quickly over the past thirty years. During the 1980s and 1990s, most funding campaigns were organised through institutional mobilisation efforts. Most non-governmental organisations (NGOs) initiated by the government made the best use of the existing government administrative system to raise funds from SOEs or celebrities and to implement and monitor programmes.

Meanwhile those NGOs founded by private forces – by individuals, institutions or religious entities – approached their fundraising in different ways. Some raised funds from INGOs, others from overseas diasporas or individuals, others from other local resources, etc.

Since the year 2000, the government has adopted a more positive policy on philanthropy, passing more laws and regulations to give more space and flexibility to NGOs. As a result, the total number of NGOs registered has almost tripled. Between 1999 and 2008, the total number of social organisations in China increased from 142,655 to 413,666, an increase of 290 percent.

## Part two: The main players and their functions in the process of philanthropic development

### Government

The Chinese government, from the national to the local level, is the primary driving force of philanthropy and has played a vitally important role in promoting it in China through policy making, grant provisions, advocacy, and nurturing new forms of social organisations out of its own system. The Chinese Youth Development Foundation, the Chinese Poverty Elevation Foundation, the Chinese Red Cross Foundation, the Soon Qingling Foundation, the Chinese Charity Federation, the Shanghai Charity Foundation, the Chinese Association of Social Workers, and the Chinese Association for NGOs represent the most active and influential NGOs with strong government backgrounds.

Some government-operated non-governmental organisations (GONGOs) have successfully, innovatively and effectively created new ways of mobilising large amounts of funding by making use of the existing government administrative system in China to help those in need. The Chinese Youth Development Foundation has raised over 350 million United States dollars (USD) to help three million children and youths from poor families to continue their education, has built thirty thousand Hope Schools and has trained over one hundred thousand rural school teachers. The Chinese Poverty Elevation Foundation has implemented the biggest microfinance programme in China helping millions of farmers eradicate poverty. They have also made more impact on policy than other NGOs due to their specialised background.

## Grassroots NGOs

Grassroots NGOs founded or initiated by individuals and institutions are the second largest driving force in promoting philanthropy. The Amity Foundation was created by a group of religious and educational leaders to initiate philanthropic giving by people from other countries and regions. By the end of 2008, Amity had successfully raised donations of 300 million USD from overseas to help the most disadvantaged groups in China including the handicapped, children in need, poor ethnic groups in remote areas, disaster victims, etc. The Beijing Red Maple Psychological Consoling Center for Women was founded by a scholar in 1988 to meet the needs of urban women in a transitional time.

Grassroots NGOs have facilitated many innovative methods both in programme implementation and service delivery. Fundraising is a hard chore for most of the grassroots NGOs. Resources come from different avenues: some from overseas, some from individuals, others from corporate or diaspora sources. The Amity Foundation started many pilot programmes in China such as blindness prevention, mainstreaming education for the blind, foster care programmes for orphans, and community-based rehabilitation for the handicapped. Though most grassroots NGOs are weak in policy advocacy, we have still witnessed some grassroots NGO successes. The Chinese Anti-Domestic Violence Network has tried to work collectively and collaboratively with the Women's Federation, the media, and the judiciary to advocate for revising the law in terms of protecting women and children from domestic violence. Now domestic violence is widely perceived as illegal and this has been incorporated into the related law by the People's Congress.

## Corporate

In the 1980s and 1990s, state owned corporations (SOEs) played very important roles in philanthropic giving. A large percentage of the giving to GONGOs came from SOEs. One of the characteristics of SOE giving was that the quantity of giving was high. Grants by SOEs to GONGOs were often high-profile media events, and received extensive publicity across the country.

Now more private and multinational corporate groups are playing active roles in giving. Since 2005, over 460 corporate foundations have been created; most of them were founded by private corporate bodies and high net individuals. The Narada Foundation, the Vantone Philanthropy Foundation, the Xiangjiang Philanthropy Foundation and the Taoyuanju Community Philanthropy Foundations are among those with larger endowments, exceeding 100 million Chinese yuan (CNY) (equivalent to 14.3 million USD). Education, health, welfare, environment are the areas on which most of the corporate foundation funding is concentrated.

Corporate groups often act as donors for those they trust or those with the most influence. During the 1990s and 2000, most corporate bodies used the act of making donations as a way of marketing or advertising. Now these companies include philanthropy as part of their corporate responsibility. Staff involvement is encouraged in addition to grant support.

## Diaspora

The Chinese living overseas are the fourth most actively involved force in philanthropic giving, especially in response to large-scale disasters such as the Sichuan earthquake and important events such as the Olympic Games.

By June 2009, total philanthropic giving in China over the previous twenty-eight years had exceeded 20 billion USD. In 2008, the total giving for the Sichuan earthquake and other events of this nature was about 1.4 billion CNY (approximately 205 million USD). This does not include other benevolent forms of giving such as time, service, and donation in kind, etc.

The diaspora has been active in philanthropic giving ever since the beginning of the 1980s. At this time, most of the diasporas preferred to give funds back to their hometowns to build schools, hospitals, roads and libraries. Now the younger generation of diaspora prefers to build their own foundations in order to implement programmes or deliver services in accordance with needs.

**International NGOs**

The total number of INGOs operating in China is estimated to be between five and ten thousand. This is not a big number in comparison with the GONGOs and the grassroots NGOs, yet they play a very unique role.

Between the early 1980s and the mid-1990s, INGOs had a very difficult time establishing programmes in China. The earliest INGOs chose to enter China either by partnering with the government (for example, Orbis International partnered with the Ministry of Health), or with NGOs (many with GONGOs such as CANGO, whilst some religious-based INGOs chose the Amity foundation as a partner). Others such as Oxfam, World Vision and Save the Children chose to work with local government as partners, whilst some, such as the Ford Foundation, which was one of the very few INGOs to receive permission to register as a non-profit organisation for its Beijing office, chose research institutions as their partner,. INGOs centred mainly in big cities like Beijing. Most of them concentrated on education, health, welfare, poverty issues and disaster relief.

Between the mid-1990s and early 2000, more INGOs gained access to China after the Beijing Women's conference and China's entry into the World Trade Organization. More INGOs chose to register as corporate representative offices in order to obtain legal status. New forms of operation were adopted: the building of their own local programme branches, or working together with other grassroots NGOs or research institutions. Many big INGOs such as Save the Children, Oxfam, World Vision, and the Salvation Army moved their China headquarters to Beijing and left the programme offices in Yunnan in order to gain visibility. Additionally, more areas in need of funding were taken into consideration such as the environment, legal aid, micro finance, etc.

Since 2004, more INGOs have come into China, setting up in different parts of the country. Now in almost every province, municipality and autonomous region, INGOs exist. HIV/AIDS and labour issues are additional areas on which INGOs now focus.

Today, over thirty INGOs including the Bill & Melinda Gates Foundation have their China Office registered in the Ministry of Civil Affairs.

INGOs have played a unique role in the development of philanthropy in China through the transformation of ideas, funding provisions, skills and knowledge transformation and human resources training. Christian Blind Mission International, based in Germany, and the biggest INGO in the world working for the handicapped, has worked in partnership with Amity since 1986 to help people with all types of handicaps. They sent teams of experts in all fields to train ophthalmologists, nurses, technicians, special education school teachers and community health workers to provide better service to the handicapped. The Ford Foundation provides 20 million USD per year on average to support a wide range of projects from education reform, natural resources management, gender issues, arts and culture, etc. In the early days, INGOs recruited most of their staff from GONGOs and/or grassroots NGOs. Now however, we are witnessing a reverse flow of human resources as more INGO leaders and professionals are leaving INGOs to join the domestic NGOs as leaders or managers, or are starting their own NGOs. This is helping to enhance the leadership of local NGOs.

Last but not least, all types of NGOs have been playing increasingly important roles in providing a new channel of work opportunities for young graduates, the retired, and people between jobs from corporate and professional agencies.

## Part three: Personal observations – as a witness, a participant and an active constructor

I have been involved in the non-profit sector for over twenty years, starting as a volunteer at the Amity Foundation, a church-initiated foundation based in Nanjing. I joined Amity as a full-time staff member in 1990 after completing my master's degree, instead of continuing my teaching career as a university teacher, and became an NGO practitioner, program director and later NGO executive. In 2004, after obtaining my Masters in Public Administration concentrating on non-profit organisations in Harvard's Kennedy School, and a Doctorate in Law from Nanjing University, I founded the NPO Development Center Shanghai. This was the first of its kind in Shanghai and the second nationwide: a support organisation promoting capacity and accountability building in the non-profit sector in China through training, coaching, networking, research and programme support.

Over the past twenty years, I have been a witness, a participant and a hands-on constructor in the process of philanthropy in China.

### As a witness

As a witness, I have observed significant changes in this sector over the last twenty years. The attitudes of people and government towards philanthropy have changed dramatically. In the early years of my career in the non-profit sector, social recognition was low. Very often, people simply did not understand what I was doing. On one of my field-trips by train to visit the north of Jiangsu Province, passengers did not understand what my career entailed. When I told them I was working for a foundation, they took it as security on the stock market; I then tried to explain it as "social work", and people laughed and said what everyone else did was also social work. Finally I used the term "charity" which the passengers understood as "doing something good". Yet they were puzzled because to them only the rich and senior did "good things". They believed that my decision to give up teaching was not a wise choice. In the early years of my career at Amity which was faith-based, I was quite often perceived as a missionary by the government officials at the first few programme field visits, even though I was not a Christian.

### As a participant and constructor

In the past twenty years, I have been widely involved in many areas as a philanthropic practitioner, advocator and researcher. I have covered many areas including education, health, welfare, rural development, services for the handicapped, capacity building, etc. So far, I have been directly involved in over six hundred programmes, raising 8 million USD in funds, conducting about eighty training courses for five thousand NPO leaders from over six hundred NGOs, and providing one-to-one coaching and consultancy to over one hundred NGOs. I have also facilitated approximately two hundred networking activities, promoting sharing, dialogue and collaboration for maximising the limited resources available for philanthropy. I have led over a dozen research projects, and provided professional support to grassroots programme implementation for youth, handicapped, and disaster victims. I am also very active in advocating for multi-sector collaboration for sustainable development. I am the primary researcher on NPO management, especially regarding capacity building of NPOs in China.

## Part four: The trend of philanthropy for the future

The next ten to twenty years will be vital for China economically and socially. China not only needs to maintain its economic development, but also needs to ensure the delivery of diversified high-quality social services to meet the needs of a population of 1.5 billion. Therefore, the scale of the philanthropic sector will inevitably increase as China further develops.

### A vision for the future

Changes will be necessary in many aspects. In the legal environment, more laws and regulations will need to be developed. Registration for non-profit organisations will thus be made much easier, and all non-profit organisations will benefit from tax-exemption. Therefore, the total number of foundations, member associations and social service organisations will increase by at least three-fold. NPOs will play a more active role as their capacity increases. The third sector will become stronger. More NPOs are needed to provide more diversified high quality services to people in need. NPOs are the main service provider. More constructive relationships with the government will be formed as the third sector grows more capable and accountable. NGOs will have more say in policy making.

The support system for philanthropy will come into being. Therefore, more support organisations will be able to provide assistance to all kinds of NGOs including training, management consultancy, networking, information technology support, financial and administrative advice, human resources services, etc. A Council on foundations and a council on non-profits will also come into being. The quality of these organisations will be enhanced as the level of leadership increases.

As the scale of the middle class increases and the quantity and quality of corporations are enhanced, the volume of giving will be increased at least by ten-fold as more corporate groups and individuals are able and willing to give.

JANE FRANCIS, ALEXANDER JACKSON
& SHIVANI SATIJA

# 8 India

# FUSING THE OLD AND THE NEW: THE SIR RATAN TATA TRUST AND PHILANTHROPY IN INDIA

Throughout its long history, the Sir Ratan Tata Trust has prided itself on its pioneering approach to philanthropy. Founded in 1919 by Sir Ratan Tata, the Trust has consistently been a leader in the field of philanthropy in India. Today, it stands between the "traditional" model of community-led charity and innovation in strategic giving. The Trust is well-placed to fuse India's rich charitable history with new approaches to addressing the country's social and economic challenges in the twenty-first century.

## Sir Ratan Tata

Born in 1871, Sir Ratan Tata was the second son of Jamsetji Tata. Jamsetji was one of India's leading industrial magnates, the founder of the Tata business empire which thrives today. Sir Ratan, like his father, was a true Indian nationalist, convinced of his role in developing a prosperous future for the country. He was also kind-hearted, generous and broad-minded and throughout his lifetime he championed a number of philanthropic causes, and devoted his time and money to them. These early donations cast a light on the present grant-making policies of the Trust.

## Sir Ratan Tata's early philanthropy

Sir Ratan Tata was a personal friend of Gopal Krishna Gokhale, who set up the Servants of India Society in 1905. Through the society,

Gokhale – one of the leading figures of the Indian independence movement and a future mentor to Mahatma Gandhi - sought to promote social progress, bring an end to discrimination, and encourage the reform of society through peaceful means. Identifying himself with this vision, Sir Ratan gave the Society a ten-year endowment fund to support its welfare work for the poorer sections of society. The same interest in welfare and social reform still inspires the activities of the Trust today.

Sir Ratan later supported Mahatma Gandhi in his struggle to end discrimination against Indians under the South African government during apartheid. Under pressure from the South African authorities, Gandhi's movement was in dire straits. As well as providing his moral support to the cause, Sir Ratan Tata disbursed the substantial sum of 1.25 lakhs (125,000 Indian rupees (INR)) to Gandhi between 1909 and 1913.

Sir Ratan's desire to support research into the causes of poverty and its amelioration led him, in 1912, to propose that the London School of Economics set up a Chair for investigating poverty and finding solutions to it. Towards this Chair he paid fourteen hundred British pounds (GBP) every year until his death in 1919. The trustees of the Sir Ratan Tata Trust, recognising the work of the London School of Economics, extended this grant until 1931. Today, the Sir Ratan Tata Foundation is a permanent part of the university, offering yearly fellowships on research into South Asian issues.

## The founding of the Trust

Having acquired a reputation as a philanthropist by these early acts of giving, in 1913 Sir Ratan began to think about establishing a charitable Trust which would receive the bulk of his fortune after his death. To that end, he laid out his plans for the way in which such a Trust's funds could be used:

> "... for the advancement of Education, Learning and Industry in all its branches, including education in economy, sanitary sciences and art, or for the relief of human suffering or for other works of public utility..."

> "To engage qualified and competent persons to investigate into matters that pertain to the social, economic or political welfare of the Indian community, the object being to design schemes of a practical nature calculated to promote the welfare of the said community, care being taken that such work is not undertaken from the stereotyped point of view but from the point of view of fresh light, which is thrown from day to day by the advance of science and philosophy on problems of human well being..."

He also directed that *"No experiment and no venture should be aided or undertaken unless the scheme thereof is carefully prepared..."*

*"No institution or organisation should be aided of which the accounts are not subject to periodical audits and are not regularly issued and which would not be open to inspection and examination..."*

Sir Ratan passed away in England, in September 1918. In the following year, the Trust which bears his name was set up with an initial endowment of 8.1 million INR, with his brother Sir Dorabji Tata as Chairman. Sir Ratan's widow, Lady Navajbai Tata, also played an active role in the Trust.

## The early years of the Trust

In its early years, the Sir Ratan Tata Trust focused its activities in the city of Mumbai (then known as Bombay), predominantly on education and medical relief. The Trust also made grants in the fields of women's development, and one of its biggest initiatives in these early years was the Sir Ratan Tata Industrial Institute. At a time when few women could work in the industrial sector, the Institute gave needy women the chance to work and gain skills by manufacturing clothing.

In 1932, the trustees turned to Mr S.M. Markham from the Carnegie Trust in America, and sought his advice on how best to focus the Trust's grant-making activities to fulfil the vision of its founder. Markham advised the trustees to "embark on a definite three or five year policy with the intention of securing the greatest possible advance in one or two directions." Accordingly, the Trust began to expand its operation from individual grants to include large projects which had a real significance for national welfare.

## The growth of the Sir Ratan Tata Trust

Throughout the next few decades, the Trust focused its activities on large-scale institutions in Bombay which contributed to India's welfare and development. Medicine was one key area of focus. In the early 1940s, the Trust helped set up the Tata Memorial Hospital, which became one of India's premier institutions for cancer treatment and research; the Tata Memorial Blood Bank; and the Lady Ratan Tata Medical and Research Centre, established in Mumbai in the 1980s as an advanced medical facility, staffed by renowned consultants and experts.

Continuing the industrial legacy of its founding dynasty, in 1948 the Trust supported the foundation of the National Metallurgical Laboratory at Jamshedpur, which has since proved to be a cornerstone of India's industrial and technological development. In cooperation with the Sir Dorabji Tata

Trust (which was set up by Sir Ratan's brother), in 1936 the Sir Ratan Tata Trust established the Tata Institute of Social Sciences (TISS). Unlike a conventional university, the TISS was designed from the outset to promote social justice, social welfare and equitable development. Through research and education, it has consistently supported the growth of India's third sector.

The late twentieth century saw the rapid expansion of the Tata Group. With the opening up of the Indian economy in the early 1990s and the Tata Group's continued growth, the income of the Sir Ratan Tata Trust increased significantly. The trustees realised the need to utilise this income in an intelligent, effective and prudent manner.

To this end, in 1994 the Trust prepared its first strategic plan. To do so, it brought in the veteran social entrepreneur Vijay Mahajan. As a key consultant, Vijay Mahajan recommended changes in the operations in the Trust, to make the vision of Sir Ratan Tata more relevant to modern India.

Five key areas were established: education, health, arts and culture, rural livelihoods and communities, and public initiatives. It was decided that, instead of responding to individual requests and making *ad hoc* grants, the Trust would focus its grant programmes on these five themes. To fulfil its new mandate, the activities of the Trust gradually assumed pan-Indian proportions, shifting away from its traditional emphasis on the Mumbai region.

By the late 1990s, the Trust had expanded its activities across India, made grants in eighteen states, and had begun striking significant partnerships with key non-profit organisations. To build on these initiatives, the Trust enlisted the assistance of Deep Joshi, a renowned social activist and champion of the Indian third sector.

Deep Joshi mandated the Trust to go beyond "resource transfer" and begin full, strategic engagement with the non-profit sector in India. The Trust had undertaken a lot of good work and had made a significant difference to the lives of many, but it was still focused on making grants, rather than developing and supporting Indian philanthropy.

It was decided that relationships with grantees would change, through encouraging effective "intrapreneurship" (the process of entrepreneurship within an organisation or within a sector). Even if a grant itself was short-term, the relationship between the Trust and a grantee could be longer and deeper through building the capacity of the non-profit organisation.

## The Sir Ratan Tata Trust in the twenty-first century

Having adopted this plan, the Trust began moving forward into the twenty-first century with a new, innovative approach towards engaging the Indian philanthropic sector. As it did so, its resources grew, and consequently between 2001 and 2009, the Trust's grant making grew sevenfold.[1] This financial windfall was used to implement the "intrapreneurship" plan developed by Deep Joshi, through six nationwide initiatives aimed at boosting the lives of rural Indians.

Partnerships have been established with state governments, and alliances with international institutions and multilateral donors have been built. The Trust has begun working through five broad programme areas: rural livelihoods and communities; education; health; enhancing civil society and governance; and arts and culture.

The Rural Livelihoods and Communities programme focuses on two key themes, which are essential for the development of modern India – land and water development, and microfinance. The Trust has emphasised inclusiveness in growth and retaining agricultural dynamism as its two overall objectives, recognising the central role that agriculture will continue to play in India's economic and social life for many years to come.

The Water Sector Research project supports cutting-edge research initiatives which seek solutions to India's water crisis. Nearly a third of the country is drought-prone, whilst a quarter is also prone to flooding. Ensuring innovative and impactful water strategies is essential to agricultural growth and preserving health as India's population grows.

Other initiatives in this programme seek to improve land management strategies in India. Through supporting scientific research into food security and sustainable livelihoods, the Trust's initiatives act to preserve and distribute vital knowledge amongst governments, non-governmental organisations (NGOs) and local communities.

The Trust's Microfinance Initiative was created as a response to the need for efficient and reliable financial services for the development of the economy. For those who live on the margins of the economy, such access can enable an increase in the scale of their operations, or diversification into a new source of livelihood. To this end, the Sir Ratan Tata Trust operates a number of projects which seek to improve the access of the rural poor to microfinance. For instance, the Centre for Microfinance uses qualified professionals to provide a range of technical and support services to microfinance institutions. It emphasises research, networking, and building relationships between microfinance institutions, local communities, and government departments.

---

1 From 210.43 million INR in 2001 to 1,533.64 million INR in 2009.

The **Education** programme seeks to strengthen India's educational system at all levels, in keeping with the Trust's mission to build up capacities in key sectors. The country has made great strides towards universal elementary education; the Trust seeks to build on this by improving the quality of elementary education. It also provides grants to higher education institutes, and supports links between elementary and higher education institutes.

The **Health** programme has two aims: to provide rural health development, reflecting the Trust's goal of improving the wellbeing of India's rural poor; and to improve the quality of specialised, high-level clinical care. Rural India still suffers from serious shortages of adequate medical care, and serious health problems. To address this, the Trust seeks to support innovative health solutions which will empower local health service providers. And by helping to fund specialised clinical institutes, the Trust supports India's efforts to become a leader in advanced medical care.

In its **Enhancing Civil Society and Governance** programme, the Trust seeks to fulfil one of its most important objectives – to build India's non-profit sector, and to make it more effective in its work to address the challenges facing the country. Civil society in India is still evolving, and the Sir Ratan Tata Trust is assisting that evolution. For instance, through its Youth and Civil Society Initiative, it educates young people about the importance of citizenship, community development, and participation in civil society.

The **Arts and Culture** programme emphasises institution-building in the arts as its main goal, recognising the contribution of the arts to Indian society. There is still a serious lack of human resources in India's cultural sector, as well as a lack of exposure to, and understanding of, the vast and diverse field of arts and culture. This is one of the major reasons hindering the professional development of many art institutions in India – a concern that is shared by many artists and art institutions in the country. Through supporting existing institutions and fostering new ones, the programme seeks to build a rich artistic infrastructure for India.

Through all of these initiatives, the commitment of the Trust to innovation and impact shows that one of the guiding principles of Sir Ratan himself – that "[no] experiment and no venture should be aided or undertaken unless the scheme thereof is carefully prepared" is still adhered to today.

Today, Mr Ratan N Tata is the Chairman of both the Sir Ratan Tata Trust and the Sir Dorabji Tata Trust, as well as of the Tata Group itself. He was born in 1937 to Naval Hormusji Tata, the son of Sir Ratan Tata. He worked his way up through the Tata Group, becoming Chairman in 1991, and has been instrumental in transforming the Group into a globe-spanning commercial giant. As recognition for his services to India's development, he has been honoured with the Padma Bhushan, one of India's highest civilian awards.

True to his forefathers' legacy, he is a prominent figure in business and philanthropic circles, in India and around the globe. He is Chairman of the Indian Government's Investment Commission, serves on the Board of Trustees of the RAND Corporation, and is a Board member of the Bill and Melinda Gates Foundation's India AIDS Initiative, to name just a few of his many roles.

At the end of the first decade of the twenty-first century, the Sir Ratan Tata Trust continues to be a leader in innovative Indian giving. As a strong supporter of the country's charitable sector, the Trust has a central role to play as Indian philanthropy emerges as a driving force for social change and realises its full potential.

## The Trust within Indian philanthropy

Indian philanthropy has traditionally been guided by two themes – religion and nationalism. Religious giving has inspired Indian philanthropists for thousands of years. Many of the religions which flourished in India taught that charity could lead to salvation and was part of one's duty within the religious community.

As a result, much early philanthropy in India was directed towards giving to religious causes (to temples and monasteries) or to the poor and needy in the community as part of a religious obligation. India's diversity of religions – including Hinduism, Islam, Buddhism, Sikhism, and Christianity – has created a rich blend of different philanthropic traditions.[2]

In the twentieth century these religious motives for philanthropy were supplemented, and sometimes replaced, by the growing independence movement and the concept of Indian nationalism. Mahatma Gandhi played a central role in the rise of volunteerism through his call for the development of India into a modern, progressive state. Development, the reduction of poverty, education, and social justice were all essential to this vision, and were to be addressed partly through the concept of *Seva* (service).

Jamsetji Tata, and his sons Dorabji and Ratan Tata, were proud supporters of Gandhi's vision of a modern India. From the very beginning Jamsetji Tata saw his industrial empire as part of the wider story of India's astonishing development. He was one of a number of Indian industrialists who began to channel their corporate wealth towards philanthropic causes.

The Indian government also saw philanthropic organisations as a catalyst for the country's development, particularly in the turbulent years

2 The Asia Pacific Philanthropy Consortium *India*, [online], available from the World Wide Web: http://www.asiapacificphilanthropy.org/node/19

after independence. The government began to actively support Indian philanthropy, by increasing the legal space available for non-profits and by decreasing the tax burden on charitable organisations.

Over time, the financial support provided by the Government to philanthropic organisations was supported by a recognition of the third sector's role in advocacy and innovative development policies. Furthermore, as the federal government continues its policy of decentralising and empowering local authorities, decreasing the role of the cumbersome central bureaucracy, non-profit organisations have become essential development partners at the local level.

The Sir Ratan Tata Trust, as one of the country's largest philanthropic organisations, and as one with a history of innovative social programmes and a tradition of supporting India's third sector, has a vital role to play in this ongoing process.

## Prospects and challenges

The future for Indian philanthropy is bright, but there are still challenges to be faced. Despite the country's rich philanthropic heritage, its level of charitable giving has not kept pace with its breakneck economic growth. The new wealthy, educated middle class has not yet fully tapped its potential for charitable giving. According to one estimate, India's civil society sector raises just 600 million United States dollars (USD) a year, although the potential is more than 10 billion USD.[3]

The rich traditions of Gandhian voluntarism, strong local communities and religiously-inspired charity remain strong, however. Many Indians do give generously to local causes, or those which are closely related to them. Poverty, health and care of the elderly and the young are strongly supported, and receive significant donations from all sections of Indian society. The growing number of successful multinational companies operating in India – whether foreign or Indian – has led to a greater level of corporate social responsibility programmes and corporate philanthropy.

However, to an extent this "new philanthropy" is unfamiliar in India, where a focus on traditional, community development remains the norm. Giving remains personal, rather than institutional.[4] Multinationals operating in India are expected to engage in traditional, charitable activities, rather than innovative philanthropy. In addition, there is little pressure from

---

3 Economic Times, March 5 2008 'Indians are charity rich but philanthropy poor', [online], available from the World Wide Web: http://economictimes.indiatimes.com/News_by_Industry/Indians_are_charity_rich_but_philanthropy_poor/articleshow/2839166.cms

4 Viswanath, P and Dadrawala, N (2004) *Philanthropy and Equity: The Case of India' Global Equity Institute* Harvard University. [online] Available from the World Wide Web: http://www.fas.harvard.edu/~acgei/PDFs/PhilanthropyPDFs/Phil_India_Case.pdf

the third sector and from the government to "go beyond", and redefine expectations of what philanthropy should be. The third sector is dominated by religious philanthropic organisations, which are interested in preserving the traditional system; the government sometimes sees philanthropists as an unwelcome intrusion into the public sphere, despite its enthusiasm for the third sector.

The Sir Ratan Tata Trust is well placed to bridge the gap between "traditional" and "new" philanthropy in India. With its roots firmly in the community-focused, Gandhian system of public service, it has transformed itself over the years into one of the most forward-thinking, innovative philanthropic organisations working in the country. The experiences of the Sir Ratan Tata Trust hold important lessons for the future of Indian philanthropy.

As India becomes an increasingly powerful world player, its philanthropists will become more and more integrated into the global philanthropic community. India has much to teach the world, but it also undoubtedly has much to learn from other philanthropic cultures. In particular, building a broader tradition of giving amongst the emerging middle classes will be key to tapping India's philanthropic potential. In line with its eager assimilation of outside business models, India is also likely to absorb the growing trends of innovative and investment philanthropy developing elsewhere in the world.

In doing so, Indian philanthropy will be following the path trodden by the Sir Ratan Tata Trust, which today is one of the undoubted leaders of institutional giving in India. In the twenty-first century, it will continue to fuse India's rich and diverse traditions of giving with innovation and forward thinking. As the Trust's founder stated at the beginning of the last century, philanthropy must be undertaken "from the point of view of fresh light, which is thrown from day to day by the advance of science and philosophy on problems of humanity's well being".

SHAMSH KASSIM-LAKHA

# Pakistan

# PAKISTAN, A CASE STUDY: FROM CONVENTIONAL TO STRATEGIC THE INNOVATIVE ROLE OF THE PAKISTAN CENTRE FOR PHILANTHROPY

Civil society organisations, philanthropists and policy makers in Pakistan are redefining charity. The potential of using philanthropic contributions as investments for improving the quality of life of the poor, the disadvantaged and marginalised is increasingly being recognised by these stakeholders. Assisted by a structured approach to increasing the volume and effectiveness of philanthropy and an enabling environment provided by government, the shift from conventional charity to strategic philanthropy has resulted in enhanced social investments leading to the building of human and social capital.

The end of the first decade of the twenty first century saw the world confronted by one of its worst economic crises. In developing countries such as Pakistan – where citizens look to the state as the primary source of basic social services – the crisis has gone beyond simple economics. Rampant poverty and the government's inability to provide has led to disillusionment with the state's capacity to govern and administer justice. A pervasive sense of uncertainty is eating into all aspects of civic life. Compounding the situation is the added complexity arising from political instability and Pakistan's tough neighbourhoods, not to mention an increasingly radicalised population.

As the development challenge has grown tougher in recent years, an increasing number of civil society organisations (CSOs) and individuals are taking on the fight across multiple fronts; be this in education, health, gender equality, women's development, rural development, environmental protection or economic empowerment. This struggle assumes a much more complicated nature when one considers that 40 percent of Pakistan's population of 170 million is below the poverty line, 46 percent of the population is not literate and the United Nations Human Development Index for Pakistan ranks it 136th out of 177 countries.

Dismal though the situation may be, Pakistan has witnessed a growing trend of self-help through civil society initiatives. Prominent among these is the practice of giving donations and voluntary service by individuals, corporations, and Pakistan's widely spread diaspora. Assisted over the past decade by citizen efforts towards organised philanthropy, state and non-state actors alike view this act of collective and individual giving as a beacon of hope for creating much-needed social assets. The most recent example of this generosity was witnessed in the aftermath of the October 2005 earthquake in the northern parts of the country, which cost more than eighty thousand lives and brought forward the greatest outpouring of indigenous philanthropic support and voluntary effort ever witnessed in the country.

This chapter presents a case study of the Pakistan Centre for Philanthropy (PCP), established nine years ago as a civil society initiative to enhance the volume and effectiveness of philanthropy in a predominantly Muslim population. It begins by explaining the strong religious beliefs of Muslims which enjoin acts of charity, as well as the deep-rooted culture of the people of Pakistan that for centuries has encouraged support for the needy. The chapter goes on to elucidate how these attributes have conditioned and defined philanthropy in Pakistan, providing the impetus to organise indigenous generosity. It then describes the critical partnership role of the government in creating an enabling policy and administrative environment for such giving. The chapter concludes by explaining how the PCP, founded in 2001 by eminent citizens, leaders of civil society and business has assisted the process of igniting the impulse to give into a flame of philanthropy. Finally, the objectives and programmes of PCP that translate strategy into activities are described in some detail in the hope that Pakistan's experiences in encouraging a shift to strategic philanthropy, for building social assets in addition to conventional charity, may benefit other Muslim and developing countries.

## Islam as the keystone of indigenous philanthropy

*"Virtue does not lie in merely turning your faces to the East or the
West. Rather it encompasses faith in God, the Angels, the Book, the
Prophets and to give off what you have out of love for Him, to your
relatives, to the orphaned, the needy, the traveller, to those who ask
for help, and for the enslaved. It is also the keeping of prayer and the
giving of Zakat"*

Q2; 177

We are at a juncture in history, where societies are trying to pick
from times gone by – lessons and experiences that restore a semblance of
harmony – a feeling of fraternity; through which some of our modern day
suffering may be mitigated. Muslims often refer to the days of the Prophet
Mohammad, peace be upon him (PBUH), when the Islamic nation was
more of a welfare state; when the population benefited not only from the
generosity of the state but also of individuals. Nearly a millennium and a
half ago, when Islam was spreading across Arabia and beyond, the Prophet
(PBUH) and later Caliphs were practicing institutionalised philanthropy
while living in societies that seem rudimentary compared to the complex
structures that nation states have become today. In those nascent years of
Islam, the state provided separate funds from which the needs of the orphans,
the widows and the destitute were met. These social support initiatives of
the state were actively supplemented by individual philanthropists who also
created endowments for the support of "madrassas" or schools and clinics.
Interestingly, there are examples of endowments even for the upkeep of
communal physical facilities such as water wells and caravanserais for
travellers. In short, institutionalised philanthropy by the state as well as
generous individuals looked after many needs of the citizens.

The Muslim community or the Ummah in those days was not merely
a religious community in a narrow sense. It represented a context where
moral and social values of faith could be translated into action. Thus, as the
Muslim community expanded through conversion and conquest, its rulers
and scholars sought ways to implement such ethical ideals in their societies.
Though the world of Islam would ultimately encompass considerable
human, geographical, and cultural diversity, a common pattern of thought
was articulated in theological and legal discourses, translating Quranic
principles into daily social life. Questions of giving and ethics thus became
integrally connected to evolving Muslim practice, and in time incorporated
the institutionalisation of procedures for the collection and distribution of
individual charitable giving.

The Quran itself articulates a very textured and multivalent ethical concept of charitable giving. While inclusive of the notion of acts directed to the needs of the poor, the Quranic concept extends the significance of charitable giving to encompass the ideals of compassion, social justice, sharing, and strengthening. Such an ethic aims not only to be socially corrective, but also to reflect the moral and spiritual value attached to the qualitative use of wealth, property, resources and voluntary effort for the welfare of individuals, communities and society as a whole.

It is within the framework of voluntary giving, however, that the most innovative and sustainable adaptations of the Quranic spirit have occurred. Over centuries, Muslims, individually and as a community, have developed extensive networks to translate Quranic philanthropic values – along with broader humanistic values of compassion and service – into voluntary associations and charitable organisations to help the poor and the needy in many parts of the world. They generally target the most vulnerable groups in societies: the poor, unemployed, women and children and, increasingly, refugees and victims of war and violence.

Modern examples of organisations carrying out such work include the Noor al-Hussein Foundation (Jordan) whose mission is to promote individual and community self-reliance, grassroots participation in decision-making and project implementation, equal opportunities with special emphasis on women, and intersectoral cooperation. Another case is the Hamdard Foundation in Pakistan. This foundation declares as its primary mission the worldwide propagation of the scientific nature of eastern medicine, and its development in the light of modern research. Income from commercial manufacture of its medicines is ploughed back into sponsorship of lectures, scientific conferences, the creation of international networks of scholars and the publication of journals and pamphlets. In 1991, the government of Pakistan granted the Foundation a charter to establish Hamdard University.

An example of a recent, community-based initiative is the collaboration of various mosques in Zanzibar (Tanzania) to create a foundation to promote commercial activity in order to support wealth creation which can be harnessed to support social development among neighbourhoods in the vicinity of the mosques. A more global effort is represented through the work of the Aga Khan Development Network (AKDN), a contemporary endeavour of the Ismaili Imamat to improve the welfare and prospects of people in countries in the developing world, particularly in Asia and Africa. In each of the countries in which it is active, the AKDN addresses issues of health, education, economic development and culture that work holistically to enhance the quality of life of all citizens – irrespective of race, ethnicity, religion or gender.

The ethical teachings of the Quran, the example of the Prophet (PBUH) and Muslim history and tradition show how ideals related to charitable giving were translated into institutional forms and actions. Thus, historical insight offers powerful lessons for today to help Muslim societies move beyond mere rhetoric in their quest to sustain Islamic principles of giving, selflessness and compassion towards those who are in need – for the betterment of their societies and others among whom they live.

As modern Muslim nation-states and communities across the globe seek to relate issues of their heritage and faith to questions of self-identification and development, practices such as *zakat* (obligatory religious giving), *sadaqa* (voluntary giving) and *waqf* (endowment) offer opportunities to rethink the relevance of historical social welfare and charitable practices in contemporary Muslim social and economic life. As the majority of Muslims live in what is considered the developing world, the fundamental Quranic values of social justice and equitable distribution of resources figure prominently in discussions of the relevance of religion to public policies and private philanthropic action for the welfare of society.

## Philanthropy in Pakistan

The modern Western understanding of the term "philanthropy" emerged in the eighteenth century as the state and private individuals began to assume responsibility for the care and welfare of the less fortunate, a role traditionally held by religious authorities. Today, "philanthropy" is perhaps best defined as "activities of voluntary giving and serving, primarily for the benefit of others beyond one's family".[1] This broad definition is crucial, for philanthropy in Pakistan today reflects traditions and institutional structures of the diverse cultures and religions that shaped the region's history, before and after the country's independence in 1947. In particular, this definition allows for the Islamic integration of secular and religious life, and acknowledges that the central role religion has played in shaping Pakistani society has contributed to subtle differences in the meaning of philanthropy. Thus, the definition of philanthropy used here enables meaningful, cross-cultural comparisons while at the same time encompassing understandings and practices particular to Pakistani society.

It is also important, at the outset to distinguish between "charity" and "philanthropy". Charity is generally seen as providing immediate relief to some lack or need. This commonly occurs in the shape of welfare disbursements, where people "in need" are typically provided with food, shelter or money. Philanthropy has come to be associated more with the broader and longer-term connotation of "social investment". The shift

---

1 Cf. Robert L. Payton (1988) *Philanthropy; Voluntary Action for the Public Good*, NY: American Council on Education (p32)

towards social investment signifies that philanthropy should move beyond charity towards building human and social capital that would bring about sustainable development. In other words, it should invest in education, in enhancing social and economic opportunities for those who are less privileged, and in building strong organisations to address social ills over a longer period. To put it another way, the term "philanthropy" as used here is about "teaching people how to fish", as opposed to "giving them fish". Philanthropy for social investment entails a longer gestation period and is a more demanding enterprise than charity.

## Historic roots of Pakistani philanthropy

As explained earlier, religion – specifically Islam – and a local culture of supporting social needs of the poor, provide the basic context for giving in Pakistan. The cultural impetus of giving is evident from the contributions of Muslim, Hindu, Sikh, Parsi, and Christian individuals and organisations – at times working in co-operation with one another. The creation of Pakistan in 1947 brought significant changes to philanthropic activity in the region. A combination of private charity and state paternalism emerged to cope with the social problems borne of the dramatic events of the late 1940s and 1950s. The streams of refugees wrought by the partition of the sub-continent spurred a massive, spontaneous voluntary effort. Out of this effort, Pakistan gained new "social welfare agencies" working on issues of resettlement, homelessness and health.

The study of present-day philanthropy in Pakistan reveals that there is a growing gap between society's needs and society's institutional capacities. Pakistan's performance in the social fields has lagged, even when compared to its South Asian neighbours. There is wide evidence to suggest that desperately needed investments in building human capital – through education, health and welfare – are best organised through a mix of private and public institutions. Past philanthropic patterns – both governmental and private – must be reformed.

On the other hand, over the last decade and a half there has been an awakening of civil society with an exponential rise in private voluntary citizen initiatives in the social sectors of Pakistan. The two private sectors, epitomised by the concepts of the merchant and the citizen, are playing an increasingly larger and significant role in the provision of social services to poor communities in both urban and rural areas. The humble but all-important self-help efforts by poor and disadvantaged communities have been augmented through technical and financial support from a growing number of increasingly professional non-profit intermediary development organisations, generally known as non-governmental organisations (NGOs), or not-for-profit organisations (NPOs). The result has reached a scale and complexity that can begin to be measured in improvements in household incomes, and health and social indicators. While the dimensions of the diverse organisations of the emerging citizen sector are not yet well-studied or mapped out, it is abundantly clear that citizen self-organisation offers a most promising and sustainable avenue to tackle poverty, ignorance and ill-health.

Interestingly, the regulatory framework that governs such private initiatives retains laws, policies and attitudes that pre-date Pakistan's independence, or reflect concerns and situations specific to the impact of partition and conflict in the subcontinent. While some contend that this has hampered effective oversight of civil society institutions, others believe this "relaxed" regulatory approach has encouraged citizens to come together more readily in support of various social welfare causes. As so often, the truth lies somewhere in between.

## The shift to strategic giving

It is increasingly recognised that a society's capacity to shift from relief to development – from charity to social investing – is closely related to the credibility and effectiveness of philanthropy-receiving institutions. Credibility and effectiveness must, in turn, be built upon and sustained by a largely indigenous base. Pakistani society is fortunate to have a deep impulse and practice of charitable giving and volunteering.[2] Over the past fifteen years it has become increasingly clear that by focusing on indigenous resources and relying on religious beliefs and cultural traditions it is possible to decrease dependence on foreign assistance. In fact, through numerous innovative ways, Pakistani citizens and civil society institutions are helping the country to move beyond charity to sustainable social development.

Pakistan's indigenous philanthropists include both individual and corporate givers, who have donated money, goods or time to benefit others. Unique patterns of giving, reflecting diverse historical, religious and cultural influences, distinguish indigenous philanthropy in Pakistan from that in other contexts.

It is also important to define the meaning of "indigenous" with respect to the recipients of philanthropic actions, individually or collectively, of Pakistani citizens. The "indigenous philanthropic institutions" include not only those founded, developed, and sustained solely in Pakistan, but also certain organisations headquartered or initiated outside the country. Examples of this latter category are: SOS-Children's Village, Pakistan, which is affiliated with the Austrian-based, international SOS¬Kinderdorf organisation but is an autonomous, self-supporting Pakistani institution;

---

2  *Philanthropy in Pakistan: A Report of the Initiative on Indigenous Philanthropy*, Aga Khan Development Network, August 2000

and the Aga Khan University. This is chartered in Pakistan with campuses and programmes in six countries in Asia and Africa as well as the UK, and is part of a global Aga Khan Development Network, broadly international in its mission but also oriented to the development of the education and health sectors in Pakistan. While each of these organisations has historical ties or contemporary links to external institutions or funding sources, they have established strong roots in Pakistan and a generous indigenous donor base.

Mehnaz Fatima Special Education Centre which is certified by PCP

An important actor in the evolving dimensions of Pakistani philanthropy is the citizen sector. Bearing in mind the broad definition of "philanthropy", it is nonetheless important to distinguish between voluntary giving and the institutions that are the recipients of this philanthropy. By studying the recipients of philanthropy we can better understand philanthropy itself. In other words, we study the products to understand the source, the fruits to understand the tree. These fruits are themselves diverse, possessing equally varied appellations, but their comparison yields underlying commonalties that reflect the unique as well as universal qualities of Pakistani philanthropy.

Today over a hundred intermediary organisations in Pakistan provide social services through a network of grassroots groups and tens of thousands of local organisations working to address basic social needs at the community level. Together these form Pakistan's "citizen sector". The organisations vary a great deal in terms of their size, competence, transparency, in what they actually do, and in their impact. They address topics ranging from irrigation, micro-credit, and housing to community policing, consumer protection and civil rights; from health clinics and teaching hospitals to formal and non-formal education; from environmental awareness and community-based land use planning to small-scale income generation efforts.

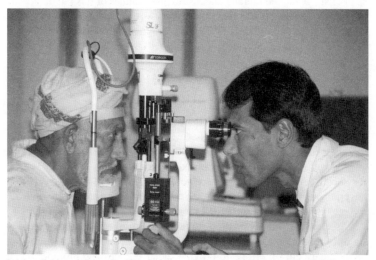

Leighton Rahimtoola Benevolent Trust which specialises in eye care and is certified by PCP

A few examples of these entities and the work they do are instructive. They include: South Asia's first private institution of higher education, the Aga Khan University, chartered in 1983, which enjoys one of the highest national and international standings in health sciences, education and health care; Lahore University of Management Sciences and some twenty-five other privately sponsored universities which followed the lead of these early pioneers in higher education; The Citizen's Foundation which runs over six hundred schools providing high quality education to eighty thousand children of low income families; Shaukat Khanum Memorial Cancer Hospital; Orangi Pilot Project for the improvement of sanitation for urban slum dwellers; and the Aga Khan Rural Support Programme, that changed the lives of millions of the poorest of Pakistanis in the northern parts of the country, and which provided the model for government-sponsored National and Provincial Rural Support Programmes across the country.

Other less dramatic though no less impressive examples include small women's development NGOs such as Khwendo Kor in the North West Frontier Province which works for the upliftment of women, and the Hamdam Development Organisation in Dera Ismail Khan, working in health and education.

In 2002, the government of Pakistan accepted an innovative private sector initiative by some distinguished members of the diaspora and sponsored the National Commission for Human Development (NCHD) and its partner institution the Pakistan Human Development Fund. In a short span of six years, the literacy and health programmes of this public private partnership reached out to over ten million women and children in almost all districts of the country. Its literacy programme earned it the United Nations Educational Scientific and Cultural Organisation prize for 2006. Contrary to past practice, the present government has continued supporting NCHD – a confirmation of the programme's effectiveness and a sign of sensible governance.

Collectively, these civil society organisations represent a significant development infrastructure across the country. Even more powerful than the material resources they generate, is the support they receive from millions of volunteers who provide social services and contribute their professional knowledge. Although these organisations constitute an effective vehicle for social development, most receive little or no financial support from government or foreign donors. On the other hand, many are benefiting from the catalysing efforts of the PCP, as will be seen later in this chapter.

As a whole, however, these organisations represent an increasingly significant development infrastructure across the country, which is drawing on voluntary citizen efforts to provide social services and promote social reform. As they take on greater organisational formality, they tend to be referred to as "NGOs"/"NPOs"/"CSOs". These terms are used without consistency in Pakistan and, among other things, there remains an important need for more careful differentiation of the many types of organisations operating under the broad umbrella of voluntary private initiative.

Thus far in this chapter we have reviewed the religious beliefs of Muslims across the globe that shape their attitude to support the needy and the cultural underpinnings of charitable giving in Pakistan. We have seen that the role of civil society in Pakistan has emerged more strongly over the past fifteen years and as economic growth has become palpable, citizens have become increasingly aware of their duty to assist the less fortunate and in doing so they have gradually banded together in groups to enhance the effectiveness of their social welfare efforts. Charitable giving has largely been applied towards traditional purposes of relief for the poor and needy. Only in recent years has there been a greater realisation by citizens, non-governmental organisations and government that generous as Pakistanis are, the impact of their giving will be substantially enhanced if more of it is invested in social assets.

How this objective is being achieved through the institutionalisation of some aspects of philanthropic efforts is described in the following sections, which elucidate on the genesis of the PCP and the enabling environment for philanthropy created by government.

Prep class in progress at the Hamza Foundation which is certified by PCP

## The Pakistan Centre for Philanthropy – from conventional to strategic

The Centre emanated from original research on philanthropy and is an outcome of recommendations of The International Indigenous Philanthropy Conference of 2000 attended by His Highness the Aga Khan and the President of Pakistan, who supported the idea of fostering an enabling environment for civil society and endorsed the creation of the PCP to promote structures and strategic approaches to enhancing philanthropy for social development. The genesis of this initiative however was much earlier in the late 1990s when the country was suffering under the effects of international sanctions and international development assistance had dried up following the testing of its nuclear bomb. It was then that thinking about enhancing philanthropic giving was initiated when His Highness asked some eminent citizens and civil society leaders, "How long will Pakistan continue to rely on external benevolence?" He wondered how Pakistani society, so strongly rooted in the ethic of the faith and with a long-standing culture of giving, could be encouraged to rely more on its own capacity to give material and human resources for the development of its needy. He observed that Pakistan's inevitable economic growth would increase the potential for harnessing the impulse to give that was innate in the religious beliefs and culture of its citizens. The question was how this philanthropic pie could be enlarged, and how the additional charity could be channelled into building social assets for sustainable development in addition to customary relief of the needy.

At His Highness' behest, the Aga Khan Foundation assembled a group of eminent citizens, CSO leaders and captains of business to deliberate how Pakistan could harness its own philanthropic potential and assist the state in improving access to social services for the poor. Known as the Steering Committee for Indigenous Philanthropy,[3] for two years starting in 1999 this distinguished group of men and women thought through the concepts of an organised and structured approach to philanthropy.

Assisted by seminal research studies on individual and corporate giving commissioned by the AKDN about the state of individual and corporate philanthropy across Pakistan, the group learnt about the situation on the ground. What Pakistanis gave, to whom and where they gave and for what purpose, was critical to understanding and charting a strategy for the next steps. Some striking conclusions of the Study of Philanthropy in Pakistan,[4] based on the methodology of an earlier Johns Hopkins survey of US philanthropy, were:

- "In 1998 alone, individuals gave an estimated 41 billion Pakistan rupees (PKR) (820 million United States dollars (USD)) in cash and goods." Astonishingly, 28 percent of this amount came from those earning less than 2 USD a day. In other words, the impulse to give was strong throughout society, regardless of personal circumstances.
- Even more surprising was the finding that in terms of per capita

3 Members of the Steering Committee - Chairman: Dr Shamsh Kassim-Lakha, President, Aga Khan University. Members: Mr Syed Babar Ali, Pro-Chancellor, Lahore University of Management Sciences and Adviser, Mr Mueen Afzal, Secretary General, Finance and Economic Affairs, Government of Pakistan, Mr Kamal Chinoy, Chairman, Aga Khan Foundation (Pakistan), Dr Attiya Inyatullah, Member, National Security Council and President, International Planned Parenthood Federation, Mr Mahomed J Jaffer, Senior Partner, Orr Dignam & Company, Advocates, Mr Shoaib Sultan Khan, Senior Adviser, United Nations Development Programme and Chairman, National/Punjab/ Sarhad Rural Support Programmes, Mr Khurshid Marker, Chairman, Merck Marker (Pvt) Ltd, Mr Shaukat Mirza, Managing Director, Pakistan State Oil, Mr Saeed Ahmed Qureshi, Former Deputy Chairman, Planning Commission, Government of Pakistan, Ms Sherry Rehman, Media Consultant, Dr Sulaiman Sheikh, Chief Executive, Sindh Graduates Association, Mr John W Wall, Country Representative Pakistan and Afghanistan, The World Bank Group

4 *Philanthropy in Pakistan: A Report of the Initiative on Indigenous Philanthropy*, Aga Khan Development Network, August 2000.

giving in proportion to their incomes, Pakistanis were at least as generous as US citizens.

- The volunteering component too is substantial, with a 58 percent participation rate, more than twice the global average. In fact, it exceeds the famously high rate of volunteering in the United States.
- The aggregate individual giving in cash, kind and volunteer time in 1998 totalled 70.5 billion PKR or nearly 2 billion USD. This is even more impressive when compared to 84 billion PKR spent aggregately by provincial and federal governments on health and education in the budget for the Financial Year (FY) 1996 – 97.

As in the United States, and as expected, a large portion of all giving in Pakistan is to faith-based causes.

A comparison with foreign assistance is even more instructive. For FY 1997 – 98 foreign aid was made up of 112 billion PKR in concessional loans and 6 billion PKR in grants, the latter representing just 5 percent of the total. Comparing indigenous giving to foreign grants, Pakistanis gave 20 billion PKR in money alone, that is, five times more than the amount their country received in outright grants by way of foreign aid.

Extrapolating in the absence of valid statistics but based on current trends, it can safely be assumed that levels of giving would have at least doubled since 2000, coming in the vicinity of 140 billion PKR in 2008, or 1.8 billion USD at current exchange rates. Note, this is greater than the largest ever US aid package of 1.5 billion USD annually for five years, approved by the US Congress under the Pakistan Enduring Assistance and Cooperation Enhancement (PEACE) Act 2009 (Kerry-Lugar Bill).

In addition to the valuable outcome of research studies, the Steering Committee on Indigenous Philanthropy reviewed best practices around the world in organised and structured philanthropy and drew lessons for Pakistan. Enriched by this knowledge, the Committee convened a major international conference in 2000, to seek the input of over three hundred delegates representing CSOs, business and eminent citizens on the way forward in institutionalising the promotion of philanthropy for social investment. The conference was particularly struck by the outcome of the research study on Philanthropy in Pakistan and the impressive levels of individual giving in support of the less fortunate.

The importance of the agenda of the conference was underlined by high-profile keynote speakers including President Rafiq Tarar of Pakistan, General Pervez Musharraf, the country's Chief Executive at that time and His Highness the Aga Khan. Following two days of intense deliberations, conference participants recommended the establishment of the Pakistan Centre for Philanthropy to promote the volume and effectiveness of philanthropy for investment in social assets.

Established in 2001, the PCP functions as an independent, non-profit support organisation with a Board of Directors composed of eminent citizens, civil society leaders and business heads in equal numbers. Core funding has come from a variety of sources including Pakistani philanthropists and businesses, Aga Khan Development Network and the Canadian International Development Agency. Programmatic support has been provided by individuals and corporations, the United States Agency for International Development (USAID), the Norwegian Embassy and more recently the Government of Pakistan.

As the credibility of the organisation grew and its impact was noticed, its Board took the bold decision to establish an endowment to provide a permanent resource to support the core operational costs (not programme activities) of the Centre. The appeal was launched with a call to corporations and individuals who gave the first 10 percent of the endowment of 400 million PKR or 5 million USD. With this critical private sector support in place, the Board was successful in securing a matching amount from the government. Recently, the PCP was fortunate enough to receive the remaining 80 percent from a foundation established by a member of the Pakistani diaspora who was motivated to support an institution he descried as "nothing short of revolutionary".

From its inception the PCP has been channelling philanthropic giving for social development and researching potential areas of growth that have led to positive differences in peoples' lives. It has helped bridge the gap between donors and the end beneficiaries in society by acting not only as a conduit between the two but also by making the public and private sectors more responsive and aware of the dividends of enhanced philanthropy.

As an example of its promotional work, the Centre has strongly encouraged giving by the corporate sector. Its latest research shows that between 2000 and 2007, voluntary corporate giving has increased eight-fold from 228 million PKR to 1.87 billion PKR. More importantly, the PCP's work with philanthropists has shown that it is possible to move from a conventional to a strategic approach to giving that encourages investment in social assets for sustainable development.

Within nine years, the PCP has created a niche for itself as the lead organisation for the promotion of philanthropy in the country. In addition to being a dialogue partner of social development networks in the country and the Pakistan government, PCP engages in regional and global activities with like-minded organisations and individuals to share, learn, explore and strengthen the promotion of philanthropy. This international networking includes interactions with: Asia Pacific Philanthropy Consortium, Global Philanthropy Forum, CIVICUS, The Asia Foundation, Give2Asia, Global Giving, Pearson's Fund and more recently the World Congress of Muslim Philanthropists.

PCP's ability to influence the creation of a more enabling legal, administrative and policy environment for philanthropy is perhaps one of its most strategic contributions to philanthropic work in the country. PCP has successfully persuaded successive Pakistani administrations to raise the size of tax-exempt donations which individuals and corporations can give to approved organisations. In 2008, it effectively convinced the government to roll back a proposal to cut by half the amount corporations and individuals can donate to approved charities. The latest example of PCP's effective voice with government was evident in the Finance Bill of 2009, wherein, "companies /associations of persons were permitted to claim tax credit on donations made; up to a maximum of 30 percent of the income. In the case of individuals the limit was 20 percent of the income" (raised from 15 percent). These fiscal concessions are among the most generous anywhere.

In an external evaluation of the PCP, undertaken by the International Business Leaders Forum, (IBLF), London, a charity established by His Royal Highness the Prince of Wales, the evaluators recognised PCP's contribution to philanthropy development in Pakistan and acknowledged that a strong and independent non-governmental organisations cadre is essential to accelerating social development in Pakistan. The IBLF report further highlights PCPs broader impact on the development front in Pakistan thus, "PCP has demonstrated that systematic and strategic investment by Pakistani corporates, individuals and government donors in Pakistani non-profit organisations (NPOs) is not just possible in Pakistan, but also something which is very much desirable. In so doing, PCP has contributed to recognition that a strong and independent NPO sector is essential to accelerating social development at the community or grassroots level across Pakistan".

PCP seeks to promote altruistic efforts of national and international philanthropists (individual, corporate and diaspora) by establishing effective linkages between the grant-maker and non-profit organisations. This requires bridging the information and credibility gap that exists between these two and is often a major impediment in the promotion of philanthropy. The Centre does not enter into direct service delivery mode nor does it receive grants directly.

Perhaps the biggest impact of PCP on the philanthropic movement in Pakistan is in the building of trust between the donors and users of philanthropy for social causes. Admittedly, these are early years but an excellent beginning has been made. Through its certification of NPOs' programmes, PCP ensures that those NPOs certified by it have the required institutional processes of using philanthropy effectively and efficiently while on the other hand it provides donors with efficient vehicles of using their contribution in the best interest of the end beneficiaries. An added trust-building area is NPO-Government relations where the PCP again has been working steadily to reduce the trust deficit that has long existed between the two. Much more needs to be done in this area but mutual confidence is gradually building up.

## PCP programme interventions

NPO Certification: Relying on best international practice, the programme seeks to evaluate NPOs on standardised parameters in critical areas of internal governance, financial management and programme delivery as well as wide dissemination of information about organisations that qualify on these parameters. Certification is essentially a "seal of good practice" for certified organisations and entitles them to receive tax exemptions on their income as well as from import duties and similar levies on goods imported for their programmatic activities. The programme has contributed immensely in addressing the trust deficit that has long existed between donors and recipient organisations.

PCP's NPO certification scheme was at the centre of controversy when it was initiated. Many civic groups questioned PCP's mandate to certify independent and self-governing organisations. Government agencies and donors were sceptical whether a certification scheme would gain the necessary legitimacy and scale. Business donors favoured their own due diligence mechanisms and were keen to retain their own independence and discretion. Over the past six years since its inception however, the certification scheme has gained legitimacy among many of those who have been involved with it from government, civil society and business. Several international donor agencies including those from Australia, Italy and Norway now make it a condition that NPOs seeking their support must be certified by the PCP. More recently, the government of Sindh province too has laid down this condition for certain NPOs seeking funding from its Community Development Programme, which functions as a public private partnership.

The NPO Certification Programme has certified 180 NPOs so far. To support this important programme, the Government of Pakistan, Ministry of Social Welfare and Special Education provided a grant of 48.987million PKR (600,000 USD) through the mechanism of a PC-1 form to be disbursed over three years, 2008-2011. Since PCP's certification fees cover only a fraction of the cost involved, this Government support has strengthened the Certification Programme and especially enabled PCP to extend its benefits to smaller NPOs.

Philanthropy Support Services are the action part of the organisation's services where partnerships are manifested in the form of actual projects. They include a Web-based development market place – Philanthropy Portal – an online facility which aims to help grant-makers find and reach the most suitable destination for their charitable funds. This mechanism is based on an engine that sifts through a databank of credible, certified organisations and returns donation options based on preferences identified by grant-makers.

Another project under the Philanthropy Services is Public Private Partnerships for Education (3Ps) for improving physical infrastructure in primary schools and enhancing access to and quality of primary education. The main objective of PCP's 3Ps programme is to harness the potential of corporate philanthropy for improving educational services for marginalised and under-served communities through an institutionalised school adoption process.

PCP interventions have contributed to improving the quality of education by facilitating the training of teachers, and by providing improved, needs-based physical infrastructure including supplementary reading materials, toilets, water supply, furniture, stationery and boundary walls for schools in the provinces of Sindh and Punjab.

By 2007, with the support of twenty four corporations, some seventy five schools had received PCP assistance through the 3Ps programme with direct benefits accruing to over ten thousand students. By 2008 over 1 million USD had been raised and spent in a three-phased program tapping a variety of corporate entities plus a sizeable USAID grant of 400,000 USD.

The successful demonstration of Public Private Partnerships for improvement of government schools opened new avenues for PCP. It encouraged the Foundation Open Society Institute (FOSI) – a Switzerland based international grant maker sponsored by the Soros Foundation – to partner with PCP to improve education in government schools. A joint proposal by PCP and the Sindh Education Foundation (established by the provincial government) received a two year grant of 181,049 USD (11 million PKR) from FOSI for "Improving Quality of Education" in primary schools in Hyderabad District. Keeping in line with its policy, PCP's role in this program is of a catalyst – to coordinate and facilitate and the programme has made good head way since May 2008.

For PCP, the programme has demonstrated the willingness of corporate partners to become actively engaged in social philanthropy ventures in a tangible way, providing inspirational examples for others to emulate. The success of the 3Ps program motivated the Federal Minister of Education to request PCP to hold several multi-stakeholder country-wide dissemination workshops at the local level to promote PCP's "Operational Policies" and "District Manual" developed under the Public Private Partnership programme.

The Research Unit at PCP operates with the objective of expanding the philanthropy knowledge map of the country. The programme, on the one hand, endeavours to expand the empirical map on voluntary giving which largely remains untapped, while simultaneously its research findings help stakeholders, particularly policy makers, plan better and more effective social investments for civic benefit in Pakistan. Since its inception, its research programme has been the corner stone of much of PCP's work and helps determine who gives, why they give and where they give. It informs the Centre about those segments of society which largely remain untapped, and provides objective information on trends and opportunities in philanthropy for social development. As mentioned earlier, the Center's annual survey of listed companies in Pakistan confirms corporate philanthropy has jumped eight-fold over the past six years. The launch events associated with PCP's corporate research reports and its annual Corporate Philanthropy Awards have helped mobilise opinion leaders from government and business to take philanthropy more seriously.

Successive studies of corporate giving, legal and policy environment for NPOs and diaspora giving have considerably enhanced PCP's reputation for providing objective information on trends and opportunities in philanthropy for social development. PCP reports are frequently referred to and cited in government, business and civil society documents and reports, as well as the media. The Centre's research provides benchmarks for those interested in promoting philanthropy across society – in government, business, academia, international agencies and civic groups. This has meant that for those interested in philanthropy for social development, PCP is the first port of call. A recent example of this is two recently commissioned research studies by the provincial government of Punjab on giving by individuals, as well as a survey of private and family foundations in the province.

The external evaluation of the PCP in 2008 conducted by the London-based IBLF recognised the Centre's research endeavours by noting that, "PCP has provided a steady stream of high-profile and evidence-based research reports on various aspects of philanthropy for social development, providing benchmarks or points of reference for policy discussion, legislative initiatives, and building confidence among both donors and beneficiaries on the value of philanthropy for social development."

While the Centre's research work has made noticeable impact, there remains a paucity of funding for conducting research to update data and address many new critical areas in philanthropy.

The PCP's Communication and Advocacy Programme aims to enhance societal understanding of philanthropy and development. The Centre recognises that all stakeholders need to be educated in the statistics and mechanics of philanthropy. For this purpose a multi-pronged media strategy advances discussions and awareness on philanthropy, including regular updates on the PCP website. While the Communications and Advocacy Programme with government is robust, for the public and the media this is one of the weak areas of the Centre. A recent perception survey has formed the basis of a revised communication strategy.

## Volume and effectiveness of philanthropy

The changes in the political and economic context of Pakistan since 2000 have also meant changes in the perception of philanthropy and the dividends it can deliver. PCP is at the heart of a growing movement among business, government, civil society, religious groups and individuals who share an interest in promoting philanthropy for social development. The launch events associated with PCP research reports have helped mobilise opinion leaders from government and business to take philanthropy more seriously.

In 2008, the Centre worked on a "Formative Research for Women Economic Empowerment Programme", a first of its kind in Pakistan. It was aimed at helping to improve the process of implementation, identifying methods to develop linkages across projects and gauging the impact on current policy. Through another study, "Government-CSO Partnerships; Towards Promoting a PPP Framework", the Centre provided a suggestive policy framework that may foster strong and effective public private partnerships between the Government and CSOs in Pakistan.

While the volume of philanthropic giving is an obvious indicator, measuring its effectiveness in advancing social development is more difficult. Providing direction or signalling priorities for philanthropic giving is a delicate matter best left to the choice of the donor. The PCP approach has been to make the choices available to public, private and individual donors clearer and more transparent.

To appreciate how PCP has grown over the years and how it has impacted on the shift from conventional to strategic philanthropy, it is important to recognise the economic and political context in which it initially had to operate and how it has adapted to the changing national scenario. Similarly, the needs and circumstances related to philanthropy for social development were quite different a decade back as compared to today. Again, the War on Terrorism has completely changed the political and economic context for promoting philanthropy in Pakistan, where NGOs have had to focus more attention on transparency, financial management and governance issues than ever before in order to demonstrate that funding them does not mean support for terrorists. PCP has both contributed to and adapted to the changing context.

## From here onwards

Today, more than ever, it is time to look into harnessing non-state resources and actors – especially those locally available – and direct them towards alleviating at least those pressure points that pertain to the provision of the basic human requirements of food shelter, clothing and health. By demonstrating that an innovative idea can be translated into a valuable institution for social development, PCP has emerged as an active development partner of the government of Pakistan.

As a continued effort to encourage and promote philanthropy, PCP organised the second Pakistan Corporate Philanthropy Awards in June 2008. As an encouragement, Prime Minister Syed Yousaf Raza Gillani hosted the event at the Prime Ministers House and presented philanthropy recognition awards to listed companies that ranked high on PCP's criteria. During the ceremony and as evidence of government's recognition of the PCP, while appreciating contributions by the business sector, the Prime Minister announced a contribution of 20 million PKR (250,000 USD) to the Endowment Fund of the organisation.

Moreover, the work of the Centre now demonstrates that even under the very challenging economic, political and regional challenges faced by Pakistan, there are noteworthy achievements to celebrate and to share with others. In fact PCP's experience in harnessing philanthropic resources for the building of social assets presents an interesting model for emulation by other developing economies. PCP has already established a collaborative arrangement with Tajikistan whose team of experts visited Pakistan to learn from PCPs experience in addressing social needs through philanthropy. A similar facilitating relationship with Afghanistan's CSO sector is also under consideration.

PCP's role in bringing together government, civil society and corporate entities is already being viewed as a replicable model for other nations facing similar needs. In fact in June of 2007, while addressing participants at the second Enabling Environment Conference in Kabul, Afghanistan, His Highness the Aga Khan recommended to the Afghan Government:

*"Let me mention in this regard a successful programme we have started
in a neighbouring country: the Pakistan Centre for Philanthropy. One
of PCP's roles is to function as a standard-setting body – a group that
certifies the effectiveness of organizations in contributing to the public
good … The story of the PCP is another sign of a recent maturing
process in the development arena. It represents another component of
a strong enabling environment."*

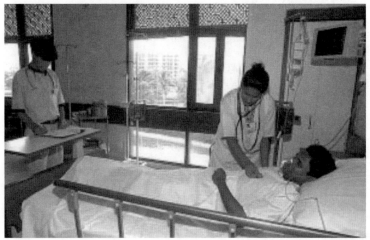

Aga Khan University Hostpital Patient Behbood Society which is certified by PCP

In terms of the future, PCP aims to focus on several new initiatives:
- First it wishes to concentrate on efforts that clearly translate into
  enhancing the quality and quantity of philanthropy for social
  development. Pursuing such a course will require defining metrics to
  measure the quantity and quality of philanthropic investment. It will
  entail more direct interaction with companies, government agencies
  and civic groups. Such metrics, if publicly reported, could then be
  used by all stakeholders to encourage more effective philanthropic
  investment.
- PCP's Board of Directors have decided to form a Philanthropic
  Network in Pakistan that will convene an Annual Forum of
  Philanthropy for Social Development, focused on understanding
  and drawing attention to existing and emerging issues, rather than
  merely on products (such as the NPO certification programme). The
  Forum will aim to generate dialogue and links between philanthropic
  investors, civic groups and government agencies. It will be used
  to highlight progress (or lack of it) in improving effectiveness of

philanthropy and to identify and articulate publicly key opportunities and barriers to philanthropy for social development.
-  Building on the role and reputation of PCP to become a convenor or facilitator of *ad hoc* forums for discussing important or emerging issues relevant to philanthropy for social development, without a formalised work plan and expectations. The focus would be on addressing "issues arising" from both the viewpoint of philanthropists and those directly involved in social development work.

*Age-old systems of religious, tribal or inherited family authority still have enormous influence in these societies. Local identities that often cross the artificial frontiers of the colonial past are more powerful than outsiders may assume. These values and traditions must be understood, embraced, and related to modern life, so that development can build on them. We have found that these age-old forces are among the best levers we have for improving the quality of life of rural peoples, even in cross-frontier situations.*

His Highness, the Aga Khan, April 23. 2009 at the Global
Philanthropy Forum, Washington D.C.

In conclusion, PCP's story in essence is that of a partnership between citizens and state, a partnership which the Centre has fostered by bringing out the best of both. Pakistan's current predicament has led to the awakening of civil society actors on the nation-building canvas. Government machinery, hitherto geared to run on paternalistic lines, is increasingly being seen to give space and accept the non-government sector as an active partner in addressing the pervasive issues arising out of lack of resources, inequitable development and poor management. PCP's role has been recognised repeatedly at the highest levels of government.

In the words of former president Pervez Musharraf at the launching of "Philanthropy by Pakistani diaspora in the USA" on August 02, 2006, I appreciate PCP's endeavour to promote philanthropy. I see the Centre playing a central role in addressing the lack of trust in citizen organisations.

On a wider theme, the Centre's facilitative services to both donors and users of philanthropic donations have been summed up in the IBLF evaluation of the Centre in 2008 as follows, "PCP has helped build confidence among institutional and individual donors in Pakistan and internationally by helping to link potential donors with beneficiaries (social development NPOs) in Pakistan. The PCP certification scheme, the philanthropy "P2P Portal" and evidence based research reports on philanthropy trends have all contributed to PCP's reputation as an "honest broker" always willing to help those interested in promoting philanthropy for social development."

As a catalyst, PCP's objective is to make clearer and more transparent choices available to public, private and individual donors, thereby fostering trust. This effort is part of the initiative to encourage a shift from a conventional to a strategic approach to philanthropy for the creation of social assets that help reduce poverty in the long term.

PCP has emerged not just as an active development partner of the government of Pakistan, but recently, it has received increasing recognition in the Muslim world for its innovative approach to promote giving. The work of the Centre has demonstrated that even under the difficult economic, political and regional challenges faced by Pakistan, its people's impulse to do good and to give of their material wealth has remained strong.

> *"The likeness of those who spend their wealth in Allah's way is as the likeness of a grain which groweth seven ears in every ear a hundred grains. Allah giveth increase manifold to whom He will. Allah is All Embracing, All Knowing."*
>
> (Holy Quran, Surah Al-Baqra, Ayat, 261).

PETER S. CLEAVES[1]

# 10 United Arab Emirates
## THE EMIRATES FOUNDATION - A MODERN RENDITION OF A FAMILY LEGACY

### Historical and context

The Emirates Foundation, created in 2005, builds upon the l ong-standing humanitarian vision of the Al Nahyan family that has ruled the Abu Dhabi emirate since 1793.

Sheikh Zayed Bin Sultan Al Nahyan (1918-2004), who forged seven separate emirates into a single nation in 1971, was a far-sighted leader with a personal history of magnanimity. He believed Abu Dhabi's oil wealth was a gift from God that should be shared with those in need. He also considered that individual good deeds should not be heralded. However, his direct and indirect contributions are well known. During trips to Africa, anguished by the sight of women carrying water long distances to their homes, he would order the digging of a well in the village center. Sheikh Zayed took advantage of every opportunity to learn, and probed visitors about the needs of their countries. He sent teams of trusted advisors abroad to check out untoward social or material conditions he could alleviate, whether in Turkey, Pakistan, Morocco, Mali, or elsewhere. He drove a Land Rover to the interior of the United Arab Emirates (UAE) visiting desert tribes to personally hear about their hardships and alleviate them. He constructed a home for care of orphaned children from countries experiencing civil unrest or wars. Wildlife likewise received his attention. He stopped hunting in the UAE and as a result free range wildlife flourished. On the island of

---

1   The author expresses his thanks to colleagues and associates knowledgeable about the Emirates Foundation and Abu Dhabi history who made valuable contributions to this chapter.

Bani Yas, he created a reserve as a sanctuary for such endangered species as the Arabian Oryx and the sand gazelle. His son and presidential successor, Sheikh Khalifa Bin Zayed Al Nahyan, continued the practice with patrolling of sanctuaries.

Officially, Sheikh Zayed created the Abu Dhabi Fund for Development and the Zayed Charitable and Humanitarian Foundation for housing, schools, hospitals, airports, and orphanages, and to assist in disaster relief when countries were afflicted by earthquakes, floods, hunger and fires. Health and education services attended to thousands of communities worldwide. His concern for the environment went hand-in-hand with infrastructure and social services, such as his commitment the "Aflaj System" (small scale irrigation canals) and his "Greening Program" (to combat desertification). He believed strongly that women should have every educational opportunity, and created Zayed University to assure their access to higher education.

Sheikh Mohammed Bin Zayed Al Nahyan speaking with his father, Sheikh Zayed Bin Sultan Al Nahyan, together with Sheikh Khalifa Bin Zayed Al Nahyan, currently Ruler of Abu Dhabi and President of the United Arab Emirates

His sons, including Sheikh Khalifa bin Zayed Al Nahyan, President of the UAE and Ruler of Abu Dhabi, Sheikh Mohammed Bin Zayed Al Nahyan, Crown Prince of Abu Dhabi and Deputy Supreme Commander of the UAE Armed Forces, continue this philanthropic tradition today. In a team effort, they enabled, among other things, the creation of the Makerere University - John Hopkins University Family Care Center in Uganda and have provided major support for the Oasis Hospital in Al Ain, UAE.

Sheikh Mohammed has personally established the Mohammed Bin Zayed Species Conservation Fund for endangered wildlife projects around the world, and has made a significant contribution to the United Nations in order to establish the United Nations Global Initiative to Fight Human Trafficking (UN-GIFT).

In 2005, Sheikh Mohammed Bin Zayed originated the idea, consistent with the national vision of Sheikh Khalifa Bin Zayed, of creating a new foundation dedicated to serving the people of the United Arab Emirates. The thinking process continued over several months beginning with a single idea – corporate social responsibility – expanding to volunteerism for Emirati youth, and then to a holistic conception across numerous fields. Among his close collaborators, Sheikh Mohammed Bin Zayed is known for his unwavering sense of duty to country – with "duty" writ large – making service to the nation the core of his personal philosophy. Among other efforts, he expected the Emirates Foundation to be a catalyst for behavioral change. In olden days, the Emirati helped the poor, who were not left to their own devices. In the *majlis* (community meetings with a sheikh), all people were respected and dignified. He wanted these values to be institutionalized in a new creation. In sum, the Foundation emerged as an expression of a larger vision of his father Sheikh Zayed – and that of his brother Sheikh Khalifa, who sees the advancement of citizenship as the cornerstone of a strong UAE society.

The Foundation has two main objectives: first to engage Emirati youth in contributing to the future of the country; and, second, to encourage businesses to adopt the principles of corporate social responsibility. The first aim seeks to address the risk that society may become too materialistic and that the young may not be sufficiently aware of their social responsibilities. The second issue seeks to secure something in return from the private sector in exchange for the many advantages they have gained from being based in the UAE.

It is important to note that the Emirates Foundation did not receive the formal "patronage" of Sheikh Mohammed bin Zayed. This was because it was felt that such patronage would only encourage business to symbolically associate itself with the organization, rather than make real efforts to ensure that it was a success. Instead, some individuals, including members of the Board of Directors, took it upon themselves to launch a fund raising campaign. Over 100 million USD was raised from a range of multinationals, local firms and government-affiliated organizations over a period of two years.

The Emirates Foundation is set in a religious and cultural tradition that includes *zakat* and *waqf*, though its orientation differs from both. According to the Quran, Islamic societies have an obligation to give to the poor. One of the five pillars of Islam is the payment of *zakat*, which means both "purifying" and "growth." Muslims are obliged to set aside a portion of their annual income to give to those in need. This act is a way of purifying one's self from greed and selfishness and also safeguarding and encouraging new income to come to the giver. In turn, *zakat* dignifies the persons who receive it because it shields them from the humiliation of begging and prevents them from envying the rich. No single channel exists for disbursing *zakat*; people are free to give *zakat* to whom they consider to be in need directly or to organizations that support the economically disadvantaged. While the *zakat* obligation would motivate some donors to support the foundation or engage in corporate social responsibility, its resemblance to charity is different from the modern philanthropic mission of the Emirates Foundation which goes beyond the giving of material aid, thus seeking to provide medium- and long-term solutions to national challenges.

The *waqf* is a form of endowment that shares many of the characteristics of a foundation. An individual owning a wealth-generating asset, such as property, can direct the profits toward an organization that performs a valuable public service, such as, for example, a school, a hospital or a charity. Under Sharia law, a *waqf* means "hold, confine or prohibit", in the sense that a wealth-generating asset is managed in such a way as to ensure that the assets proceeds are used for the public good and that the asset is not allowed to depreciate in value through the selfish pursuit of profit. The *waqf* thus stresses the virtues of longevity and reliability in terms of the generation of an income for the benefit of others. It can be seen as an example of "sustainable giving" in that its primary aim is to sustain specific beneficiaries. The terms of a *waqf*, as specified by its founder, must be respected. In this sense a *waqf* differs from a foundation in the modern sense, as the management of a foundation retains the right to sell assets such as property and even modify the original intentions of the founder.

Thus, while the traditional Islamic concepts of *zakat* and *waqf* inform the new Emirates Foundation, its aims go beyond these concepts as part of a necessary response to the reality of running a philanthropic organization in the modern world. The Decree which established the Emirates Foundation in 2005 refers to the fact that the Foundation is an independent corporate entity, with financial and administrative independence. Furthermore, while the Foundation is Abu Dhabi-born, it operates throughout the country and not just in Abu Dhabi emirate. While the Foundation is not subject to government control of its budget and programs, its Board of Directors is appointed by Sheikh Mohammed bin Zayed in his capacity as Chairman of the Abu Dhabi Executive Council. The Foundation is registered in the European Foundation Centre as an autonomous entity with multiple sources of funding. The Foundation has a very broad remit to support activities in the areas of science, technology, arts, sports, education, society and health.

## Three key initiatives

After the start-up period, the Board embarked on a strategy of more specific programs and concrete action from late 2006 onward. Sheikh Mohammed bin Zayed's personal interest lay in two programs, Takatof and Tawteen. Takatof's purpose was to support the goal of engaging more Emirati volunteers in social programs. In Arabic, Takatof means "shoulder to shoulder". Although initial expectations were modest, the program soon began to enroll thousands of volunteers (many in the 18-25 age group) prepared to carry out tasks such as hospital volunteer work. The programs activities soon expanded, to the extent that the program grew into a "social movement". Its expanded activities covered school work, support of families in need, staffing cultural attractions and assisting with major events such as the inaugural Formula One race and the FIFA football club championship. The outstanding success of Takatof was a source of pleasure for volunteers and directors, and was noted by the country's leaders.

Emirates Foundation Takatof Volunteers celebrating their role as hosts and guides for the UAE's inaugural Formula One auto race

In February 2007 the Foundation inaugurated Tawteen, a word that means "localization" in English. The idea was developed in collaboration with international companies. The intention was to enhance private sector opportunities in the region, an aim which acknowledged that companies had a role to play in cooperation with the government and education sectors. The aim was to provide support in the form of career counseling, encouragement of entrepreneurship and the development of leadership skills. The major challenge faced by Tawteen is to overcome the general attitude that employment in the public sector is a safer and financially more rewarding option than developing a career in the private sector. Nevertheless, it is clear that the Tawteen program is starting to change perceptions of the requirements and challenges of working in the private sector.

An additional element in the strategy of the Emirates Foundation are ambitious plans to develop projects that contribute to individual or institutional Emirati leadership, engagement of the private sector and the promotion of the country's cultural heritage. The five fields of interest, in accordance with the initial Decree establishing the Foundation, were Science and Technology, Environment, Social Development, Education and Arts and Culture. A consultation process led to the generation of innovative ideas that were subsequently approved by the Foundation's Board of Directors. All of these programs are intended to tap on the human resources of the UAE, namely the cohesive society and the tradition of mutual support. Other strengths were the proportion of women in higher education, attachment to cultural heritage and a rich natural environment.

At the same time, more needs to done to attract students to science and increase the influence of the scientific community. Better use needs to be made of natural resources. Improvements were also needed to enhance the national education system in the areas of Arabic literacy, math and computer literacy. The Foundation has launched a range of programs and initiatives to deal with these concerns. By the end of 2009, the number of grants awarded to various projects amounted to over four hundred. This rapid expansion has necessitated improvements to administrative and accounting systems. The Foundation has differed from all similar institutions in the region by publishing its audited reports. It has also placed a high priority on employing Emirati nationals; nearly half of the organization's employees are Emiratis. In addition, a number of senior posts are occupied by women.

Above all, the Foundation is fortunate in that it has the strong support of the country's leaders. All of the sums raised in the private sector have been matched by personal donations from Sheikh Mohammed bin Zayed with the support of Sheikh Khalifa bin Zayed, thereby providing the endowment necessary to ensure both a successful launch of the Foundation and the expansion of its growing range of activities.

Sheikh Mohammed bin Zayed has placed a great deal of importance on the active involvement of the business community. The goal of corporate social responsibility (CSR) was promoted by four broad approaches: first, the invitation of companies to affiliate with grants-related projects; second, the Foundation's own project for promoting CSR;

third, the communication of the Foundation's activities through the Arabic and English media; fourth, the provision of government funds for the Foundation's administration and the decision of Sheikh Khalifa bin Zayed Al Nahyan and Sheikh Mohammed bin Zayed to match all future private sector contributions to the Foundation. Sheikh Mohammed bin Zayed's intention was that the Foundation should work for all of the UAE. There are plans to give the Foundation an international profile; for example, Takatof has sent volunteers to North Africa. Another notable venture has been the International Prize for Arab Fiction (IPAF), which in its first two years saw more than two hundred submissions of recently published authors in Arabic.

The third turning point in the Foundation's early history was a major planning process mid-2007 to outline how the Foundation might attack its ambitious agenda. Five leading Emirati professionals and six international specialists spent two months in teams traveling throughout the UAE conducting interviews and holding workshops with local peers, university leaders, official agencies and nonprofits. Fields were Science and Technology, Environment, Social Development, Education and Arts and Culture, mirroring most of those areas mandated in the original Emiri decree. The team's remit included identifying strengths and weaknesses in their field, a strategy to meet unmet needs within a coherent strategy, and a suggested menu of projects. Each team was also asked to suggest one or more mega projects that would have a significant national impact. Finally, the array of projects needed to contribute to individual or institutional Emirati leadership, engage the private sector, and reinforce the nation's cultural heritage.

The exercise was highly successful. The consultants presented reports summarizing hundreds of meetings and addressed each of the questions, providing a well grounded set of priorities for the Foundation's future activities. The Board of Directors approved the plans and the Foundation began announcing and approving grants to individuals and organizations to implement their project ideas while recruiting senior professionals to head each of the five programs. A Public Awareness program was added to the mix to cover other mandated fields in a cost-effective manner, like health. Subsequently, the Foundation became both an "operational foundation" (Tawteen and Takatof) and a "grant-making foundation" (through open competitions, calls for proposals, and awards in each of the five main areas).

The consultancy teams found great strengths in Emirati society, including close family loyalties; untapped energy and commitment of youth; concern for people with special needs and the disadvantaged; a national legacy of assistance and generosity, and modernizing leadership receptive to social change. They noted that the country benefited from a

Ahmed Ali Al Sayegh (left) and Sheikh Abdullah Bin Zayed Al Nahyan holding an Emirates Foundation donor's trophy, when both were members of the Board of Directors. Mr Al Sayegh was the foundation's first Managing Director, and Sheikh Abdullah serves as the Chairman of the Board as well as Minister of Foreign Affairs

low student / teacher ratio, significant enrolment of women in higher education, a number of leading artistic practitioners producing major works and a widespread recognition that cultural heritage is an essential part of national life. They discovered the presence of accomplished senior scientists and goal-oriented junior scholars; advanced computational capacity in several academic institutions; a rich biodiversity in the country's arid environment; and they were encouraged by the country's official endorsement of international environmental treaties.

The Foundation took up the challenge of building on these strengths as quickly as it could. It launched programs to introduce the fun and excitement of science in schools and malls; to translate science websites into Arabic; to fund dozens of peer-refereed research projects; and to establish the basis of a national science academy. The Environmental program called for proposals to increase awareness through print, film and broadcast; to create internships for young persons in government and industry; and to strengthen the country's few environmental civil society organizations. The Education program offered opportunities for teachers to attend pedagogical conferences; for innovations in curriculum and improving reading skills; and for public schools to enhance the quality of their libraries. In Social Development, the Foundation supported programs for special needs centers, workshops on family challenges, and civil society organizations. Arts and Culture initiatives included individual awards for young artists, film makers, and writers; arts festivals; foreign residencies (France, England, Spain, and Brazil) for more established artists; and the International Prize for Arabic Fiction. Finally, in Public Awareness, the Foundation sponsored projects to encourage diabetes prevention and road safety.

Through 2007, the Foundation had made thirty-seven grants. By the end of 2009, the number had risen to over four hundred in all program areas. One of the projects directors was also engaged in reforming Abu Dhabi's largest home for parentless children changing it from an institutional model to a family care model with support from partner International SOS villages. In addition, the same projects director assisted the Urban Planning Council by involving community participation in revitalizing rural towns outside the city; and overseeing a range of MA and PhD fellowships.

## Aspiring to best practices

Expanding the programs and projects required administrative and financial organisation and placed stress on the Foundation as a startup organization. It drew up policies and procedures drawing on the experience of similar organizations and predicated disbursements on the grantee or project leader meeting milestones at each payment period. Externally, the Foundation sought other means of meeting international standards. It differed from virtually all foundations in the Gulf Region by publishing its audited financial reports. The Foundation joined the European Foundation Centre and the Arab Foundations Forum. It called the first meeting of all

UAE foundations to exchange information on their programs and discuss cooperation. It bought carbon emission credits for its air and road travel. It offered extensive training opportunities to young staff, and converted the status of some support personnel from South Asia from outsourced workers to permanently contracted employees. The Foundation placed a high priority on hiring Emirati nationals for its senior and junior positions, reaching nearly 50 percent of all employees. Two of its top executives were women, and an additional five of the six senior program officers also were women. It sought ways to engage stakeholder involvement in overseeing foundation programs, and all staff members signed a code of conduct covering conflict of interest.

## Business involvement

By 2008, the Foundation realized it needed to provide its donors with opportunities to see more clearly how their contributions were being used. It attempted to do this in three ways.

First, it invited companies to affiliate with one or more of the fifty grants-related projects resulting from the planning process. Affiliation meant consultation on the project's structure and objectives, advising on grant selection, examining the accounts on how the funds were spent, and publicity for their corporate involvement. In the selection committees, for example, companies sat with academics or specialists related to the issue area, and offered their perceptions on the relative merit of proposals, in an advisory capacity. To the surprise of some of the academics around the table, the company representatives offered telling insights on the proposals at hand, significantly improving the feedback to the eventual grantee on implementing or enhancing their ideas. The Foundation also created "councils" for each of the program areas – to which companies would be invited – with the objective of reviewing the status of all the projects.

These contributions were as valuable to the Foundation as companies' monetary donations since a private sector lens focuses on planning, project leadership, financial soundness, risk taking, ambitious goals, and a practical inclination to get things done. Some of these attributes are less evident in a nonprofit setting.

Second, the Foundation launched its own project to promote CSR or corporate citizenship. It funded research on the degree of understanding or adoption of CSR principles nationwide, conferences and workshops on CSR, and collaboration with the Dubai and Abu Dhabi Chambers of Commerce to spread knowledge and encourage engagement. The Foundation undertook the preparation of its own Sustainability Report, following guidelines of the Global Reporting Initiative (GRI), as part of an effort by the Abu Dhabi Environment Agency to promote adoption throughout the public and private sphere. Once its own report is published, the Foundation agreed to encourage similar reports among other social sector entities, such as hospitals, schools, and nonprofits.

Third, the Foundation placed greater emphasis on communicating its activities in the national media, in the Arabic and English language press, print and broadcast. With the plethora of program activities underway, the Foundation shifted its emphasis to putting reporters in touch with grantees and special projects, so they themselves would get the coverage. The strategy was appreciated by the reporters – who sought interesting copy on new subjects – and the grantees. The tactic benefited the Foundation since invariably its support would appear in the article as the key funder – helpful also as feedback to corporate donors. More importantly, the grantees' vision, purposes, and accomplishments contributed to the Foundation's own strategy. The publicity helped justify the Foundation's license to operate – which in essence involves transferring resources from one sector of society to another through the Foundation's program and project filters.

Sheikh Mohammed Bin Zayed Al Nahyan, Crown Prince of Abu Dhabi and Deputy Supreme Commander of the UAE Armed Forces, with Peter Cleaves, the foundation's first chief executive officer

## The Future

Any foundation aspiring to develop and succeed needs to (a) communicate more clearly its mission, (b) evaluate its performance, (c) build synergies between programs, as well as (d) secure its long-term financial sustainability.

In late 2008, an Argentine working in an Italian public relations firm asked at a fundraising event "Tell me about the Emirates Foundation." By the time the answer had covered the six core programs, the two major operational projects, and the steps to construct a modern foundation – the questioner's facial expression changed. "That's too much to grasp," she said.

This experience was just another proof that the Foundation needed to find ways to communicate its purposes. A series of internal discussions arrived serendipitously at the fortuitous conclusion that the Foundation was involved in only three main themes. These are Youth Development, Knowledge Creation, and Society and Culture. Each grant, project, and initiative falls into one of these headings. Youth Development encompasses Tawteen, Takatof, most educational grants, environment internships, science fairs, reading for youth, teacher training and a multitude of other projects that had the clear intention of preparing the next Emirati generation to be productive and self-fulfilled citizens. Research contributes to Knowledge Creation in basic sciences, applied technology, educational achievement, and Emirati society, as do PhD fellowships that mold the next generation of Emirati knowledge leaders. Society and Culture covers new social organizations, special needs centers, workshops on family legal issues, diabetes awareness campaigns, environmental protection, and promoting young artists – all of which together sustain and enhance social relations and strengthen national identity.

A simple statement by a grantee that "your support changed my life" is proof enough that an investment has had an impact. Notwithstanding, all boards ask their senior leadership to evaluate their activities, and this task will be a constant pursuit of the still very young Emirates Foundation. Measuring results of the three defined priorities will certainly be easier and more beneficial than seeking to consolidate the outcomes of six individual and potentially fragmented programs.

Startup organizations with high energy and an exciting mission eventually run the risk of evolving into a bureaucratic machine with strict rules, rigid organizational charts, and diverse sub-units, each with their own agenda. Spontaneity and collaboration can become lost as hierarchy, competition over budget, and status differentials induce its members to retreat into silos, fiefdoms, or separate "turfs." This outcome is deadly for an organization whose *raison d'être* is innovation, risk taking, synergy, and cross-disciplinary collaboration. Foundations as well as businesses devise preventive strategies to forestall this eventuality, postponing or avoiding the day when the organization needs to be restructured – often brutally - in a major shakeup to recapture its lost virtues.

The Emirates Foundation's preventive strategy begins with the appointment of senior program managers – already with impeccable disciplinary credentials – who value the links between science and art, environment and society, education and public awareness. The Foundation has been fortunate to assemble an outstanding contingent of professionals to lead each of its program areas, while retaining its two founding members who assume ever greater responsibility. These program professionals actively seek synergies with sister programs in pursuit of their joint missions.

The Foundation also holds two types of staff meetings each month. One meeting assembles all staff to hear a presentation on a single program, new administrative procedures, a talk by a Board member, or a discussion of next year's plans – followed by Q&A with senior managers. The meetings inform but also build familiarity and collegiality among all staff – who often enjoy a good laugh over a humorous incident and remain after the hour's meeting over coffee and snacks to chat and strengthen friendships. The second meeting is for all program staff – in a low hierarchy environment without directors – to encourage the sharing of project plans and outcomes and collaboration between interest areas. Representatives from Finance, IT, and HR attend to gain a clearer understanding of what their functions are actually supporting – and so they have a more complete idea of the overall mission when asked outside the Foundation. Eliminating hierarchy, erasing boundaries, and neutralizing a fear to speak up are keys to the success of the meetings for all program staff, as ideas are thrashed out from all quarters and all age groups. The expected outcome is for more collaboration, shared resources, new program ideas, and pride in the organization.

While many respected foundations voluntarily plan for their own demise, such is not the intention of the Emirates Foundation. It expects to continue to build up its reserves to contribute to Emirati society, incubate and spin off successful projects like Takatof and Tawteen, and eventually extend its reach to other Arab countries and beyond, all while following the best practices it can muster. The question mark is how these aspirations will be met given the financial reality that the capital reserve is insufficient for the long term. This reality helps keep the attention of Foundation management, directors, and staff focused on proving their worth – to the business community, to national leadership, and to the direct beneficiaries of its activities, all of whom continue to represent the best judges of the Foundation's performance.

Sheikh Mohammed Bin Zayed has summarized the Foundation's *raison d'être* as such: "Charity and hospitality have always been at the heart of our culture. Innovative organizations such as the Emirates Foundation and its partners continue to provide the people, businesses and government entities of the United Arab Emirates with new and diverse opportunities to contribute to that ongoing tradition. The Emirates Foundation provides a number of invaluable services to the community through its various programs and initiatives. Importantly, it is also helping to establish a much greater understanding of the benefits of volunteering among young people, the nature of modern philanthropy for local organizations, and the value of corporate social responsibility for the business community of the United Arab Emirates."

ATALLAH KUTTAB AND DINA H. SHERIF

# 11 Arab Region

## THE CASE OF THE ARAB FOUNDATIONS FORUM AND THE JOHN D. GERHART CENTER FOR PHILANTHROPY AND CIVIC ENGAGEMENT

### Introduction

Philanthropy in the Arab region dates back centuries, with a culture of giving deeply rooted in Arab cultures and within the three monotheistic religions – Islam, Christianity and Judaism – that exist in the region. Specifically for Arab Muslims (who constitute the majority of the Arab region), charitable giving in the form of *zakat* and *sadaqa*, and the establishment of *awqaf* (*awqaf* is the plural form of *waqf*, an Islamic trust or endowment) has historically been a means to maintain social justice and equity through both an obligatory and non-obligatory transfer of wealth from those who are privileged to those who are less privileged. Historically, this giving was both strategic and sustainable with the *waqf* being the main provider of essential social services such as health and education to those who were less privileged. Modern history has witnessed the overall demise of the *waqf* system, largely for political reasons, and as a result the culture of giving in the Arab region over past decades can be largely described as charitable in nature with individual giving, as opposed to institutional giving, being at the forefront. Meanwhile, over the same period of time, and again for political reasons, active displays of citizenship and civic duty have also been on the decline in the Arab region.

Over the past decade, there has been exponential growth in private wealth in the Arab region as a result of both increased oil prices and rapidly expanding private sectors. This increased wealth continues to be juxtaposed by extreme poverty, high unemployment rates and sub-standard social services such as health and education. The combined circumstances of increased wealth and impoverished communities have led to an overall shift in the philanthropic scene of the Arab region; specifically over the past decade.

Based on data collected by the John D. Gerhart Center for Philanthropy and Civic Engagement over the past three years, a number of broad trends have been identified within the philanthropic sector.[1] Among the most important is a rise in citizen activism among successful and affluent business leaders, who are introducing both innovation and entrepreneurship to their giving. Arab business leaders not only want to share their wealth and contribute to their societies in a meaningful way; they also want to ensure the sustainability of their own businesses. The fact that businesses cannot thrive if the communities around them are falling apart is no longer contested. To that end, a growing number of business leaders in the Arab region are investing their money socially as aggressively as they do financially. These same business leaders are also more willing to lobby local governments to change policies and provide greater access to public services to those who do not have access. By the same token, the private sector has been more willing to partner with the public sector with the objective of sustainable social change.

Further to the above, there has been a consistent increase in the number of foundations established in the region over the past decade whether they are family, corporate or community foundations. Those who used to give large sums of money on an individual basis are now choosing to institutionalise their giving in the form of a foundation that is sustainable and that is strategically tackling a specific problem in society in both a transparent and responsible manner.

Several broad categories of foundations can now be found in the Arab region:

- **Family foundations**, where bequests are from personal assets and management may stay at least partially among family members.
- Corporate giving (either legally autonomous through a foundation or through a division of a company) operating on annual infusions of profit or shares from a company.
- **Community foundations** that enable multiple small donors to pool their financial resources together for a common purpose, often directed to a geographic locale.
- A **partner or membership foundation** model, which includes a group of individuals who pledge founding and/or annual amounts to a foundation and serve on its board of trustees. Often these are

---

1   Refer to: Ibrahim, Barbara and Sherif, Dina (2008) *From Charity to Social Change: Trends in Arab Philanthropy*, AUC Press: Cairo

business-people who have established relationships of trust and share a common vision for the use of their philanthropy.

- **Public-private partnership foundations**, which involves the collection of funds from both citizens and the private sector that are also matched by the state or a public official.

While philanthropy in the Arab region for centuries was largely driven by faith, and funds were given through faith-based structures, the past decade in particular has pushed the sector to take on a new form. The philanthropic scene constitutes a unique mix of business leaders such as Fadi Ghandour, the chief executive officer (CEO) of Aramex International (Founder of Ruwwad in Jordan), wealthy families such as the Sawiris family in Egypt (founders of the Sawiris Foundation), companies such as Paltel who have established the Paltel Foundation, and state representatives such as Sheikh Mohammed bin Rashid Al Maktoum, ruler of Dubai and founder of the Mohammed bin Rashid Al Maktoum Foundation. The mix of government funds and private funds that created institutions like the Emirates Foundation and Dubai Cares makes the region even more unique in nature.

While it is clear that the institutionalised philanthropic sector is growing, on the whole it remains restricted. Current legal frameworks in the Arab region continue to act as a barrier to more rapid growth. The process of registering a private foundation remains complex and rigid, which often pushes philanthropists to not register at all or to register their foundation outside of the region completely. Furthermore, the lack of existing non-governmental organisations (NGOs) with a credible track record also acts as an obstacle to the growth of the philanthropic sector. Many philanthropists remain sceptical of NGOs due to the fact that by and large, civil society in the Arab region has been known to be corrupt and unprofessional. This, however, is also changing with many NGOs becoming more professional and more transparent; although for some, change is not happening at a fast enough rate, leading a number of new foundations to take the path of being operational as opposed to grant-giving. It is important to note that despite these obstacles, the philanthropic sector continues to grow slowly but surely.

For the philanthropic sector to continue to grow and develop, the provision of a support infrastructure is necessary. For this reason, in 2006 the John D. Gerhart Center for Philanthropy and Civic Engagement at the American University in Cairo (AUC) and the Arab Foundations Forum (AFF) were both established to help the Arab region develop its supporting infrastructure. The Gerhart Center was established to act as a source of knowledge and capacity-building while AFF was established to link all of the existing Arab foundations together within one network. Both the

Gerhart Center and AFF have been working together closely since their inception with the common vision to unify, strengthen and professionalise the philanthropic sector.

## The John D. Gerhart Center for Philanthropy and Civic Engagement

The John D. Gerhart Center for Philanthropy and Civic Engagement was launched in March 2006 by the American University in Cairo, with a mission to promote philanthropy and civic engagement in the Arab region by establishing the Center as a source of knowledge on philanthropy and civic engagement, a catalyst for sustainable social change and a cultivator of a heightened sense of citizenship and social responsibility, specifically among Arab youth. The Center was established out of a strong belief that indigenous problems in the Arab region could be resolved both through the social investment of indigenous wealth and through more active participation of local citizens within their communities. Former President of the AUC John D. Gerhart (for whom the Center was named), believed that if the wealth of the region was strategically invested and if citizens became more engaged in changing their own fates, the Arab region would become a different place. To achieve this, he believed that an academic center needed to be created to provide the knowledge and training required to move the sector forward.

With the above in mind, the key strategic goals identified by the Center in 2006 included:
- Advancing an enabling environment for strategic giving and social action in the Arab region;
- Producing and sharing knowledge about philanthropy and civic engagement regionally and internationally;
- Promoting a more responsible corporate sector; and
- Encouraging youth to become civically engaged.

Despite such an ambitious mandate, the Center started out as a small operation with a growth strategy that was gradual but consistent.

### Structure and operation of the Gerhart Center

From its inception, the Gerhart Center's work has been guided by an international Advisory Board, appointed by AUC's president. The Board is composed of eminent educators, Arab philanthropists, and civil society leaders from around the world. The president, provost, and Center director act as *ex officio* members. The Advisory Board meets face to face once per annum with various members communicating regularly with the Center director on important matters throughout the year.

The Gerhart Center is administratively affiliated to the provost's office, signalling its engagement with all academic units of the university and its commitment to interdisciplinary modes of work. In 2006, the Center started with a director, an associate director, an administrative assistant and an intern. In early 2007, a communications and outreach manager position was created to be followed by the creation of a philanthropy advisor position in late 2007. By 2008, the Center had also added a program assistant position, and in 2009 a director for the Community Based Learning Program at AUC was created. Throughout, the work of the Center has been supported by part-time staff and consultants when necessary. In 2010, the Center remains a fairly small operation. Discussions are currently taking place regarding the staff expansion required to reach the Center's goals.

For the first four years of the Gerhart Center's existence, the key components of work fell under two main themes: promoting philanthropy in the Arab region and promoting civic engagement on Arab university campuses, starting with the American University in Cairo.

Most recently, at the start of 2010, the Center began to tackle the goal of promoting a more responsible corporate sector. While on the surface it may appear that promoting philanthropy and corporate social responsibility are in fact very different from promoting civic engagement on university campuses, it is important to stop here and explain why they are linked. The Arab region has the largest percentage of youth in the world today. If values related to social responsibility and community engagement are not instilled among Arab youth, it will become difficult to sustain either the philanthropic sector or a socially responsible corporate sector in the long term. The Gerhart Center believes that by focusing on university students and in finding ways for them to engage with their surrounding communities in meaningful ways, the Arab region will start producing young leaders who will remain dedicated to social change both in their personal and professional lives.

## Promotion of philanthropy in the Arab region

As a first step towards establishing itself as a strong, regional knowledge-base on Arab philanthropy, the Gerhart Center launched a year-long research project, supported by the Boeing Company, in November 2006 to identify the varying forms of philanthropy and its scope of practice in eight Arab countries (Egypt, Jordan, Palestine, Lebanon, Qatar, Kuwait, Saudi Arabia and the United Arab Emirates (UAE)). A research team comprised of seven individuals from around the region was identified and went on to interview key figures from foundations, NGOs, media organisations, government officials, and business leaders in each of the aforementioned countries. The project culminated in a comprehensive study that highlights innovation and best practices in philanthropy across the region, and also charts the "way forward" for key stakeholders on how to further promote strategic philanthropy in the region.

The results of this first phase of research were presented at a regional consultation on Arab philanthropy from January 20-21, 2008, organised in partnership with the newly established Mohammed bin Rashid Al Maktoum Foundation in Dubai, UAE. The Mapping Arab Philanthropy (MAP) study, entitled *From Charity to Change: Trends in Arab Philanthropy* and later published as a book by AUC Press, concentrates not on individual giving, though it is widespread throughout the region, but on the ways in which philanthropic giving is currently formalised into sustainable institutions.

As a follow-up to the above-mentioned study, in-depth case studies on philanthropy in both Egypt and Jordan are currently being carried out. Case studies will include the forms of philanthropy that exist, approximately how much money is being invested philanthropically, what areas are attracting the most philanthropic dollars, the impact of philanthropy on the ground, and identification of partnerships being forged. At the start of 2010, it was also decided that an in-depth case study on the Kingdom of Saudi Arabia would also be carried out.

Further to the research mentioned above, and in order to promote strategic philanthropy in the region that is both sustainable and innovative, the Gerhart Center joined forces with the Institute for Philanthropy in London to launch the Arab Forum for Social Innovation (AFSI). The overall objective of AFSI was to bring together a small network of individual philanthropists with the skills, commitment and imagination necessary to make a significant contribution to the Arab region. The overall aim of the Forum was to deepen the understanding of critical social issues in Arab communities and propose effective models for tackling them.

The first AFSI meeting was held in September 2007 in London and was sponsored by Arcapita (an investment firm headquartered in Bahrain). The forum was attended by key philanthropists from Egypt, Kuwait, Lebanon and Palestine. The second Forum was sponsored by the Mohammed bin Rashid Al Maktoum Foundation and was held in Dubai in January 2008 preceding the aforementioned regional consultation on Arab philanthropy. The second AFSI meeting, which focused on innovation in philanthropy, was attended by philanthropists from Egypt, Jordan, Lebanon, Kuwait, Saudi Arabia, and the UAE. At the meeting, participants agreed to share hosting responsibilities on a rotating basis and to arrange field visits to deepen collective learning. While the start of AFSI was successful, a strategic decision was made by the Gerhart Center to discontinue the Forum and put all of its efforts into supporting the Arab Foundations Forum, the official network representing Arab Foundations and strategic philanthropy in region.

## University-based civic engagement

Higher education institutions, which have bases in every nation and adopt similar roles, are perhaps the only kind of global institutions capable of instilling a more moral and caring dimension in the youth of today. Colleges and universities are in a strategic position to shape the thinking and values of future leaders: to shape them into responsible citizens with a will to continuously give back to their communities and work for social change. To that end, the Gerhart Center has focused on creating a culture of civic engagement on the campus of the American University in Cairo and throughout the Arab region. The main initiatives include: the Community Based Learning Programme at AUC; and the Ma'an Arab University Alliance for Civic Engagement.

### Community-based learning program

Since its inception, the Gerhart Center has been working to promote community-based learning (CBL) as a teaching pedagogy at the American University in Cairo. CBL is a teaching methodology that purposefully engages students in a community-service experience to advance their learning goals. It is based on principles of community empowerment, mutual respect, reciprocity of gain, and sustainability of output. Since September 2008, the Community-Based Learning Program has developed in a variety of ways. Most specifically it now has a full time Director appointed to manage and expand the idea of CBL into a program across the AUC campus.

### The Ma'an Arab University Alliance for Civic Engagement

At a time of immense regional challenges, universities are called upon to contribute more directly to social and economic development. On October 13 and 14, 2008, the Gerhart Center, in partnership with Innovations in Civic Participation (a Washington, DC-based non-profit organisation) and the Talloires Global Network of Universities, hosted a regional conference on the incorporation of civic engagement onto Arab university campuses entitled, Tadamunn: Towards Civic Engagement in Arab Education.

In March of 2009, as a result of this conference, the Gerhart Center launched the Ma'an Arab University Alliance for Civic Engagement (Ma'an Alliance). With the launch of the Alliance, the Gerhart Center has begun recruiting heavily for member institutions, and has recently launched its own website, which includes a glossary of civic engagement terms in English and in Arabic, along with various other resources for university administrators and students. The Ma'an Alliance has the potential to be an incredible resource for universities in the region and already has fifteen university members from around the region in its network.

## The corporate sector and sustainability

A by-product of the research on Arab philanthropy has been a deepening interest in the role the private sector can play in contributing to sustainable development. Firms can do this not only by socially investing in the surrounding community, but also by changing their overall business conduct through the application of a "corporate sustainability" lens to the management of their companies.[2] In order to cultivate this change in the private sector, the Gerhart Center has launched a comprehensive Corporate Sustainability Capacity Building Program with the support of three key corporate players in the region; Abraaj Capital, Aramex International and the Mansour Group.

The idea of launching a corporate sustainability capacity-building program was born out of a clear need for the private sector in the region to not only understand what corporate sustainability means to their business, but to acquire the skills and know-how to go about integrating it in a manner that is effective and will serve the bottom-line of their companies. The belief of the Gerhart Center is that businesses can contribute to sustainable social change in a more meaningful manner if they use a sustainability lens in the overall management of their businesses. The corporate sector, through more socially-aware policies and work decisions, can have a positive impact on poverty, inequality, climate change, and building more participatory societies.

### The Arab Foundations Forum

The founding of a network of Arab foundations stemmed from the need to create an infrastructure for philanthropy that would support sustainable solutions to the chronic problems of the region. In 2006, the Arab region remained the only region without a network. While this can be seen as unfortunate, there is an advantage to being the late-comer. The Arab Foundations Forum (AFF) was able to learn from the mistakes that other networks went through. The most significant lessons were derived from the experience of the South African Grantmakers' Association (SAGA) as will be further explained below.

---

2  The principle of sustainability, often invokes what is referred to as the triple bottom line of economic, social and environmental performance. In sum, companies should operate in ways that secure long term economic performance by avoiding short term behaviour that is socially or environmentally detrimental. Sustainability also puts emphasis on community stewardship and the need to "socially" invest in communities using the same principles of sustainability as a backdrop.

## Chronology of events and meetings

AFF was founded with the aim of strengthening the capacity of Arab philanthropy by promoting dialogue, networking, learning and collaboration among foundations and with partners within the Arab region and beyond. It all started at the European Foundation Centre (EFC) meeting in Budapest in May 2005, where the absence of Arab philanthropic organisations was felt. Three organisations attended: the Arab Fund for Human Rights (represented by coordinator Yousry Mostafa, and board members Fateh Azzam and Atallah Kuttab), Universal Education Foundation (represented by Secretary General Marwan Awartani) and the Welfare Association (represented by Director General, Atallah Kuttab).

In Budapest the three organisations agreed it would be a good idea to convene a meeting of Arab foundations to discuss the possibility of forming a network. The Welfare Association took the lead in creating a network of foundations and committed to hosting the forum in its early stages. This was made possible by a grant from the Ford Foundation which included the cost of a part-time coordinator and basic activities in addition to the commitment from the Welfare Association to provide all other support costs such as office space, secretarial support, equipment, etc. Although the Welfare Association's mandate is to support Palestinians, its management justified its support to such an initiative as part of its commitment to support the philanthropic environment in the Arab region.

The inaugural meeting of the AFF took place one year after Budapest, in May 2006 in Jordan, as an initiative of the Welfare Association. During this first inaugural meeting, the objective was to agree on the definition of the foundation in order to differentiate the group from existing networks of NGOs in the region. Also, it was discussed whether the group would be named a network, alliance or forum. The meeting also resulted in a stimulating dialogue on key issues concerning the benefits of networking, and thus linking the Arab foundations sector with the global philanthropy sector. This meeting was attended by five organisations: namely the three organisations that were at the Budapest meeting as well as the Qattan Foundation based in Palestine and the Makhzoumi Foundation from Lebanon. A basic definition of "foundation" was formulated with emphasis on having a reliable source of income either from an endowment or committed annual funding. Also, each foundation agreed to take the lead role in their own country in marketing AFF and attracting new members.

After that first meeting in Jordan, under the leadership of Dr Atallah Kuttab and with seed money from the Ford Foundation, seven more meetings took place between 2006 and 2009. During that time the AFF was able to draft and adopt its bylaws, elect a Board of Directors, articulate a mission, vision, and strategic objectives as well as establish a strong membership base. By October 2009, AFF succeed in having over fifteen full member institutions, all of whom were paying an annual membership fee of three thousand United States dollars (USD) to sustain the network.

## Analysis and lessons learned

It is important to reflect on and analyse the experiences of the last three years to acknowledge the strength that the AFF has acquired, and actual or potential weaknesses, in order to minimise their negative impact on the progress of the AFF in the future. These reflections and thoughts can be summarised as follows:

### Linkages and learning from other similar networks in other regions

From its inception, communication was undertaken with the European Foundation Centre, Council on Foundations (CoF), TrustAfrica and the World International Networks of Grant Makers (WINGS) on their experiences, including similar experiences on their own continents. Most revealing and enlightening was the experience of the Southern African Grantmakers' Association (SAGA) for its rich experience in successes and failures. The latter provided important lessons, which had led to the closure of that experience. From the authors' reading of SAGA's history, its main drawback, among others, was a lack of ownership by its members. It is hoped that the concept of ownership of AFF by its members will remain pivotal and will continue to guide the AFF experience into the future. The experience of SAGA influenced the decision to keep the AFF small, the grouping informal, and build a strong core group of similarly minded/committed foundations in the early stages and up to the third meeting.

### Hosting of AFF at the Welfare Association

The fact that AFF was hosted by the Welfare Association meant that the cost of its operation and setup was minimal, and allowed the initial core group of founders to not be distracted by the establishment of the network's infrastructure. This enabled more time to be spent in defining added value of such a network, developing its membership, and agreeing on the bylaws. This meant a solid start for the AFF with quality time focusing on issues that mattered rather than the bureaucracy of setting up an operation. The development of bylaws gave clarity to newcomers on the intent of the AFF and made it relatively easier to recruit new members.

## Name of the AFF

The name of the AFF took around three meetings to agree upon. The conclusion to that discussion was an excellent team-building exercise that enhanced trust and set the tone in our relationship to respect each other's opinions. There was a tendency to be dismissive of spending too much time on such a topic, but it became clear that the name was important to the overall identity of AFF. It is not just a name, but what the organisation stands for and is a reflection of how it operates. Initial ideas were geared towards the building of a "network". Soon after, it became clear that a number of members were wary of networks and had bad experiences. A network to those members meant that their contribution starts and ends in the regular meeting, be it once or twice a year (most probably once annually) with a secretariat doing most of the work. Members wanted a grouping where everybody remained engaged with the workload and responsibility was distributed among all members – not just a few. It was argued that the word "forum" served members better than network and the word was adopted.

## Sustainability and covering cost of core operation

Reviewing experiences of existing networks it is very clear that dependence on external donors for core costs (meaning costs of coordinator, offices, etc.) always places strain and stress on the organisation and can result in financial difficulties. The AFF from its inception followed two strategies to mitigate this: AFF meeting costs should be kept as low as possible by asking members to cover their own costs. In addition, member foundations of host countries were to cover the cost of the meeting venue. Membership fees, fixed initially at one thousand USD annually, were later raised with the full support of new members to three thousand USD annually based on a target of twenty members to cover core costs.

## Embracing diversity

This was a critical topic. In the first three meetings it was initially planned that the AFF should focus on linking foundations that focus on social justice. Early objectives stated this, and excluded foundations that followed purely charitable approaches. However, following the addition of new members, it became clear that the AFF should not contribute to the fragmentation of the philanthropic sector but be inclusive of all foundations in the region. It became clear that nobody has the right to decide what is right or wrong in giving and there has to be to a dialogue on the effectiveness of giving ranging within the spectrum of social justice to charity.

## Level of representation

Experience from other networks shows that foundation collaboration can work, but that it takes time – and most of all – commitment from participants. Also, participants should be decision makers in their own organisations to move agendas forward. The AFF from the outset has emphasised two criteria for participation: high level participation (at the level of executive director or one level below) and consistency in terms of who is delegated to attend if the assigned representative cannot attend. This served AFF in the last period as key decisions needed to be taken, whether on mission/vision/objectives document, bylaws, membership fees, etc. Decision-making was prompt and acted upon due to the high level of representation.

## Risks moving into the future

Lebanese poet and philosopher Jubran Khalil Jubran once said; "Climbing starts when reaching the top". The last three years have been slow and cautious but also without serious setbacks and with continuous growth. Existing members deserve a pat on the back for their perseverance, commitment and tolerance. Most textbook mistakes on networking were avoided. However, the bar has been set high and with a surge in membership and attendance in meetings (attendance demand for meeting planned in Cairo in October 2009 exceeded seventy which, by any measure, exceeded planned expectations and was even slightly overwhelming) the leadership of the AFF needs to tread carefully, and study the following positive past practices to avoid risks that lie ahead:

- Maintaining cooperation among members and avoid competition at all costs;
- Embracing diversity at all levels: language, types of foundations (operating, grant-making, hybrid, etc.), size of foundations (small and large), geographic mandate (across the Arab region or specific to one country), approach to giving and philanthropy (spectrum of social justice to charity), etc.
- Ensuring that new members are brought in from the Western part of the Arab region (Maghreb) and increase members from the Gulf region, so that the AFF will not end up being an eastern Mediterranean-plus-Egypt grouping of foundations;
- Avoiding lowest common denominator decisions stifling creativity and effectiveness;
- Continuing to be meaningful to members; the previous period focused on bylaws, governance issues, setting expectations. The next period will focus on activities and therefore needs to ensure those are useful to members;

- Continuing to fund core expenses and not depend on outside funding for that component;
- Avoiding moving faster than the majority of the membership to avoid losing commitment, engagement and most important of all trust (as the saying goes "more haste, less speed");
- Continuing to define the importance of the AFF to the infrastructure of philanthropy in the region, making sure the AFF stays relevant.

## Conclusion

According to the American University in Cairo Provost Lisa Anderson, our "future is about networks of concern, about philanthropy and engagement, about mechanisms and vehicles for sustaining our fellow citizens – those who are with us and those who have yet to appear – in this new world". Strategic philanthropy is on the rise in the Arab region with organisations like the Gerhart Center and AFF working to support its growth and development. Given the global nature of today's problems, it will be important for different regions around the world to work together more closely. This can be done through networks like the AFF, to identify ways and means to collaborate on solutions to common challenges and learn more from each other. The knowledge base that is being created by the Gerhart Center, in addition to the capacity-building programs being implemented, and the movement the Center is slowly beginning to create towards a more civically engaged Arab region, will serve to support the work being carried out by the Arab Foundations Forum and its growing membership base.

To this day, while there are a number of consultancy firms who are now providing services specifically in the areas of philanthropy and civic engagement, the John D. Gerhart Center for Philanthropy and Civic Engagement and the Arab Foundations Forum are the only two established institutions in the region working to create a support infrastructure for the rapidly growing "new" philanthropic sector. Moving forward, it will be essential for both organisations to work closely together and mobilise the resources required to carry on with this important work. The challenges that exist in the Arab region are many, and each of these challenges will require a more engaged and more strategic philanthropic sector for real social change to take place in the region.

## Bibliography

- Asia Pacific Philanthropy Consortium *Review of Operations (1994-2004)*
- Council on Foundations (1999) *50 years timeline (1949-1999)*, USA
- Council on Foundations (2004) *Funder Networks in Action*, USA
- Council on Foundations (2004) *Collaboration through Funder Networks*, USA
- Hamdan, Luma and Sherif, Dina (2009) "Report on AFF-Gerhart Center meeting at EFC Preconference meeting" *Trends and Challenges to Networking*, Rome
- Hodgson, Jenny (May 2009) *Strategic framework for the Global Fund for Community Foundations*, South Africa: unpublished working paper
- Ibrahim, Barbara and Sherif, Dina (2008) *From Charity to Social Change: Trends in Arab Philanthropy*, Cairo: AUC Press
- International Society for Third-Sector Research (ISTR) (2002) *Celebrating ISTR's Tenth Anniversary: Its Past, current Progress, and Future Prospects*, USA
- Kuttab, Atallah (December 2009) *Arab Foundations Forum: the advantage of arriving late*, London: Alliance-online
- Milner, Andrew and Hartnell, Caroline (September 2006) *SAGA – The end of a roller-coaster ride*, London: Alliance-online
- Nyegosh, Dube (Spring 2009) "Effect Magazine" *Exploring the world of Nordic Foundations,* Brussels: European Foundations Centre (pp 30-39)
- Playfair, Emma (Spring 2009) "Effect Magazine" *Renewed Vitality in Arab Philanthropy*, Brussels: European Foundations Centre (pp 40-41)
- Reed, Leslie and Alberg-Seberich, Michael (September 2008) "Alliance Magazine, Vol. 13, Number 3" *Initiative for Learning Democracy in Europe (ILDE)*, London

TARIQ H. CHEEMA

# Muslim Philanthropy

## THE WORLD CONGRESS OF MUSLIM PHILANTHROPISTS: A STRATEGIC APPROACH TO STRENGTHEN MUSLIM GIVING

Muslim philanthropy is at a crossroads. It faces the challenge of building new, global models of giving, whilst refining the old methods embedded in Islam's vibrant religious and cultural traditions. It must also address the pressures and suspicions which have fallen on Muslim philanthropy as a result of tensions and extremism in the Islamic world.

To guide and strengthen Muslim philanthropy on the global stage, the World Congress of Muslim Philanthropists (WCMP) was established in 2007 by a small group of dedicated individuals. The WCMP aspires to bring together donors to exchange ideas, deepen their understanding of challenges, and to institute an environment of enduring engagement in which knowledge, wealth and influence is leveraged strategically and effectively.

### Muslim philanthropy at a defining moment

Islam has a long and legendary culture of generosity. As the Aga Khan has said,

> *"One of the great principles of Islam, in all its interpretations, is the elimination of poverty in society, and philanthropy's centrality in this duty."*

The messages of compassion, of giving, and of support of the destitute and oppressed are intrinsic to the Islamic faith. They have a long history in the Muslim world; charitable giving actually started right from the beginning of Islam as we learn from The Qur'an and the tradition of the Prophet Muhammad, and it will continue forever, since it is a Qur'anic principle ordained by God and His Prophet. The principle of *zakat*, the annual tax of purification of wealth, is one of the five pillars of Islam, and is obligatory for all Muslims who are wealthy and are capable of paying. Although the rate of giving has been debated by jurists over the centuries, most Muslims accept that 2.5 percent of an individual's accumulated wealth for a year is an acceptable rate.

One portion of the *zakat* is used as a public welfare system, providing support to poor members of the community, and was therefore part of a Muslim's communal duties. It was, and is, also a spiritual act: giving allows one to purify oneself of material selfishness, whilst the recipient is purified from envy and jealousy.

The practice of *zakat* is not just intended to temporarily alleviate suffering. By demonstrating an example of virtue and duty, granting *zakat* encourages all members of society to work harder, to be compassionate, and to improve the welfare of the community. *Zakat* is, therefore, both spiritual and profoundly social.

Although *zakat* is one of the most fundamental tenets of Islam, it is just one aspect of Muslim philanthropy, which is a broad and diverse phenomenon reflecting centuries of change in very different cultural, social, and economic contexts around the world.

Another is *sadaqa*. Unlike *zakat*, this is discretionary, and is the personal choice of each individual Muslim. It is also not necessarily monetary in nature. *Sadaqa* is in fact a broad term, and may mean anything from a kind word, to voluntary service, to clothing and feeding the poor.

The third, rarer form of Islamic philanthropy is *kaffara*: charitable donations given as part of a penance after breaking an oath.

The fourth aspect of Islamic philanthropy is the contribution of donations for building mosques, schools, and hospitals, by establishing one of the strongest social manifestations of Muslim giving, *waqf*. The word originally meant a religious endowment, but over time the word has shifted meaning, and is now more likely to simply mean a foundation. Many of these foundations act for the public good – schools, hospitals, and mosques. Others act in a similar way to Western family trusts, allowing philanthropic wealth to be safely protected from tax and passed between generations.

Through these different forms of giving, philanthropy binds Islamic communities together, and serves as both a demonstration of faith and of community spirit. It is religious as well as social, and it illustrates the idea that in Islam, it is not soley the responsibility of the government to help disadvantaged members of society – it is the responsibility of all Muslims, as members of the community. That is why Islam legislated *zakat*, an annual tax levied by the government, and *sadaqah*, charity, given voluntarily to whomever we see fit; priority is given to family members and relatives.

Given the myriad types of Islamic philanthropy worldwide, judging the scale of Muslim giving is difficult. However, some estimates hold that total Islamic giving falls between 250 billion United States dollars (USD) and 1 trillion USD annually. This is a vast sum, and it underlines the need to distribute this wealth in the most effective, strategic way possible.

## Under pressure

In recent years, Islam has come under pressure around the world. The spread of extremism and political tensions created opportunities for some to question the very nature of Islam and to portray it in a negative light. Muslim philanthropy too came under suspicion.

In the United States (US), the aftermath of the September 11 attacks saw moves to clamp down on cross-border giving to charities that were seen as suspicious. Some were Islamic charities which gave to causes in the Middle East, such as the Holy Land Foundation, which had its assets frozen by the US Treasury in late 2001. The Foundation and its executive leadership were arrested and found guilty for giving charitable donations to *zakat* committees in the Palestinian territories which, the prosecution alleged, were controlled by Hamas, a designated terrorist organization under US law since 1998.

Although the Holy Land Foundation remains the only Islamic charity that was tried and convicted on terrorism related charges, such prosecutions have led to fears that create a blanket suspicion of all Islamic charities, and traditional *zakat* is under threat in some countries. Newly elected, US President Barack Obama acknowledged the problem in a major speech in Cairo in June 2009, saying that, in the US, "rules on charitable giving have made it harder for Muslims to fulfil their religious obligation".

This pressure and negative publicity – for Islamic giving and, unfortunately, for Islam itself – limited Muslim philanthropy's ability to tackle global challenges. These aggressive efforts have discouraged donors from giving and made it more difficult for existing donors to give. The difficulties in addressing social injustice, poverty, extremism, environmental degradation and illiteracy have led some to question whether Muslim philanthropy requires a new set of assumptions, of operational giving, and of innovative practices which could meet these challenges.

## The need for global, strategic giving

Despite ongoing efforts to tackle the social needs of the Muslim world, Islamic philanthropy has yet to be properly institutionalised. Muslim philanthropies which are intended to address the world's challenges are generally limited by skill sets, training, and development. There is a shortage of qualified, experienced philanthropists, which reduces the value and impact of each dollar which is donated.

Many donors also prefer to try and alleviate issues through short-term, *ad hoc* solutions. There is a distinct lack of focus on strategic investment and the development of the philanthropic sector – this makes it difficult for a long-term infrastructure of giving to develop, and creates barriers to achieving the real goals of Islamic philanthropy. We must move "from charity to change", away from individual giving and towards addressing the root causes of the problems through strategic social investment.

## The World Congress of Muslim Philanthropists

These circumstances prompted the formation of the World Congress of Muslim Philanthropists in 2007. The first initiative of its kind, the Congress is a forum for a common voice, and seeks to encourage collective action to guard and strengthen Muslim philanthropy.

The WCMP aspires to bring Muslim donors together, in order to exchange ideas and deepen cooperation on projects of vital importance for global philanthropy, not just for Islamic causes. By doing so, it hopes to encourage a strategic framework for giving and to establish Islamic giving in its rightful place within the global philanthropic community.

WCMP believes that strengthening the Muslim philanthropic sector must be a priority, and from the outset we have committed ourselves to strategic thinking about necessary change in the field.

## The first Congress – facing challenges and finding solutions

The annual conference of the WCMP brings together philanthropists, government and business leaders, visionaries, and industry experts from across the world, to offer pragmatic insights and constructive responses to the global challenges of today. The forum moves beyond existing initiatives, which often simply seek to give money to problems in Islamic societies. The conference instead promotes intellectual debate and deep analysis of social challenges within Muslim societies.

The inaugural conference of the Congress was held in Istanbul in 2008. Istanbul was chosen for its historic symbolism as a bridge between the Muslim world and Europe – between east and west. Istanbul serves as the symbol of modern Turkey, a nation which has built a thriving democracy without losing its Islamic faith and culture.

More than two hundred participants attended, representing over a hundred foundations and non-governmental organisations (NGOs) from around the world. The theme chosen for the conference was "Facing Challenges and Finding Solutions", reflecting both the enormous difficulties faced by the Islamic world – conflict, poverty, social injustice, environmental degradation, educational problems, human rights, and religious extremism – and the possibilities created by the institutionalisation, and the globalisation, of Islam's traditional culture of charity and generosity.

Prime Minister of Turkey Recep Tayyip Erdogan, at the first World Congress of Muslim Philanthropists in Istanbul, 2008

The conference was attended by influential figures from all walks of life: the Secretary General of the Organisation of Islamic Conference, Professor Ekmeleddin Ihsanoglu; the Prime Minister of Turkey, Recep Tayyip Erdogan; Dr Nafis Sadiq, Advisor to the UN Secretary-General; Her Royal Highness Sheikha Al Mayassa bint Hamad Al-Thani; and the United Kingdom's Minister for International Development, Shahid Malik.

Underlining the urgent need for the conference, Professor Ihsanoglu stated that "the World Congress of Muslim Philanthropists has convened at a very critical juncture; it comes at a time when need to increase credibility, accountability, and capacity is paramount in the Muslim world".

Through three days of addresses, roundtable discussions, research presentations, and networking opportunities, the conference made real progress towards a new, strategic way of giving for Muslim philanthropists. Ten key lessons were drawn from the conference:

- The worldwide community of Muslim philanthropists should be proactive in reaching out to the needy, irrespective of their race or religious beliefs.
- The work of Muslim grant-makers could be greatly improved through enduring, sustained international engagement amongst philanthropists
- Muslim philanthropists should take a closer look at potential new challenges, ranging from the environment to political conflict, and from "Islamophobia" to extremism, and set their giving priorities according to these challenges.
- While compassion is the most powerful driving force behind helping victims of natural and man-made disasters, there is a need for capacity building, mutual cooperation and communication among Muslim humanitarians for ensuring coordinated, economic and effective relief operations.
- Developing benchmarks – such as establishing a clearing-house of information, creating best practices, and helping charities to leverage the available capital and human resources through effective consulting and training – are vital for the growth of Muslim philanthropy.
- Accountability and transparency must be essential in any grant-making process. Educating and updating grantees on compliance and cross-border giving regulations must be a part of the responsibilities of existing Muslim philanthropists.
- Besides donating to faith-based, educational and health-care institutions, it is essential to fund initiatives that promote research, leadership development, economic and social entrepreneurial advancement, environmental stewardship, religious and cultural tolerance and effective responses to the negative aspects of globalisation.
- Muslim giving needs to shift its focus from conventional to strategic, making its impact long-term rather than short-term, through building endowments and incorporating strategic planning. As important as emergency assistance will always be, Muslim philanthropy must also engage the root causes of poverty and conflict and be ready to invest in longer term solutions.
- Strategic partnerships and alliance building with mainstream philanthropies on common global issues should be encouraged.
- Gatherings of Muslim philanthropists through annual conferences, roundtables and workshops must be promoted.

## The second Congress – conventional to strategic: A new paradigm in giving

Building on the interest and enthusiasm shared at the first conference, as well as endorsements from across the world, a new conference was convened in March 2009. The forum took place in Abu Dhabi, and again drew a diverse mix of political figures, leading philanthropists, international donor representatives, and academics from around the world.

The second conference took place under the theme "From Conventional to Strategic: A New Paradigm in Giving". This theme emphasised the overall purpose of the WCMP – to improve the conduct of Islamic philanthropy and to prepare it for the challenges of the twenty-first century.

The conference served as a forum to discuss innovative policies, using advanced research and practical tools to enhance philanthropic impact. As a result, the conference aims to encourage a more informed and professional workforce of Muslim philanthropists in the field; to increase collaboration between individuals as well as between institutions; and to create new philanthropic initiatives to strengthen regional and global philanthropic communities.

The conference paid special attention to the philanthropy of the Gulf Cooperation Council, the six countries that make up the Persian Gulf states. Philanthropy in this region contributes 15-20 billion USD every year: it is one of the most generous regions in the world. However, less than 2 billion USD of this is institutionalised.[1] Most available funding is not properly planned, distributed, collected, or measured – it is simply passed through informal channels with no attempt at the strategic measurement which institutionalised philanthropy is able to provide.

Malaria was an area of particular focus at the conference, with Mr Ray Chambers, special envoy of the UN Secretary-General for Malaria, in attendance. A high-level dinner on the subject was hosted prior to the conference itself. At this dinner and at the conference, participants acknowledged the dangers that malaria posed to the Muslim world. Over 40 percent of malaria victims in Africa are from Muslim states; malaria affects societies as well as health and must be addressed. Islamic philanthropists have a vital role to play in addressing the problem.

Poverty and a lack of education – not just in Muslim societies, but around the world – were also recognised as serious challenges. Despite more than 1 trillion USD in aid over the past half century, nearly half of the

---

1 McKinsey and Company (2009) *Increasing the Impact of 'Giving' in Saudi Arabia*

world's population lives on less than 2 USD per day.[2] Seventy-five million children around the world are not in school. Three-quarters of a billion adults are illiterate.[3]

Philanthropy, and Muslim philanthropy in particular, will be essential to reducing poverty and improving standards of education. As a philanthropic culture which is rooted in the developing world, and which has a strong history of countering social injustice, Muslim philanthropy must work with national governments and international agencies to meet the challenges of poverty and poor education.

In particular, educational institutions should be established which strengthen Islamic scholarship and teach inter-religious relations. Such cultural initiatives are essential to preventing growing religious extremism and "Islamophobia". Supporting inter-faith action to promote peace and development is an important area for Muslim philanthropy to support in the current political climate.

## The road ahead

The issues and challenges addressed at the conference encouraged the WCMP to begin facilitating new initiatives in the field. These initiatives form the Congress's strategic framework, The Road Ahead, which aims to strengthen Muslim philanthropy through innovative structures and policies. The WCMP has identified seven critical goals which it can achieve to move the field forward.

The first is holding its annual conferences to bring together Muslim philanthropists, government representatives, researchers, and leaders from NGOs from across the world to discuss significant issues and trends in the field of philanthropy and social justice. The conference will be held in a different location each year in order to expand knowledge and learning across borders. Building on the first two successful conferences, the WCMP will hold its next conference in Doha, Qatar, in March 2010.

Second is the need to establish "giving networks". There is heightened interest in the development of funds that are created for the purpose of "pooling" resources and targeting them toward a common purpose, such as education or health. The Congress believes "pooling" is a creative and promising trend, and would like to expand a broader development of such funds. These newly created networks have the advantage of sharing risks

2  Chen, S and Ravallion, M (2008) *The developing world is poorer than we thought, but no less successful in the fight against poverty,* World Bank [online], available from the World Wide Web: http://siteresources.worldbank.org/JAPANINJAPANESEEXT/Resources/515497-1201490097949/080827_The_Developing_World_is_Poorer_than_we_Thought.pdf

3  UNESCO (2008) *'Education For All Global Monitoring Report'*, Oxford: Oxford University Press [online], available from the World Wide Web: http://unesdoc.unesco.org/images/0017/001776/177683e.pdf

commonly found in grant making activities, as well as the learning that stems from this work. The WCMP has begun moving forward by establishing the first pooled fund on global hunger known as "Hasanah Fund".

This fund will seek to gather information and expertise on the problem that global hunger poses, and the ways in which philanthropists, by sharing their expertise and resources, can seek to address this.

Third, the WCMP has identified the need for consulting and operational assistance, in order to help Muslim philanthropists be more strategic in their grants. The WCMP intends to establish a culturally diverse pool of talented consultants that are able to deliver services to both grant making foundations and individuals. For example, consultants can help to identify potential grantees who are compatible with a foundation's vision and goals; they can help wealthy individuals to establish foundations, and inform them of the value of giving institutionally rather than individually; and they can provide technical assistance and training to NGOs and charities around the world.

The fourth critical goal for the WCMP is to support the work of these consultants by producing in-depth, innovative research and analysis on the current practice of philanthropy in the Muslim world. Currently, the level of information remains unacceptably low. The Congress will address this need by conducting research on critical questions and issues in the field, and disseminate the material through the media and through conferences and university programmes. To ensure that the research produced is truly global, the WCMP will translate the material into several languages.

The fifth critical goal is to publish a quarterly journal, alongside these occasional research papers. This journal, *Muslim Philanthropy*, will help to fill the gap in literature which currently exists on contemporary Islamic giving. It will educate readers on the latest research and trends in Muslim philanthropy, and provide information on the latest news and events occurring in the field.

The sixth goal is to establish an Academy of Philanthropy. The Academy will provide educational services that promote the professional development of Muslim philanthropists, taught by experts who can advance the effectiveness of practitioners in the field. The educational content will incorporate the best of both traditional and contemporary Muslim philanthropic practices, including the intersections between faith and social responsibility. The Academy's offices will be strategically located in both the East and West in order to effectively connect learning resources across the world.

The seventh goal, and one of the most essential, is to establish a global charity clearing-house. This clearing-house, known as *SecureGiving*, will inform philanthropists and foundations across the world about other participating charities. By acting as an intermediary to donors seeking to invest in the Muslim world, *SecureGiving* will help to identify the most effective and relevant channels of giving in an increasingly crowded field of non-governmental and civil society organisations.

While countries have adopted rules and regulations for governing the development and operations of NGOs, the regulations which govern global giving are not uniform or consistently applied. Along with the pressures which Muslim philanthropy is under today, this has charged philanthropists with the onerous, costly task of ensuring that charities and other organisations receiving their support are not linked to terrorism in any way. There is an underlying supposition amongst some regulators that charities in the Islamic world are "guilty until proven innocent".

Former UK Prime Minister Tony Blair at the second World Congress of Muslim Philanthropists in Abu Dhabi, 2009

*SecureGiving* will help to address this. Its listings of grantees and organisations will be based on meaningful standards of transparency which are accepted and adopted by NGOs on a voluntary basis. This will make the task of verifying each grantee's credentials much easier for philanthropists. In other words, this clearing-house is intended to facilitate secure, sustained, and strategic giving.

## The future for the World Congress of Muslim Philanthropists

In only two years, despite limited resources, the World Congress of Muslim Philanthropists has demonstrated its ability to engage world leaders and Muslim donors at the highest levels. As it moves from a convening role into a catalyst for social investment, it needs to build strong partnerships across sectors. The WCMP has begun working with a number of reputable institutions such as the United Nations, the Organisation of Islamic Conference, the Islamic Development Bank, Actionaid International, the King Khalid Foundation, the Tony Blair Faith Foundation, the Network of European Foundations' Mercator Fund, and other leading philanthropists and foundations from the Muslim world. These partnerships illustrate the important recognition that the WCMP is receiving on the global philanthropic stage, and suggests an even more promising and engaging future lies ahead.

WCMP is an emerging organisation that holds enormous potential for positive change in Muslim philanthropy. Its track record to date, that of delivering highly successful international conferences that bring together leaders in the field, is impressive.

In the words of Her Excellency Sheikha Al Mayassa bint Hamad Al Thani of Qatar:

*"Now is the time to examine how we can metamorphose our generations-old culture of spontaneous, massive, personal generosity which we are so good at, so that it incorporates the kind of planned and realistic philanthropic giving which can be a powerhouse of lasting change."*

The sense of "philanthropic identity" that is emerging among practitioners and supporters of Muslim philanthropy is encouraging, and must be built upon in the years to come as we move towards truly strategic Islamic giving. The future looks bright, but this future will only be realised through building and strengthening the Congress to face the challenges of the twenty-first century.

NAMIK CEYLANOĞLU & ZEYNEP MEYDANOĞLU

# Turkey
# FOUNDATIONS IN TURKEY: VEHICLES OF PHILANTHROPY, AGENTS OF CHANGE

## Introduction

The foundation institution has been the major philanthropic vehicle in Turkey for thousands of years. Its most significant characteristic has been its ability to adapt to major societal changes at this crossroad of civilisations. Today, Turkish foundations are once again emerging as agents of change in the context of the country's development and democratisation agenda.

This chapter aims to give readers a better understanding of current philanthropic practices in Turkey by providing them with a background; to hint at possible transformations the philanthropic sector is likely to go through in the next decade; and to share the authors' admiration for the sector's current vitality within the global philanthropic community. It must be noted that "the foundation" will be the focal point of the chapter, due to its significance as the major philanthropic medium in the region and the availability of information on its origins and history.

The first section of this chapter aims to offer an analysis of contemporary philanthropic practices in Turkey by linking them to their roots in the Ottoman era (1299-1922). Through this historical perspective the role of foundations will be analysed from two separate perspectives: their role in these three empires' governance structures, and their effects on the everyday lives of the people who lived in this geographical area. The focus will be on the classical Ottoman period as it is often perceived as the golden age of foundations.

The second section will focus on the twentieth century – the Republican era – and will provide an overview of how philanthropic practices evolved during this period of intense modernisation. Important themes that will be explored include the persistence of traditional philanthropy through the "old" Ottoman foundations and the "new" charitable foundations; the impact of social movements and political turbulence; the emergence of a more enabling environment for philanthropy in the last decade; and foundations' role in Turkish citizens' lives today.

The final section will explore three new trends in Turkish philanthropy that came hand in hand with the more enabling environment of recent years, which has made experimentation possible. These are the establishment of Turkey's first community foundation, the institutionalisation of diaspora philanthropy and the discovery of corporate social responsibility by Turkish firms. These new practices, although now considered traditional in Western European and North American contexts, promise to bring about significant change and innovation for Turkish philanthropy.

## Age of empires

The origins of Turkish foundations go back thousands of years. More than thirty-five thousand foundations were established and operational throughout the Ottoman era. In fact, the foundation was the most important philanthropic institution throughout the Ottoman realms. All the services one can expect to have in a civilised society, except for defence, were financed, organised, built and maintained by this system. Not only did foundations facilitate many public services but they also administered property holdings (the majority of Ottoman Istanbul property was administered by foundations). With some of their tasks, one can argue that they were not only part of civil society but also early examples of civil society organisations (CSOs).[1]

As such, by the eighteenth century, the foundation institution had established itself as the major provider of social services such as education and health. These organisations also provided a space for socialising and cultural exchange, generating social capital in the multi-cultural Ottoman Empire. In this context, foundations touched on the lives of every individual – rich or poor, Muslim or non-Muslim, old or young. One can argue that these organisations allowed for a dynamic, de-centralised and independent administration net, which was the only way such a diverse and vast empire like the Ottoman state could survive over seven centuries.

Yet, as the late Ottoman era unfolded in the nineteenth century, so

---

1  Çizakça, Murat (2006) "Economic Dimensions of Foundations in the Ottoman Era" in Bikmen and Zincir Eds (2006) *Philanthropy in Turkey: Citizens, Foundations and the Pursuit of Social Justice*, TÜSEV Publications

did a darker age for foundations. During this time, the Ottoman Empire was obliged to rapidly westernise and centralise for its survival. The foundations, located at the very centre of all social life, naturally had their share in this change. One crucial step was the establishment of the *Evkaf-ı Hümâyun Nezareti*, the Central Foundation Administration, which heralded the end of the local and decentralised foundation system. A similar trend was followed by the Ministry of Finance on the collection of some foundation revenues. Furthermore, the sultans' desire to legitimise their reign in the public eye and the outside pressure to dismantle the foundation system brought about the end of the state-foundation cooperation in the Ottoman context. The sultans started to ignore the traditional foundations and preferred to implement direct philanthropy on a massive scale.

The impact of these policies of centralisation can be seen clearly in the number of foundations that existed during these periods: while during the eighteenth century there were about twenty thousand foundations in the Ottoman Empire, the Republic inherited a mere 5,859. Yet, as argued above, the foundation as an institution was able to adapt to the trends of centralisation and modernisation, which is how it managed to remain relevant in the Republic that followed the Empire.

## The Republic

With the advent of the Turkish Republic in 1923, a series of significant political, cultural, social and economic reforms were implemented under the leadership of Mustafa Kemal Atatürk, the founder and the first President of the Republic of Turkey. During this era of intense modernisation and state building, the understanding and work of foundations also acquired new dimensions.

Instead of being the sole provider of key social services, foundations became catalysts and supporters of the modernisation process. Some contributed to the country's development and modernisation through institution building, while others focused on achieving social justice through policy reform. As a result, the country's leading universities, hospitals and museums continue to be foundation investments, while a diverse set of social fields such as education reform, youth, women, children and the environment are tackled by foundations of great expertise and large human resources. It can be argued that taking its strength from the Ottoman foundation system, the "new" Turkish foundations added a democracy and development perspective to their work – be it institution building or advocacy.

A chronological overview of the foundation institution in the Republican era gives a clear illustration of how this institution has evolved and adapted itself to society's needs. For instance, in the late 1950s and

1960s, Turkey's rapid industrialisation came hand in hand with the establishment of charitable foundations by the country's first industrialists. Now around fifty to sixty years old, these institutions have mainly focused on buildings, institutions and scholarships that facilitate access to education, health and other social services, resembling their Ottoman ancestors in their fields of activity. As a consequence, they have made great contributions to the infrastructure and social service delivery in every corner of the country.

Following the politically turbulent years of the 1970s and 1980s in Turkey, the 1990s saw the establishment of a new wave of foundations. Rather than focusing on the infrastructure and access to social services, these organisations focused on the quality of these services, the use of public resources and social justice issues; their areas of concern ranging from education reform, issues concerning youth, women and children, to the environment. Their methods also differed from their earlier counterparts, in that they used expertise, advocacy and lobbying rather than directly channelling significant amounts of funds to aid the social problems at hand. In this sense, their work complemented and affected the work of the more traditional foundations that were established decades ago.

Turkey's European Union integration process has been the most recent demonstration of how Turkish foundations are able to re-invent themselves and remain relevant during times of rapid societal change. The foundation institution emerged as an important player in Turkey's EU integration process in the twenty-first century, and actively benefited from a number of transitions that came about with Turkey's candidacy. As a result, the government has been eager to conform to EU demands; legislative reform packages involving amendments concerning foundations and civil society have been passed; new and vast financial resources for civil society have emerged, accompanied by new channels to affect policy making at the national and EU levels. Thus, a large number of foundations and civil society organisations (CSOs) have benefited directly or indirectly from the above-mentioned transformations and increased their capacities both in service delivery and advocacy to affect public policy in a way that was not possible before.

In short, the foundation continued to be the major philanthropic vehicle in the Republican era – channelling private wealth for public good through the lens of development and democratisation. Foundations were able to adapt as the definition of public good changed and evolved, and continues to play a critical role in citizen's lives.

## The new millennium

The new millennium has brought about a number of significant changes to the work of foundations in Turkey. Partly related to the emergence of the more enabling environment mentioned above, foundations have been *mobilising* and *experimenting* like never before.

Bringing together the country's leading foundations, TÜSEV (Third Sector Foundation of Turkey) was established in 1993, which has brought about significant changes in the work of Turkish foundations. For the past fifteen years, TÜSEV has been a leader in improving civil society laws, generating research and policies for the sector's future, and encouraging dialogue and cooperation among private, public and third sector actors. Today, TÜSEV's members – consisting of one hundred Turkish foundations and associations – continue to share a vision of strengthening civil society in Turkey.

As for experimentation and innovation, there are countless examples. Yet perhaps recent developments in the areas of community, diaspora and corporate philanthropy deserve a closer look.

Turkey's first community foundation, Bolu Community Foundation, was established in June 2008, in a town of approximately eighty-five thousand inhabitants and presents an important milestone in Turkey's third sector. The foundation aims to promote the well-being of the town by supporting critical projects put forth by non-profit organisations which address the critical social and economic development of the community. It is established and operated by a group of thirty-two local business and civil society leaders with the technical support of TÜSEV. As Turkey's first pilot community foundation, it is already serving an important role in mobilising resources, engaging donors, and convening stakeholders. Over the past year, the Foundation has gained some experimental experience in fundraising for and administrating small grants, yet its support has mostly been charity-oriented in nature. The Foundation's management has expressed their wish to provide more support for social justice issues in the coming years.

The Turkish diaspora is more present than ever in channelling resources to the country's rapidly expanding non-profit sector. Though their support has been largely in line with the traditional foundations' tendency to build institutions and physical infrastructure, the emergence of Europe and US-based diaspora organisations with mandates for social change is encouraging. Some of these diaspora organisations place a strong emphasis on creating opportunities that empower people while having a lasting impact for future generations in areas such as environmental sustainability, gender equality, women's empowerment, arts and culture and civil society empowerment.

Local corporations are also emerging as new actors with an eye for social justice philanthropy, as companies in Turkey appear to be increasingly aware of their role as donors and supporters of the third sector. Until recently, Turkish companies lacked sound strategic practices in making grants and working with civil society organisations beyond a "one-off" sponsorship level. Today, leading companies and holdings are not only increasing their capacity in working with CSOs, but they are also broadening their involvement through employee volunteering and donor programmes. Most importantly, CSOs and some leading companies are creating partnerships for project funding with a view to aligning mutual objectives and respective strengths to address critical development challenges such as education reform and environmental sustainability. However, such best practices are not widespread yet and need to be better promoted and expanded.

In conclusion, Turkish foundations will continue to re-examine their role in society and acquire new dimensions in their work. Given their strong roots and having already demonstrated their adaptability in the face of major societal changes, it seems reasonable to assume that the foundation institution will continue to be the major philanthropic vehicle and agent of change in the following millennia.

OLGA ALEXEEVA

# 14
# Russia
# A HISTORY OF TRUST IN DISTRUSTFUL TIMES

## A brief history of philanthropy in Russia

Philanthropy in Russia is an "old new" phenomenon. For centuries before the Bolshevik revolution that broke the tradition of giving for nearly eighty years, most Russians donated part of their income to charity, either through the church or through established charitable institutions, which usually had the royal blessing. The Orthodox Church was the only source of organised charity and the main recipient of donations up until the eighteenth century. The Church established shelters for the homeless, hospitals and orphanages. Just like in Catholic European countries, monasteries were key providers of social welfare and education. In the eighteenth century, inspired by Western European examples of secular giving and charity, the Russian aristocracy began to play a much more active role in philanthropy. Catherine the Great, probably the most famous Russian Empress, established the first universities in Russia, created the first system of secular secondary schools and a range of secular social welfare institutions, all funded by a combination of state funding and donations, mainly from the aristocracy. That tradition continued into the nineteenth century and by 1900 Russia boasted a whole range of charitable organisations and institutions under royal patronage or with royal blessing; some with state funding, some without. The Institutions of Empress Maria alone included over three hundred organisations providing social support to thousands of people in need through orphanages, hospitals and schools.

In the 1860s the liberal reforms of Alexander II which freed peasants from serfdom and boosted business activities in Russia also created legal opportunities for new forms of philanthropy to flourish outside the realms of the aristocracy. Compared with the Church-led charity of the Middle Ages and the royal-led charity of the eighteenth and early nineteenth centuries, as the result of liberal reforms the second half of the nineteenth century saw a surge of "merchant" giving: philanthropy by the newly rich owners of mills and factories, trade posts and banks. By the end of the nineteenth century Russian merchant donors provided millions of roubles to museums and theatres, universities and schools, social institutions and even to movements that today may be called human rights organisations such as the movement for women's rights. Pavel Tretyakov, the founder of the famous gallery of Russian Art in Moscow; Savva Morozov, the main donor to the first children's hospital in Russia – still called the Morozov hospital; and many others donated significant sums annually to charity.

However, certain characteristics of Russian philanthropy that we see today were already manifesting themselves. First of all, Russian philanthropy at the end of the nineteenth and beginning of the twentieth century was not institutionalised. By 1917 Russia had thousands of operating charities but no private or family foundations or trusts. Major Russian donors preferred to support or even create from scratch institutions of direct assistance to the needy such as hospitals or shelters, cultural and educational establishments, instead of giving grants and donations to other charities – a trend that continues today. Secondly, despite the fact that the reforms of Alexander II allowed Russians, even of non-aristocratic background, to create charities without the royal blessing, Russian donors still sought royal approval of their giving, and when not creating their own institutions, preferred to give to state run or supported organisations. This trend of seeking government blessing in philanthropy is again very strong today.

In 1917 after the Bolsheviks took power in Russia, charity and philanthropy were declared "obsolete" by the winning Communist Party. In the new workers' state where all people were equal, it was considered that nobody needed charity. However, well into the 1920s charities existed in Soviet Russia to combat homelessness and famine and extend education to the poorest of peasants. Then, by the end of the 1920s and even more so after Josef Stalin took firm hold of the country, charity was defined as "cynical acts of capitalists trying to cover their exploitation of the working classes" (Ozheghov Thesaurus, 1976, Moscow) and was forbidden altogether, even for the Church.

However, it would be a mistake to consider that non-profit volunteer activities or even charitable activities were completely absent in the Soviet Union. The Soviet system, for example, greatly encouraged volunteering

Children at the Theatre

for causes deemed important for the building of communism, and while many people, especially in the late 1970s and early 1980s were forced to volunteer for such causes, there were always thousands of people who believed in the ideas and ideals of communism and donated their time and effort in a truly voluntary manner. In the 1940s and almost certainly until the 1960s the majority of Soviet people believed in communist ideals and donated and volunteered on a voluntary basis, not out of fear or due to pressure. Then in the 1970s and 1980s such belief in communist ideas all but evaporated and along with it the truly voluntary donation of time and money nearly ceased to exist, replaced by forced volunteering and giving. The aftertaste of that forced volunteering when, for example, obligatory work on collective farm fields by the urban population was called "voluntary", poisoned the whole notion of volunteering in Russia for many years. The true meaning of volunteering only started to recover in the public view after 2003-2004 with the growth of the new young middle class's engagement in philanthropy.

Marias Children

Michael Gorbachev, hailed in the west as the "father of perestroika" can also be called a "father of new charity" in Russia. It is under his supervision and with his blessing that charities were allowed to be formed again in Russia: first with mega semi-governmental institutions. The Children's Foundation and the Culture Foundation were created, for example as early as 1987. In 1989 the first independent parliament in new Russia, the Council of Deputies, adopted the Law on Public Associations which opened the door to the creation of thousands of charities and non-governmental organisations (NGOs), without the need for the Communist Party sanction.

Volunteers of the Donate Life programme visit patients at child cancer unit

Simultaneously, the first private companies and cooperatives started giving donations from their very first profits to charity: to help children in orphanages and to save ailing hospitals and schools.

## The Russian charitable sector: From self help and democratic development to populism and civil movements

The Russian non-profit sector has come a long way since the first independent non-profit organisations (NPO), or as they are more often called, NGOs were allowed to register.

The very first modern Russian non-profit sector was predominantly focused on self-help. The first Law on Public Associations adopted by the Soviet Supreme Council of Deputies allowed people for the first time since 1917 to form associations to pursue non-profit goals. Up until 1995–1996 public associations were the only legal forms of non-profit, non-governmental organisations allowed. But even before the first 1989 law was adopted, the first associations were already formed. These included the All Soviet Union Association of Disabled People and several other organisations. After 1989 thousands of smaller associations at the regional and local level were registered in Russia.

In parallel, the state inspired colossal foundations such as the Soviet Children's Fund and the Soviet Fund for Culture which, as soon as they were formed, started attracting their first donations. In the public eye, initially only those foundations were associated with "charitable organisations" or "charitable foundations". Because these organisations were linked with top state officials and state support, these semi-governmental institutions formed the first public and media image of the charitable sector. Numerous small public associations were not considered by the general public to be charities despite the charitable nature of their work. This early confusion over the notion of "charity" or "charitable", inseparable from the state and state blessing, later created considerable challenges for the sector in its recognition by the general public.

In the 1990s public associations comprised over 70 percent of the Russian non-profit sector that may be defined as "public benefit". The first associations – of single mothers, large families, the disabled, parents of disabled children and war veterans, (including veterans of more recent wars such as the war in Afghanistan), brought together the most deprived and the poorer segments of society; those who could not survive alone in the "wild market" times of the 1990s. These associations provided moral support and a sense of community, and fought for and distributed among their members humanitarian aid from the West, which was at first abundant, and then more and more scarce. In most cases, the activities of such associations ended there: in basic mutual help, humanitarian aid distribution and later on local government support distribution (delivering goods and services funded by the government) and occasional events for their members. But a number of associations grew to develop much more sophisticated services and established the first rehabilitation centres for children with cerebral palsy, job training programmes for adults in wheelchairs, or became campaigning and human rights organisations such as the Soldiers' Mothers Committee which initially united families who had lost their sons to internal violence and crime in the Russian army.

However, the membership nature of public associations also resulted in the Russian charitable sector turning inwards, to focus on certain vulnerable groups without exposure to or dialogue with the wider population. The sector in fact existed on the fringes of society and very few associations tackled the problems faced by the general public: catastrophic unemployment, loss of savings by the majority of the population, degradation of medical care and general loss of direction in comparison with the previous tightly regulated life – where to go, how to live, and what to aspire to. As a result, in the 1990s, the time of the biggest growth of the registered charitable sector in Russia, most Russian people did not come across new Russian charities in their daily lives and hardly knew that they existed. At the same time, several scandals surrounding charitable foundations created by the state destroyed public trust in the notion of "charity" and formed a view that all charities are just mechanisms for laundering money by dirty officials. The public, even those who knew of or were even members of public associations did not make the connection between their own associations, and other charities and did not consider other public associations as charitable organisations.

So, by the end of the 1990s the Russian charitable sector, while considerable if compared with Soviet times, (from twenty registered charities in 1986 (all government initiated) to over three hundred thousand NGOs in 1999), still played a marginal role in Russian society. It comprised four distinctive groups of organisations with their own sources of funding, groups that hardly communicated even with each other, let alone with the public at large.

The first and the largest group – public associations – were composed of people who got together to help themselves. These charities were often the smallest and poorest but still the biggest part of the Russian charitable sector. The majority of public associations did not have staff or premises, their budgets rarely exceeded five to ten thousand United States dollars (USD) a year, and funding came from local authorities and local businesses, often in the form of in-kind contributions. Paradoxically, those charities were the most self-sustainable, simply because they became used to functioning with practically no resources.

The second group of charities was those created by "professionals": teachers, doctors, psychologists. This much smaller group of charities was born out of the professionals' disillusionment with the state system of social care and a wish for Russian social workers, educational and medical professionals to build more modern and effective services. These charities in fact created modern social services in Russia: for disabled people, especially children, for orphaned children, for the homeless, and other vulnerable groups. But while these services were of much higher quality than those provided by the government and also engendered major changes in government attitudes towards social welfare, they were only available to tiny groups of people and again existed on the fringes of society, serving a small, marginal part of the population. The "professional" charities were also funded by *ad hoc* contributions from local business and occasional foreign grants. The lack of scale in the "professional" sector in Russia was and continues to be a result of the lack of consistent funding.

The third group of public benefit organisations, such as, for example, the Moscow Helsinki Group which existed "underground" even during Soviet times, were human rights organisations. In the 1990s human rights organisations flourished, their numbers increased tenfold and there were no restrictions on their operations. Human rights charities focused on political rights, including the right to vote, something very new to most Russians at that time; or on the most violent and noticeable abuse such as the violation of human rights in Russian prisons, in the police system and in the army. However, just like the previous two groups in the sector, they failed to connect with the wider population and they did not by and large address human rights issues that concerned the general public – namely economic and social rights: employment rights, benefits, property rights, etc. Later, by the beginning of the new millennium, many human rights organisations had learned that lesson and began to address economic and social rights in addition to political rights. But it was too late: Vladimir Putin came to power in 2000 and significantly decreased the freedom and space for manoeuvre for human rights organisations. What also impaired human rights charities in Russia was that the majority of them were funded exclusively by foreign donors. Human rights charities did not even make an effort to fundraise from the public, but were fed abundantly by various democratic development programmes and US private foundations. As a result, while addressing burning issues in Russian society, Russian human rights groups did not have any real connection with that society, were not known to the wider public and in reality did not represent the public interest.

Finally, the fourth group of charities formed in the 1990s consisted of so-called "roof" institutions, fake charities created mostly by government officials, local bureaucracy or sometimes local businesses to launder money or achieve political capital. Such charities did hardly anything for public benefit, often only existing on paper. Some, however, undertook certain activities, usually in partnership with the authorities, of a completely populist nature. By and large, those who actually did conduct some activities created one-off events, such as the public distribution of humanitarian aid, usually connected with some calendar date such as the anniversary of victory in the Second World War or Christmas. But in comparison with the rest of the charitable sector, those charities received full support from the authorities (being created largely by them), the attention of the media, and although the least useful and least transparent, were most known to the general public. In 1990s these semi government-operated non-governmental organisations (GONGO – organisations that are legally independent and non-governmental but in practice are created by the government), semi money laundering charities ended up in scandals practically every day, and as a result only added fuel to the strong public distaste for any "charitable" institutions or organisations.

The 1990s ended abruptly with the election of Vladimir Putin as President of Russia. The ten years following this, from 1999 until 2009, have been characterised by the significant decrease of political freedom in Russia, the shrinking of democracy and an increase in violent attacks on the non-profit sector by the state, especially on human rights groups. At the same time, the past ten years have also seen significant economic growth in Russia and the creation of a young educated vibrant middle class which, after gaining some material prosperity and status, turned its attention to the public good and began giving.

The past ten years have become another turning point in the history of the Russian charitable and philanthropic sector. This period has displayed four key tendencies that have completely re-shaped the sector in Russia and laid both opportunities and challenges for its future:

- Firstly, the decrease and degradation of the institutionalised charitable sector;
- Secondly, the growth of middle class giving and along with it so-called "direct help" and "assistance funds";
- Thirdly, the explosive growth of giving by Russia's ultra-wealthy and the birth of the Russian foundation sector;
- Fourthly, the redefining of the notion of "self-help" and the development of self help organisations not by the fringe or most vulnerable groups of the population but by the wider public – to address much wider, very common public interests.

It is still questionable whether the institutionalised charitable sector in Russia is deteriorating or not. I am sure some of my colleagues working in the sector today would not agree with me and would demonstrate examples of the fantastic achievements made by charities, and their ability to finally connect with the public.

Truly, I would be one of the first to provide great examples of exceptional work and sustainability in the Russian sector, resilience to pressure and an ability to transform and to adapt to new environments. I would name, for example, the Early Intervention Institute in Saint Petersburg, the AIDS charities in the Urals, the Maria's Children Studio in Moscow. But these examples only highlight the main problem of the institutionalised Russian charitable sector today – they are very few and far between. The majority of Russian NGOs – we would rather use this term – are struggling to survive under the new registration and reporting regime, introduced by Putin's Kremlin, and they face more and more challenges in their fundraising. Public associations, the spinal cord of the registered sector in the 1990s, are closed down or stop operating with the speed of one an hour; their members are either disillusioned with the progress of their work or, for purely economic reasons, need to find other means of survival.

But first and foremost, the registered sector today does not really know where it is going and what it wants to achieve, or why it exists. The former goals of public associations of self-help and joint survival no longer apply, and even the economic crisis does not appear to be redressing this pattern. Professional social services are expensive to provide, and without a steady stream of funding, with the ever increasing cost of providing services, professionals' charities face a dilemma: either they begin to charge for their support, thus moving towards commercial enterprise and cutting out the poor and most vulnerable families, or they reduce their help. Some professionals' charities such as DOWNSIDE UP, Maria's Children and several others have learned how to fundraise for their work from the general public but the majority of registered Russian charities, despite years of sponsored fundraising training, still have no idea of how to connect with the public and how to ask for support from ordinary people. This means that they are not tapping into this valuable source of funding although they do gain funds from foreign foundations, corporate philanthropy or the state.

I keep referring to the "registered" sector – creating, I am sure, a lot of confusion among readers of this book. But such referral has its specific meaning and is linked to the second trend in the development of charity and philanthropy in Russia today – the "direct help" and "assistance funds", which are mushrooming in the country at an incredible rate.

Substantial economic growth in the last ten years has created a young educated vibrant middle class in Russia. Whilst concentrated mostly in big cities, the new Russian middle class is starting to play a more significant role in all aspects of Russian life – from the recent explosive growth of domestic consumption to philanthropy. Since 2004-2005, the Russian middle class has turned its attention to charity and giving. However, due to a nearly total lack of trust by the Russian public in existing charitable organisations, the new Russian middle class donors are choosing a different route for their giving – so-called 'direct help'. Instead of giving donations to operating charities, Russian donors have decided to help individuals in need: children who require expensive medical treatment and are not covered by any insurance or state support, poor families that face grave problems, or indeed governmental institutions such as orphanages or hospitals that strangely attract more trust and recognition from the general public than the far more transparent and effective independent charities.

In response to such public demand, numerous so-called "assistance funds" have been created in Russia in recent years, many of them by the media, the others by or with the support of celebrities. Assistance funds, while also now being registered as NGOs, pride themselves on having zero or little administrative costs (in truth often funded by one or two generous wealthy donors), and on creating a transparent channel of giving directly to people in need, which is usually understood as one-off financial assistance in medical or family emergencies. At the time of writing, nearing the end of 2009, Russia had over thirty nationwide so-called "direct assistance funds" that all proclaimed direct aid to people in need, and in each region similar local funds have begun to emerge. It is estimated that in 2009 alone, the year of the economic crisis, over 45 million USD have been donated by the general public to assistance funds, a massive amount for Russia, and all these funds in reality bypassed the more traditional charitable sector.

Today, assistance funds are starting to register as charities themselves, some of them as "Donate Life" foundations which initially proudly stated that they had no bureaucracy and do not implement "dubious projects", in fact have large staffs ("Donate Life" alone has over fifty employees), and are extending their programmes to pay attention to the root causes of problems such as the lack of access to highly skilled medical care. But the majority of assistance funds follow the public preference and cure symptoms rather than problems, for example, paying millions of roubles to save one child while not paying any attention at all to the overwhelming ills of the Russian health care system.

The development of direct help assistance funds goes hand in hand with another trend in the Russian non-profit sector – the creation of so-called "movements" of non-registered associations comprised of people who are united by some common problem such as the nearly total corruption of the traffic police in Russia. In contrast with the self help groups of the 1990s who united very vulnerable and the poorest of the poor, these new associations bring together a much wider range of people, many of whom are young and successful, regarding issues that resonate in the souls of every Russian. The Russian drivers' association, consumer groups, associations of owners of summer houses – so-called "dachas" – and so on, reflect and address problems that nearly every Russian family faces. As a result, they receive significant support from the public and are gaining public trust.

The Russian charitable sector today is dying and at the same time being reborn. It is shedding its old inward-looking, narrow-minded foundations of self-help, and dependency on a few institutional donors such as foreign foundations or big businesses, and it is reaching out to the general public and finally starting to address its interests. At the same time, it still lacks a sustainable funding base and an independent voice that can be heard by the government and the public alike, and because of this it is losing good people.

## The Charities Aid Foundation in Russia

The Charities Aid Foundation (CAF), one of the largest foundations in the UK, founded in 1924, opened its office in Moscow in 1993. It was a time of political turmoil (the Russian parliament was bombed just two months after CAF opened its office), wild and sometimes violent growth of independent business, and exponential development of the charitable sector.

CAF Russia started its operation with programmes to support and encourage emerging Russian NGOs by providing training and free legal aid, space for meetings and reference publications. By 1997 it became clear to us that the time had come to start talking about domestic philanthropy in Russia. Few back then believed that chaotic and non-transparent Russian business would donate money to charity, but our first events, which focused on corporate social responsibility (CSR) and corporate giving, gathered as many as ten to twenty corporate participants. The situation changed after the financial crisis of 1998. The crisis played a role of a "cold shower" for growing Russian businesses who prior to that gave money to anyone who asked without considering the impact, results or needs. Instead of killing philanthropy in its infancy as many feared, the crisis pushed corporate donors to think more strategically about where they gave, how they gave, and what needed to be done to make their giving achieve better results with fewer resources. By 2001 CAF Russia had worked with over a dozen large Russian companies who decided to restructure their corporate giving and reach out to the non-profit sector.

Private giving followed, first by the ultra-wealthy with the Vladimir Potanin Foundation becoming the very first private foundation in Russian history, followed by the "Dynasty" Foundation of Dmitri Zimin and others. We worked with many of them, helping to design giving programmes and understand priorities. In 2003-2004 it became clear that focussing only on giving by the ultra-wealthy was not sustainable, and that we needed to reach out to the wider public and talk to ordinary people; to create opportunities for the middle classes to give. Soon after we introduced employee giving as a straightforward and convenient way of giving, and later launched several successful campaigns to promote philanthropy, recently opening an online giving platform – www.blago.ru.

We drew some important lessons from our work in Russia and have also tended to move somewhat differently from many other international foundations. For example, we started to work with small public associations, parent's groups and social welfare projects when most of the foreign donors were concentrating on human rights and democratic development. We understood that people would rather acquire the notion of civil society and democracy through issues they are concerned with in their daily lives, than through politics or theoretical constructions. We started working with Russian businesses when they looked quite ugly. But we always remembered that the famous Rockefellers and Fords were not angel-like creatures in their lifetimes either, and we needed to start with the donors that we had. And while we created one of the first assistance funds in Russia – Life Line, with the aim to boost giving among ordinary people – we became the first to urge others to move forward from primitive payment for operations and raised concerns over the lack of connection between new donors and the public. We see turbulent but exciting times ahead and now debate what else will happen in the next decade that we need to start addressing today.

## Philanthropic giving in Russia

### Corporate giving: the haunt of "one company towns"

Corporate philanthropy in modern Russia started at practically the same time as the first independent co-operatives and private companies were permitted to open in 1986-1987. That philanthropy was mostly *ad hoc*, reactive and mostly included small donations and in-kind gifts to local schools, hospitals, or directly to people in desperate need (e.g. in need to cover expensive medical costs or victims of disaster). It remains the same for thousands of small and medium size enterprises. However, giving priorities and patterns of large national companies in Russia differ significantly from small and medium size enterprises.

It is possible to identify at least three types of philanthropic behaviours of companies in Russia:

**"State" oriented industrial companies and banks:** these are either companies where the state is the majority shareholder or companies that have a close connection with the government or particular officials. These companies tend to align their philanthropy with priorities of the Kremlin and/or local authorities in regions where they operate and very often give money directly to the government or through government agencies.

**Independent industrial companies and non-retail banks/financial companies:** these tend to be the most proactive in corporate giving, implement major corporate community programmes, create corporate foundations, and aspire to model their corporate philanthropy on the best international standards.

**Retail companies:** their corporate giving is closely connected to their business interests: brand promotion, sales, advertising, customer retention and loyalty; they prefer to engage customers in giving, and tend to focus mostly on cause-related marketing options. However, Russian retail companies are much less proactive and experienced in cause related marketing than the international retail brands active in Russia such as Avon, who are current leaders in the cause related marketing field in Russia.

There are also some specific issues of the Soviet corporate welfare legacy that Russian companies have to deal with in their corporate giving. In the Soviet Union enterprises historically subsidised a significant part of social welfare; regional housing, health and recreation provision, especially in the less accessible regions of Siberia, the North and the Far East. After privatisation in 1993–2000, the new owners of industrial enterprises faced growing demand to sustain the basic social safety net in the so-called "one company towns": towns where their enterprises were the main employer, tax payer and provider. Sustaining local welfare which the government could not finance became the main item on the corporate philanthropy agendas of all industrial companies in Russia. Some companies just continued to fund the ailing social infrastructure in their towns, others tried to shy away from this responsibility by transferring social assets to the balance sheets of local authorities (mostly without much success). Some independent private companies spent considerable resources to re-structure and modernise the social infrastructure and involve local communities and small businesses in supporting social welfare, education, health and other issues in their areas.

While corporate philanthropy is wide spread, CSR is still very much a debated concept in Russia. The majority of large national companies only started taking an interest in CSR in about 2001-2002. CSR conferences attract hundreds of corporate representatives and a dialogue about the nature of corporate responsibility in Russia exists on different levels, but in reality only a handful of private nationwide companies make an effort to implement best practice in CSR, report on CSR and even understand CSR beyond pure corporate giving.

### Private giving: the wealthy

While analysing private giving in Russia, it is important to differentiate between giving by ultra-wealthy Russians and the rest of the population. Directions, patterns, motivations and forms of giving by the ultra-rich are distinctively different from those of ordinary middle class people or even other wealthy people. In Russia the "ultra-wealthy" category is usually applied to individuals included in the Russian Forbes list, for which in 2008 one needed to amass over 400 million USD in personal wealth to be listed. More generally high net worth (HNW), however, is taken to mean a wide range of wealth levels from one hundred thousand USD per year family income in provincial areas to up to three to four hundred million USD of personal assets in Moscow or Saint Petersburg.

From the initial surge in private giving in 1987-1988 and until 2004–2005 individual giving by ordinary people, including small and medium business owners, the middle classes and the poor practically did not exist. Donations by small and medium size enterprises indeed included funds given directly by the owners of those enterprises, sometimes such "hidden" donations comprising up to 50 percent of the total annual giving by a company. But by and large most of the Russian population preferred to throw coins to beggars than give to charities.

In 2004–2005 the situation started to change very rapidly: from less than 5 percent of the population considering giving to charity in 2001 (CAF Russia research on individual giving, 2001) to over 56 percent stating that they considered giving as an important "duty" of every person, and 40 percent willing to support charitable causes regularly in 2006 (VTSIOM (ВЦИОМ) – the Russian Center of Sociological Research and Public Opinion Survey, 2006). However, as mentioned above, the principle charitable giving by individuals was mainly to directly support people in need, and the new flow of donations from the Russian middle class bypassed the registered charitable sector.

What is also important about new Russian private philanthropy, both from the middle class and the wealthy, is that it is distinctively secular, and its growth is not at all connected with the restoration of the Orthodox Church in Russia. According to the reseach, *BRIC Giving (Individuals Giving in Brazil, Russia, India and China,* CAF, 2009), typical motives for giving by Russians, include compassion, a sense of personal duty and responsibility, and even curiosity, as philanthropy or volunteering are very new elements of social life in Russia.

However, we can also identify "de-motivating" factors that are hindering the growth of private giving in Russia. Apart from considerable distrust of the Russian public in any organised institutions, let alone in "non-governmental" organisations, there are some other factors that impact the growth of individual giving by the general public in Russia:

-   Lack of tax benefits for individuals: there are a few options of some tax benefits that an individual donor can receive but only if he or she gives to a government institution such as an orphanage or a school or a hospital, and the procedure for obtaining such benefits is very complicated;
-   Russians do not have cheque books and a direct debit system: in order to make a donation to a charity, individuals must go through the tedious procedure of a bank wire transfer;
-   The overall majority of Russian charities are not yet active in raising funds from the general public.

Motivations and patterns of giving by ultra-wealthy individuals, however, are somewhat different from those of the general public. While many ultra-wealthy people in Russia enter the philanthropic field because they are moved by compassion similarly to the middle class donors, this almost "accidental" giving quickly gives way to philanthropy driven by clearly defined personal or corporate interests.

"Interest based" giving is the key driving force of ultra-high net worth philanthropy in Russia. Interests of the ultra-wealthy include for example the need to promote a corporate brand of a privately owned company, or expand business to a new territory or a country, or simply to buy the loyalty of politicians especially when donations are given to charities under the patronage of such politicians. For a number of Russian ultra-wealthy donors, interests may also include their wish to improve their image abroad, especially in the USA and Western Europe. In recent years, since Vladimir Putin became the President and then Prime Minister of Russia and significantly reduced options for open policy dialogue and political contest, philanthropy for some ultra-wealthy donors also became an instrument of policy influence and an alternative to direct involvement in politics.

If one draws a progression pattern of ultra-wealthy donor motivation in Russia, it would start with an "accident" – an *ad hoc* act of giving, an emotional reaction to an event or a person in need; it will then continue with giving based largely on short term interests; and for some it finally transforms into giving based on newly formulated or discovered values. In the case of the ultra-wealthy in Russia such a change in motivation is often very pronounced and evident and expressed in all aspects of private giving: what donors support, how they give, whom they invite to run their philanthropic projects, whom they choose to advise them, and of course how, if ever, they talk about their giving.

## Foundations

Foundations are an even more recent phenomenon in Russia than philanthropy in general. It is important, however, to differentiate between a legal form of a "foundation" in Russia and the true meaning a foundation would have in the United States or in Europe.

In Russia a "foundation" is one of the legal forms in which charities can register. There are generally very few specific requirements for foundations in comparison with other legal forms of charity; among these are, for example, the requirement to have a board of directors and an advisory board. In reality anyone can register a foundation, even without any initial funds. As a result of a very "loose" legislation in relation to foundations, there are over 35,000 foundations registered in Russia alone but only a handful of those foundations could be defined as foundations according to US or European standards.

The Russian Donors Forum (RDF), a voluntary association of donors in Russia, estimates that there are in reality just over one hundred private foundations in Russia, forty corporate foundations and thirty community foundations; so approximately one hundred and seventy foundations which would be considered "foundations" by US or European standards, meaning institutions that have assets, independent governance and generally act as funding institutions providing resources to other charities or implementing projects they fund themselves.

The RDF 2008 analysis of activities of twenty private and corporate foundations showed that:
- 10 percent of foundations surveyed by RDF are grant-making foundations;
- 80 percent are operating foundations, meaning that they implement charitable programmes themselves instead of giving grants to other charities, or some of them combine grant-making and operating programmes;
- In 10 percent of cases it was not clear what foundations actually do or they were still in the early planning stage.

Main priority areas of foundation giving in Russia in order of importance are:
- Children's welfare – twelve foundations out of twenty surveyed
- Education
- Science
- Culture

Such priority areas as the protection of the environment, human rights, health (except paying directly for the medical treatment of children or people in need), or more "sensitive" subjects of social welfare or health such as mental health, HIV and AIDS, human trafficking, and abuse (including drug or alcohol abuse) are absent from agendas of private and corporate foundations in Russia. Poverty alleviation as a specific topic is also not addressed by private foundations; donors prefer to pay attention to some specific groups of the needy such as orphaned children without getting into a discussion of poverty as a problem. Various models of encouraging economic activities by the poor, such as microcredit, social entrepreneurship recently (2008) started to gain some interest but such interest is still very remote and Russian donors either do not know how to implement such initiatives in Russia or in most of cases are afraid of the political consequences of moving towards the "poverty agenda".

Relations between foundations and the state in Russia vary significantly depending on the nature of their founders, source of funds, and even geographical location. In general, foundations created by companies tend to build more close ties with the government either on the national (if a company is a major national corporation) or local level. Private foundations, even ones created by individuals openly loyal to the Kremlin, tend to distance themselves from the government and sometimes opening a private foundation becomes the only opportunity for a particular ultra-wealthy individual to retain some form of independence in philanthropy, when in corporate giving such independence becomes more and more of a problem.

## Conclusions and perspectives, the role of Russia in the global philanthropy development

Today Russian philanthropy stands alone in the whole post-socialist space of Eastern Europe and the former Soviet Union. Compared with other post-communist countries, it is massive, fast growing and constantly evolving. However, the majority of domestic giving bypasses the registered and organised non-profit sector and goes either directly to individuals in need or to government institutions such as schools or orphanages. Russian philanthropy is an incredible mix of generosity and distrust, creativity and stereotypes, bravery and complacency. It operates in a non-favourable and an often openly hostile legal environment, with no tax benefits for donors, and yet donations from Russian corporates, for example, often reach up to 17 percent of their pre-tax profits, the highest percentage in Europe. Russian philanthropy is generous but very inward looking: Russian donors do not as a rule support projects outside Russia, unless such projects ultimately will benefit their homeland. Russian people *en masse*, while substantially wealthier than in the Soviet time, still mentally consider themselves poor and under-privileged and therefore do not see themselves helping other countries, for example, in Africa and in Asia.

The history of Russian philanthropy and the non-profit sector draws some important lessons for other emerging markets or countries on the road to more strategic giving and an efficient voluntary sector. It shows that however poor your public is, it is imperative to raise funds from the public and engage in a dialogue with this public from day one, even if initially this yields few material results. It highlights the significance of stereotypes and the long lasting echo of even a small scandal and misuse of funds in fragile and vulnerable societies, and thus the importance of transparency for all NGOs, big and small. It shows enormous potential for domestic giving and an opportunity to engage even first generation rogue entrepreneurs in strategic philanthropy, and that it is possible to raise funds in any country, thus decreasing dependence on foreign funding. And it also shows what happens to NGOs dependent on foreign funding when their foreign donors withdraw.

Russian philanthropy is complex and constantly evolving. It will one day cross Russian borders and support projects outside its homeland, and therefore it needs to form partnerships and learn lessons from international experience today.

LUC TAYART DE BORMS & GERRY SALOLE

# 15 Europe

# THE EUROPEAN FOUNDATION STATUTE: END-GAME OR THE ULTIMATE BRUSH-OFF?

## Introduction

This year marks the twentieth anniversary of the European Foundation Centre (EFC) which was founded in November 1989 by a group of seven, forward-looking European foundations. The sector is at an important crossroads, the anniversary not being merely an important milestone but, coming in the wake of the financial crisis and in the anticipation of a stronger and more cohesive European Union, it provides a compelling opportunity for those of us involved with the sector to take an analytic and frank look at how far the sector has come and how far it still has to go. We believe, moreover, that we have finally reached the end-game in the long, sometimes baffling process towards the adoption of the European Foundation Statute, a critical cornerstone which will enable the sector to perform more coherently and visibly. The next few decades thus promise to be exciting and crucial times for European philanthropy.

Reflecting on the past decades, we believe that the European foundation sector has evolved into a major economic force that is making significant contributions to Europe's development at both national and European levels. The sector is rich in its diversity and has evolved over centuries. Rooted in diverse models of civil society, it has also remained contemporary and has moved with the times as societies respond to the forces of globalisation and the re-defined role of the state.

Most recently, for example, the sector has proven itself to be resilient during the economic global downturn and tapped hidden strengths that have enabled it to show both responsible leadership and to realise ambitious creativity. The sector is moving forward into the future with self-confidence. This self-confidence is a recent phenomenon. Until a few years ago European philanthropy seemed somewhat overshadowed by, and continued to define itself by reference to, US philanthropy. Recently, there has been a marked and genuine consciousness of home-grown and historic capacity that seems to have liberated European foundations from their timidity and hesitancy about embarking on completely new paths.

In the future, we can expect European philanthropy to continue to adapt its work programmes to reflect current realities. Globalisation is re-shaping our world and blurring national boundaries. Governments are re-defining themselves, creating space for the private sector to undertake service delivery. This is also a space where foundations are taking on new responsibilities, as convenors and agents of advocacy, together with NGOs, trade organisations, and other actors.

At the same time, Europe is preparing for a new generation of philanthropists. Young people are becoming increasingly engaged. A study undertaken by the King Baudouin Foundation (KBF) in 2008 – *Youth and Philanthropy* – reveals that better educated young people are more inclined to want to engage in a good cause and are often motivated because they want to see quick, visible results. Giving is also about self-respect and self-image – it is both "cool" and normative to engage actively in good causes.

## A major economic but hitherto "invisible" force

Many experts and private sector specialists were surprised to learn that the European philanthropy sector is larger than its American counterpart in terms of assets and expenditures. According to the European Commission's Feasibility Study on a European Foundation Statute:[1]

> *"[We] estimate that the European foundation sector has assets of between €350 billion and €1.0 trillion, and annual expenditures of between €83 billion and €150 billion. By contrast, US foundations have assets of approximately €300 billion and expenditures of €29 billion."*

The study, which was released in February 2009, also reported: "The European foundation sector is a major economic force and makes significant contributions to the public good of Europe." It estimates the number of

---

1 *EUROPA – the official website of the European Union* [online], available from the World Wide Web: http://ec.europa.eu/internal_market/company/eufoundation/index_en.htm

foundations in the European Union (EU) ranges from ninety thousand to one hundred and ten thousand, or around four hundred foundations per million inhabitants. There is a wide variation in the number of foundations between European countries, ranging from a high of more than sixteen thousand in Hungary, fourteen thousand in Denmark, and over ten thousand each in Germany, Spain and Sweden; to lows of three to five hundred public benefit foundations in Belgium, Greece and Portugal.

The European Commission study also reveals that philanthropy in Europe is quite different from in the US; it favours operating programmes over grants, engages directly with national governments and the EU institutions. European foundations often take on the role of convener, as described below.

A 2008 book on European philanthropy[2] showcases the work of a selection of foundations across Europe. The book reveals that foundations have a "brilliant" track record and play many valuable roles in their societies and beyond. The sector has earned much credibility in many crosscutting areas.

Many foundations work cross-border to grapple with migration, science, culture, human trafficking, HIV/AIDS, and poverty in innovative and multifaceted ways. Others play the role of catalyst, facilitator or convener as they work closely with civil society organisations, governments, scientific and cultural institutions, and others. In this role, foundations bring together stakeholders in a multidisciplinary forum to debate issues and formulate policy recommendations that are delivered to national governments and European policymakers and parliamentarians.

Then why the surprise about its size? Why such a low profile? The European philanthropic sector is not very well known, compared to other parts of the world, notably the US. The public, policymakers and politicians remain, unfortunately, largely unaware of the huge amount of assets at play in the sector – and their potential for impact in the future. Despite the current economic downturn, these assets are set to grow exponentially with the wealth transfer of the current generation.

There may be many reasons for this low profile, including the fact that in the European environment today, foundations are perceived as relatively small players, but it continues to be a sector that seems to be somewhat invisible to journalists, politicians, law-makers and European pundits and think-tanks. It is almost as if there is something about the ubiquitous nature of these civil society institutions that makes them somehow less visible.

The EFC is working to change this perception of the European philanthropic sector, addressing particularly the sector's uncanny ability

---

2 MacDonald, N Tayart de Borms, L (2008) *Philanthropy in Europe: A rich past, a promising future*, London: Alliance Publishing Trust.

to operate below the radar. This is rapidly being replaced by the necessity to combine efforts, prove impact and be better understood as stakeholders and their partners demand that foundations become even more effective and transparent by working in partnership with other organisations and foundations. Hence the current focus on a European Foundation Statute which will do much to put European philanthropy on the European map.

The diversity of the philanthropic impulse across history has resulted in a dynamism that still fuels the sector today. This dynamism took root within Europe's different religious contexts and has been shaped by varying degrees of secularisation over several centuries. The separation of church and state in most countries has allowed philanthropy to find its space in modern societies in different ways.

*Philanthropy in Europe: A rich past, a promising future*,[3] notes that for European foundations to fulfil their obligation to create value, they must fully understand the context in which they assume their various roles and how best to meet the economic, cultural and social needs of the societies in which they operate, whether in their own communities or beyond. To do this, foundations must take into consideration the policy environment in which they work. In defining this environment – and responding to it through grant-making or operational programmes, projects and initiatives – it is critical to evaluate the interplay of roles of the state, the market and civil society.

European foundations operate in very different societal contexts, which inevitably means that they are actors within a framework created by different models of civil society. They are also using a broad range of methodologies that go beyond traditional grant-making to taking on operational roles, using tools such as advocacy and communications strategies or running their own scientific and cultural institutions.

Civil society is quite a different animal in the north of Europe than in the south, as it responds to different realities and cultural paradigms. Consider that despite the forces of secularisation and post-modernism that have swept across Europe, cultural paradigms die hard, which in part accounts for the different civil society models. For example, southern European society is still characterised by a very Catholic paradigm, while in northern Europe Protestant ethics generally prevail.

Three models of civil society can be identified across Europe outside the Anglo-Saxon model – the Rhine, the Latin/Mediterranean and the Scandinavian. These models are of course evolving and changing, as are our societies, but distinctive characteristics can be identified. To better

---

3   This description of civil society is from: MacDonald, N Tayart de Borms, L (2008) *Philanthropy in Europe: A rich past, a promising future*, London: Alliance Publishing Trust (p. 8-10).

understand the rich diversity of the European sector, it is important to consider how foundations act within various civil society models, and against the backdrop of globalisation, the changing role of the state and shifting socio-economic patterns.

We believe, however, that the diversity and mutability of civil society is even more complex than even these models allow for. There is, for instance, sometimes as much difference between foundations within a given country as there is between those in different countries. Indeed, it is clear that foundations have always had complex responses to different contexts and it stands to reason, therefore, that foundations are constantly changing and adapting to contexts. The example of Italian foundations of banking origin is illustrative in this regard. There are some eighty foundations of banking origin, with total assets in excess of 65 billion euros and an annual expenditure of over 1.5 billion euros as of 2006. These foundations were all created simultaneously when the Italian state privatised state-controlled savings banks. The fact that these organisations were created at the same time, with the same strict fiscal and legal framework with comparable, if not identical, governance structures could encourage the casual observer to regard these entities as the same. However, there are already palpable differences between these close cousins, ranging from the miniscule to more substantive. Variations include governance, decision-making processes, the autonomy of staff, the focus or interpretation of their missions, investment policies, different perspectives on their mandate and international grant giving. If this is true of such close cousins over a relatively short period of time, what could evolve over a considerably longer period?[4]

## Today – a community of resilient organisations

European foundations have been described in as many ways as the forms they take. Critics may view them as "aloof, opaque, bureaucratic, unaccountable, self-contained, and run by old boys' clubs", but the current economic downturn is proving such critics wrong. Instead of unveiling a shambolic, opaque collection of national philanthropic institutions, the crisis has revealed a sector that is composed of a community of dynamic, growing and highly resilient organisations. Tough times have also revealed hidden strengths. When faced with adversity, foundations mustered the self-confidence to look beyond the immediate financial crisis to creatively and ambitiously identify new ways to fulfil their missions.

This is indeed a pivotal time for foundations and their reputation and the sector will be marked by how they react over the next couple of years.

---

4  Salole, G (2008) "The resilience of Civil Society and its implications for Policy: The European Experience" in *Civil Society at the Crossroads*, edited by Taye Assefa and Barhu Zewde, Forum for Social Studies, Addis Ababa

In October 2008, in the midst of the global financial meltdown, the EFC launched a survey among its members to better understand the impact of the unstable economy on their activities and future prospects. Just over half the respondents reported that the financial crisis was not affecting their organisations. The majority of the EFC's European members saw a drop in assets in the range of 15 to 25 percent in 2008. This is less than our American counterparts, many of which suffered losses between 30 and 45 percent. In fact, the majority said that they would still be able to meet all grant-making programme commitments in 2009.

However, nearly half of the respondents expected their foundations' budget for grant-making and/or operating programmes to decrease in the next two years, while two-thirds said they were considering significant changes in their investment strategy and asset allocation in the future.

## Responsible leadership in tough times

Many of the EFC's members regard the economic downturn as a strategic opportunity. They are certainly not panicking but rather are undergoing a serious rethink regarding their long-term investment policy and strategy. What the crisis brought home to most foundation leaders is the driving principle of responsible leadership in tough times. Foundations have responsibilities to the communities they serve – in bad times and in good times.

KBF, for example, decided to take an anti-cyclical approach. It took the position that as an investor in equity markets, it must ride the ups and downs of the real economy. It also believed in its responsibilities to the foundation's donors and beneficiaries. Like many foundations, it was awash in a sea of conflicting financial and investment advice. Its board of governors wanted to avoid the "expert trap" because in the short-term, no one knew – or knows – what the best strategy is. The foundation decided to weather the storm by regularly rebalancing its portfolio and making some staff cuts. However, KBF did not waver from its commitment to keep the same level of spending in 2009 through to 2010 and 2011.

Many EFC members are taking this opportunity to examine more closely the effectiveness of, and approaches to, funding with a view to increasing their impact in the longer term. As a result, they are engaging more closely with their grantees and partners and exploring new ways of working together. In doing so, they are developing new collaborative models where they can benefit from shared expertise and infrastructure.

There are many examples of foundations weathering the storm and extending a helping hand to others. The financial crisis and increasingly unexpected budget cuts have placed NGOs and other civil society organisations in an insecure position with dramatically decreased funding.

The Open Estonia Foundation has launched a call for project proposals to help civil society organisations survive these difficult economic conditions. The Open Society Emergency Fund of one million euros will finance social projects in twenty countries in Eastern Europe, the Balkans, Central Asia and Caucasus aimed at supporting the most vulnerable groups of society affected by the global economic crisis, as well as innovative initiatives promoting the values of open society.

## The curious paradox of perpetuity

There is a misperception that because foundations are typically organisations that have been set up in perpetuity – with endowments that donors intended to last in perpetuity – they are unable to change or evolve. Over the years, this concept has led many in the sector to ponder a key existential question: "How do perpetual organisations grapple with change?"

Other questions foundation leaders and others think about when considering their obligation to create value, and their role in society because of their privileged tax treatment, include: should foundations spend down? Could they make a greater impact by committing assets as well as income to fighting for their causes? Or should foundations provide stewardship for their assets in order to last in perpetuity?

The financial downturn has forced many foundation leaders and their boards to stop thinking about such questions and leap into action. Many have had to find new ways to achieve their missions and objectives, while at the same time providing immediate support to those who need it most.

## Participating effectively on the European stage

Looking ahead to the next twenty years and beyond, we believe the European foundation sector must do much more to build on the work it is doing to meet the challenges ahead. But therein lies our conundrum. To do so, we must become even more European and more global, while working in closer partnership with other organisations and foundations. But the sector's operating environment is restricted, something that could be remedied to a large degree within the parameters of a European Foundation Statute (EFS).

Legal and tax impediments across the EU's twenty-seven member states hinder the cross-border work of foundations. Since 2001, the EFC, individual foundations and national associations of foundations have advocated that the European institutions propose and adopt an EU regulation, known as the EFS. The EFS would enable foundations and donors to advance their work and cooperation across national borders.

The EFS proposed by the EFC would create a new European legal instrument as an optional tool, complimentary to existing national legislation. Foundations could register as European Foundations and be mainly governed by European law. The status would only be available to foundations pursuing public benefit purposes across national borders.

After some initial foot-dragging, the European Commission launched the *Feasibility Study on a European Foundation Statute*, which supports the long held position of the EFC that the EFS is the best policy option for addressing cross-border barriers and thereby stimulating foundation activities. Key findings of the study[5] include:

- Among the twenty-seven EU member states, there are considerable regulatory differences in the treatment of foundations. However, with regard to public benefit foundations – foundations that promote public benefit purposes only – there are important similarities in treatment that are more substantial than the remaining differences.
- Cross-border activities of foundations face civil and tax law barriers due to legal differences and uncertainties leading to higher compliance costs.
- Estimates of the measurable costs of these barriers to cross-border activities of European foundations range from 90 to 101 million euros per year. There are also incalculable costs (including the cost of foundation seat transfer, cost of duplication, and costs of failure) that are certainly higher.
- There are five policy options for addressing cross-border barriers to stimulate foundation activities. The EFS is the preferable policy option.
- In addition to reducing the cost of cross-border activities, an EFS "would have additional positive effects on the general governance of foundations and trusts; on the behaviour of donors and giving; and on the European economy, especially in the field of R&D."

For many reasons, some of which we note below, the EFC continues to strongly support the creation of the EFS as an optional legal instrument for European foundations engaging in cross-border activities.[6] Based on the clear recommendations of the feasibility study, the EFC is calling on the Commission to complete its impact assessment in 2009 and to promptly issue a proposal for the EFS.

---

5   Ibid; *Feasibility Study on a European Foundation Statute*; (p.1.)

6   For more information about the EFC advocacy for an EFS, see http://www.efc.be/efs/.

## Characteristics of European foundations

The EFC believes that European foundations under an EFS should have the following characteristics:
- A legal personality
- Promotion of public benefit purposes only
- An open list of public benefit purposes
- No formal membership
- Supervised by a state or national authority
- Established by registration
- A minimum capital requirement
- A European dimension, i.e., some cross-border activities.

## Current barriers to cross-border activities of foundations

The EFC has analysed existing civil and tax law barriers to the cross-border activities of foundations in Europe. These barriers result from differing civil and tax laws across the twenty-seven member states and include:
- The lack of possibility to transfer the real or registered seat of a foundation to another member state;
- Difficulty in obtaining recognition of the legal personality of a foreign foundation;
- Legal insecurity regarding national recognition of the "general interest" or "public benefit" nature of a resident foundation's cross-border work;
- The administrative burdens and costs imposed on foundations in dealing with differing national rules, and in setting up branches in other countries, both of which require continuous legal advice;
- The lack of trust by national administrators of foreign-based foundations, causing foundations to incur the costs and burdens of establishing branches in other member states;
- Tax incentives are generally only granted to resident public benefit foundations;
- Cross-border activities can put a foundation's tax-exempt status at risk in some member states;
- Individual and corporate donors receive tax relief in most, but not all member states. In most EU countries, donations to foreign foundations do not qualify for tax relief for the resident donor; and
- Only a minority of member states grant inheritance tax exemptions for donations to non-resident public benefit foundations.

Legal scholars have suggested that some of the existing tax barriers may conflict with the European Community Treaty, including failure to provide tax incentives to donations to charities established in other member states, higher inheritance or gift tax for legacies and gifts to charities in other member states, and higher taxation on foreign-sourced income of charities.[7]

## Other options for dealing with the problem are inferior to the EFS

The feasibility study considered options to the EFS, including; maintaining the status quo with soft law instruments; harmonisation of national foundation laws; and bilateral or multinational treaties. The study correctly concluded that the EFS is the preferable policy option. Maintaining the status quo would leave foundations and donors with existing barriers.

Soft law approaches such as information campaigns, codes of conduct or accreditation models would not reduce costs. Harmonisation of foundation laws is neither wanted nor feasible. The differences among the member states are rooted in history and culture and such diversity is viewed as valuable. Bilateral or multinational treaties are unrealistic, as not all countries will sign such treaties.

The EFS is the only real option to overcome existing barriers in the most effective way. It would remove existing legal and administrative barriers and lead to the highest cost reduction. The EFS would be an additional, optional public benefit tool governed mainly by European law, complementing national and regional laws. The EFS would allow foundations and funders established or operating in more than one country to adopt the legal form of a European Foundation registered in one member state, but recognised in the other twenty-six member states. These European Foundations would be able to operate EU-wide under a single set of rules and a coherent management and reporting system.

## Benefits of a European Foundation Statute

A European Foundation Statute would bring many benefits to the European foundation sector and to Europe, its people, and its companies.

### For foundations

An EFS would facilitate and increase cross-border work and cooperation. This European tool would simplify and facilitate foundations' cross-border

---

7   Ibid; *Feasibility Study on a European Foundation Statute*, (pp. 140-149)

activities. Foundations from different countries or regions address issues that do not stop at national borders. These issues are dealt with more effectively in cooperation with foundations in neighbouring countries, or communities facing similar situations. The EFS would encourage them to add a European dimension to their entities and activities.

An EFS would offer legal certainty and significant cost savings through uniformity throughout the EU and would be a trusted legal tool easing cross-border operations. It would provide foundations and funders with a flexible European legal instrument to design internal governance structures, group their organisation and further develop it and its activities. An EFS is needed to ensure that foundations receive equal treatment in regulation of the internal market.

An EFS will bring clarity to the concept of foundations and will provide a common definition of "public benefit purpose foundations" across the EU where currently the term "foundation" is much too loosely used to refer to very diverse undertakings, ranging from personal benefit to commercial endeavours.

### For donors

An EFS would help mobilise and channel private assets for public benefit across Europe. It would advance the international interest of founders, their rising geographical mobility during their working life and upon retirement, and the increased geographical spread of their assets across Europe and beyond.

### For citizens

An EFS would serve as a robust and flexible management tool to support citizen action at EU level and beyond.

### For companies

An EFS would simplify the task facing international companies seeking to fulfill their corporate social responsibilities through the creation of foundations. Currently they must often create separate foundations in the various countries in which they operate, causing the complexity of maintaining a coherent policy and management among the different company branches.

### For the public good

An EFS would advance the European public good, by facilitating cross-border activities and cooperation between foundations as well as encouraging EU competitiveness and reinforcing the sector through the knowledge that social action will be more effectively promoted. An EFS will promote the pooling of private resources to address pressing needs and global policy issues in areas such as research, education and innovation, mobility and migration, the environment, cultural and linguistic diversity and dialogue, security and development.

There is a special role for European foundations to play in the field of research, as many advocate placing research funding at the heart of philanthropic activities. In presenting the results of a 2005 expert report,[8] *Giving More for Research in Europe: The role of foundations and the non-profit sector in boosting R&D investment*, Dr George Papaconstantinou noted:

> *"To promote the role of foundations in financing European R&D, the EU needs to initiate a regulation on a European statute for foundations and national governments need to reconsider their fiscal policies, legal and regulatory framework and matching policies."*

In a speech at a conference in March 2006, Giving More for Research Funding for Europe, European Research Commissioner Janez Potočnik confirmed:

> *"The Commission's approach to tackling research and innovation under-investment in Europe is to mobilize all policies and factors, and this includes philanthropy. Philanthropy has a long history in Europe. Think only of the Middle Ages, and the Enlightenment, when rich supporters of artists and scientists were numerous. Perhaps the time has come to revive this debate in the research field."*

An EFS can lead to a benchmark of accountability, transparency and good governance of foundations and channel domestic and foreign funds for public purpose across the EU and beyond.

## A European Foundation Statute is long overdue

There is another compelling argument for a European Foundation Statute. Looking ahead to the next twenty years, we also expect to see the philanthropically inclined "baby boomer" generation transferring a large slice of their wealth to activities for the public good, which coincides with the very areas in which European foundations have expertise. As these Europeans have grown up in a European Union where they have enjoyed mobility, they will expect to be able to give and engage in cross-border

---

8  *EUROPA – the official website of the European Union* [online], available from the World Wide Web: http://ec.europa.eu/invest-in-research/pdf/download_en/rec_5_7800_ giving_4_051018_bat.pdf

philanthropy.

We believe now is the time for Europe's institutional machinery to get into gear and to facilitate the sector's ability to participate properly on the European stage by moving forward with a European Foundation Statute. It is long overdue.

Rayna Gavrilova

# 16 Europe

# THE CHALLENGE OF PARTICIPATION: THE TRUST FOR CIVIL SOCIETY IN CENTRAL AND EASTERN EUROPE EXPERIENCE

## Introduction

The Trust for Civil Society in Central and Eastern Europe (CEE Trust) is a grant-making organisation, established with the purpose of supporting the development of a strong civil society sector in seven post-communist countries in Eastern Europe – Bulgaria, the Czech Republic, Hungary, Poland, Romania, Slovakia and Slovenia.

The term "civil society" can encompass a broad spectrum of activities but almost always it implies civic activism and democratic participation. Therefore, encouraging citizens' engagement has always been a priority in our work. For example, 40 percent of all grants awarded by the CEE Trust in 2008 had the direct or indirect objective of fostering or supporting participatory democracy. This is not surprising: non-participation, apathy and reluctance to engage are increasingly seen as major threats not only to functional democracy but to the very well-being of societies.

Unlike many other kinds of support (humanitarian help, developmental aid, social services, advocacy work, watchdog activities, etc.) support for participation by default relies on the response, feedback and engagement of the so unpleasantly named "target groups" it is aimed at. This paper will review the experience of the CEE Trust, examine the main observations of the organisation and make some suggestions for further reflection.

## The approach of the Trust for Civil Society in Central and Eastern Europe

The Trust for Civil Society in Central and Eastern Europe was founded in 2000 by a group of major American private donors active in the region after 1989 with a special interest in supporting the growth of civil society and democracy. At this time the likelihood of the eastern European post-communist countries joining the European Union (EU) and completing the transition to democracy appeared certain and several American donors, private and public, had started preparing their exit from the region.

The model of the philanthropic trusts, pooling resources from several donors, was tested first with the Baltic-American Partnership Fund, created jointly by the United States Agency for International Development (USAID) and the Open Society Institute (the Soros Foundation) in 1998 and registered as a public charity in the United States. It was intended to operate for ten years with a capital of 15 million United States dollars (USD) contributed by the two founders.

The Trust for Civil Society in Central and Eastern Europe was established by five American private foundations: the Ford Foundation, the German Marshall Fund of the United States, the Charles Stewart Mott Foundation, the Open Society Institute, and the Rockefeller Brothers Fund. These were later joined by the Atlantic Philanthropies. By the end of its existence on 31 December 2012, the total assets of the CEE Trust will have reached 75 million USD. The model of the Trusts proved to be a good transition mechanism and two more Trusts were established by various groups of donors: the Balkan Trust for Democracy and the Black Sea Trust.

The CEE Trust was conceived as a legacy mechanism, founded on the assumption that democratic transition was nearing its successful completion and that the infrastructure of civil society (associative forms and practices) was more or less fully (re-)established. The foundations which established the CEE Trust and the individuals serving on the Board of Trustees had vast experience in philanthropy and a deep understanding of the role and the needs of civil society. This helped them to frame their mission to support the long term sustainable development of civil society. This mission is based on three pillars. Firstly, to support the maturation of an environment conducive to the development of a strong civil society (very broadly taken to mean the legal, fiscal, social, and cultural environment), secondly, to strengthen the capacity of civil society organisations (CSOs), and thirdly to promote the development of indigenous support for different forms of civic activities (private foundations, public mechanisms, individual and corporate philanthropy).

Since its conception it has been clear that the CEE Trust is a supporting mechanism, an intermediary with high sensitivity to the changes, the messages, the needs, and the requests that come from civil society itself. The first four years of its existence followed a funding strategy, which faithfully carried out the founding objectives of the Trust and concentrated on the infrastructural needs of the non-profit sector. At the end of the first period of operation and the first broad evaluation, however, it became clear that it was necessary to introduce more flexibility and to link the strategic goals of the organisation to concrete objectives, which have significance and importance for both the citizens and their organisations.

In 2006 four thematic areas were announced for the first time in an attempt to prioritise needs and establish some criteria for assessing funding applications. The priority areas were identified following extensive consultation with a wide variety of personalities from different sectors in the seven countries where the CEE Trust operates. There was nothing revolutionary about them and they were marvellously consistent from country to country. The defined priority areas of need were seen to be: more accountability of the state to the citizens, more participation, more solidarity, and the improvement of the environment within which civil society operates.

The CEE Trust's operational approach is based on two main principles: maximum flexibility and responsiveness to the needs and ideas of civil society actors, and maximising the impact of our work by sharpening its focus. This balancing act has proven to be difficult but not impossible.

We run a yearly call for proposals with clearly defined themes or priorities, which help us to achieve a more focused intervention. In parallel to this and in order to guarantee flexibility, we consider requests outside these defined areas, and grant (on a limited basis) support to projects which fall outside of the call. Another characteristic of our approach that we find effective is direct communication and discussions with individual organisations or groups. This approach is labour intensive but we believe that its two main benefits vastly outweigh its disadvantages: it provides the staff of the CEE Trust with access to a vital source of knowledge and experience, and this knowledge is especially valuable in submitting the project proposals for evaluation to our advisory committees.

## Why this theme (again)?

As a citizen of one of the young democracies in Europe and the senior executive of an international foundation supporting civil society, I often hear the same serious concerns being voiced concerning civil society: the passivity of citizens, insufficient social capital and low levels of participation. The phenomenon is by no means confined to the new member states of the European Union or to Europe. In an article about civic participation in the United States, Allan Luks, the Executive Director of Big Brothers Big Sisters of New York City, claims that the creation today of an initiative such as the Big Brother mentoring network that was developed in 1904 would attract few if any participants at all: "surveys over the last decade regularly show Americans saying that the decline in civic life is a serious national problem ... If a country's social capital – the collective strength of the relationships and interactions between citizens – is allowed to weaken, people will retreat into their own groups, and that nation will become more polarized and less able to enact new social changes."[1]

Political scientists and practitioners in Central and Eastern Europe share the same anxiety.[2] This is reinforced by the acute awareness that a low level of participation and trust have different consequences in old and in new democracies. Furthermore, it appears to be a shared understanding that the flaws and disappointments of these democracies are closely related to the existence of an immature or handicapped political culture both in terms of shared values and democratic practices (in the two forms of democracy, representative and participatory). It comes as no surprise then, that the motives of organisations seeking support to redress social ills very often mention the deficit of participation – almost 50 percent of the requests the CEE Trust receives are related in one way or another to different aspects of participation, inclusion, activism, and mobilisation.

It seemed, therefore, imperative to revisit the issue of participation from the perspective of a philanthropic organisation. In this paper I would like to offer some observations stemming from the experience of the Trust for Civil Society in Central and Eastern Europe in supporting active citizens and then suggest some lines of thinking and planning for philanthropy that have, I hope, broader relevance. The definition of participation adopted in this paper is the broader one: "Citizen participation is the active involvement of individuals in changing problematic conditions in communities and influencing policies and programs that affect the quality of their lives".[3]

---

1 Luks, Allan (May 2004) "Building Civic Participation: Regaining a Social Voice", *World and I*, Vol. 19, 5, p. 280 ff. News World Communications, Inc. Farmington Hills, Michigan: The Gale Group

2 See for instance, most recently, a collection of opinion pieces by Codru Vrabie, Mila Mineva , Andrzej Waśkiewicz Chris Worman, and others, published on the CEE Trust website. [online], available from the World Wide Web: http://www.csf.ceetrust.org/rnd/

3 Encyclopedia of Social Work, Quoted by Mary L. Ohmer, "Citizen Participation in Neighborhood Organizations and Its Relationship to Volunteers' Self-and Collective Efficacy and Sense of Community", *Social Work Research*, Volume 31, Number 2, June 2007, pp. 109-120. Washington DC: National Association of Social Workers (NASW)

## The needs as seen by civil society actors

From 2006 to 2008 the CEE Trust received 2,435 requests for support in response to our calls for proposals, 350 of which were approved. It came as no surprise that the project proposals which could be linked to our first two priorities (more accountability of the state to the citizens, more participation) were by far the most numerous (with all the reservations concerning the arbitrariness of the attributing of "live" projects to fixed categories).

The perceived needs and proposed instruments to address them, listed in the applications for support, represent an incredible wealth of information. In their entirety they could be compared to a big qualitative survey, which is of course non-representative, but its diversity of perspectives is in fact comparable to the real richness of social life. Applications came from big and small entities; national (even international) organisations and small grass-roots groups, (sometimes not even registered); non-governmental organisations (NGOs) with twenty years of experience and groups established yesteryear by high school students; think tanks and environmental coalitions; social service providers and academic researchers; universities and media; individual citizens. This information is invaluable for anyone interested in addressing societal needs and for this reason I have made an effort to filter and analyse the information concerning citizens' participation from close to one hundred projects in Bulgaria, the Czech Republic, Hungary, Poland, Romania, Slovakia, and Slovenia, supported by the CEE Trust between 2006 and 2008 and addressing different aspects of participation. The texts of the applications quoted below have been subjected to hard simplification and more or less subjective classification for the sake of arriving at broader observations.

The first substantive part of the CEE Trust application form is called Problem Identification and Context Analysis and calls for arguments as to why a given organisation is applying for support. The reading of these analyses immediately revealed an omnipresent concern about citizens' participation, albeit spelled out in different ways and with emphasis on different elements.

Most organisations phrase the problem they see in general terms using the current discourse of the third sector/public service environment: "effective participation" or "social and economic inclusion of marginalised groups".[4] Some organisations are interested in the wider picture and adopt a broader sociological/political perspective, using phrases such as the "profound changes of authority and social trust", "the disintegration of the

---

4 This and all the following un-attributed quotations are taken from the application forms and are available in the short annotations of all supported projects on the CEE Trust website. [online], available from the World Wide Web: http://www.ceetrust.org

connection between the capital and the regions, between the central elites and the local public, between the civic culture and politics" or "the crisis of trust in public institutions".

For many organisations the community is the key element of a good life, democracy and civil society and is, consequently, the focus of their efforts. Their long term goal is to "strengthen the spirit of belonging", "consolidate local community for common integrative actions" or "stimulate civic engagement in local communities". The community approach is often closely tied to efforts to improve relations between citizens and local authorities and community participation in decision-making, to "stimulate participation of local activists in decision-making".

The language of the proposals reveals to the careful reader the different understandings of participation – direct and for all (referenda, town hall meetings) and indirect or representative (either political or corporatist). Some organisations obviously see participatory culture as a direct result of economic or sustainable development and perceive their task as being to enhance the development of local communities.

An additional approach might be defined as activation or mobilisation to "activate the members of the local community in order to improve the living conditions" to "mobilise local public" or to "structure, provoke and support active civic behaviour". A few organisations in different countries have adopted a strategy to achieve community unity and participation by identifying, developing and supporting "small emerging grass-roots initiatives" or "informal civil associations and enterprising groups in the remote districts and settlements".

A significant number of projects place special emphasis on young people, who are seen as the drivers of change or as the source of a future good society that will take some time to come. The most frequent problems relating to youth are perceived either as "apathy and non-participation" among the young in general or the lack of outlets for the voice of young people. Frequently heard demands call, for example, to "involve young people in local government" or "in public debates" or to "raise young people's participation in civil society". In reality, projects aimed at introducing or reforming civic education and targeting young people are so numerous that they could be regarded as a separate group. It is quite possible that the big and well-publicised programmes of the EU such as the YOUTH Programme have not only raised the visibility of the issue, but created a buzz of excitement and somewhat opportunistic behaviour. Numerous conferences, seminars, publications and conversations with different individuals point to the overwhelming evidence that educating the new generation of citizens is becoming a task of paramount importance for many analysts and practitioners in the public sphere.

The experience of the twenty years of post-communist transition has demonstrated that the acquisition of civic culture and social capital should start early in life; that they take a long time to develop, if indeed they ever do. Even adults, especially in remote, smaller, more homogeneous communities, have little incentive and face serious psychological and cultural difficulties to change their attitudes and public behaviour. Quite often they are exposed to limited positive stimuli and at the same time consume all the negative trappings of liberalisation, mostly through television. These groups have enormous weight not only in social terms but also at the polling stations and in surveys about readiness for engagement. Not surprisingly, in many places the actively engaged minorities (often associated in diverse CSOs) see the most salient problem as the lack of adequate socialisation mechanisms. As we read in one project, the people behind it are striving to make citizens "tolerant, open minded, creative, acquainted with the rules of democracy; with high moral and social sensitivity; able to organise themselves".

Association City Culture – Gdańsk, Poland. Partnership for Wrzeszcz Project

## The proposed solutions

The proposed remedies to the deficit of participation, perceived, as we saw at the beginning of this chapter as a major threat to democracy and good society, are quite diverse. It is, however, possible to identify certain trends.

Creating opportunities to participate is by far the most popular solution, proposed by many organisations and this approach is based on sound and justified assumptions. Opening up the social channels or society in general, as advocated for more than twenty years by George Soros, the biggest philanthropist in Central and Eastern Europe, is the basic prerequisite for a participatory democracy.

The legislative reforms and the constant improvements of normative documents in post-communist countries have provided the necessary framework for participation. This, however, remains an empty shell as long as citizens do not obtain or wrestle for opportunities to avail themselves of their right to participate. It is fair to say that governments and supranational bodies, such as the EU Commission, have established programmes to encourage the growth of different participatory mechanisms and yet today it is still a recognised fact that the intermediaries – mostly non-profit organisations – are best positioned to conceive and create opportunities for citizens' participation in the context of everyday life, with all its constraints and unexpected challenges. It is by no chance that several surveyed projects are directly aimed at preparing and strengthening these organisations to be real representatives instead of citizens by proxy, encouraging them to "develop the capacity of the foundation that concentrates on community development and public participation through funding, training and experience sharing". One great advantage of the CSOs in comparison to the governmental mechanisms is their potential to generate new ideas. The challenge for foundations might be seen as how to allow for experimentation, while staying on mission, and how to accept that failure

Project group work — Nowy Sącz, Poland. Public Achievement goes to Visegrad Countries Project

or less than spectacular success is a normal part of the process of growth and knowledge accumulation.

On the practical side, the CEE Trust has supported several ideas on how to "establish common space" and "develop mechanisms for effective interaction". These include public debates, "interactive Internet media for civil action", and the "inclusion of young people in public debates by direct participation in the media". The most interesting ideas are the ones proposing specific activities, organised and facilitated by the CSOs themselves and involving participation.

Some of these activities are issue-oriented. For example, the establishment of "networks of local watchdogs who monitor local administration" or the "mechanism of on-going citizens' control around environmental rights" have figured in proposals alongside the idea of groups of diverse stakeholders working together "to find alternative models to work with children at risk, using the model of World Café". Other proposals suggest the "participation of communities in violence-prevention education at school" or "to deal with the rising popularity of nationalistic discourse", to stir reflection on the communist past. Quite often organisations place not issues but inclusive physical spaces and entities at the centre of their mobilisation drive - volunteer centres, youth clubs, "citizens' initiative groups", local youth councils. The creation of an independent social space that connects young activists and the local community was proposed by a Hungarian non-profit organisation engaged in improving quality of life and empowering local people in the largest continuous metropolitan poverty-stricken area in Budapest. They used available derelict and cheap space in the neighbourhood and the work of twenty volunteers to create a hub and turn it into a meeting place and educational centre. The staff and the volunteers created their own games and installations, organised community discussions and a young people's festival in the summer of 2009.

A popular approach to encourage participation is the establishment of different communication and consultation mechanisms linking different social actors (citizens, administration, businesses, media, etc.) in order to "establish links with government and to ensure that voices ... are heard and questions are answered". In the member states of the European Union these initiatives are met halfway by strong encouragement and financial support by the European Commission to establish consultative mechanisms at all levels of governance. The biggest issue is of course representation. Both the advantages and disadvantages of corporatism and the relationships between organisations and constituencies are subject to scrutiny and an ongoing debate that transcends the scope of this paper.[5] Suffice it to say

---

5  See for instance Oldersma, Jantine (1997) 'The corporatist channel and civil society in the Netherlands', in *Private Groups and Public Life: Social Participation, Voluntary Associations and Political Involvement in Representative Democracies*. Jan W.Van Deth, ed. New York: Routledge, (p. 144-162)

that in young democracies the jury is still out on the effectiveness of these formal mechanisms, but it seems important to instil the understanding that citizens have the right to be present and to have a voice.

The leading motive in proposing and fighting for such opportunities is to give voice to the citizens and generate dialogue or discussion. Many practitioners are fully aware that dialogue in public does not come naturally and they work to overcome this difficulty. The favoured approach is, of course, training or the development of skills (often subsumed under the much abused term, "capacity building"). These include strengthening citizens' communication and conflict resolution skills, developing the ability to monitor institutions and budgets, enhancing proficiency in project drafting, raising awareness and knowledge about specific issues, rights and documents, etc. It is no secret however, that many projects with perfect planning, curricula and teachers are quite disappointing in instigating change in the actual public behaviour of citizens, not least because they have an inherent contradiction: they are based on classical knowledge-transfer relationships (teacher-pupil, but minus the motivation of a professional trainee or an A-grade student), whilst aiming to achieve in fact the very opposite of this relationship - empowerment. Higher chances of success seem to be found in projects embracing smart interactive training (mock elections, "walk in my shoes" days, simulations, etc.) and/or responding to the real readiness to engage, which is often impeded solely by a lack of confidence, knowledge and/or skills.

Some organisations propose a more systematic (sometimes academic) approach, which starts with the "mapping of citizens' needs". These diverge in their ideas on how the exercise should be performed – by experts (sociologists, accountants, economists, social workers) or by the public - "providing and diffusing a set of practical tools to be used by local communities and citizen groups to self-diagnose their needs and potential in terms of agenda-setting and provoking change in a given locality by mapping". The latter of course is the preferable option as it includes actual participation. An issue that deserves special reflection is the fact that while citizens often identify their most pressing needs as the different aspects of living environments, social services and the performance of governmental and judicial offices that directly affect their lives, the experts see bigger chunks of the puzzle and point at structural problems. It is no surprise that this divergence creates communication gaps that are not easy to fill and has greatly contributed to the dissatisfaction and low trust of citizens in non-profit organisations, perceived sometimes as living in a world of their own.

A next step in the transformation logic that a number of organisations propose is to "prepare innovative mechanisms to mobilise" or to "research, develop and use new strategies and methods; test their applicability and sustainability". Some prefer to start with a blueprint for public participation and to "define strategy for the future". To this systemic approach belong many projects and activities related to formal civic education that aim to "integrate core concepts and practices into the students' curricula and professors' schedules as internships and traineeships" or "develop capacity of educators through steering committees, trainings and campaigns". Part of the efforts to educate the public at large can be found in the numerous campaigns intended to "promote the public participation concept" and inform citizens of their rights.

A very different form of intervention is embraced by a small number of strong organisations who see "providing seed project funding and training to grassroots community initiatives" to "stimulate and support the initiative of the small NGOs and local initiative groups through organising campaigns" as a means of achieving their objectives or who suggest organising competitions for "small grants to realise ideas for improving their areas of life".

Association City Culture – Gdańsk, Poland. Partnership for Wrzeszcz Project

Yet another successful method of encouraging participation, dialogue and the acquisition of skills, is the use of arts and culture to provide a space to bring people together and frame messages in a compelling way. Initiatives such as organising a "human rights film festival as an impetus for activating young people" or "consolidating the creative potential of filmmakers, journalists and media professionals, connecting them with institutions endorsing social rights and civil society" have been suggested, as has the use of local museums as "centres for public debates and incentives". The use of traditional cultural clubs as community centres and the "involvement of young volunteers in preserving and valuing the immovable and movable cultural heritage" by using theatre for education and the collection of oral history have proved consistently successful and popular. The experience of one Bulgarian organisation working to curb domestic violence illustrated the possibilities of this type of experimentation. Based in a mid-size town with a high degree of preservation of traditional morals and concepts about privacy, where even talking about domestic violence is socially inacceptable, the activists decided to stage and run the theatrical representation of fictional domestic conflicts. They asked the audience to take roles in ending the fictional story, using this opportunity to deliver their message. The project was so successful that the organisation was invited to perform in four more towns and cities.

None of the activities summarised above can claim to be particularly innovative or even extraordinarily effective, nor does this paper have the purpose of assessing the effectiveness of different participation techniques and approaches. The short-term results seen from these projects should be regarded as unstable until the opposite is proven at a later date. Both the survival of a mechanism (platform, council, procedure) and the establishment of the habit of using them should be checked at least one year after the termination of a given project if a donor organisation is interested in the "outcomes" of its activities. Assessing the long-term social effects of a project to change the way people feel and act is an exercise in futility; theoretically indefensible and practically undoable. The existing quantitative measurements are a useful tool to "take the temperature" of a society or community but are by no means an instrument to judge the success of short-term programmes. Based on my subjective assessment formed as a result of my close acquaintance with many projects, I would say that good, sound initiatives do deliver when an organisation (or group) is familiar and mindful of the context (I am tempted to use the word "embedded") and uses its social capital. When it is prepared to be consistent and persistent and when it seizes the opportunities as they appear (even if not listed in the project application). Needless to say, the second and equally important element is people. It takes motivation, integrity and communication skills to bring people in.

This overview of the field as presented by the operational organisations clearly reveals that while the problem with participation (very much like another broad category – corruption) is all too familiar, the vision of what constitutes a good society (inclusive and participatory among other things), is not uniform and reflects both articulated and non-articulated attitudes, political ideas and contexts. Not surprisingly, the proposed approaches to improve participation are quite diverse, not only in their specific activities but in their underlying assumptions. It seems to me beyond any doubt that encouraging and maintaining this diversity is a good strategy for philanthropic organisations interested in participation, because they are the only conceivable form of authentic representation and also because the outcomes of civic and philanthropic efforts become visible at the meta level, in the complementarity of the different initiatives.

Most organisations with experience in community development, environmental protection, sustainable development, social work, promotion of democracy, social solidarity building and others, who have different, often diverging and occasionally conflicting agendas, are acting on the intuitive or rationally constructed premise that associative life is based on social ties and that social ties grow, among others, out of common activity and/or common values. Therefore they concentrate their efforts on creating opportunities to strengthen social ties by organising different activities. Where participation is concerned, philanthropy places its trust in the diverse actors whose work will gradually change societal dispositions.

## A few observations

The comments offered in the previous paragraphs can be summarised in a few observations that might be useful for foundations in the process of planning and developing strategies for their engagement in the improvement of societies. First of all, it seems to be advisable not to adhere to a single paradigm or explanation of the "logic" of social life and to offer space for civil society actors to experiment and investigate for themselves. Individually they might be wrong; as a group they will know best, provided that their ideas are not pre-selected through one single filter.

Another observation that I would like to share is what I perceive as an inherent though unarticulated belief in the automatism of results - the expectation that good ideas and practices are like water flowing from places of plenty to places of need. Numerous organisations have discovered the hard way that efforts need to be placed in maintaining, propagating, advertising and promoting good ideas and/or practices, and philanthropic supporters should consider some (more) space for similar post - or para - project activities.

And closer to the topic of this paper, the root problem of participation is motivation. All approaches, even the most astute and creative techniques, will remain only superficially participatory unless they stimulate the motivation of individuals. Participation is at its root a matter of individual choice. Then comes culture (the social voice which incites or stifles participation), and finally, opportunity. So far, Central and Eastern

Europeans have witnessed the might of negative motivation, transforming this into positive motivation appears to be one of the biggest challenges of the future. From a practical point of view, however, convincingly demonstrating the benefits of joining in participation seems to me one of the best potential inroads. Another recommendation would be the consistent effort to bring together different people – exposure to diversity is a major factor in stimulating change in thinking. The two other well known motivators, role models and real success, can be added to this list as small as these may be.

Instead of a conclusion, and as an argument of the need to not fall prey to hegemonic paradigms, I would like to use a quotation from Ralf Dahrendorf, which returns this discussion on participation in its broader social context, "The loss of social binding forces has been a topic of social sciences and politics as well for 150 years … Certainly that is a particularly weighty matter today … but I am concerned with the other matter, freedom, the full unfolding of freedom. It is a question of not being taken in by false ties, replacement religions, virtual ties, for that is the risk when too strong a focus is placed on this motive for ties".[6]

---

6  This Century's Review [online] [Accessed 19 October 2009]. Available from the World Wide Web: http://www.thiscenturyreview.com/ralfdahrendorf.html

TAMZIN RACTLIFFE

# 17 South Africa
## SOUTH AFRICAN SOCIAL INVESTMENT – A GIVING MODEL BEYOND "PHILANTHROPY"

> "We must appreciate that all over the world, right down the centuries, there have been great religions that have encouraged the idea of giving – of fighting poverty and of promoting the equality of human beings – whatever their background, whatever their political beliefs. That spirit has lived not only in the world but in South Africa as well."
>
> Nelson Mandela[1]

"Philanthropy" is not a word that has much positive resonance for many South Africans. It speaks of affluence beyond the average person's reality and is largely viewed as the terrain of the exceptionally wealthy. For the very poor, it carries unwelcome images of the beneficent few (who in South Africa are – or have typically been – white) who have much, and who bestow "alms" on the poor, who are typically black. That the majority of South Africans don't relate to the term philanthropy may be best evidenced by the fact that there is no direct translation for the word in many of the official South African languages.

The term "charity" has similar connotations with respect to the distribution of "gifts" from those who have to those who do not. It may be that the religious imperative that it is important to be charitable in one's life

---

1 Kuljian, C (2001) "South Africa: Tapping Local Resources to Address Local Needs", In *In Focus*, Prepared for Charles Stewart Mott Foundation, October 2001

in general, irrespective of one's personal circumstance, which makes this term somewhat more acceptable. Notwithstanding, neither term seems to sit comfortably in South Africa.

Perhaps it is against the implied passivity on the part of the receiving poor that South Africans rebel. Or perhaps it is a rejection of the generosity of the rich elite, whose very riches are perceived to have been achieved on the backs of the poor. The reality is likely to be more complicated than either explanation. In a post-apartheid South Africa, where the focus is on redistribution and redress, the idea of a rich elite bestowing their generosity upon the poor, who are poor as a result of an unjust system, raises the spectre of a past inequality that has retained the right to dictate where there is access to, and distribution of, resources. Indeed, some believe that those who can afford to be philanthropists are unlikely to have suffered as victims of apartheid, at least in terms of accessing resources or amassing wealth. Thus, implicit in the image of a philanthropist is the person who may well have "overlook[ed] the circumstances of economic injustice that make philanthropy necessary".[2] "Aid" is another such term with similar connotations.

## The language of philanthropy in South Africa

When talking about philanthropy in South Africa, it is often assumed that one is referring to "corporate social investment" (CSI). This term has wide application and is often equated with philanthropy because, in essence, it refers to grant-making practices that are designed to address socio-economic development and transformation needs in the country. The term CSI gained currency after the first democratic elections in 1994 when it became a "must-do" (indeed, in some cases mandatory) practice within the South African business sector. This served a number of purposes: to demonstrate visible support for the new democratic government; to safeguard and build reputation as a good corporate citizen; and to maintain an informal "licence to do business", while also contributing to the critical needs for redress and socio-economic transformation of South African society and social structures. This is not to say that there was no "corporate philanthropy" – or charitable giving – during apartheid. However, giving practices under apartheid were largely restricted to charities, as opposed to organisations addressing social justice or socio-economic transformation.

Indeed, legislation at the time[3] prohibited any real form of social justice philanthropy. Under apartheid, the South African non-profit sector worked

---

2  Collins et al. (2001) *Robin Hood was Right; A Guide to Giving Your Money for Social Change*. (p.31). As quoted in Setkova. (2004): (p.10)

3  See opposite page

around these restrictions to provide a social welfare safety net to the disenfranchised and, at the same time, became a significant force for social justice and change in the country, often serving to channel Scandinavian and American foundation funding.[4]

Beyond the social investment practices of the corporate sector, there is also in South Africa, as in Africa more broadly, a deeply rooted tradition of giving and mutual helping. It is perhaps these terms that are best able to describe the philanthropic activities of the large majority of the populace. Indeed, "giving" resonates much more strongly within South African society on a broad level, covering everyday acts of kindness as well as planned giving by ordinary people within and between communities. That these terms are more accurate ways of understanding philanthropy in South Africa is well evidenced in the monograph *The Poor Philanthropist*[5] where it was the notion of "helping" that was best understood within communities to explain their philanthropic activities. This study makes significant distinction between "philanthropy of community", being "relations of 'help' among and between" communities and "philanthropy for community", being "the conventional philanthropic orthodoxy of 'vertical resource transfers from rich to poor". The difference between philanthropic "giving and helping" behaviour of the masses, on the one hand, and social investment practices, on the other, largely fits into these two categories in South Africa.

## GreaterGood South Africa: Integrating "philanthropy of" and "philanthropy for" communities

*"By acknowledging that South Africans contribute to their communities in many different ways, and on many different levels, we value ordinary people and empower them to connect with fellow citizens and make a difference where it counts."*

Bheki Sibiya, Chair, GreaterGood SA Trust (Annual Report 2007-08)

---

3 The Fundraising Act of 1978 made it "a crime to solicit or receive donations from the public unless this had been authorised by the Director of Fundraising. Any donation from outside South Africa was deemed as having been donated by the public within South Africa." As sourced in Budlander, G. (1993) *The Role of Voluntary Organisations in Emerging Democracies: Experiences in Eastern and Central Europe and in South Africa*, Copenhagen: Danish Centre for Human Rights

4 Habib A & Taylor R (2005) 'Anti Apartheid NGO's in transition', In: Anhieier H & Kendall J; *Third Sector policy at the crossroads: An international non-profit analysis*, Routledge

5 Wilkinson-Maposa S, Fowler A, Oliver-Evans C & and Mulenga C F N (2005) *The Poor Philanthropist: How and Why The Poor Help Each Other*, Cape Town: Compress. [online], available from the World Wide Web: http://www.efc.be/ftp/public/CPI/Publications/Poor_philanthropist.pdf

In the early days following the first democratic elections in 1994, there was great fervour around the potential for, and commitment to, transformation. Both corporate South Africa and the general public were excited about the potential to build a new democratic, equitable society, and committed to finding the ways to engage in social and economic transformation. At the same time, however, there was a significant lack of available information, tools or infrastructure to facilitate engagement or foster widespread connections for effective giving.

The founding activities of GreaterGood South Africa began in early 1997 though the organisation as it appears today was only launched in 2004. A non-profit organisation, GreaterGood established itself in order to address the need for information to strengthen civil society in South Africa, to grow connections between communities and people and to facilitate and encourage giving activities of all kinds. From the outset, GreaterGood was focussed on building a "philanthropy of community", whilst at the same time creating the infrastructure, database and information that would ultimately also respond to the needs of the corporate sector wanting to engage more meaningfully with the imperatives of social investment. GreaterGood adopted a dual focus by building the networks and connections within and between communities concurrently with the infrastructure conducive to the provision of effective social investment advisory services.

Ahead of its time, GreaterGood used technology from the outset to build the framework within which research, social networking and giving ("social investment" activity) could begin. The initial GreaterGood platform provided access to information in an online form, although outreach activities facilitated growing networks and connections offline as well. This helped develop the kind of infrastructure foundation necessary to bring coherence to "giving" activities. Essentially, GreaterGood acted as an intermediary or honest broker, serving to bring people together, to create connections between "good causes" and willing givers, and to overcome the dislocation between the privileged and the disempowered communities all over South Africa by encouraging new ways of thinking about social change and development. GreaterGood's real innovation was to provide a range of ways for people to connect with their community: giving time, surplus or previously loved goods; skills or knowledge; reward points; and, yes, even money.

At its heart, GreaterGood promotes the message that "everyone has something to give". This helps to change mindsets and reinforce the idea that giving is not just about money and that "investing" in social development can deliver real "returns".

## Beyond philanthropy: Social investment in transformation

The idea of acting as a "giving, or social investment intermediary", coupled with the need for advisory support for corporate South Africa, led to the creation the South African Social Investment Exchange (www. SASIX.co.za) in early 2006. In the absence of any real understanding or information on which to base their decisions, CSI managers were looking for better advisory services to assist them. SASIX filled the gap in the market for this advice, through pre-screening and rigorously analysing opportunities for social investment in specific community-based social development projects, while also fulfilling a monitoring and evaluation function to report on impact throughout.

Over the past fifteen years, a significant amount of money has been channelled into social development through corporate social investment. A Human Sciences Research Council survey on giving in 2005 reported that corporate social investment commits an estimated 5 billion rand per annum, whilst regular citizens give roughly 12 billion rand each year from their own pockets.[6] However, despite this active programme of redress and transformation, things do not seem to be getting substantially better for the very poor in South Africa. Major challenges, such as access to quality healthcare, education and food security, show few signs of being adequately addressed.

In the face of this observation – true not only for South Africa but for Africa as a whole – it is increasingly accepted that philanthropy alone, while noble and very much needed, is not enough to lift people out of poverty and address South Africa's historic imbalances. We need to find new ways of empowering poor communities to uplift themselves. The growing consensus that Africa needs "more trade than aid" is also driving a new investment agenda, one focused not only on creating new wealth, but on creating wealth in ways that maximise social transformation and economic empowerment of all members of society while minimizing environmental impacts. This means giving people access to capital and providing the tools for them to manage it effectively. This resonates strongly within the South African government's legislative framework for corporate sector contributions to socio-economic development. The Broad Based Black Economic Empowerment (BBBEE) scorecard, spearheaded by the Department of Trade and Industry, sets out minimum standards of achievement for corporations across seven essential elements of transformation, including skills development, preferential procurement and enterprise development. The growing understanding that philanthropy

---

6 Human Sciences Research Council (2005) *State of Social Giving* series, commissioned by the Centre for Civil Society, National Development Agency and South African Grantmakers' Association, South Africa

alone is not sufficiently able to enable transformative social change is driving the agenda for socially responsible investment across South Africa, the continent and, indeed, the globe.

Despite a huge socio-economic backlog and good potential for real and multiple returns on investment, South Africa significantly lags behind international trends in the use of commercially viable socially responsible investments for pension fund portfolios. In the United States (US) and in most member countries of the Organisation for Economic Development, 10-15 percent of retirement assets were invested in socially responsible investment strategies.[7] This figure is around the low double digits in the United Kingdom (UK) and Australia, and slightly lower in Continental Europe. By contrast, the South African financial services sector manages a national endowment of approximately 1 trillion rand in life and pension fund savings, with only a very small proportion of this – less than 1 percent – being directed towards investing in a socially responsible manner,[8] despite compelling international evidence of the strong nexus between investment performance and performance on environmental, social and governance issues.

How can one explain the low take-up of financially rewarding socially responsible investing in South Africa when there is such a high emphasis placed on social investment as a means of corporate philanthropy? South Africa has an exceptionally well-developed financial sector and a crying need for social spending. Throughout the country, there is a wealth of social entrepreneurs who have created social enterprises in a wide variety of sectors including healthcare, education for all, affordable housing, alternative energies, clean technology and microfinance. Yet with the partial exception of microfinance institutions, South African social enterprises have found it difficult to access growth capital. Most for-profit social enterprises have borne the extra burden of not being able to benefit from traditional grant funding, since they are usually categorised with "pure profit" driven entities that operate without any metrics – positive or negative – related to social or environmental implications.

A key absence in South Africa has been the lack of a transaction platform to provide committed, socially minded investors with an efficient and effective mechanism by which to identify and direct their capital into impact investments which provide for risk management. The kind of intermediary mechanisms necessary to facilitate a meeting of demand and supply of such funds are weak in South Africa and establishing such a framework may mobilise just a small portion of the available pool for

---

7    Jackson, H (2009) 'ESG Processes: Come to the Party' In: *Today's Trustee*, September-November 2009 [online], available from the World Wide Web: http://www.totrust.co.za/010909_esg.htm

8    Jackson, H, Ibid

social impact investment, but this could have a major impact on addressing the country's development challenges.

In response to this progression in the social investment field, the South African Social Investment Exchange (SASIX) developed beyond grant-making for corporate social investment. In 2007, it entered into a joint venture with Cadiz Asset Management to provide social investors with opportunities for investment in social transformation initiatives that would provide a real financial profit over and above their social impact. Today SASIX Financial has established itself as an intermediary that can effectively broker social and responsible investments and provide accessible, well researched, analytical data on social development activities, initiatives and investment opportunities. This can assist companies and individuals to make decisions around responsible investment and determine the basis upon which they can allocate their social investment and socially responsible funds, whether these are grant funds, pension funds or programme related investments. In the past twelve months, SASIX Financial has brokered commitments of around 250 million rand in social impact financial investments.

## Building a bridge between developed and developing worlds

The phrase "social investment", when referring to corporate philanthropy, has been mostly regarded as a misnomer and increasingly seems to cause confusion with the growing field of socially responsible investment. Nonetheless, it has had the benefit of implying – even if only in principle – due consideration and thoughtfulness to the allocation and managing of philanthropic funds as investments. Whilst this was slow to realise any immediate advantage after 1994, it established a foundation for transformative social investment which is now beginning to reap rewards.

South Africa has, by necessity, encouraged a different way of thinking around philanthropy – as social investment – in order to bridge the chasm between the developed and developing worlds within one country. This dichotomy within the newly democratic South Africa, with the legacies and injustices of apartheid and the commitment to change and real socio-economic upliftment, has demanded not only philanthropic investment from the public and corporate sectors, but also that communities themselves step up to the plate and demonstrate the return and benefit they are generating with the investment being made in them. By assuming "investment" and not "giving"; by assuming there are "social profit", rather than non-profit, organisations, there is a relationship of action and responsibility on both sides of the giving/receiving line. This approach to development or socially transformative philanthropy could also encourage similar transformation and increased levels of responsible, socially transformative for-profit investments.

Viewing philanthropy as social investment provides an alternative framework which, coupled with the recent global economic crisis, has played an important role in maturing philanthropy and responsible social investment practices. The model of SASIX and the infrastructure it has encouraged within the field of social capital intermediation has been a significant catalyst not only in South Africa but increasingly across the globe. SASIX has been an active protagonist at the forefront of building the momentum for a global model of social investment extending along the full continuum from philanthropy through to market rate social investment.

In this regard, SASIX assumes social investment to be any kind of investment that delivers at minimum a social return – achieved by investing money for no financial return, as in a grant – or by investing money for a range of potential financial returns in addition to the social return. This is not to say that philanthropy is dead. Philanthropy has, and likely always will have, a place in society. There are many charitable organisations – as opposed to development organisations – whose work is critical for our society. However, what is also evident is that we need a new model of "development philanthropy" that will more actively address the inequitable distribution of resources, integrate philanthropy both of and for communities, and empower communities to achieve their own sustainable prosperity.

## From a social investment platform to a social stock exchange

The global shift in the practice of philanthropy and calls for reform in philanthropic infrastructure have demonstrated a desire for new social capital systems, better measures of impact and performance, more cost effective and comprehensive analysis and research information and more efficient social investment. It is this shift, combined with an understanding of the need for investment as opposed to pure philanthropy, which has led to the South African Social Investment Exchange capturing the imagination of organisations, investors and intermediaries around the world.

SASIX is by no means the only innovative online transaction platform – there are a growing number of these. Indeed, the first decade of the twenty-first century has seen a great deal of innovation in building financial markets that value and emphasise social, environmental and financial returns. This innovation is marked by great variety, but can be collectively described as elements of emergent social capital markets. All of these social capital markets suffer from much higher transaction costs than financial markets, significant information bottlenecks and a lack of intermediaries that meet a known, agreed-upon standard. In response, organisations are emerging to address various elements of these market-specific challenges.

Within the universe of these emerging organisations, are online giving marketplaces or "philanthropic giving" portals that facilitate knowledge sharing and transactions between two groups: grant-makers, philanthropists and other social investors, and the social benefit non-profit organisations or micro-social enterprises working on the ground. At a minimum, such platforms exist or are under development in Brazil, Canada, Colombia, Denmark, Norway, Switzerland, Germany, India, Israel, Italy, Kenya, Thailand, the Philippines, South Africa, the US, the UK and through the United Nations Development Programme. SASIX itself has already facilitated the development of the United Nations' South-South Exchange and is currently assisting a number of other countries with the establishment of their online transaction platforms for social investment.

There remains, however, significant variation within these efforts ranging across services provided, capital sources sought and type of businesses/enterprises supported. Together they cover the full spectrum; from non-profit organisations accessing grant or donation capital, to for-profit social enterprises and other social purpose businesses accessing debt or private equity finance for a blended financial, social and environmental return.

What these efforts share is a commitment to the language and practice of the financial capital markets applied to the social sector, coupled with a focus on transformative social and environmental development to address poverty. It is this dual focus that is taking these platforms into new territory and encouraging a natural progression, as is increasingly anticipated, to a social stock exchange.

There is a growing movement in many parts of the world to develop true social stock exchanges – publicly regulated financial markets that would enable for-profit social mission businesses to trade in listed equities. In the social stock exchange model, it is proposed that those companies that are aimed at addressing social or environmental missions into their bottom lines meet investors interested in enterprises that satisfy business standards whilst actively addressing global social problems. This is different from traditional socially responsible investment in that it does not consider companies that involve socially responsible business practices to effectively "do no harm". Rather, it looks at those social purpose businesses that actively seek to do good by promoting social change and social impact. The intention in creating a separate social stock exchange is to attract investors who believe in social mission as much as profit potential.

The approach of developing a social stock exchange is not without its critics.[9] Some believe that such an exchange may import the values and conflicts of the for-profit sector, most especially if social purpose businesses are put in a head-to-head competition for funding. Indeed, most social entrepreneurs tend to stay away from capital markets because they fear mission drift or the erosion of their social values. Others believe that this is precisely why there is a need for an alternative social stock exchange that is tailored to social businesses and like-minded investors. For instance, in a survey of social-purpose businesses in the UK, the London Social Stock Exchange initiative found that roughly half were planning to raise capital in the next twelve to eighteen months, some of them to the tune of 7 million dollars or more. Almost 20 percent said that if a social stock exchange existed, they would want to list their companies on it. Interestingly, the survey also found that investors really liked the idea of a dedicated social stock exchange, with more than ten percent of pension funds and socially responsible investors applauding the idea and a further fifteen percent saying they would move between one and three percent of their assets, many within a year.[10]

A core question that remains unanswered is whether a social stock exchange should be part of an existing stock exchange or whether it should be entirely separate. There are those that contend that existing stock exchanges are the most cost-effective mechanism through which to highlight these businesses, and that creating a separate listing will isolate them and take them out of the mainstream. Others believe that the traditional exchanges, with their focus on financial returns as the only metric, will sideline and marginalise social purpose businesses. Proponents of this position also question why traditional businesses can have their own exchange but social businesses cannot.

Whether independent or part of an existing framework, what a social stock exchange offers is the potential to act as a market maker between socially conscious impact investors and social/environmental businesses, to provide capital-raising tools for social enterprises and to act as a market entry/exit mechanism for investors. It would meet the needs of impact investors looking for a transparent, regulated and accountable mechanism by which they can:

- reduce search costs by providing a single point of entry for investment into social enterprises across Africa (listed and unlisted)
- access traded instruments that offer liquidity

9  Clearly So, Social Business Blog, *Why a social stock exchange is a bad idea* [online], available from the World Wide Web: http://www.clearlyso.com/sbblog/?p=14

10  Pradeep Jethi (as quoted by Janet Paskin) (2009) 'Markets with a social mission', In *Ode Magazine*, May 2009 [online], available from the World Wide Web: http://www.odemagazine.com/doc/print/63/markets-with-social-mission

- receive transparent and rigorous reporting on the financial and social return generated by each entity listed on the exchange, according to globally accepted standards and metrics.

Ultimately, the innovation offers so-called "hybrid investments"; products with financial returns in exchange for high measurable ecological and/or social impact. Investors win because they receive transparent, liquid, social investment opportunities in publicly regulated social purpose businesses with a high level of comparability between the non-financial impact of their investments. Social purpose businesses benefit as they can substantially lower their cost of capital by using an effective intermediary and market trading infrastructure.

## Slowly, slowly: A privately regulated alternative trading system as an interim step?

The challenges of developing a fully publicly regulated social stock exchange may take longer to overcome than anticipated or desired. In the immediate term, however, another mechanism could serve both to defragment the multitude of individual and uncoordinated efforts for social investment and to raise the standards for trust, credibility and comparability across these efforts.

A preliminary requirement for a successful social stock exchange is the existence of an electronic trading platform that can provide a single entry point to pre-vetted and certified opportunities, presented by certified "affiliate" listing sponsors from across the globe and a significant capital-raising marketing force to ensure the meeting of investors and investments. This can be achieved through the creation of a regulated alternative trading system. GreaterGood South Africa is working to achieve this by creating the NeXus for Impact Investing (NeXii).[11]

NeXii is a social enterprise that addresses problems facing impact investors and social enterprises seeking investment capital, while also effecting positive social and environmental impacts. Investors looking for a more positive impact on society will access an expanding local and global list of new and secondary private offerings on NeXii's secure transaction and communication platform. This will allow impact investors to identify and invest in targeted companies, funds, projects, non-profits and environmental credits strategically based on their portfolio management needs and objectives.

The unification of these fragmented markets for investment and donation opportunities will draw a widening range of investors and increase financing

---

11 *NeXii* [Online], available from the World Wide Web: http://www.NeXii.com

opportunities for those seeking social capital. Ultimately the efficiency gains and the increasing focus on the social, environmental and financial opportunities in this underserved capital market will increase capital flows and improve the impact and accountability of social organisations and businesses. The virtuous cycle created by increasing the quality of investments that in turn increases investment capital and the availability of capital drawing in more investment opportunities will eventually place NeXii at the centre of this expanding market.

NeXii will create and support a regulated and transparent impact capital market that brings together investors seeking a combination of financial, social and environmental returns with pre-vetted organisations and enterprises in search of capital from around the globe. NeXii facilitates the appropriate investment – from philanthropic gifts to market rate social investment – to match the organisation or enterprise's needs. Because a wide range of opportunities will be available to investors, investors will be able to tailor their investment portfolio to match their risk profiles and investment objectives, while maintaining a clear focus on the impact of their investments.

A woman harvests grass on a farm outside White River to make grass mats and handbags to sell at the craft store supported by SASIX-listed organisation, Khumbulani Craft, at the gates of the Kruger National Park

As a precursor to a publicly regulated social stock exchange, NeXii can provide an ongoing pipeline for listing on such an exchange while also providing appropriate earlier-stage investment opportunities and capital-raising mechanisms – whether these be on the basis of philanthropic grant to programme-related debt or social venture capital as private equity ahead of a listing. NeXii could create an entirely new social capital market system within which global philanthropy, social investment and responsible impact investment can blend for maximum impact upon the world's most pressing social and environmental problems.

## What about standards?

Whether it is NeXii, SASIX, the London Social Stock Exchange initiative or any other social investment trading platform, the critical need for improved philanthropic and social investment is directly related to the standards applied in listing, determining impact and building auditable measures of change on the ground. There is already a growing professionalization within the emerging industry of impact investing. Experts acknowledge the value of developing common standards for benchmarking, comparable measurement tools and coordination among stakeholders over and above listing standards. Terminology is another key area requiring clarification and standardisation. This is demonstrated in the words of Geoff Burnand, chief executive of the UK-based Investing for Good, who has argued that, within impact investing, "there is a need for consistent language and appropriate mainstream investment products to enable the wealth management community to understand the interrelationship between impact, financial return, and investment risk."[12]

The number of requests to GreaterGood for assistance in replicating SASIX, the need for pulling together multiple approaches to social investment transactions and for developing a regulated trading exchange platform, all raise the question of how these efforts can be integrated under or within a single globally applicable social investment framework that would provide comparability, credibility and trust.

For the past two years, GreaterGood has considered this issue under the rubric of its the Global Federation for Social Investment Exchanges (GSIX)[13] initiative, which proposes developing a global federation of impact investing exchanges that can set standards, build brand awareness and new markets and advocate for clear, consistent regulations that foster global impact investing.

GSIX is intended to be a non-profit, multi-stakeholder association of social investment exchanges and enterprise analysts, brokers, impact investors and financial intermediaries focused on *growing sustainable*

---

12  Burnand, G (2009) *Investing for Social and Environmental Impact*, Monitor
Institute [online], available from the World Wide Web: http://www.monitorinstitute.com/impactinvesting/documents/InvestingforSocialandEnvImpact_FullReport_004.pdf
13  GSIX – the Global Federation for Social Investment Exchanges – is still a working title for this initiative.

*impact investing* globally. GSIX will strive to provide impact investing exchanges and their ancillary service providers with a member-run federation to:
- guide global support for vetted non-governmental organisations and other social enterprises;
- set, monitor and disseminate standards for impact;
- express its voice to policy makers, the media and the public on the power, range and results of the social economy; and
- act as a key deliberating body on regulations and transnational social investment.

Why is this necessary? It is more than evident that the current social capital landscape contains inchoate and fragmented sets of players on both the investor and enterprise sides of the equation. Investors may be foundations, social venture funds, individuals, family offices, public grant-makers, corporations, social investment funds or any mix of these. Enterprises include everything from purely charitable not for profits to social businesses with non-distributed financial returns to businesses seeking both market-rate financial returns and social/environmental impact. Similarly, the types of transactions that investors use to support enterprises run from grants to loans to debt guarantees and equity investments.

This innovation and diversity in the market is a good thing, but it has stretched past the boundaries of our existing ecosystems of support. This is where social investment exchanges come in. Various models have developed over the years, often focused on single points on the landscape, for example, facilitating grants or allowing loans to be made. These specialised systems are necessary and useful, but none of them are in a position to organise on behalf of the movement as a whole or to help newcomers – both enterprises and investors – find their best position. GSIX will provide that voice for the whole – supporting independent elements to thrive while also advocating on behalf of the ecosystem. As such, GSIX will contribute to organising, improving and growing social investment exchanges and the analysts, brokers and financial intermediaries who depend on them.

Supported by NeXii to provide capital raising, investment intermediation and data services, GSIX will contribute directly to improving the social capital marketplace. As a global membership body, GSIX will promote the full range of social investments, from not-for-profit to market rate returns plus social/environmental benefits. This is particularly important at this stage, as the funding needs of emerging enterprises, especially those serving the poor, are still evolving. Enterprises may start with grant funding, advance to managing debt and eventually issue equity stakes. At the same time, the financing sources – individuals, foundations, companies, government agencies, pension funds, banks, and multi-lateral organisations

– often offer more than one kind of financial product. The ecosystem depends on all of these sources, enterprises and financial vehicles and GSIX will serve organisations that work across these spectra.

Like NeXii, GSIX will promote an effective social capital market that focuses on investment in high social/ environmental impact opportunities with varying levels of social and financial return. The members of GSIX are those intermediaries of varying shape and form that all seek out opportunities that will have a measurable, life-changing impact on people and their communities. As GSIX members, these intermediaries will commit to conducting standard and comparable due diligence procedures, listing opportunities according to shared standards and reporting in ways that investors can understand, compare and trust.

## It all started in Africa

In all that it does, from facilitating giving and advising on social and responsible financial investment, GreaterGood South Africa promotes "vertical" and "horizontal" exchanges of support within and between local communities, as well as between these communities and broader social/corporate structures. It provides opportunities for "philanthropy for community" through the South African Social Investment Exchange and GreaterCapital, a social investment advisory consultancy operated by GreaterGood. It also provides opportunities for "philanthropy of community" by building social networks and giving circles and facilitating giving campaigns of all kinds – whether these are giving time to help a child learn to read, redistributing clothing, offering alternative gifts for family and friends or presenting opportunities to give money to an organisation to fund its work. As an intermediary, it is focused on all forms of philanthropy, without stressing only the act of giving. As an organisation it has remained committed to fostering the empowerment of communities through access to knowledge, ideas and decision-making.

The unusual mix within South Africa – of a middle-income country with a significant social and economic transformation agenda – has provided valuable experience in defining and developing systems for the traditionally developed world of investors whilst addressing the pressures and demands of the traditionally developing world of beneficiaries. Industry Charters and the legislative framework governing the corporate sector's input into socio-economic empowerment in South Africa require that corporations bring tangible results to the communities in which they operate. In particular, the Broad Based Black Economic Empowerment (BBBEE) scorecard awards points not just for the transformation of ownership or management but also for a company's investment in building skills, boosting enterprise and developing local communities.

South Africa's unique situation has created an imperative for flexibility and rapid change. Whilst the country still has a long way to go to address critical developmental challenges, this dynamic environment offers particular opportunities for social investment that stretch far beyond conventional philanthropy.

Emílio Rui Vilar &
Rui Hermenegildo Gonçalves

# 18 Lusophone Africa

# Foundations in Portuguese-Speaking African Countries: Preparing the Future

*"My message is simple: rather than a technically skilled generation, we need a generation that is capable of questioning the technique itself; young people who are able to think about the country and the world afresh. Rather than people able to give answers, we need those with the capacity to ask questions"[1]*

## Philanthropy is also a Portuguese word

In 2003, as part of the European Foundation Centre's 14th Annual General Assembly and Conference, which took place in Lisbon, the *Centro Português de Fundações* (Portuguese Foundation Centre) organised the first Meeting of Portuguese-speaking Countries Foundations.

Focussing on the general theme of "The Role of Portuguese-Speaking Foundations: Preparing the Future", the main goal of the meeting was to discuss the role of foundations in Portuguese-speaking countries in three areas, identifying the main problems and challenges that foundations faced in these countries; understanding the activities, priorities, strategies and best practices of these foundations; and, finally, discussing and promoting a more effective cooperation. For the first time ever, representatives of foundations from all the Portuguese-speaking countries met: Angola,

---

1   Mia Couto (2006), *Oração de Sapiência* opening speech at ISCTEM, Maputo, published in E se Obama fosse africano? E outras interinvenções (2009). Editorial Caminho, 2nd edition.

Brazil, Cape Verde, Guinea-Bissau, Mozambique, Portugal, São Tomé and Príncipe and East Timor.

The meeting was geared towards emphasising the importance of the Portuguese language as a factor in unifying and developing the communities of these countries and the role of foundations – as civil society organisations with their particular responsibilities and missions – in doing their utmost to organise activities that promote Portuguese in scientific, cultural and economic areas, thus contributing to the development of their respective populations.

Portuguese is the seventh most-spoken language in the world (250 million people speak it), the third European Union language most-spoken in the world and the eighth language of the Internet. Although Portuguese is the official language in only eight countries, the various global diaspora ensure its presence on all continents, permitting and sustaining a universe of communication and truly global relationships.

Sharing a language that spans various continents and economies in a communicational and networked society means that those who speak it have greater freedom and choice in the future. However, we should also defend the principle that Portuguese is not the sole preserve of any of the countries that adopt it as their official language, but rather, it is a common asset jointly owned, without any restriction whatsoever.

A language, any language, should be seen and function as a factor or an element that consolidates the identity and culture of those who speak it. It should also be seen from other perspectives, such as a means of accessing knowledge or as a human development factor. A shared language means shared markets and the free movement of people and goods; it facilitates peace and stability, influences international agendas and international events, thus contributing to the creation of wealth and greater international integration of economies, as well as the promotion of knowledge. To this end, Portuguese is of unquestionable strategic importance for the activities of foundations on numerous levels.

The Community of Portuguese Language Countries (CPLP) Foundations Meetings, as they are currently called, in as far as they coordinate their activities with those of the CPLP,[2] contribute to consolidating a platform of civil society organisations that, in their diversity, work and express

---

2 The Community of Portuguese Language Countries (CPLP) is an international organisation, with its head office in Lisbon, which was set up in 1996 by the heads of state of Angola, Brazil, Cape Verde, Guinea-Bissau, Mozambique, Portugal and São Tomé and Príncipe. East Timor later joined after achieving independence from Indonesia. According to its founding declaration, the fundamental goals of the CPLP are to consolidate the domestic and multinational culture that gives the Portuguese Language Countries their own particular identity, thus reflecting the special relationship between them and the increasing international importance of this set of countries, which are geographically dispersed but identified by a common language.

themselves in the same language, sharing common aims with a growing spirit of cooperation. The number of foundation representatives has increased from twenty at the first meeting to over fifty at the sixth meeting in São Tomé and Príncipe, in September 2009

## Portuguese-speaking African countries (PALOP)

The CPLP Foundations Meetings are particularly important within the context of the five Portuguese-speaking countries on the African continent: Angola, Cape Verde, Guinea-Bissau, Mozambique and São Tomé and Príncipe. Despite their geographic, demographic, social and economic differences, we can say that these countries constitute a regional bloc, sharing a certain cultural identity, of which philanthropy and the foundations are a part.

Previously Portuguese territories, they emerged as independent states between 1974 and 1975 after the military revolution of the 25th April 1974 deposed the dictatorial and colonialist regime in Portugal. In Angola and Mozambique, independence was followed by violent and long-lasting civil wars that postponed the consolidation of democratic regimes and social and sustainable economic development. In addition, the difficult social situations and inequality brought on by the different political contexts and autocratic regimes naturally prevented the creation of an emancipated civil society with the capacity to ensure their rights or self-organise.

Apart from the first meeting, which was attended by the Fundação Bispo Settímio Artur Ferrazzeta (ex-bishop of Bissau), this was the reason why no other foundation from Guinea-Bissau, a country seriously affected by political instability and the collapse of different state institutions, has attended the meetings.

The creation of foundations in these countries is a recent and rather unequal phenomenon. Beyond the foreign foundations that operate on a permanent or regular basis there, three major types can be distinguished: asset-based foundations, which boast an initial endowment or continued funding from domestic or foreign companies; person-based foundations that are associated with individuals from civil society, normally without an initial endowment or assets and, as such, dependent on funding from external bodies (public or private, domestic or international); and lastly, politically-based foundations, which are created from within different political parties. Whilst the first type is more similar to or identifies with typical foundations, boasting a certain financial autonomy, the second type is more like a non-governmental organisation (NGO), and is normally involved in fundraising.

In the first category, we find foundations that are set up as part of the social responsibility policies of public companies in these countries, like

Fundação SONANGOL (set up by SONANGOL, Sociedade Nacional de Combustíveis de Angola) or Fundação Brilhante (set up by ENDIAMA, Empresa Nacional de Exploração de Diamantes de Angola). In the second category, there is another kind of foundation – those without permanent financial capital but with valuable human capital. These have been set up by dynamic and entrepreneurial personalities or as a tribute to historic figures and heroes of independence, like Cape Verde's Fundação Amílcar Cabral. Two other examples of this kind are Mozambique's Fundação para o Desenvolvimento da Comunidade set up by Graça Machel, or the Fundação Joaquim Chissano, set up by the country's former president. In Cape Verde, the Fundação Infância Feliz, headed by the current First Lady, has had a major impact on mother-child protection in the country, and in São Tomé and Príncipe, the Fundação Mãe Santomense, which was set up by public health medical specialist and current Minister of Foreign Affairs, Carlos Tiny, helps underprivileged children with potential to receive a better education and proper training.

We know that foundations are a feature of economically and financially advanced societies and their existence reveals an intrinsic redistribution of wealth. However, foundations do not adhere to pre-defined models and, in terms of an organisational model of collective interests, they can display different characteristics that are determined by particular social and cultural, as well as political, legal and even religious factors. Nonetheless, what they all have in common is an inherent individual or collective solidarity that benefits the less fortunate sections of the different communities in which they operate.

## Global conscience, local action

Foundations exist to apply civic action to solve social and human problems and these meetings are useful for expanding the ways in which that action occurs. They are also useful in demonstrating how foundations are an important mechanism for promoting public interest and social intermediation as an alternative or complement to the work of governments, whose importance and intervention in these countries is almost exclusive.

Through their work in the Portuguese-speaking African countries, foundations and other organisations in civil society are a crucial influence on decision-making and action in social contexts where their work can have a real impact and added value. Thanks to the freedom provided by democratic regimes and the redefinition of the state's role, there is greater room for civil society to intervene. This is why it is even more necessary and urgent to reflect on what, how and why foundations do what they do.

Philanthropy's sphere of influence has become more demanding and the work of foundations in particular requires permanent reinvention. If this is not the case, they risk losing their main attribute, namely the ability to innovate, anticipate and influence public policy.

Currently, the numerous institutions that make up "civil society" can act as a catalyst for important social changes. By being players in a private collective participation, in which group objectives surpass mere individual interests, these institutions are creating a new awareness of the importance of sharing certain values of community life. Democracy is also achieved with the participation of citizens within the structures of civil society, although this participation is not simply a right but also a duty for citizens that accept their responsibilities in relation to the communities they are part of.

Some of these countries boast advanced sectors of civil society organisations, as is the case of Cape Verde, where the Plataforma das ONG de Cabo Verde (Cape Verde's NGO Platform), which was formed in 1996 by eighteen organisations, now boasts over two hundred NGOs and community and/or development associations, including ten foundations.[3]

## Philanthropy as a movement

In today's world, philanthropy is no longer an isolated act and has essentially become concerted action between institutions. This is based on economies of scale in relation to available resources (which are sometimes financial but mainly human), presupposing the social and geographical dispersion of problems, whilst aiming to maximise the impact of the activities of the agents involved.

The scope and effectiveness of foundations' philanthropic activities therefore depend on an instrumental capacity to create partnerships geared towards solving problems and founded on an informed understanding of their causes. Their work is necessarily more strategic and structured, focussing on investment in long-term interventions coupled with a rationale of gradual and permanent learning, experimentation and adjusting trajectories when necessary.

Philanthropy is a process of persistence, a veritable laboratory of social responses, where errors signify opportunity and not fatality. Analysing how successful foundations are in achieving their mission depends on the ability to identify mistakes in a timely fashion and being flexible enough to change the courses undertaken. This is why mechanisms for monitoring projects and assessing their results are so important and why sharing experiences collectively is crucial to avoid duplication and replicate success. There

---

3   Moniz, M (2009 Plataforma das ONG, *Referência obrigatória no panorama dos actores não governamentais em Cabo Verde*, in Cooperação Descentralizada, ACEP, July 2009.

must be a collective mobilisation to meet the important global challenges that legitimise the activities of foundations and constitute their raison d'être.

A globalised society is essentially a networked society and today we have tools that allow us to, if not eliminate, then at least drastically reduce geographical barriers and facilitate an approximation based on common elements. Portuguese is a very important work tool and a unique facilitator for the conceptual and critical alignment of these common denominators.

It is here that the CPLP Foundations Meetings can help create a solidarity network that speaks the same language. It has been very satisfying to see common projects and partnerships forged between the foundations that would not have existed otherwise, had it not been for their participation in these meetings. They have also functioned as an observatory on development, having organised and been involved in the interim assessment of the Millennium Development Goals in all Portuguese-speaking countries, for example.

## Conclusion

The CPLP Foundations Meetings are an important opportunity to reflect upon the role of foundations in countries with a common language and a tradition resulting from a long historic process. However, it is not the job of foundations to judge history but rather to understand it using objectivity and rigour, in order to avoid repeating the same mistakes. Foundations should showcase it using the best of what it has bestowed upon them: a cultural identity shared by eight countries, united by a past experienced together, by a language that, enriched in its diversity, is recognised as one alone, as a tool that is valuable within the context of development and for asserting their international standing.

A common language, in itself, is not a solution for the difficulties facing the Portuguese-speaking African countries. The necessary ingredients for solving the problems of development in the societies to which foundations are accountable can be found in their individual and collective capacity for entrepreneurship and for taking responsibility; essentially, in the ability to ask the questions that Mia Couto mentions. Because of their unique characteristics, foundations can play a crucial role in this area. They can encourage and create the right conditions so that entrepreneurial ability and the capacity to take responsibility emerges, preferably within the more underprivileged and neglected social groups in these countries, for social, economic or cultural reasons.

In Portuguese-speaking African countries, foundations can be crucial drivers of development, taking on the role of important interlocutors or intermediaries between communities, states and international organisations.

This is why the CPLP Foundations Meetings as learning and sharing experiences are instrumental for what is achieved by philanthropy in the field. From what began as a small gathering in Lisbon in 2003, these meetings have become an essential platform for philanthropic capital to circulate throughout the Portuguese-speaking countries.

# 19 Africa
## PHILANTHROPY IN AFRICA: FUNCTIONS, STATUS, CHALLENGES AND OPPORTUNITIES

## Introduction

Philanthropy in Africa, at least from the perspective of those societies I am familiar with – of which I am a part – is perhaps best captured in the framework of *birth, life, death* and *rebirth*. I explain briefly below how these concepts, strange as they may seem, interface with philanthropy both in terms of its meaning and practice in an African's life, (although of course this might not be peculiar to Africans alone and may well apply to many other societies). I use this framework very cautiously, however, because some African societies may not fit within it and its use here is therefore illustrative rather than representative.

I am also aware that this framework might not capture all dimensions of societies in Africa – but neither does the term philanthropy. Many in Africa would rather not use the term; instead they prefer to use simple expressions such as "helping" or "giving". Limited as these might appear to be, they capture the essence of what in other parts of the world would clearly qualify as philanthropy.

Although this article does not seek to give a comprehensive definition of what philanthropy in Africa is, it may be useful at the outset to point out some of the features of what can be classified as philanthropy in the continent. As stated in an entry in the *International Encyclopaedia of Civil Society, "The term philanthropy is not generally understood nor is it preferred in Africa-simply because it is not inclusive both in its scope and reach."[1]*

Given this, the term is used rather carefully here, intended to capture both the nature and character of philanthropy in the African continent, which revolves around two dimensions – the horizontal and vertical. Some writers have preferred to call the horizontal forms of philanthropy (or giving) "African philanthropy" or "philanthropy with African characteristics". Is there a difference between these two definitions, though? "African philanthropy" would perhaps imply philanthropic action that is specific and unique to Africa, and researchers in the continent have made some attempts to define the very essence of this type of philanthropy: it is mainly indigenous and usually informal, although there have been movements towards institutionalising some of its forms. Some research and clarification, however, is still needed to define the concept of "philanthropy with African characteristics" and this might in fact overlap with the concept of "African philanthropy".

More dominant and prominent are the vertical forms of philanthropy in Africa, which have normally been in the shape of formal and institutionalised mechanisms such as foundations, trusts, community chests and other societal mechanisms through which communities help each other.

Given these variations in definition and description when one speaks of philanthropy in Africa, not everyone agrees on its features. Often, priority is given to modern and formal institutions of philanthropy at the expense of the informal ones. And where there is an encounter between the two types, formal and institutionalised philanthropy often overrides everything else. Let me illustrate this point through a story.

In 2008, I attended a workshop that brought together a number of *philanthrocrats*[2] in Africa, mainly from the community foundations movement. The workshop facilitator began by asking each participant to share his or her experiences of working in philanthropy. As each participant spoke, I realised that many drew a clear line between their profession in philanthropy and their day-to-day lives. In other words, philanthropy as practice was not necessarily embedded in their personhood. For many, their experiences ranged from two, four, ten and even twenty years in the field of philanthropy or development in general. One gentleman, who was probably in his early sixties, even went as far as saying that he had been in other fields before, but had just joined the philanthropic world less than

---

1   Moyo, B (2009) 'Philanthropy in Africa' *International Encyclopedia of Civil Society* (eds. Helmut K. Anheier and Stefan Toepler) [online], available from the World Wide Web: http://www.springerlink.com/content/j62k806410114239/fulltext.html

2   This is a term coined to refer to those who work in the bureaucracy of disbursing philanthropic resources.

two years earlier. He was probably the least experienced in the area he professed. I sat there wondering what this exercise meant to me and whether or not I was reflected in the discussions that had gone before me. It was at that point that I decided I would frame my response to the question of experience by using the concepts of birth, life and death. I have since revised my framework to include rebirth – for it is when there is death that new life begins again. So instead of being a linear framework, it is now cyclical.

In order to define what philanthropy meant for me and others I know, I juxtaposed my date of birth and my experience of philanthropy. I was thirty-five years old at the time. And I had thirty-five years of experience in philanthropy. This perplexed many in the room who by mere calculation of my age would have found it very difficult to understand how I had worked for thirty-five years in the philanthropic sector, when in fact I looked thirty-five or so years old. My point was that for me there is no clear line between my life as I live it everyday and my professional occupation when it comes to philanthropy. Even if I did not have a professional job or career, I would still have given the same answer. And this is why.

**Birth**: When I was born (and before then) many people gave my parents all kinds of assistance which was by definition and nature philanthropic. At the time of my birth, which I am told included a naming ceremony, all manner of gifts – both financial and in-kind – were extended to me and my parents in ways that today would be defined not just as charity but as "development". Thus I immediately became a recipient of some benevolence from both my community and those from afar, as did my family and parents. At that point, I could not become a philanthropist but I certainly benefited from philanthropic acts. There is no doubt that my parents were philanthropic already.

**Life**: As I was growing up, I continued to be the recipient of many forms of philanthropic acts at home, from the community, and increasingly from the international world. I still am today. I have been a recipient of religious gifts, financial support and other forms of philanthropy. However I have not just been a recipient. I have also been a philanthropist in my own way to others, in terms of my time, money, and in-kind contributions to others. Thus I have partaken in both the horizontal and vertical forms of philanthropy. There is no clear line between my life and being philanthropic or being a recipient of philanthropic acts. At any moment in my life, I am one or both of these.

**Death/rebirth**: This is the most controversial to some people and yet it is the clearest phase in one's lifetime where philanthropy is best illustrated. Either, one is a recipient of philanthropy, aimed at covering the costs of burial and other funeral arrangements (including consoling the bereaved), or one is also a philanthropist at death through wills and bequests. A number of philanthropic institutions normally benefit at the death of some rich people who give a certain part of their estate to philanthropic causes. It is through such a process that new life begins – either a foundation or trust is established, or other forms of institutionalised philanthropy are born.

So my definition of philanthropy is very simple. My experience of philanthropy coincides with my age. Thus birth, life and death/rebirth are defining philanthropic moments for me as an African. I am yet to meet an African, or any human being for that matter, who would not identify with this. Therefore, whatever form philanthropy takes, it has some manifestations at a personal level at each of these life moments.

The main challenge, however, has been the lack of information regarding both the scope and size of philanthropy in Africa. The paucity of information has led to many myths and untruths about philanthropy, leading some to view Africa as lagging behind both in terms of its understanding and practice. There are very few institutions that have dedicated resources and personnel towards the research and study of philanthropy on the continent. No continental studies have been conducted in this field – it is a field that is under-resourced and seriously understudied.

There are however some studies that have been conducted at a national level. These include those in South Africa,[3] Southern Africa,[4] North Africa,[5] East Africa. I have also since contributed a chapter on Philanthropy in Africa to the 2009 *International Encyclopaedia of Civil Society*.[6]

To close this gap, TrustAfrica developed a philanthropy-specific project which among other things seeks to:
- Ascertain gaps and opportunities as well as produce a resource base and a mechanism for building an "infrastructure of and study of philanthropy" in Africa;

3 Everatt, D., & Solanki, G. (2005) *A nation of givers? Social giving among South Africans*, Durban: Centre for Civil Society. Friedman, S., Hudson, J. & Mackay, S. (2005) *Like cheese, like chalk? 'Professionalism' and 'Whim' in corporate giving at Anglogold Ashanti and Pick' N' Pay*, Durban: Centre for Civil Society. Habib, A. & Maharaj, B. (2008) *Giving and solidarity: Resource flows for poverty alleviation and development in South Africa*, Cape Town: HSRC Press. Mahomed, H. (2009) Conceptual frameworks influencing social justice philanthropy: A study of independent funders in South Africa in *The state of philanthropy*, in Africa. Dakar: TrustAfrica.

4 Wilkinson-Maposa, S., Fowler, A., Oliver-Evans, C. & Mulenga, C.F. N. (2006) *The poor philanthropist: How and why the poor help and give each other*, Cape Town: Compress. Moyo, B. (2004) *Dimensions of philanthropy in Southern Africa*, Paper prepared for the Ford Foundation Retreat, Jinja: Ford Foundation

5 Daly, M (2007) *Philanthropy in Egypt: A comprehensive study on local philanthropy in Egypt and potentials of directing giving and volunteering towards development*, Cairo: Center for Development Services

6 Moyo, B (2009) 'Philanthropy in Africa' International Encyclopedia of Civil Society (eds. Helmut K. Anheier and Stefan Toepler) [online], available from the World Wide Web: http://www.springerlink.com/content/j62k806410114239/fulltext.html

- Understand local forms of philanthropy within the broader discourse of philanthropy.

This project has specific focus on an annual publication called *The State of Philanthropy in Africa*, whose main aim is to measure the state of philanthropy in the continent by gathering all necessary data, in order to locate the philanthropic discourse in proper context.

## The current philanthropic landscape

This section addresses briefly what exists in Africa. It draws heavily from a recent publication by the same author.[7] As stated above, the philanthropic landscape in Africa is generally characterised by both horizontal and vertical dimensions of philanthropy. Because the term "philanthropy" is not popular with the people in the continent, and neither is it useful in capturing what exists, the emerging body of literature on philanthropy in Africa prefers to define philanthropy as "help" or "giving".[8] In the informal realm, philanthropy manifests itself in what Wilkinson-Maposa *et al.* have called the "philanthropy of community". In this realm, philanthropy refers to giving by the poor to other poor individuals of the community. More often this manifests itself in cultural and linguistic underpinnings – hence it normally takes on indigenous expressions such as cooperatives, rotation and savings clubs (normally called stokvels), communal collective efforts and burial societies.

In the formal realm, philanthropy takes forms such as private foundations, trusts, corporate foundations, family trusts, community chests and community foundations. More often this is understood – or misunderstood for that matter – to mean the rich giving to or helping the poor. I say misunderstood because this is, however, a form of disempowerment for the poor. The rich are made patrons for the poor, and yet the poor are philanthropic too, as my story earlier on demonstrated. The added danger with this interpretation is that it also takes away the poor's agency in giving and developing themselves and others, around and far beyond.

As I write this chapter, Haiti has been struck by one of the most disastrous earthquakes in recent history. African civil society organizations led by Mrs Graca Machel, TrustAfrica, CIVICUS and the African Monitor have put together a campaign called Africa for Haiti[9] which appeals to all Africans, poor and rich, to make contributions that would be channelled

---

7  Ibid.

8  Wilkinson-Maposa, S, Fowler, A, Oliver-Evans, C, & Mulenga, C F N (2006) *The poor philanthropist: How and why the poor help and give each other*, Cape Town: Compress

9  www.africaforhaiti.com

towards rebuilding Haitian communities. Such an approach is informed by existing research which increasingly shows that giving is not the exclusive domain of the wealthy.[10] This is also informed by the fact that Africans more often give to local causes, and very few give to international causes. This might be due to the fact that many developmental challenges are right in front of them, for example the HIV/AIDS pandemic; wars and conflicts; unemployment, particularly for the youth; and the general levels of poverty. But with a disaster like the one in Haiti, Africans are being called upon to give to international causes. In other words, this campaign has the potential of turning what is normally considered local and informal, as well as indigenous, into an international mechanism.

There are many factors that motivate people to give. Many are motivated by what in Southern Africa is called "*ubuntu*" – literally referring to humanity or humaneness. There are also significant numbers of people who help and give both financially and in kind because of their religion. In return, these people expect spiritual blessings. But there is a group of people that give and help because they think that their philanthropic activities are geared towards tackling poverty and development-related matters. An interesting defining characteristic feature of philanthropy in Africa is that there is a thin line between short-term and long-term philanthropic actions. Charity is not just charity, it is very much linked to development.

This thin line is also to be found in diaspora remittances, which are fast becoming critical levers of development on the continent. Existing research on remittances seems to conflate contributions made to families with philanthropy. There is no doubt that the diaspora phenomenon is an emerging and interesting development in philanthropy, particularly in Africa. It is estimated that there are more than thirty-five million citizens of African descent in the United States alone, whose collective purchasing power amounts to about 450 billion United States dollars (USD) per annum.[11] According to the World Bank's 2007 report, remittances to Africa amounted to 4 billion USD for Sub-Saharan Africa.

Individual giving and foundations play a major role in Africa in terms of defining the philanthropic landscape. Below I give a snapshot of individual giving and foundations.

---

10   Everatt, D, & Solanki, G (2005) *A nation of givers? Social giving among South Africans,* Durban: Centre for Civil Society. Wilkinson-Maposa, S, Fowler, A, Oliver-Evans, C, & Mulenga, C F N (2006) *The poor philanthropist: How and why the poor help and give each other,* Cape Town: Compress

11   Bridgewater, P. (2003). *The African diaspora and its influence on African development,* Remarks at Kentucky State University March 28, Frankfort, KY

## Individual giving

There has not been much research conducted in Africa on individual giving. However, there are considerable resources that come from individuals, either to other individuals or to formal institutions. The only study so far on giving which was conducted at a national level is by the Centre for Civil Society at the University of KwaZulu Natal. This study is instructive of what is generally believed to be the case across Africa.[12] It concluded that South Africa was a nation of givers. Over half of the people who were surveyed gave money to charities or other causes, a third gave food or other goods to charities or other causes, while almost a fifth volunteered time for charity or other causes. The study adds that slightly less than half of the respondents gave money or goods directly to the poor, while the majority preferred to give to formal structures rather than to individuals.[13] Elsewhere throughout the continent, similar trends can be observed. More studies need to be conducted however, to avoid the tyranny of anecdotes.

Many individuals are motivated by religion when they give either money or in kind. Most religions require the poor be taken care of. However, another motivating factor for individual donors is the need to tackle poverty. As such, individual giving is not the exclusive domain of the rich, the poor also give. Because of this realisation, emerging institutions such as community foundations are finding that they can also raise resources from local communities. Individuals also give time. According to a study of the nonprofit sector in South Africa,[14] the sector has the highest number of volunteers. In 1999, more than 1.5 million volunteers contributed their time to the sector. Their contribution was equivalent to the work done in 316,991 full time jobs and accounted for almost 49 percent of the nonprofit sector's work force. Volunteers were active in culture and recreation, religious institutions and politics or advocacy. There were 70,740 volunteers in the culture and recreation sector, 64,457 in the politics and advocacy sector, 52,743 in the religious sector and 50,450 in social services.[15]

Individual giving can be enhanced if the tax regime is enabling. In most countries, the tax environment does not provide incentives for voluntary

---

12  Everatt, D, & Solanki, G (2005) *A nation of givers? Social giving among South Africans*, Durban: Centre for Civil Society. Wilkinson-Maposa, S, Fowler, A, Oliver-Evans, C, & Mulenga, C.F.N

13  Ibid.

14  Swilling, M, & Russell, B (2002) *The size and scope of the non profit sector in South Africa,* Durban: Centre for Civil Society

15  Ibid.

giving in the public interest.[16] This is a challenge that confronts many countries, but an opportunity exists to reform tax laws: this would serve as a significant step forward in encouraging private individuals to donate parts of their estates to philanthropic activities. Already Africa is witnessing an increase in new foundations being created by individuals, and more are likely to emerge if the environment for individual giving is improved.

## Foundations

The speed at which African foundations are sprouting right across the continent points to the fact that the philanthropic landscape is developing and maturing faster than was anticipated. In the last few years, foundations working in Africa were mainly international in nature and orientation. Today, however, there is an emergence of African-founded and led foundations, most of which also focus on areas which, previously, only international foundations addressed. These include, but are not limited to, grant-making to civil society and the private sector in fields such as development, governance, human rights, community development, HIV/AIDS, and peace and security.

These new foundations include TrustAfrica, the African Women's Development Fund, the Mo Ibrahim Foundation, the Nelson Mandela Foundation, the Joaquim Chissano Foundation, the J.A. Kufuor Foundation, the Solomon Tandeng Muna Foundation and the Youssou N'Dour Foundation, among many others. Some of these have been created and supported by international foundations such as the Ford Foundation. Others have been formed by former heads of states. Others, like the Mo Ibrahim and Dakota Foundations, were created by rich Africans who made their money mostly from the private sector and are now giving back to the communities. Sports personalities and others have also created their own foundations right across the continent, and these focus on issues that are dear to them. The Mutola Foundation in Mozambique is a classic example of a foundation set up by a sports personality. Because there are many sports personalities – mostly working in Europe – there is potential for more foundations to be set up according to the specific interests of the founders.

Foundations are the biggest constituents of institutional philanthropy in Africa. The highest concentration of foundations is still in Anglophone countries, mainly in Southern Africa (South Africa mainly), East Africa (Kenya) and parts of West Africa (Nigeria and Ghana). North Africa, particularly Egypt, has also developed a number of foundations. In these

---

16 SAGA (2004) *South Africa philanthropy and the Fiscus,* A SAGA position paper: Johannesburg: SAGA.

countries, there is a growing development of family trusts, about which very little is still known.

In South Africa alone in 2002, there were 3,891 non-profit organisations that were registered as trusts or foundations, representing 4 percent of the non-profit sector overall. For a subsector about which relatively little information exists, the number of trusts and foundations would appear to be quite high. And research conducted into a sample of family foundations in South Africa showed that they are all very diverse in terms of the projects that they support and their overall modes of operation.[17]

Although foundations appear to work in many different areas, the majority work in the fields of education, welfare and health. Equally, very few family foundations are in areas that could be described as transformative, such as social justice, democracy, rule of law, gender and civil rights and so on, and much of their work would seem to focus on ameliorating the effects of poverty, for example, rather than addressing its causes. This tendency towards "charity" among family foundations is not only true of family foundations in South Africa, but is a common feature of much institutional philanthropy across the world.[18]

Over the last ten years, there has been an increasing interest and growth in the number of community foundations. In 1998, there were only two such foundations across Africa: today there are more than fifteen such institutions on the continent.[19] The highest concentration is in South Africa. Others are found in Kenya, Tanzania, Egypt, Malawi, Uganda, Mozambique, Lesotho, and Zimbabwe. There are other community-like institutions in Africa, and these have not been studied. The growth in community foundations is an illustration of the importance of such community-based institutions for development purposes; through community foundations, communities feel that they own their own development. The Kenya Community Development Foundation is a classic case, illustrating how communities can rally around a particular development imperative and pull their resources together.[20]

Despite the interest in community foundations (even the World Bank has been developing community foundations across the world – the four

17  Moyo, B (2006) *Family foundations in South Africa*, paper prepared for the State of Social Giving in South Africa Report Series. Durban: Centre for Civil Society

18  Chen, L (2002) *Philanthropy and social change in Latin America,* Strategies and lessons. Workshop presentation, The David Rockefeller Centre for Latin American Studies and The Hauser Centre for Non Profit Organizations, Harvard University

19  Global Status Report (2008) 2008 Community foundations global status report [online], available from the World Wide Web: www.wingsweb.org/Information/publications_ Community_2008_Main.cfm

20  Mutuku, M (2006). 'Process makes perfect'. In Katharine Pearson (Ed.), *Donors ourselves: Rural development philanthropy from East Tennessee to East Africa and beyond*, Whitesburg, KY: The Center for Rural Strategies. (pp. 31–43).

community foundations in Tanzania were developed through a World Bank project), a number of challenges still abound around the community foundation concept. These include the very understanding of the term "community", which if not properly defined might lead to exclusion rather than inclusion. The other challenge has been that community foundations have tended to bypass their communities and depended mainly on international sources of funding.

Philanthropy in Africa therefore takes many forms including indigenous mechanisms, foundations (private and public), community foundations, corporate philanthropy and individual giving. As highlighted previously, giving is not the preserve of a few rich people, but is a domain that also includes the poor, who are taking an interest in their own affairs. Hence a significant number of individual givers include the poor who are driven by the need to address poverty, charity and their religious beliefs. There are a significant number of foundations, including international ones like the Charles Stewart Mott Foundation, the Ford Foundation, and other new entrants. There has been an important development in the continent which has seen African foundations sprouting up everywhere. This development is very important, for it has the potential to reverse power relations that exist between the global North and the global South. Also, there is a possibility that these new foundations can break the dependency cycle that currently characterises relations between the non-profit sector and international foundations. Lastly, it is possible that the new foundations can work on an equal footing with their counterparts from the north. But equally important is to caution that the same African foundations could, within Africa, recreate the same imbalances that currently define relations between the north and the south.[21]

TrustAfrica and other philanthropic institutions such as the African Women's Development Fund, the Southern Africa Trust and the Kenya Community Development Foundation have been in the forefront of developing a philanthropic platform in Africa. For example, after many years of consultations, planning and preparations, the African Grantmakers Network (AGN) was launched in Accra, Ghana in July 2009. This network was formed by major African grant-makers on the continent, as a platform for collective action with the potential to reverse some of the imbalances of the past. At the same time, the AGN has the potential to propel Africa's development through an effective use of philanthropic resources. Currently guided by a steering committee of seven organisations and located at TrustAfrica, the Network will, among other things, be a platform for peer-learning and good practice. It will serve as a force to amplify African

---

21   Moyo, B (September 2008) *Can the new African foundations break the dependence syndrome?* Alliance Magazine (pp. 40–41)

voices and advance African perspectives in development and global platforms. It will also cultivate productive relations with other civil society formations in Africa.

However, the AGN faces a number of tasks to not only maintain the momentum but to remain relevant. Among these, the first is information generation about grant-making in Africa, including the general map of what exists and the architecture of philanthropy on the continent. The second task relates to managing collaborations and partnerships. The wide acceptance of the launch has the potential to fast-track the AGN's growth beyond natural laws of expansion. Thirdly, the AGN will have to be innovative, and think outside the box in connecting the various initiatives across the continent in ways that contribute to an effective development approach.

In addition, TrustAfrica has supported efforts aimed at securing the conditions for democracy and equitable development in Africa. This has been possible through grant-making, technical assistance and provision of mobility support for groups and individuals who under normal circumstances would not be able to operate effectively. Thus as an African foundation, TrustAfrica has not only focused on building an infrastructure for philanthropy but has used its philanthropic resources to address challenging developmental questions facing Africa. From transitional justice issues to economic governance and the promotion of human rights, TrustAfrica has attempted to give ordinary Africans the capacity and voice to hold their governments accountable. Working at the regional and continental level, TrustAfrica has used the treaty system to advocate for good governance, free and fair elections, agrarian reform, gender equity and civil society protection.

## Conclusion

Philanthropy in Africa is a field that still needs further probing. For example, Africa still needs more research and studies that track philanthropic flows, as well as studies which explore their impact on development and transforming societal structures. More important will be the alignment of philanthropy with national priorities as well as with the activities and processes of traditional philanthropy. New studies in the continent, such as the focus on diaspora philanthropy, the focus on indigenous philanthropy and optimising institutional philanthropy will prove useful in defining the philanthropic terrain in Africa within the next five to ten years. With more philanthropic institutions emerging and more research being conducted continentally, the philanthropic map is slowly being drawn.

FERNANDO ROSSETTI

# 20 Brazil
# FROM PHILANTHROPY TO
# PRIVATE SOCIAL INVESTMENT

## A brief history

From the colonisation by Portugal, in 1500, until the nineteenth century, Brazilian philanthropy was essentially related to the Catholic Church. Most education, health and social assistance services were delivered by religious, Catholic institutions, funded by individual, family and royal donations. Some of these initial organisations continue working, although with renewed sustainability challenges – such as the "Santa Casa de Misericordia", a large network of philanthropic hospitals, which today is funded mainly by public resources.

With independence from Portuguese rule, in the 1820s, newly created public institutions also began to offer social services, such as education – a process that accelerated with the adoption of a republican political system, in 1889. For many decades, waves of immigrants, particularly from Europe, took to this syncretistic country new cultures and ideas on how to organise the state, the market and civil society.

In the mid twentieth century, a few families that had grown rich with the rapid industrialization of the country created some of the first indigenous Brazilian private foundations. Most were oriented at the time to deliver social services to the workers around their own businesses – since state assistance was and frequently continues to be precarious. Other social movements, also sparked by the industrialization process, laid the foundations for the universalization of health and education public policies which was achieved at the turn of the twentieth century.

The military rule, from 1964 to 1985, strengthened the grasp of the state over civil society organisations (CSOs), which either continued to be linked to the Catholic Church – although with strong Marxist influence – or were related to left wing, anti-dictatorship political movements. With a few important exceptions, businesses supported the military rule. And philanthropy, in general, continued to fill in the many gaps left by the state.

The so called "democratic opening" of the country, from the mid-1970's onwards, and especially the wide social mobilisation that led to the 1988 Constitution, set the political and legislative stage for a historic transformation in the organisation of Brazilian civil society and philanthropy.

At the same time, Brazil started globalizing its economy and a wide range of multinational businesses established themselves in the country, influencing the culture of corporate philanthropy and individual giving. Brazilian businesses also became more global in their activities, promoting new kinds of relationships between the industrial elite of the country and other societies.

Education became the main national private social investment area, driven by the demand for a more qualified workforce to meet the stringent competitiveness of the global economy, and by the perception that opportunities are better distributed through a qualified public school system.

## The birth of the third sector

Figure 1, below, started circling around the world in the second half of the 1980s. It is a good illustration of the ideological aftermath of the fall of the Berlin Wall in 1989, or the collapse of the USSR in 1991. Instead of dividing society into two groups, capital and labour, which dispute hegemony over the state, this iconic image proposes three sectors: state, businesses, and civil society organisations. Around the same time, the American sociologist Francis Fukuyama proposed the *End of History*, claiming the victory of economic liberalism over state-run economies.

In Brazil, as in most societies, the roles and workings of the state, businesses and civil society organisations had already been undergoing structural transformation for many years. In the 1990s, the concept of the third sector gained momentum in many societies. In general terms, this concept means that the public sphere is not only a state-run issue, but should also include the participation of the private sector – both for-profit (second sector) and non-profit organisations (third sector).

Some opposed this movement, calling it, especially when related to the economy, the "Washington Consensus", or "neoliberalism", and accusing it of disseminating a generally small-state ideology, less regulation in the markets, and wider business and civil society participation in public policies, such as education and health. Most Latin American countries, having their economies strongly linked to the United States (US), have been influenced by these concepts and practices.

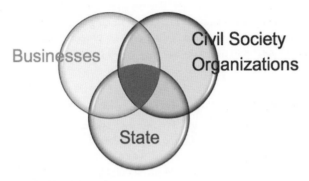

Figure 1: The birth of the third sector

With its new, more participatory 1988 Constitution, Brazil took a lead in this process in South America. The country finally started to seek a more sustainable economic policy, which initially consisted of privatisation, opening its market to other countries, reorganising the state and regulating the financial sector, to counter the acute economic crisis experienced in the 1980s and 1990s. This tighter financial legislation helped to shield the country from the 2008 global meltdown.

For the creation and monitoring of its social public policies, Brazil institutionalized a series of councils on municipal, state and federal levels, which included the participation of representatives from the three sectors. New major laws were approved by the National Congress for children and adolescent rights (1990), consumer rights (1990), social assistance (1993) and education (1996), among others.

In the early 1990s, a corruption scandal involving a philanthropic organisation led by the Brazilian First Lady tainted forever in the country the meaning of the word "philanthropy" – which became linked either to tax evasion through civil society organisations or to less strategic ways of contributing to social issues – and even to programs that reinforce the dominance of the elite over poorer communities in society.

Soon afterwards another, wider corruption scandal led to the impeachment of the Brazilian President Fernando Collor de Mello, in 1992. But democracy consolidated in the country, and businesses and civil society organisations began to thrive.

A pioneering example of the profound changes happening in the third sector is offered by the Abrinq Foundation, linked to the association of toy industries in Brazil. Created in 1990 to promote the new legislation on children and adolescent rights, this foundation, led by businessmen, launched in 1995 a "children-friendly business" stamp, which was given to enterprises that confirmed that no child labour was included in any part of its production chain. For the first time in Brazilian history, a business-related foundation instead of taking care directly of their beneficiaries – "since the state doesn't do it" – proposed and implemented a program that, more than a decade later is still producing significant social and economic changes.

## The foundation and association boom

In 1995, with its democracy reinforced and a new, social democrat President elected, the long-lasting hyperinflation was finally controlled. For the first time in decades, Brazil was able to collectively envision a better future. Foundations and civil society organisations (framed legally as non-profit associations) acquired a kind of panacea position in society.

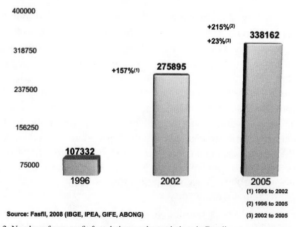

Figure 2: Number of non-profit foundations and associations in Brazil

From 1996 to 2005 (therefore in only ten years), the number of foundations and non-profit associations tripled, from 107,332 to 338,162. In the same period, the number of businesses grew by 68 percent, to 5.4 million. And the population in the country approached the two hundred million mark – an outstanding emerging market in many senses.

Although among the 338,000 non-profit foundations and associations, a quarter were related to different religions, which were also booming in the country (161 percent expansion in ten years), the group that grew the most were the non-governmental organisations (NGOs) related to rights advocacy and development (a startling 437 percent from 1996 to 2005, totalling 60,000 organisations). In 2005, the number of workers in the sector reached 1.7 million, or around 6 percent of all Brazilian formal labour.

This growth was accompanied by a similar proliferation of intermediary civil society organisations. In 1991, the Brazilian Association of NGOs (Abong) was created. At the same time, foundation and business leaders started to hold monthly meetings to reposition the way their organisations worked in the country. Initially gathering at the American Chamber of Commerce, with the support of the Kellogg Foundation, these leaders went on two international benchmarking tours in the US and Europe. They ended up creating the first philanthropy association in South America in 1995: the Group of Institutes, Foundations and Enterprises (GIFE) – initially with twenty-five members and today with one hundred more.

In 1998, some of the same business leaders that had created the Abrinq Foundation (1990) and GIFE (1995), among other organisations, launched the Ethos Institute on Business and Social Responsibility. The 2001 UN Volunteer Year also accelerated the building of local and regional volunteer centres around the country, most of them linked to rich Brazilian families, to national and international businesses or to both.

## Building a sustainability crisis

To understand the profound Brazilian third sector sustainability crisis, that was catalysed by the financial meltdown in 2008, one has to investigate how the foundation and association boom was funded and what are the limits of this kind of funding. GIFE has also been trying to uncover what new resources are available, or could be made available, to consolidate the rich constellation of civil society organisations that have grown throughout Brazil in the last twenty years.

There are at least five main sources of funding for CSOs, including foundations (see Figure 3 below).

First of all there is the state, with its public money, conveyed through tax incentives or exemptions and through public policies run by CSOs with government funding. In the 1990's, and especially throughout Fernando Henrique Cardoso's presidency (1995-2002), there was a strong drive towards business and civil society participation in the delivery of social services.

The President's anthropologist wife, professor Ruth Cardoso, was a strong proponent of public-private partnerships in actions ranging from illiteracy eradication to wealth generation in poor communities. The

Figure 3: Funding resources for the third sector

expansion of the nursery school system in Brazil has been achieved in great part by non-profit organisations, funded mainly by municipal governments. The Brazilian public health system involves government, private and non-profit organisations, and many of the children and adolescent rights policies engage CSOs, with public-private funding.

A second group of funders could be described under the heading of "international cooperation". The association and foundation boom in Brazil (especially some more complex expressions of this movement, like the creation of intermediary organisations such as Abong, GIFE and Ethos) was driven by core seed funding from international organisations. Some of them are linked to other governments, such as the United States Agency for International Development (USAID), the European Commission or German foundations maintained by political parties.

There is also another important type of international player that, although small in number, has a tremendous impact. The history of Brazilian philanthropy would probably be different without the funding for CSOs offered by American independent foundations such as Kellogg and Ford, and by European ones such as AVINA.

Thirdly, NGOs and foundations also raise funds through religious institutions which, as discussed above, have been proliferating in the country. Fourthly, CSOs might sell products and services, from Christmas cards to training programs and consultancy services, which constitute a increasingly important source of cash for them. Social ventures are a global trend.

Lastly, there is philanthropy itself, or private social investment as this kind of activity came to be called in Brazil at the turn of the century. And this is where Brazil follows a unique path. The whole tax exemption/incentive system created in the 1988 Constitution establishes that only certain kinds of businesses or individuals can match funds with these resources – notably the ones that make more profit and, because of that, have more complex forms to relate to government tax bodies.

The number of businesses that most benefit from tax incentives is estimated by government at around 7 percent of all private enterprises in the country. The number of individuals benefiting from most incentives is also lower than 10 percent. This reiterates that much of the wealth in the country is concentrated in the hands of few.

The third sector boom has received a strong contribution from the business sector and its leaders, who were relevant for the professionalization of the sector, introducing planning and evaluation tools and methodologies. However, the lack of incentives for endowments makes most philanthropy budget planning a yearly procedure.

More research is needed to allocate the exact role of each of these types of funders in the Brazilian civil society organisation boom. But the funding environment of the early 1990s has changed considerably in the last decade: a larger state ideology gained hegemony; international cooperation is moving out of Brazil or simply fundraising in Brazil rather than providing funds from outside; businesses are directly operating their social investments, so there is less traditional grant-making. This has led to a structural sustainability crisis for CSOs.

## Confronting a conceptual confusion

Close to the end of the 1990s, there were so many new organisations, programs, projects, networks, alliances, books, courses and so on that it began to be difficult to tell who was who and what was what in the new economic sector which had surfaced from Brazil's democratisation and globalization.

This conceptual confusion moved GIFE and Ethos – two of the main intermediary organisations – into opposing positions, and they started to dispute ideas which started to dispute ideas on social change and members. The solution was to agree on a conceptual division: GIFE's members would gather around the concept of private social investment – defined as "the voluntary giving of private resources in a planned, monitored and systematic manner for social, cultural and environmental projects of public interest" – and the Ethos Institute identified its work with the American-inspired concept of Business Social Responsibility, creating and disseminating a tool for corporate assessment to be divided into seven broad subjects:

- Values, transparency and governance
- Workforce
- Environment
- Suppliers

- Consumers and customers
- Community
- Government and society

So GIFE focused on what in the northern Hemisphere is still called philanthropy, or social investment, predominantly with corporate members, but also with independent and family organisations. And Ethos concentrated on building a corporate responsibility ideology and tools for the dissemination of new business practices. Today, many of the corporate members of Ethos have their philanthropic body associated with GIFE.

Nevertheless, the conceptual confusion continues – aggravated by the emergence of the sustainability movement, which is sometimes understood only in its environmental aspect, others referring to the "triple bottom line" of economic, environmental and social sustainability.

Many businesses still call their community work "corporate social responsibility" – although Ethos disagrees with this use of the concept. Sometimes social services delivered to the business' workforce are called "private social investment", although this kind of work is not considered so by GIFE.

In the business philanthropic sector a new phenomenon started to develop around 2005. The foundations and institutes, created by companies to look outwards to the community and its needs, were summoned by their maintainers to help them introduce social responsibility practices in business, blurring the more clear-cut conceptual division that had been introduced by GIFE and Ethos in 1999. The social investment staff became a kind of "social intelligence unit" for these businesses.

By the end of the first decade of the twenty-first century the main trend in the corporate sector has been alignment between business social responsibility practices and social investment activities. The largest Brazilian companies have started to dispute international sustainability rankings, to position their brands globally as socially and environmentally responsible. Much like some American companies investing in Brazil, Brazilian corporations working in Africa, for example, have begun introducing social investment actions in the communities where they are building roads or dams.

## Social investment tools

One could summarise the development of philanthropy in Brazil in the last two decades in only three steps:
1. Giving fish.
2. Teaching how to fish.
3. Reorganising the fishing production chain.

Today, the more complex and sophisticated social actions developed by institutes, foundations or businesses have in fact built systemic approaches to social change, taking into account governmental public policies and their many stakeholders. In one Brazilian region a corporate foundation literarily reorganised the fishing production chain, generating wealth for poor fishing families, more income for the municipalities involved, and opening new markets for the products.

But these three steps do not cover the many different arrangements of philanthropy in the Brazil. So in 2005 GIFE developed a new tool which classified philanthropic institutions into five different types.

Figure 4: The Private Social Investment Typology

The first type of philanthropic work is the more traditional and, up to today, the prevailing kind, which deals more with the symptoms than with the causes of social problems, such as giving food, clothing, shelter or gathering and distributing toys at Christmas. This is sometimes called charity or social assistance. Research conducted in 2005 by IPEA, a federal government think tank, showed that around two-thirds of the businesses in the country undertook some kind of philanthropic work; and that two-thirds of these have very incipient, more charity-like practices.

In a country with the level of misery still encountered in Brazil, this kind of philanthropy is fundamental, but not sufficient to change the root causes of inequality. The Brazilian sociologist Herbert Jose de Souza, known as Betinho (1935-1997), tried to bridge this approach to community with more complex social programs, declaring in the 1990s that, "One cannot educate a hungry child".

The second type of social investment, and the second-most frequent, is called multi-project social investment. It is very visible in bigger institutions which develop many different projects and programs without much alignment between them. Usually the programs in a multi-project organization illustrate some of its history. For example, a project may have started working with kids in the streets, then discovered that a program was needed for their families and opened one. This program is then overseen by a new CEO who likes arts and develops a museum, then the government may create a tax incentive for sports programs and the organisation opens another program in this field, and so on.

Foundations, institutes and businesses usually make their initial contact with GIFE in this second stage of organization of their social investment. Their first requests are for tools to evaluate the effectiveness of their programs, usually prompted by board members or by people linked to the business.

The need for evaluation in this phase is a misguided hypothesis in most cases, because one cannot evaluate a multi-project institution, due to the organic development of its activities – which emerge without much planning or prior establishment of measurable goals. What multi-project social investment organisations usually need is thorough strategic planning.

The third type of philanthropic institution is transitory from the second to the fourth, and involves the search for focus in its activities. For bigger institutions this can take from many months to a few years. It usually causes a kind of an "identity crisis" in the organisation; what do we do, and why? This crisis is aggravated by the fact that to focus does not only mean to have a clearer vision on one's social investment, but also to concentrate activities in fewer, better-planned programs. Sometimes traditional activities of the institution have to be closed down and pioneer staff have to be sacked. The main symptom in this phase is that the organisation tends to allocate most of its energy and resources inwards, not outwards.

When there is a clear vision, mission, objectives, an action plan, and an adequate, specialized staff to deliver this, the institution becomes strategic or professional – the fourth type of social investment. In businesses there is also a greater alignment in these cases between its private and public interests: information technology corporations build global digital-inclusion programs; food companies develop nutritional education methodologies; telecommunication groups train teachers to use the internet in the public schools they have cabled.

The fifth type of social investment relates to strategic organizations that endeavour to scale-up their impact and outreach. To scale-up implies intra and inter sectoral partnerships, frequently working in the building or improvement of public policies. Due to their relatively small investment power compared to governments, many of these organisations adopt a research and development (R&D) approach, building methodologies, training programs or what has come to be known as social technologies which, once tested, can be scaled up through public policies or disseminated through governmental or non-profit institutions, such as schools or hospitals.

More than 80 percent of the 125 members of GIFE invest in education, many developing social technologies that range from managerial tools for schools to complex and broad training programs for teachers.

A scheme such as the GIFE Social Investment Typology is always limited. The choice of building a typology was due to the fact that these types do not represent a linear evolution, from the first to the last. On the contrary, all the five types are important, the first one, for example, having the potential to develop social capital in a community.

Besides, many organisations have characteristics of all the five types – especially the larger institutions. Depending on leadership and other variables, a strategic organisation can very quickly become multi-project, or a R&D program can have difficulty in scaling up its impact. But this typology is usually helpful for a day-to-day description of a foundation or institute. The staff at GIFE frequently resort to these types, sometimes combined, to describe its members or prospective members.

## 2010 scenario

As described above, Brazilian civil society organisations are undergoing a structural sustainability challenge. Besides tripling in number, the easy, "spread and pray" money that flowed out from businesses and their foundations in the 1990s is now used in a much more strategic, professional and focused way – an important achievement for intermediary organisations such as GIFE and Ethos.

Civil society is no longer seen as a panacea for social challenges – sometimes it is even reported as part of the problem. The endemic corruption in Brazil has tainted the relationship between governments and CSOs in the public eye. When distributing funds, governments tend to simply outsource public policies to CSOs, with very rigid contracts and lower costs, rather than invest in the development of the autonomy and quality of these civil society organisations.

Businesses are also responsible for the damaged image of civil society organizations, including foundations and institutes. Although there are many notable counter-examples, in general businesses tend to prioritize their private interest. Corporate projects with more investment in visibility than in the social action are not rare.

It is quite frequent for a corporation to lose all memory of its private social actions. Sometimes, with the turnover of the staff in the corporate philanthropic sector, the whole organization literally forgets all the activities it had been developing and the partnership relations involved in these actions. At GIFE we call this "systemic amnesia".

The Brazilian-based private social investment institutions linked to businesses were affected in different ways by the global economic crisis in 2009. The downturn would have been much worse if it had taken place ten years earlier, when social responsibility was more a discourse than a practice. Now it would be difficult to just cut all philanthropic programs if these have become part of the culture of the corporation. So in many businesses, social investment underwent cuts in budget similar to all other areas.

Many businesses that had their social investment classified in the initial phases of the typology simply cut, almost altogether, their social investments. The most globalized Brazilian industries, such as mining and steel, conducted major cuts in their philanthropic budgets, since they project a diminished income for years. But many maintained, and some (like a few Brazilian private banks) even increased their funding.

Brazil became an investment-grade country in most international rating agencies in 2008-2009, while many more developed economies were caught by their biggest crisis in decades.

Global philanthropy is also undergoing structural changes, due to many, complex variables. International cooperation has decided either to move out of the country to more deprived societies in Africa or Asia, or to reposition their sustainability model, maintaining their work in the country with national resources. American foundations are focusing more in their own country and its borders, especially Mexico. Haiti is also drawing attention and resources.

The Kellogg Foundation closed its Brazilian office in August 2009. Ford Foundation re-focused from more than ten programs to only four. Oxfam has announced it will move out. Since 2008 USAID has been using its social responsibility money mainly to promote American corporate social investment achievements in Brazil.

Since 2008, the UK-based Charities Aid Foundation (CAF) has been delivering services to wealthy families through the local support organisation IDIS (Institute for the Development of Social Investment). In 2009, Save the Children merged with the Abrinq Foundation – the social investment branch of the Brazilian toy industry association quoted above.

The overall perception is that there is wealth and opportunity in the Brazilian third sector marketplace. Provided that the global economic crisis does not break out again, the 125 members of GIFE will probably invest more than 1 billion USD in 2010 in social, environmental and cultural projects. Recently the pop star Madonna fundraised more than 10 million USD for her charity work in Brazil. In 2011, Worldwide Initiatives for Grantmaker Support (WINGS) will move its secretariat to São Paulo.

A recent Ford Foundation research on the sustainability of its grantees showed that these social leaders perceived many challenges and threats to their organisations, but with a few exceptions were generally optimistic about the future and planning expansions of their work.

In politics the whole American continent has shifted in the last ten years, from a small to a large state ideology. The Argentinean president Carlos Menem (1989-1999) is a good representative of the 1990s hegemonic vision of a small state. Venezuelan president Hugo Chaves is now a leading, strident political voice. Menem's policies led to the bankruptcy of

Argentina. Chaves' impacts are not yet clear, but Venezuela does not seem to be in good shape. Menem had his continental counterparts: Vicente Fox (Mexico), Fernando Henrique Cardoso (Brazil) and in the US Bill Clinton and later George W. Bush. Chaves is the caricature of a wider movement: Luiz Inacio Lula da Silva (Brazil), Evo Morales (Bolivia), Rafael Correa (Equador), Felipe Calderon (Mexico), and in the US, Barack Obama.

In the 1990s there was a predominant drive towards market and civil society autonomy throughout most American societies. In the 2000s the trend is towards a stronger state presence. In the long term, it might be more sustainable to try to balance these political forces.

## The 2020 vision for Brazilian social investment

The underlying question for Brazilian private social investment is how to continue developing and professionalizing the sector, and at the same time make new resources available for thousands of CSOs which were created and sustained in the last twenty years by sources that are either leaving the country or being refocused into new kinds of action.

During 2009, GIFE conducted a participatory planning process with its network leaders to build a ten year vision for the private social investment sector in Brazil. This process was still underway when this article was concluded. The main results were planned to be presented in the 6th GIFE Congress on Private Social Investment – Visions for 2020, in Rio, in the first week of April 2010. Around a thousand participants were expected at the reunion, one of the largest of the Brazilian third sector.

The GIFE Vision for Private Social Investment in 2020 consists of three main axis, or objectives:
- Social legitimacy and relevance
- Thematic and geographic scope
- Diversity of social investment

The first axis is related to the more traditional activities of a foundation association or support organisation. To build legitimacy and relevance for social investment practices in society, the sector has to improve its managerial and governance models, to articulate its actions with other social actors in the field, to measure the impact of its different programs, and to communicate these activities in a clear way to all stakeholders.

The second axis deals with the present concentration of Brazilian social investment in some thematic areas – such as education, culture and youth – and in specific regions of the country, usually nearer to where the wealth is produced – like São Paulo and Rio – than where it is most needed, such as the north and northeastern regions of Brazil.

The thematic and geographic concentration of Brazilian social investment is due in great part to the predominance of corporate philanthropy in the country. This happens because of the legal framework that gives more incentives for these corporations, and to the fact that most of Brazilian businesses are still run by their founding families – so these tend to operate their social investment through their business and not through a family foundation or institute.

Corporate philanthropy, even the most sophisticated and social justice-oriented, has a very palpable limit – the brand. It is rare for a corporation to get involved in polemic causes or in social actions that might generate any conflict. So the main tendency is to invest in consensual fields, such as education and culture, rather than in potentially riskier themes such as human rights, corruption control or rural land property.

The NGOs related to more polemic issues have been funded in the last twenty years either by the government or by international cooperation – which, as demonstrated above, is moving out of the country. Today there are very few resources available for watchdog organisations in any field. The structural sustainability challenge for civil society organisations in Brazil has been striking especially those which deal with more complex issues of social justice and develop their work in regions where there is less visibility for the investment's results.

The main viable solution for this concentration of social investment in more consensual themes and richer and more visible geographical regions is its diversification in the country. Brazil has some of the most interesting and innovative corporate social investment experiences in the world – and needs to continue developing this field, which has been contributing significantly to the qualification of certain public policies in the country, notably education. But only a more diversified sector, with new family, community and independent foundations, can make resources available for other social issues and regions.

This diversification of philanthropy has already been sparked by the emergence of family foundations and the creation of some independent thematic funds that invest in projects ranging from human rights and environment to gender and race relations. The first phenomenon has to do with the rapid development of Brazilian businesses, which are globalizing and professionalizing, with many of them going public through national and international stock exchanges. Recently one of the main Brazilian cosmetic industries went public, introducing its three owners into the Forbes ranking of billionaires; a year later, two of these three billionaires created their own family foundations.

The Kellogg Foundation's exit strategy from Brazil is to leave a multi-million endowment to fund NGOs with programs linked to race relations. Kellogg is also partnering with the Ford, Oak and AVINA foundations in the recently created Brazil Fund for Human Rights – also with an endowment-building, long-term strategy.

The approval of new legislation for non-profit organisation endowments could have a very significant effect on the diversification of Brazilian social investment – which at present depends on yearly budgets and fundraising procedures. There is also a need for a revision and qualification of the present practices in the funding of civil society organisations by the state.

If in the next ten years Brazil is able to implement actions to achieve these three overall objectives, it might in 2020 have a more relevant and legitimate social investment sector, which invests its resources in a wider range of themes and geographic areas, including other countries, through a diversified assortment of sustainable philanthropic institutions.

MARIA ALICE SETUBAL

# 21 Brazil

## COMMUNITY PARTICIPATION AND LOCAL DEVELOPMENT: THE WORK OF THE TIDE SETUBAL FOUNDATION IN SÃO MIGUEL PAULISTA, SÃO PAULO

*"Individuals need to be made aware that they, as citizens, are responsible for their own communities."*

This statement was made in the 1970s by my mother, Tide Setubal, when she founded the Municipal Volunteer Group, which works in the São Miguel Paulista region, on the eastern side of the city of São Paulo.

When discussing philanthropy, I always make reference to my mother as a source of inspiration behind the establishment of the Tide Setubal Foundation. When my father Olavo Setubal was the local prefect, she dedicated her time to promoting human values. The aim of her work was to bring public authorities and the community together to catalyse social change, a pioneering concept in the times of standard welfare programmes which focused on low income communities in Brazil.

The inspiration which led us to follow in her footsteps goes back to the Christmas of 2004. After a conversation with my brothers, I decided to compile stories about my mother and her thoughts for publication in a book. The idea was to enable my children, nephews and nieces, who had never met her, to see the strength of her personality for themselves through the many accounts given by people who lived and worked with her. I started an in-depth reading of her many diaries. Her notes and thoughts showed me just how much real concern she had for human development.

The book went on to be published for the family, and the stories it told inspired a journey around São Miguel Paulista to resume her work to contribute to local development and the empowerment of the community. As a result of this first visit to São Miguel Paulista, in 2005, the Tide Setubal Foundation was set up with this mission as its goal and its work based on the principles of justice and social equality.

Located on the eastern outskirts of the city of São Paulo, in 2006 São Miguel had a population of 379,000 people, and very little in the way of infrastructure and public services. For example, to give the reader a clearer understanding of the conditions in the city, the United Nations Human Development Index (HDI) is 0.843 for São Paulo and 0.451 for São Miguel Paulista. Yet at the same time, its heritage includes the seventeenth century Saint Michael the Archangel Chapel, the oldest in the State of São Paulo. A real, intangible sense of heritage can also be observed in the inhabitants who are proud to belong to the region. Research which we conducted, with the aid of the inhabitants, showed that 56 percent are satisfied with life in the neighbourhood. Commerce is cited by 58 percent as a positive point, especially for ease of access and diversity. Education was highlighted by 41 percent as a positive point in the region, mainly because of the number of schools and kindergartens. Safety, however, was perceived as being the most negative aspect in the region, followed by health care at 23 percent and lack of leisure spaces at 21 percent.

We started field work in 2006 with the aim of inspiring, encouraging and motivating local communities. It is within these communities that the institution seeks to improve the quality of life and to build and/or strengthen the act of citizenship. This commitment is clearly outlined in our mission statement and in the vision of the Tide Setubal Foundation.

## The mission of the Foundation

*"To contribute to the sustained development of a given place through the social empowerment of the community so as to achieve an improvement in the quality of life and the enhancement of citizenship."*

## The vision of the Foundation

*"To be recognised by the community, government authorities, civic leaders and other institutions in civil society as a vital partner organisation in the attainment of sustainable development of the regions in which it acts."*

The Foundation's mission and vision are rooted in the following principles:
- Construction of a fair and supportive society, working on the basis of the democratic and participative inclusion of all members of society
- Respect for different customs, habits and cultures
- Promotion of culture, tradition, experiences and the customs of the community; and
- Promotion of voluntary work

The source of inspiration for the four principles above was the social work of Tide Azevedo Setubal and they have acted as the guidelines for all the relationships and activities of the Tide Setubal Foundation since it was founded. They succinctly express the commitment of the institution to design and carry out its actions in a participatory manner and with a view to promoting the culture and experiences of the community in which it works.

A statement of principles has become an imperative in today's world, even for profit-making organisations. The greatest challenge, however, is to apply such statements in an effective manner in the day-to-day activities of an organisation, especially in relation to the community.

## Working at the local level

Local territory is the basic starting point and focus for the work of the Tide Setubal Foundation. The Foundation's programmes are based on diverse theories which define local territory as the area where social, economic and political relationships take place. It is an area which is alive and in which inter-subjective and communicative relationships coexist, and is a place overflowing with memories and meanings.

Within such a definition, each local territory contains elements that are at the same time local and "global". Local traditions are shaped by global influences, but are always based on their own unique characteristics which are built within a specific local context of values, ways of being, working and relaxing – in essence, each local territory has its own culture.

The option to use a broader meaning to define local territory, and this new context of social architecture taking place on the periphery of large metropolitan areas, results in an enormous challenge for the Tide Setubal Foundation: when implementing our projects, how do we take into consideration the "bigger picture" when addressing local issues? Being "local" in a global world could indicate a sign of need, especially for economically disadvantaged areas or for the outskirts of large cities which are areas with less mobility.

With this in mind, when carrying out its work, the Foundation places emphasis on local skills and production, but is always aware of the interaction of the location with the varied and multiple facets of globalisation. These facets include language, the cultural industry and the process of standardisation, all of which create norms, remodel local habits and tie those habits to globally accepted behaviours within the different aspects of life.

Based on our mission statement, guiding principles and general objectives, this is our Plan of Action for the two year period of 2008/2009.

- Propose and participate in forums, meetings, events and debates which focus mainly on the topic of sustainable local development and the empowerment of highly vulnerable communities.
- Promote and participate in inclusion/expansion in the media of the topic of sustainable local development and the empowerment of highly vulnerable communities.
- Consolidate and expand partnerships, especially with schools, universities, companies and local authorities.
- Develop, systematise and inform on actions and working methodologies which favour the autonomy of local and community leadership.
- Promote discussion on what a Community Foundation is and mobilise local partners and community representatives to help establish such an organisation in São Miguel Paulista.

## Our definition of local development

Development can be thought of as a process through which wealth is generated and social relationships are oriented to meet the needs of people, for the achievement and expansion of their potential and for the extension of their freedom. Development is therefore a social and individual phenomenon.

As such, we can see that development is a process which seeks to improve human life and citizenship, a term which we interpret as meaning the comprehensive attainment of human rights, or in other words, civil, political, social and general rights.

From this general framework, three central values are employed for development – substantial equality, freedom and democracy. The adjective "substantial" is used in a different way to the formal/legal meaning of these values. We recognise the importance of the legal guarantees behind rights, such as, for example, formal freedom. However, development will only be effective if those rights are evident in the real life experiences of individuals and groups. For example, freedom will only be substantial if it is in fact experienced by individuals who are allowed to make their own choices and decisions. Substantial freedom is understood to mean the expansion of the capability of people to orientate their own lives based on their needs, their values, their desires and their potential.

Substantial equality is understood here to mean equality of access to the resources of life (material and symbolic) and to the social relationships which are necessary for people to undertake their life projects. This understanding of equality takes into account the possibility of the diversity of ways of life and the assertion of individuality. As this definition accepts the diversity and the development of individuality as values, it does not seek under any circumstances to standardise forms of living and thinking.

Substantial democracy is another key value. It refers to the participation of society in decisions which concern all those involved. It therefore implies, among other things, criticism of the concentration of power in a limited number of people as well as the mobilisation of people and/or partners for the ratification of decisions already made; the promotion of mechanisms which guarantee that different voices and interests will be heard; and the promotion of contra-power mechanisms.

Traditional Orchestra during the CDC's Popular Culture Meeting

## The challenges of citizenship in Brazil

One of the characteristics of citizenship in Brazil is that, in our country, social rights preceded civil and political rights. Under authoritarian and/or populist governments, a number of social rights were expanded while the channels of participative democracy were restricted.

This political history has had numerous consequences. It was through this history that our state was formed, based on creating property, serving specific interests and providing welfare. It was also through this history that the groups of society were created which are dependent on the choices of the person in power and/or the numerous bodies which lie between the ordinary person and public power.

At the same time, as this tradition weakens political participation, it also promotes the political leader who shows himself or herself to be determined and with a strong personality, capable of taking charge of the wheels of power and acting with "political will".

One of the more visible faces of social inequality is the shortage of necessary supplies and services. In areas suffering from poverty, the weakness of the public policies which universalise rights allows the appearance and replication of practices for serving specific interests and providing welfare. Because of this, instead of creating widespread rights, the necessary supplies and services appear as though they were a personal gift, a favour which must be paid for through political ratification and/or the vote. Socioeconomic inequality and the weakness of public policies provide the social basis which makes the serving of specific interests and welfare possible and gives them meaning.

Therefore to counteract our political history, we believe that it is important for a strong and duly empowered civil society to exist. This strengthening of society and the consolidation of public democratic life is important for the establishment of local development because, as local communities gather power, they increase their capacity to demand public policies which create rights for all and demand a guarantee of their levels of income, two important aspects of development in our society.

We also believe that the state has an important role in the promotion of development. We are in favour of the strengthening of civil society and also in favour of the strengthening of the presence of the democratic state in the lives of people. From our point of view, the state has responsibilities and has the power to intervene. These are characteristics which are specific to the state and which cannot be transferred to other agents in society. It is the state's responsibility, for example, to coordinate public policies and create universal rights.

For these motives, the Foundation seeks to act in cooperation with other agents in civil society and with public power, respecting the limits and the responsibilities of each of the actors.

Development has to take place on the ground. The Foundation opted to work on the outskirts of São Paulo and more specifically, in São Miguel Paulista. It is well known that the centre-outskirt relationship in city of São Paulo is complex. During the twentieth century, various centres were formed in the city, in addition to the main centres, the Old Centre, Paulista Avenue and, more recently, the Faria Lima-Berrini axis. Examples of places which play a role of regional centre are the Parish of Ó, Santana, Vila Maria, Tatuapé, Penha, Santo Amaro and São Miguel Paulista, among others. Each of these regional centres has its own immediate peripheries; in each of these areas there are regions of greater poverty and, in many of these regions, islands of wealth.

Similarly, in the central area of São Paulo, there are regions of poverty and concentrations of slum tenements and favelas. However, it is also important to understand the specificities of the regions in which work is carried out and their complex relationships with the city in order to avoid a simple generalised view of a specific outlying area.

Despite acting locally, the Foundation does not seek to restrict itself to local goals and problems. The Foundation's mission refers, above all, to a city project and, in a broader definition, to a project for society.

If we recognise that we are social beings, we should also recognise that an accentuated reduction in the freedom of some social groups and the consequences of inequality and the lack of democracy affect not only those groups but also society as a whole and each of us individually.

Therefore, work on the outskirts of the city of São Paulo is not just a job for someone else. Nor is it an altruistic action by someone without any problems. Work on the outskirts is just the opposite; it is part of an intervention in response to problems which affect everyone. It is an intervention in the city for the city. In turn, an intervention in the city can be seen as an intervention in broader terms affecting a wider society, such as the Metropolitan Region, the State or the Country.

Development is a process which takes place over time and, as such, it has a duration and rhythm. Development will be effective if conditions exist which allow it to take place and which will continue to exist in the future. In essence, development has to be sustainable.

The term sustainability can be seen in different ways. These include environmental sustainability, economic sustainability and political-administrative management sustainability.

One of these more modern ways of defining sustainable development refers to its environmental aspects. The debate on sustainability started in the early 1970s, springing from concerns relating to the environmental impact caused by the growth in the market economy.

Therefore, an environmentally sustainable society would be one in which the expansion of human potential would allow future generations to continue to develop. In other words, the development achieved by one generation would not impede the development of following generations.

Sustainability can also be seen from an economic viewpoint. Development would be economically sustainable if it found ways of obtaining the resources it requires to produce and transform without harming environmental sustainability.

The term sustainability can also include the political and administrative management of the initiatives which seek to promote development. An undertaking is politically and administratively sustainable when its participants possess the resources, capabilities and knowledge they need to provide the project with continuity and to transform it in line with requirements.

## The multi-faceted character of development

Development cannot be reduced to just one facet, but rather a range of facets. They include the environment, with a sustainable relationship with natural resources and healthy conservation, with spaces which promote and stimulate social relationships; humanising sociability, which strengthens social relationships and which recognises needs and potential; and health, with a guarantee of conditions so that people can enjoy a long and healthy life, both physically as well as on a psychological and social basis.

In a broader definition, education, another essential factor, is a series of practices which societies establish to transmit to their children the knowledge which is considered important for life. Other aspects of development include access to cultural heritage which is socially valued, along with the establishment of conditions that allow the cultural heritage of different social groups to be brought up to date and integrated into both the present and future.

One of the important aspects – and the condition *sine qua non* – for development is the economic aspect. It refers both to the right to creative and humanising work as well access to the necessary goods and services for what is considered to be a dignified existence, along with the realisation of the needs and potential of people. Finally, participation in the decisions which affect the life of the wider group must take place in order for people to recognise their dreams, their projects and their expectations.

## The Foundation and its work in São Miguel

When we arrived in São Miguel, our idea was not to position ourselves as all-knowing or to implement a ready-made formula. We sought the opinions of local leaders, non-governmental organisations (NGOs), local inhabitants, young people, teachers and public authorities, from a perspective of getting to know local requirements and, above all, to start their story by establishing a relationship which is orientated around their work – to work with the community and not for the community.

Although the name of Tide Setubal was not unknown in the region, as there is a school, a hospital and a community club which bear the same name, our proposal to act in a new way brought with it a challenge; the challenge of being "welcome".

Very often, we were received in a hostile manner. Meetings were scheduled but did not take place, work was initiated but did not continue, and proposals for collective action did not obtain the involvement of those who were to be our partners. We saw this attitude as being born out of adherence to tradition. The resistance was towards a new way of acting, a model which sought participation, transparency, communication and collective decisions as opposed to actions which seemed to be guided by a specific person. Moreover, vulnerable communities are used to "receiving" support only during times of elections, without continuity, and to feeling as though they are being used as assets.

With our proposals for change and the desire for real participation and articulation from the people, we always explained our position stating, "Look, the Foundation is here to stay, the Foundation isn't leaving." We had the distinct feeling that they wanted us to leave – that they wanted us to give them money and then leave. We saw this attitude mainly in those who felt that they were the owners of the spaces, the desires of the community and even the territory itself.

The change in this attitude and the established position on the ground started as we managed to achieve our project goals. Firstly, we opted not to have our own headquarters. We chose to invest in the improvement of a community club's infrastructure, a public space operated by the São Paulo Municipal Department for Sports.

As well as carrying out reforms, we also decided to manage the Clube da Comunidade (CDC) – Tide Setubal in partnership with the Brazil Recreation Association, a local organisation. Faced with the community's observations and under close scrutiny, we expanded a proposal which was initially only sporting in nature and aimed specifically at football. We started projects in which girls could also have their own place at the CDC. In a community almost entirely dominated by males, we implemented the Menina Mulher Project (a project focusing on girls and women) which aimed to discuss and reflect on topics such as sexuality, drugs, work, citizenship, the body and family, among others.

We expanded the sports project to include other sports. Football also took on a new perspective through the inclusion of a discussion group at the end of matches to analyse team work, respect, health and citizenship, among other topics.

Cultural programming, which also initially faced resistance and lack of participation, gained ground with a proposal to set up a community commission responsible for jointly drawing up a monthly programme. This commission was expanded and transformed into a consultative council which was responsible for decisions relating to the community club and its management.

Families were also brought into the scope of service through the Family

Action Programme, in partnership with the Municipal Department for Development and Welfare.

In the same way we arrived at the House of Culture and Citizenship, another place in São Miguel, but located in the Jardim Lapenna neighbourhood. Here, we also invested in joint action with the local organisation – the Jardim Lapenna Friends' Society. In this case, we encountered a very strong local leadership which was at times welfare driven and at other times interest-driven.

Our relationship with this organisation symbolises how challenging it really is to establish a partnership. The approach we used here is used in all the Foundation's partnerships. Establishing a partnership means integrating into institutional cultures which are very often totally different and learning how to hear what others have to say. The declaration below shows how this local leadership defines its partnership with the Foundation.

> *"And I learned with the team, with the Foundation. I started . . . to get better . . . I heard them, that I am a good student, and that I was learning. Today . . . the Foundation has also transformed my knowledge, my life, my way of being. I learned to live with people . . . live with people because that's the way it is . . . when you work with a lot of people sometimes, you do not know how to deal with a lot of people, to live with a lot of people, to live with people. This you acquire if you want to learn. Today, all our work . . . the people who are with us, the children who are here learn a different style of education, being in the company of people because the Foundation brought this to us through the professionals, the technicians."*
>
> José Nário Pereira do Santos, presidente da Sociedade Amigos do Jardim Lapenna

Since its inauguration, the House of Culture and Citizenship has been reformed twice, with the expansion of the space where activities for young people and adults take place. The young people participate in projects for community communication at the *São Miguel no Ar Centre*, for music and musical instrument care at the *ArteCulturAção Centre* and in debates and themed meetings on what it means to be young at the Youth Centre. The adults are in training and information programmes to help improve their quality of life on the Family Action Programme. There are also courses on generating income at the School Culinary Workshop and an expansion of skills provided through access to reading at the Reading Point, in partnership with the Municipal Department for Culture.

The direct action projects form one of the lines of work on the ground for local development and the empowerment of the community. It is our hope that they can become local centres, creating greater institutionalisation for the region, and that they are sustainable, managed by the community itself and that they have direct contact with local inhabitants.

Another important role, part of the relationship of credibility established with the community, is that of articulating and mediating in local issues. Here, we are involved with public authorities, with local inhabitants and leaderships in the "Our East Zone Movement", which seeks to discuss and demand changes to improve the quality of local life. Within one of our groups, a proposal to revitalise the São Miguel Municipal Market was made, a space which has become run-down by time and under use. We also took part in the project to restore the Saint Michael the Archangel Chapel, the oldest in the city.

Youths at the São Miguel public schools visit the Tide Setubal CDC Book Fair

*"I feel the arrival of the Tide Setubal Foundation in the São Miguel region has been very important because it has brought a perception, and perhaps I will not say a model, but a type of management, of organisation, which up to now people did not know from an NGO perspective, and I feel this to be important. The Brazilian state is still a state which excludes and which is not very participative from the point of view bringing people together, hearing from them what they think would be important for the whole city. I think that this is a challenge for us in São Paulo, São Miguel, Brazil. I really think that this is a challenge."*

Eduardo Dantas, local leader and public school teacher

In the course of four years of work, it is possible to see that the current scenario has new dynamics. The credibility of actions has walked hand in hand with a persistence to build together in transparency, in financial correctness, and in the clarity of objectives. Our non-political posture has legitimised and expanded our role and mission to contribute to local development.

Our next steps will be to build a Community Foundation experience in the region. In Brazil, this type of action has been undertaken in small municipal regions and also in rural communities. The challenge is to implement a fund which can invest in actions which drive development.

MICHAEL SELTZER AND KAREN MENICHELLI

# United States
## EMERGING TRANSPARENCY AND ACCOUNTABILITY PRACTICES AMONG NORTH AMERICAN FOUNDATIONS

*Until quite recently philanthropic foundations were shielded from public oversight. They operated beyond a veil of privacy long defended by founders, their families, and the fiduciaries appointed to oversee them. Foundation trustees regarded their endowments as private domains for which they were accountable to no one. Over the last forty years, however, that veil has been gradually lifted, an inch or so at a time, sometimes voluntarily and occasionally under threat of government regulation.*

Mark Dowie (2001), *American Foundations*, Cambridge: MIT Press

With the continuing economic turmoil in financial markets, the global movement to make public and private institutions more transparent and accountable has reached new proportions. It is therefore not surprising that charitable foundations have also found themselves the object of keen-eyed regulators, the media and the public. The recent foibles and transgressions of some donor institutions have fueled a new clarion call for reform.

For example, a scion of one of Boston's most prominent Brahmin families informed the Boston Globe that he had paid himself more as a trustee of his family foundation one year than the foundation had paid out in grants due to the expenses of his daughter's wedding.[1] That same year, the chief of the New York State Charities Registration publicized a "baker's

---

1 Boston Globe staff writers (October 9 2003) "Some officers of charities steer assets to selves", *The Boston Globe*

dozen" list of family foundations that regularly flaunted state and federal oversight regulations. Under such circumstances, it was not surprising that the field of U.S. foundations would draw renewed Congressional scrutiny.

In the United States, in June 2004, Senator Charles Grassley (Iowa-Republican) and chair of the Senate Finance Committee convened hearings on charitable giving problems and best practices among both foundations and non-profit organizations.[2] While averting new oversight legislation, the threat of such legislation stimulated a rich new body of accountability and transparency practices across the non-profit sector. Has the era of minimal legal oversight and reporting requirements ended?

## Background

Since their inception in the United States, foundations periodically find themselves in the crosshairs of Congressional committees. In the late 1960s, according to Peter G. Peterson, they were accused of serving as "partisan political instruments", using "bad judgment bordering on folly", and "promoting extreme ideologies both of the left and, to a lesser degree, of the right".[3] Usually, some foundation trustees and chief executives see the warning signs facing their institutions, while others choose to ignore them, and neglect to take timely measures of necessary self-correction. However, in the recent decade, more have taken voluntary steps to demonstrate their willingness to expose their work to the public. Some are driven by a social justice framework that informs both why a foundation chooses to make grants in certain fields of interest but also how it makes its decisions.

Today, transparency and accountability have become nearly ubiquitous terms to describe a variety of public matters in both the for-profit and non-profit sectors. While there is an assumption that all institutions in a democracy have a duty to explain themselves to the public, there is rarely a consensus on whether such actions should be regulated or voluntary.

Sometimes external circumstances push the pendulum in one direction or the other. In the current financial economic crisis, for example, legislators and advocates have advocated measures to increase accountability in the financial services sector. On Friday, September 26, 2008, the chairman of the Securities Exchange Commission acknowledged that "failures in a voluntary supervision program for Wall Street's largest investment banks

---

2 U.S. Senate Finance Committee (June 22 2004) *Charity Oversight and Reform: Keeping Bad Things from Happening to Good Charities* [online], available from the World Wide Web: http://finance.senate.gov/sitepages/hearing062204.htm

3 Commission on Foundations and Private Philanthropy (1970) *Foundations, Private Giving and Public Policy; Report and Recommendations of the Commission on Foundations and Private Philanthropy*, Preface, xii-xiii, Chicago and London: The University of Chicago Press

had contributed to the global financial crisis."[4] In both the business and non-profit sectors, voluntary initiatives are historically floated to preempt government regulation. The most recent collective action by California's largest foundations came in response to California Assembly Bill 624, which would have required large California foundations to report the race, gender, and ethnicity, of its staff, board members, and grant recipients. The foundations instead created a mechanism whereby this information could be made available through voluntary action without governmental oversight.[5]

## Annual reports: The traditional reporting mechanism

For most of the twentieth century, most U.S. foundations did not perceive any responsibility to report to the public. In 1969, foundations were required for the first time to file two annual information returns with the Internal Revenue Service (Forms 990-AR and 990-PF),[6] make them available for inspection to the public, and file copies of the forms with the charity authorities in their state of incorporation. In practice, it was quite rare for any individual to actually request an opportunity to visit a foundation and view its Form 990.

In subsequent decades, larger numbers of foundations chose to produce annual reports. Yet, by 2007, only 8 percent of the nation's 82,000 private foundations reported publishing an annual report.[7]

## Expanding the roster of print and online publications as communications tools

Examples have emerged of foundations augmenting annual reports with other publications to draw in readers and engage them in learning more about their work. Some publish magazines, journals and newsletters.

**The Atlantic Philanthropies**, based in Hamilton, Bermuda, publishes via email and its website a bi-weekly column *(Atlantic Currents)* which provides a platform for its chief executive officer, Gara LaMarche, to

---

4 Labaton, Stephen (September 28, 2008) "S.E.C. Concedes Oversight Flaws Fueled Collapse", *New York Times*

5 Robert K. Ross, M.D. *Bob's Blog*, California Endowment [online] [Friday, September 5, 2008]. Available from World Wide Web: http://tcenews.calendow.org/pr/tce/blog-post. aspx?id=1523

6 Beginning in 1982, U.S. foundations have been required to file only one form, a revised Form-990 PF

7 The Foundation Center, *Foundations Issuing Publications and Maintaining Web Sites, 1997 to 2008* [online] [2008]. Available from World Wide Web: http://www.foundationcenter.org/ findfunders/statistics/pdf/12_fs_fr/2008/reporting/rpub_08.pdf. Based on foundations with at least $1 million in assets or grants of $100,000 or more that also received the Foundation Center's annual survey of the largest U.S. foundations.

talk about the foundation's work and impact. Of late, foundations more commonly publish FAQs about how they operate, how their decisions are made, how to contact staff, and how to submit a proposal. **The Robert Wood Johnson Foundation** (Princeton, New Jersey) has, since 1997, published an annual book series *(RWJF Anthology)* to disseminate lessons learned from its grantmaking.[8] Acting on its responsibility to share information on its impact, the Foundation also generates more than two hundred reports a year about its closed grants. These reports are posted on the website under "Grant Results."[9]

**The Lumina Foundation for Education** in Indianapolis, Indiana, concerned with Latinos' access to and success in education beyond high school, created the Camino a la Universidad initiative which produced an interactive, sharable multimedia report on the research about Latinos and higher education.[10] **The John D. and Catherine T. MacArthur Foundation** (Chicago, Illinois) has experimented with using two or more databases ("mash-ups") to reveal new insights about its grantees. Combining geographic data with text and photos, its website presents a global clickable map of all of its grants.[11]

Foundations are also creating a presence in virtual worlds to engage readers. Second Life, an Internet-based 3D virtual multimedia world, enables its "residents" to interact through avatars that explore, socialize, and participate in group activities. **The Rasmuson Foundation** based in Anchorage, Alaska, decided to use Second Life as a new way of telling stories about Alaska's creative communities. It has created the Rasmussen Gallery of Alaskan Artists in Second Life that enables a global audience to explore representations of the art, music, and video work of Alaskan artists and socialize with others.[12] During his time as president of the MacArthur Foundation Jonathan Fanton gave a speech in Second Life about philanthropy in virtual worlds as part of the Foundation's initiative to explore the impact of digital technologies on learning.[13]

8 Robert Wood Johnson Foundation, *Robert Wood Johnson Foundation Anthology* [online], available from World Wide Web: http://www.rwjf.org/pr/anthology.jsp

9 Robert Wood Johnson Foundation, *Robert Wood Johnson Foundation Grant Results* [online], available from World Wide Web: http://www.rwjf.org/pr/grr.jsp

10 David Brotherton and Cynthis Scheiderer, Brotherton Strategies (September 2008) *Come On In. The Water's Fine. An Exploration of Web 2.0 Technology and Its Emerging Impact on Foundation Communications*, (prepared for The Communications Network) [online], available from the World Wide Web: http://www.comnetwork.org/resources/brotherton_new_media_091608.pdf

11 MacArthur's use of mash-ups to tell its story [online], available from the World Wide Web: http://macarthur.webitects.com

12 See Rasmuson Foundation video on Second Life gallery [online], available from the World Wide Web: http://www.rasmuson.org/index.php?switch=viewpage&pageid=195&highlight=seco nd%20life

13 Speech available on the MacArthur Foundation [online], available from the World Wide Web: http://www.macfound.org/site/apps/nlnet/content3.aspx?c=lkLXJ8MQKrH&b=1142275&conte nt_id={7297F122-C239-471E-BD2F-B1C94B58D190}&notoc=1

## The ascendancy of the internet web-based technology

Starting in 2000, the changing electronic environment provided a new toolbox for foundations to use as many sought to transform themselves into more accessible institutions. Communications became global, instantaneous, and around the clock. The capabilities of the Web created an expectation of openness, sharing, and participation. Pervasive bloggers are publicly scrutinizing everything imaginable and forcing firmly shut doors wide open. At the same time, the social, networked nature of the Web has shifted how people communicate, providing the tools for two-way dialogue instead of one-way broadcasting, allowing institutions to build relationships with formerly passive audiences and to promote understanding of their inner workings.

In the charitable sector, more foundations have put their annual reports and their tax returns (PF-990s) online, have allowed electronic submission of proposals and grant reports, and created e-newsletters. A few have begun to use their websites to stimulate interactivity. By building such relationships (either online or in person), foundations are deriving benefits from the collective intelligence of an online community.

Starting in the late 1990s, foundations began to augment the information that they made available to the public through the creation of websites. By 2007, 2,775 U.S. foundations comprising 13.4 percent of the sector had websites.[14] Annual reports and websites, however, do not generally shed any light on a foundation's intellectual and analytical decision-making framework, theories of change, logic models, and program strategies. Recently, the Ford Foundation, the nation's second largest foundation, added information about its grantmaking strategies in its thirteen fields of interest to its website.

Website audits have helped a number of foundations improve their utility to grantseekers. For example, the Commonwealth Fund, based in New York City, conducted an iteractive process to assess its audience's needs and desires and get feedback on changes it could make in its website. Using staff feedback and user testing, it received suggestions that improved site navigation, search functions, and access to timely content. The Fund is now adapting the site for more user customization.[15]

---

14  The Foundation Center, *Foundations Issuing Publications and Maintaining Web Sites, 1997 to 2008*, [online] [2008]. Available from the World Wide Web: http://www. foundationcenter.org/findfunders/statistics/pdf/12_fs_fr/2008/reporting/rpub_08.pdf

15  Barry Scholl (September 2008) *You Talking to Me? Understanding Your Web Site's Audience*, presentation to the 2008 Conference of the Communications Network

## Ascendancy of Web 2.0 technology[16]

What is termed "Web 2.0" encompasses the newer social features of the World Wide Web – open, participatory, collaborative, networked – which empower the audience to be part of a collective intelligence and content creation, not just the downstream recipient of information. An argument can be made that Web 2.0 epitomizes transparency and accountability by taking seriously the perspectives of audiences/constituencies and involving them in a foundation's pursuit of their mission. Like opening up the boardroom and decision-making process, it offers some tools to expose one's initial thinking, assumptions, and internal deliberations for scrutiny and feedback. It's also a mechanism for bringing in many more diverse perspectives.

The social, networked nature of the Web has shifted how institutions can communicate, providing the tools for two-way dialogue instead of one-way broadcasting, fostering relationships with formerly passive audiences and promoting understanding of internal processes. By building such online relationships, foundations can create and benefit from the collective intelligence of their online community. The **W.K. Kellogg Foundation**, based in Battle Creek, Michigan, hosted an online community forum for four months – "What helps vulnerable children succeed" – to encourage the public to comment on one of its program priorities.[17] It framed the online conversation with several questions rather than leading with its own assumptions. The feedback included some perspectives that the Foundation disagreed with but also points of view it would not have heard otherwise.

Similarly, the **Open Society Institute** (OSI) office based in Baltimore, Maryland, on its Audacious Ideas blog solicits input and suggestions from community members and issue experts about how to change Baltimore for the better. OSI staff elicit blog posts each week, and their postings are open for public comment. Postings have generated loyal readers, as many as twenty-five comments each, and reprint requests from the Baltimore Sun.[18] Similarly, the Robert Wood Johnson Foundation launched a blog called "Pioneering Ideas" for their Pioneer portfolio to solicit novel, high-return ideas that may have far-reaching impact on people's health, the quality of care they receive and the systems through which that care is provided.[19]

---

16  For an excellent summary of emerging practices, see David Brotherton and Cynthia Scheiderer, Brotherton Strategies (September 2008) *Come On In. The Water's Fine. An Exploration of Web 2.0 Technology and Its Emerging Impact on Foundation Communications*, (prepared for The Communications Network)

17  Authors' conversation with Kathy Reincke, communication associate, W.K. Kellogg Foundation, October 14, 2009

18  *Open Society Institute* [online], available from the World Wide Web: http://www. audaciousideas.org/

19  *Robert Wood Johnson Foundation* [online], available from the World Wide Web: http:// www.rwjf.org/pioneer/

**The Daniels Fund** in Denver, Colorado, provides scholarships to college-bound high school graduates and non-traditional students in Colorado, Wyoming, New Mexico and Utah. It wanted to communicate more effectively with its scholars and encourage a community of Daniels Scholars, so it created a community on Facebook after assessing the utility of email and listserves.[20]

**The Skoll Foundation**, based in Menlo Park, California, has created "Social Edge," an online community by and for social entrepreneurs – philanthropists, non-profit professionals, and the business community. Every week, the site hosts two online discussions led by experts in their field and encourages comment. The site offers video podcasts of interviews with global social entrepreneurs, which are also distributed through YouTube, iTunes, and Yahoo! An Expert Advice tab permits registered members to ask burning questions of fellow members about their social benefit venture. The resources wiki invites contributions from members. The site provides community guidelines for "creating a congenial, professional community" and "fostering a useful and spirited discussion."[21]

## New standards of practice

Over the last ten years, the US-based **Council on Foundations**, regional associations of grantmakers, and a body of fifteen major foundation leaders have all developed new standards and a body of informed practices. Such practices encompass decisions regarding grantmaking, management, operations, communications, legal, finance, mission and strategy, personnel, public policy, and governance. A few, such as the **Minnesota Council on Foundations**, have made agreement to its set of principles a requisite of membership.[22]

**The Community Foundations of Canada** developed a self-assessment tool for staffed private foundations. Subsequently, in the United States, a similar questionnaire was developed. It drew on generally accepted good accountability practices from a number of sources, including the Forum of Regional Associations of Grantmakers, Independent Sector, Aspen Institute, Association of Charitable Foundations-UK, Minnesota Council on Foundations, Council of Michigan Foundations, and the Donors Forum of Chicago. The tool is thirty-four pages long, and includes 233 questions covering grantmaking, management, operations, communications, legal,

---

20  Brotherton and Scheiderer, ibid

21  Social Edge, *Social Edge Community Guidelines* [online], available from the World Wide Web: http://www.socialedge.org/about-us/site-information/community-guidelines

22  *Minnesota Council on Foundations* [online], available from the World Wide Web: http://www.mcf.org/mcf/about/principle.htm

and finance, mission and strategy, personnel, public policy and governance practices.[23]

Despite these efforts, widespread changes in "retail" practice are scarce and disjointed. While some foundations are testing new strategies and policies, the sector lags behind overall. Watchdog organizations, such as the **National Committee for Responsive Philanthropy** (NCRP) and others, dispute that foundations are making a sufficient effort to earn the public's confidence in their stewardship of charitable resources. NCRP notes that "foundation dollars are partially public dollars because of the tax exemptions foundations are granted, and thus policy makers and the public are entitled to expect exemplary practices. Put differently, foundations are the ethical stewards of the partly public wealth entrusted to them, rationalizing significantly increased transparency and accountability to the public at large."

In addition to the work of philanthropic infrastructure organizations, other various external stakeholders, including journalists, federal, state and local officials, and grantseekers themselves, have created the impetus for foundations to change their practices.

Some foundations resist making more public information on their grantmaking strategies. They argue that if they do so, applicants will simply play back the language that a foundation uses in their proposals rather than state their case in their own language. They have also used that argument as a rationale for not using a common application form, which was introduced by many regional associations.[24]

Others do not ascribe to this line of reasoning. They have produced an emerging body of new practices worthy of consideration. These efforts have ranged from grantee perception reports, whistleblower policies, expanded websites, and in a few cases, ombudsmen.[25] Some, such as the creation of audit committees, have been deemed best or preferred practices by such bodies as the National Panel on the Nonprofit Sector, convened by **Independent Sector**.[26] Others can be found in the set of standards

---

23 See for instance "Using the Accountability Self-Assessment Tool with Your Members" on the Forum of Regional Grantmakers website [online], available on the World Wide Web: http://www.givingforum.org/s_forum/search_new.asp?CID=35&DID=42

24 Madeline Lee, during her tenure as executive director of the New York Foundation, spearheaded this effort in New York.

25 Although many professions are using gender-neutral terms like fire fighters, those in the ombudsman field have not followed suit in changing the name of their profession. The word ombudsman has Nordic roots. According to the Office of the Irish Ombudsman, "The word ombudsman is not gender specific. It is a Swedish word meaning "agent" or "representative" of the people" Although the word is historically gender-neutral, some writers have replaced ombudsman in speech and writing with "ombuds officer", "ombudsperson", or just "ombuds", or "ombud," or, in cases where the person in question is a woman, "ombudswoman".

26 *Independent Sector* [online] [October 12, 2004]. Available from the World Wide Web: http://www.independentsector.org/media/sector_panel.html

that the **National Committee for Responsive Philanthropy** released in 2008.[27] All of these efforts fall squarely in the category of what might be broadly described as self-regulation, as opposed to increased government regulation and oversight. At the same time, there is a larger body of practice outside organized philanthropy. In fact, governmental units, universities, newspapers, hospitals and even businesses have been experimenting with different strategies for a longer period of time than foundations. And more lessons might be gleaned from the practices of these institutions.

## The ombudsman experience

In the late 1990s, twenty Northern California foundations that awarded grants in San Mateo County instituted a pilot two-year ombudsman program. Six elders in the field from around the country, selected with an eye towards race and gender diversity, were enlisted to serve as ombudsmen. Grant applicants and grantees alike were invited to call a toll-free number where they would have the opportunity to select which ombudsman they would like to contact. Strict confidentiality was enforced. The ombudsmen would provide feedback to the participating foundations, while the names of those who contacted them were not disclosed.

The ombudsmen often found that some complainants did not understand how foundations operate; in these cases, the ombudsmen educated the callers about the ins and outs of general grantmaking. They also looked for patterns in calls to be able to detect and report back to all of the foundations, and to the particular foundation whose practices were called into question. The practice was discontinued after a few years since few organizations chose to avail themselves of the service.

A few examples exist where a single foundation has created an ombudsman position exclusively for its own institution. The Open Society Institute created the position of ombudsman in the 1990s to provide a channel for grantees and applicants alike to seek redress when they believe that there has been an "abuse of authority." Its president, Aryeh Neier, referenced how a government ombudsman operates in Sweden.[28] He or she is responsible to the Parliament and makes an annual report to it. Its purpose is to provide a channel for grantees and applicants alike to seek redress when they believe that there has been an "abuse of authority". Generally, three to five complaints are raised and investigated each year. While the number of complaints has been modest, they have been important in a number of countries where OSI operates through intermediary

---

27  See National Committee for Responsive Philanthropy, *Criteria for Philanthropy at Its Best*, (2008) [online], available from the World Wide Web: http://www.ncrp.org/index.php?option=com_ixxocart&Itemid=41&p=product&id=47&parent=6.

28  Interview with Aryeh Neier, President, Open Society Institute, August 5, 2008.

organizations. The current ombudsman is a highly respected individual in Central and Eastern Europe. She will investigate individual complaints, and provide a report to OSI's president. In addition, she makes an annual report to the OSI board of directors.

Drawing on his past university experience, after assuming the presidency of The John D. and Catherine T. MacArthur Foundation, Jonathan Fanton instituted an ombudsman-like procedure. He designated a senior member of his management team as the point person to receive complaints. When applicants feel that they have not been treated with fairness and professional courtesy at any time, they are invited via the Foundation's website to bring their concerns to the pertinent staff member, the vice president in charge of the program or area, or to the president. Alternatively, they can contact the appropriate member of the management team. The Foundation website provides a phone number and an email address[29] to reach him. It is his responsibility that any matter is understood and addressed, where appropriate, by relevant Foundation staff and he reports back to the concerned party. If asked, he will keep confidential the name and organization of the person submitting the feedback. His office is not a second venue, however, for the appeal of decisions about grant proposals. In actual practice, the number of actual complaints that are received is relatively modest.

## Other current practices to foster feedback

Besides these scattered examples of ombudsmen, foundations have utilized other mechanisms to solicit input from their core stakeholders to inform their work and further their impact and effectiveness. They have utilized a variety of approaches to accomplish this aim, ranging from simple applicant surveys to commissioning grantee perception reports.

A common mechanism is an annual grantee perception report on dimensions of communications and interactions between grantees and grantmaking staff that the **Center for Effective Philanthropy**, based in Cambridge, Massachusetts, conducts at the behest of individual foundations.[30]

Since the early 1990s, **The Otto Bremer Foundation**, based in Minneapolis, Minnesota, has elicited "real-time" feedback from its grant applicants. It polls each grantee and declined grant applicant on their experience with the foundation.[31] One week after its bimonthly trustee meetings and the mailing of transmittal and declination letters, a thirteen-question survey form with a stamped self-addressed envelope

---

29  concerns@macfound.org.

30  *The Center for Effective Philanthropy* [online], available from the World Wide Web: http://www.effectivephilanthropy.org/assessment/assessment_gpr.html

31  www.ottobremer.org

is mailed to both newly minted grantees and applicants whose proposals have been declined. The anonymous responses go directly to one of the foundation's three trustees. Over the years, the response rate has averaged about 50 percent. Roughly one-third of respondents provide concrete feedback, while the remaining two-thirds are merely complimentary and discounted. Working with the information technology professional staff, the trustee presents a quantitative and qualitative quarterly report for both board and staff discussion. Results are used to remedy individual problems that might arise and to improve the Foundation's overall practices. In a given year, the Foundation processes approximately 1,200 requests for support, and awards 32 million dollars in grants.

Employees of **The David and Lucile Packard Foundation** examined their procedures around six phases of the grantee relationship: proposal and selection process; development, oversight and evaluation; implementation of work; final reporting/evaluation of grantee work; renewal process; end of project/relationship. The review process yielded four standards that clearly set out what grantees could expect from program staff.

## Enhancing the communications capacity of grantees

Part of a foundation's transparency rests on the ability of its grantees to tell their story in the context of the foundation's work and funds. The Robert Wood Johnson Foundation, based in Princeton, New Jersey, has long invested in building its grantees' capacity to communicate with one another and the larger public through annual meetings of its national programs, technical assistance workshops on communications strategies and tactics, and the creation of an extranet (NPONet) to offer research and convening resources to grantees. Others have followed its leadership, especially as it related to the new tools of the Web.

The **Overbrook Foundation**, based in New York, New York, commissioned an online survey and discussion groups about how the Foundation and its US-based human rights grantees are using the Web and might better take advantage of its 2.0 tools. The survey found that most grantees used the Web largely as tool for information dissemination not interactivity to engage constituents. Discussion groups showed that exhaustion and fear lead groups to ignore new tools. The report recommends that the Foundation should:
- serve as hub of information and resources for grantees;
- help grantees increase their technology capacity;
- use provocative questions and expectations in application process to stimulate grantee thinking; and

- convene discussion groups of grantees to share technology strategies.[32]

The foundation has undertaken this final recommendation.

## Creating civic meeting grounds

A barrier to transparency is the relative isolation in which foundations operate, since they are careful to keep a distance from the non-profit community from which grantees are drawn. Foundations have sought to bring down that barrier by providing opportunities for staff to interact with grantees and provide feedback on its accessibility, strategies, and decision-making.

One way to make the foundation more approachable is to provide access to its space. **The Bauman Family Foundation**, based in Washington, DC, offers its conference space for grantee activities as well as holding program meetings to which grantees are invited. **The Daniels Fund**, which serves Colorado, Wyoming, New Mexico and Utah, makes its Denver meeting spaces available free of charge to non-profits. **The Meadows Foundation**, based Dallas, Texas, owns and operates the twenty-two acre Wilson Historic District, a non-profit office park that preserves Dallas' Victorian structures and encourages the non-profit community to work collaboratively in rent-free space.

## Using expert outside teams, committees, and peers to inform work

On its fifth anniversary, the **Doris Duke Charitable Foundation**, in New York, New York, formed several panels of "wise persons" to act as visiting committees charged with the task of evaluating the Duke Foundation's past grantmaking and advising on future directions. It recruited six to eight distinguished leaders from Duke's four grantmaking fields – the arts, environment, medical research and child-abuse prevention, and invited them to look at both current and future plans. Staff prepared extensive briefing materials on the Foundation's strategies and initiatives and provided a *rapporteur* for the all-day meetings. The resulting reports were first presented to both staff and trustees and are being used to tailor Duke's strategies, including how to make better use of funds.

The Packard Foundation's Conservation and Science Program sought

---

32 Allison Fine (September 2007) *Web 2.0 Assessment of the Overbrook Foundation's Human Rights Grantees*, The Overbrook Foundation [online], available from the World Wide Web: http://www.overbrook.org/resources/opn/pdf/Overbrook_Foundation_Web2point0_Report.pdf

expert input on its evolving strategy to address nitrogen pollution from multiple points of view, including environmental, scientific, technological and economic. For two months in 2007, the Foundation created and ran a wiki, or web page that enables collaborative work through user contribution or modification of content, as a way to gather this input. There a network of people contributed, discussed, and built on ideas of others.[33]

## Archiving foundation history[34]

The ultimate accountability of foundations is to history. Some foundations have begun to create archives or to donate their papers to research libraries, and thus to open their records for examination by historians and other scholars. Foundation record-keeping practices vary widely. They are changing rapidly in our digital world, with fears growing that foundation stories that ought to be told are being lost.

When foundation records have been well maintained, made available in archives, and wisely used by scholars, the story of US foundations – their creation, their decision-making, their relationships with other organizations and government, their successes and failures – has been well told. Their activities have been discussed in books and articles on the early public health campaigns of American philanthropies, the reforms of medical education and nursing, the transformation of higher education and schools for African-Americans, the assault on global hunger in the Green Revolution, and the role of foundations in the public policy debates of the 1960s, 1970s and 1980s.

Foundation archives have taken various forms. Some are housed within foundation offices; some collections are in libraries or university research centers. One of the most exemplary archives was opened in 1975 to house the papers of the Rockefeller family and the many philanthropic institutions they created. **The Rockefeller Archive Center** now holds the records of all the major Rockefeller-funded organizations as well as those of the Russell Sage Foundation, Commonwealth Fund, Markle Foundation and a growing roster of foundations and non-profit organizations, including the Foundation Center and Council on Foundations. Over the years some five thousand scholars from around the world have made use of these collections, writing about every field touched by American philanthropy. Documenting foundation activities, preserving the records, and making them accessible for future generations of researchers places accountability

---

33 *David and Lucile Packard Foundation* [online], available from the World Wide Web: https://nitrogen.packard.org/default.aspx

34 This section is based on a communication on (September 25, 2009) with James Allen Smith, Vice President and Director of Research and Education, The Rockefeller Archives Center

in a different context. It suggests that foundations should be accountable to future generations, especially to those who want to learn from their predecessors and to carry on with their work.

## Conclusion

Will foundation self-regulation efforts preempt new state and federal government reform efforts? To what extent will foundations across the globe also experience greater demands for transparency and accountability? We can't answer these questions with any assurance. However, we can say with certainty that due to the size of foundation assets, the notoriety of some donors, and their growing numbers, there will always be legislators and charity regulators prepared to draw attention to those institutions that fail to maintain the public's trust.

The actions described in this chapter certainly illustrate how foundations can make a dual and robust commitment to transparency and accountability, and that such measures will also translate to a higher degree of effectiveness and impact. Their practices certainly are an illustrative menu of what efforts donors can put in place to advance public understanding of the overall field of organized philanthropy. At the same time, they also enrich our understanding and broaden our interpretation of accountability and transparency.

In some cases, transforming charitable institutions will simply require modifying existing practices while in other instances, a sea change in organizational culture will be necessary. Such measures are more likely to take root if they are made integral to a foundation's *raison d'être* rather than simply add-ons. The rewards are a higher degree of intellectual exchange about theory, practice, initiatives and strategies among a larger community of internal and external stakeholders, and a renewed confidence in the value of organized philanthropy.

*The research for this chapter was made possible through the support of The Atlantic Philanthropies.*

# United States

## GLOBAL PHILANTHROPY IN AN AGE OF TURNER & GATES: COLLABORATION, SCALE AND LEVERAGE RE-IMAGINED

### Introduction

Ted Turner's 1 billion U.S. dollar (USD) gift to create the United Nations Foundation in 1997 (the largest ever at the time) ushered in a new era of philanthropy:

- An era that, over the last twelve years, has been marked by the availability of unprecedented levels of philanthropic dollars from self-made new industry billionaires.
- An era marked by living and "engaged" mega-philanthropists, who define their giving through an aspiration that problems can be solved, not merely studied – a mindset wholly in line with their rise, resources, and global influence.
- And, finally, an era where mega-philanthropists are striving to achieve goals so large that humility is a prerequisite to progress and, thus, there is also the recognition that money alone cannot solve problems – people and partnerships do.

The concept of "partnership", forever in the parlance of philanthropy as a means to define relations between grantor and grantee, has evolved to an impressive new level of reality. Philanthropic partnerships today are becoming increasingly commonplace between governments, businesses, individual philanthropists, non-governmental organizations (NGOs) and foundations, all of which desire a more literal and outcome-oriented leveraging of one another's ideas and resources, along with an admission of gaps that others can help fill.

Such a partnership approach is the core of what the United Nations Foundation was created to do, and (once again) places Ted Turner "ahead of the curve". Ted knew from the beginning that his resources, large as they were, paled in comparison to the issues the world faced. Joined by a distinguished, ambitious, but also frank and humble global Board of Directors, Ted helped create an institution that embodies the concept of aligning big ideas, big resources, and all parts of society to, in their own way, contribute to big outcomes. The United Nations Foundation also made a significant operational decision early in its implementation to create a dedicated partnership capacity with staff able to play a proactive facilitative role. I was fortunate to be a part of this.

Ted Turner and UN Foundation Board members lay a wreath at the Hiroshima memorial in 2006. From left to right: the late Ruth Cardoso (Brazil), Emma Rothschild (UK), Ted Turner, Muhammad Yunus (Bangladesh - the day after he won the Nobel Peace Prize), Timothy E. Wirth, President, and Ambassador Hisashi Owada (Japan)
Photo: United Nations Foundation

In the sphere of global philanthropy and partnership, Bill and Melinda Gates obviously also come to mind. On a scale never before seen, the Bill & Melinda Gates Foundation has the opportunity – and the challenge – of defining a role for private philanthropy, influence, and convening that is entirely different from, yet on the scale of, governments. The Foundation has had the foresight to appreciate the value of being nimble, but of greater importance, recognizing the limitations of acting alone. Thus, beyond the undeniable scale of its grant making, partnerships form a central role in the development of its program strategies and their implementation. I am fortunate to have been a part of this organization as well.

Through the lens of my time at the United Nations Foundation and the Bill & Melinda Gates Foundation, this chapter seeks to reflect, informally, on the evolution of global philanthropic partnerships over the last ten years. It is in no way exhaustive or researched, it is merely perspective drawn from personal experiences and observation.

## 2001-2004

### Few players

The United Nations and Gates Foundations' early association with global public-private partnerships reflect a strategic choice far more common today than during 2001 through 2004. The emphasis of this strategic choice is a departure from looking at a foundation through the lens of what it can accomplish based solely on its available budget. It instead focuses on understanding a major problem and recognizing that sustainably solving that problem will involve far more than money. Effective public-private partnerships that involve a foundation tend to position the philanthropic value proposition firmly beyond finance; they tend to formalize capabilities historically tapped in a more *ad hoc* fashion, such as being co-designers of programs, joint planners, neutral conveners, or influencers of public and political will.

While there were several domestic U.S. examples of foundations participating in public-private partnerships and in playing a role beyond finance, fewer examples existed internationally during this time. Most international philanthropy activities were financial in nature and were defined either through efforts of a small number of big institutional foundations, or through private giving by individuals through large charities. The most notable exceptions are the Rockefeller and Ford Foundations. In the 1960s, Rockefeller and Ford partnered to incubate and finance the first "Green Revolution", which helped alleviate starvation for millions in developing countries. Separately, Rockefeller's provision of its Pocantico and Bellagio facilities as neutral forums led to the formation of various global partnerships, including the International AIDS Vaccine Initiative (IAVI).

## Limited capacity to execute, skepticism across sectors

In the early 2000s, the capacity to execute – to literally manage global cross-sector partnerships – was inhibited by a lack of skilled facilitators versed in the languages of business, government (donor and developing country), civil society, philanthropy, and multilateral institutions; or even proficient in a subset of these categories. As a result, opportunities for collaboration were missed because of misunderstood intentions and general skepticisms. Informal perceptions I often heard included:

- *Government and multilateral institutions* were intellectually interested in philanthropy partnerships but viewed most funding of this nature as too small to take seriously (beyond receiving a check to add to their own existing programs). They were skeptical of the true impact potential;
- *Philanthropists,* though intellectually understanding leverage and problem solving, did not want their ideas or money to be drowned out by big public money and bureaucracies in all places and at all levels;
- *Business leaders* understood the regulatory importance of governments on their businesses, but as more companies looked strategically at what they might do that was both good for them and development, they tended to see bureaucracy before best practice;
- *Multilateral organizations* liked the idea of new money, but with limited capacity, they needed to focus on where the "big money" was – the public sector. This was combined with an inherent skepticism of the motivation of business, and a limited view of philanthropy's impact value (i.e., only looking at it from a finance perspective). It would take some time before I observed a meaningful number of multilaterals taking a broader perspective of the convening and advocacy opportunities provided by philanthropic or corporate leadership; and
- *Civil society* often distrusted business, saw multilaterals as bureaucratic and inefficient (unless they were already receiving huge resource flows), and were often frustrated by philanthropy seeking engagement in program planning and design, versus "just writing the check".

## Seeds of opportunity

Leadership from across sectors played a vital role in the evolving landscape of public-private partnerships during this period. Bill and Melinda Gates and Ted Turner chose leaders with skill sets from outside the philanthropic community. Patty Stonesifer's leadership of the Gates Foundation did not draw on a career in philanthropy, policy, or development, but from her private sector experience and leadership.

Tim Wirth's leadership of the United Nations Foundation, while surely leveraging his knowledge and engagement on many global issues, more importantly tapped his political acumen as a former U.S. Congressman and Senator, and his lead representation of the U.S. in various bilateral and multilateral settings. Patty and Tim's experiences and backgrounds brought a different perspective to global philanthropy and, with that, new ways of looking at and defining collaboration.

In the other sectors vital to building global partnerships, a diverse cadre of leaders had also begun to emerge.

In the multilateral space, leaders who understood the importance of such partnerships but also the structural challenges their bureaucracies faced in order to successfully engage:

- Kofi Annan, who, as Secretary General of the United Nations (and in 2001 was at the height of his influence), called for cross-sector cooperation to, among other things, establish a "war chest to fight diseases of poverty" (this led to the creation of the Global Fund to Fight AIDS, Tuberculosis and Malaria). He moreover strived to make more operational the ability of bureaucracies like the UN to partner with others, creating the Global Compact and the UN Fund for International Partnerships;

- Gro Harlem Brundtland, former Prime Minister of Norway and then head of the World Health Organization (WHO) beginning in 1998, leveraged WHO's partnership on polio eradication with Rotary International as a reference point for WHO to give a home to numerous cross-sector platforms such as Roll Back Malaria, Stop TB, and other initiatives. Many of these would take years to gain vitality, yet nevertheless reflect tangible commitments to multi-sector cooperation;

- Richard Feachem, as the first head of the Global Fund to Fight AIDS, Tuberculosis, and Malaria, had to work hard to preserve the Global Fund as a true public-private partnership. The early years were difficult, as the value proposition of business and philanthropy, as well as providing developing countries and civil society seats at what normally would be a governance table of donors, were groundbreaking in their importance but also their complexity.

Heads of State, such as President George W. Bush, Prime Minister Tony Blair, and President Jacques Chirac, all endorsed new vehicles for cross-sector engagement, and developed special projects that cut across sectors. Examples range from Bush's creation of the President's Malaria Initiative and the Global Development Alliance at USAID, to the Blair-led Africa Progress Panel, to French leadership on the creation of UNITAID, which initiated a levy on French airline tickets to generate funds to buy

AIDS, tuberculosis, and malaria medicines for developing countries.

Simultaneously, a cadre of new and expanding NGOs identified gaps in knowledge and cooperation between the sectors, and worked to fill them. Noteworthy examples include the Global Philanthropy Forum, Center for Global Development, Debt Aid Trade Africa (DATA, which eventually merged into the ONE Campaign), the Schwab Foundation for Social Entrepreneurship, the Acumen Fund, the Charities Aid Foundation, and the Japan Center for International Exchange.

Corporate social responsibility (CSR) was also beginning its migration away from pure community relations, charitable giving, cause marketing and product donation, to being used by innovative CEOs as a potential strategic lever for doing good while also building future markets. Bill Roedy of MTV International, Antony Burgmans of Unilever, Hiromasa Yonekura of Sumitomo Chemical, Lord John Browne of BP, E. Neville Isdell of Coca Cola, are important examples of leaders in the movement but they are not alone.

There are some terrific examples of CSR from this period, including: the Coca-Cola Company providing, in-kind, its distribution capacity for the delivery of polio vaccines and HIV prevention tools, Sumitomo and Exxon Mobil's transfer of technologies to help establish the first manufacturing facility in Tanzania for long-lasting insecticide treated bed nets to prevent malaria (A-Z, Inc.), and Unilever producing detergent sachets as a sustainable enterprise product for the poorest. In parallel, important ventures like the Global Reporting Initiative, UN Global Compact, and the UN Environmental Programme's Division of Technology, Industry, and Economics were starting up, and aiming to provide companies with sustainability minded planning tools and cross-sector partnering platforms.

The World Economic Forum, at its 2003 Annual Meeting in Davos, also began to raise the profile of public-private partnerships for development. The Forum's Global Health Initiative and the United Nations Foundation co-developed an early publication on the subject, and hosted a working "side-event" that, to everyone's surprise, was moved to a larger venue because of the interest.

In sum, much was beginning to happen and actors from every sector were emerging. Experience eluded most in terms of how such partnerships could work, and as mentioned above, few within each sector had staff with true experience – or a dedicated mandate – to pursue cross-sector cooperation. Within the foundation community in particular, "partnership" still tended to look like a standard grantor-grantee relationship, or foundations essentially pitching each other on projects.

A vignette on the subject: I recall a major institutional foundation president calling around to raise 100 million USD for new investments on a specific global health issue. This president wasn't necessarily looking to build a joint plan or single partnership, but to optimally raise money for that foundation's plan or to just bundle existing investments others had made to help reach the number around which a press release had already been issued.

Similar challenges were also faced by the private sector during this early period. A second vignette: at the Global Fund for AIDS, Tuberculosis, and Malaria board table, the "private sector" board seat was routinely pilloried for being of fictional value. And, candidly, in those early days management of the seat often felt (to me) more like a trade association block than a contributing partner. What did the waters look like:

- On the corporate side the message was, "Don't ask us for money, it will never be as much as a government; if you (Global Fund bureaucracy and NGO community) can't figure out a way for us to make in-kind donations that would save you purchasing hundreds of millions of dollars of drugs that we could just give, it only underscores your bureaucratic mindset and penchant for wasteful spending";
- Civil society suggested companies were trying to use product donation as a distraction from not giving even minimal funding, and moreover suggested that corporations were really trying to establish market reliance of poor people; and
- On the government side the message was, "You (the private sector) bring no money to the table, this is an exercise in public relations or market building."

Such acrimony has subsided for the Global Fund (mostly). Some of this has been offset by efforts like (Product) RED, which has provided nearly 140 million USD to the Global Fund and raised massive global public awareness around AIDS in Africa to undergird political will; Chevron has also become a corporate champion with a 30 million USD donation; many companies provide significant and routine corporate technical assistance to the Fund; and a private sector leader, Rajat Gupta of McKinsey & Co., assumed the Chair of the Fund from 2007 to 2009. On a different but related note, a 650 million USD commitment from the Gates Foundation to the Fund, coupled with regular technical assistance and constructive board representation by the Foundations' constituency, helped philanthropy avoid similar venting about resource levels.

In short, and putting a more positive spin on it all, this was a messy creation phase for international partnerships, including philanthropy's role in the space. A phase where establishing the idea of blending capacity from different sectors would take more time. A phase where few had concrete and successful experience with such partnerships, and where translating the diverse lexicons of business, government, multilaterals, civil society and philanthropy had only just begun.[1]

One very exciting and early international public-private partnership during this period was developed between the Gates Foundation, Rotary International, The World Bank, and facilitated by the United Nations Foundation. The idea was to use private capital to buy down (convert into a grant) highly concessionary World Bank loans, made to countries that normally would not be willing to seek a loan for global public (health) good due to competing priorities. The leverage for the private capital was nearly 3:1. A single 100 million USD loan could be converted into a grant with approximately 38 million USD of private capital paying off its "net present value" (the value of the 100 million USD in today's dollars, were it to be paid over its full thirty-year term.). It took nearly three years for a trust fund to be created with 50 million USD in private capital (25 million USD from the Gates Foundation and 25 million USD from Rotary International). The funds gave the assurance necessary for countries to take out the loans, knowing they would be written off their books. Approximately 140 million USD in such loans were able to be made from that initial trust fund of 50 million USD, and the model has since been replicated and expanded.

## 2005-2007

### Building bridges between sectors

Philanthropic engagement in global cross-sector partnerships experienced prolific growth during this period. More and more, skepticism around such partnerships was giving way to outcome driven and tangible examples of successful initiatives. The following are just a few examples:

- *The International Finance Facility for Immunization (IFFIM).*
  Building on the interesting, but in many ways modest World Bank "buy-down" example, the Gates Foundation championed with the United Kingdom, France, Norway, Spain, Italy, Sweden and the Global Alliance for Vaccines and Immunization (GAVI), a mega-finance initiative to scale funding for immunization programs. The IFFIM concept was to float bonds on the capital markets to

---

1 It is vital to acknowledge that pre-existing this period were some hugely impactful global public-private partnerships, especially in the global health sphere. Notably, though, institutional philanthropy did not play material roles in these initiatives until this period. Most of these efforts derive from service organizations, such as Rotary International and its partnership with the World Health Organization and UNICEF around polio eradication. One major exception would be the 1999 Gates Foundation investment of 750 million USD to create the Global Alliances for Vaccines and Immunizations (GAVI). From the outset GAVI was structured to become a major public private partnership, and, today its board comprises over twenty five representatives.

generate immediate funding for immunizations that would be paid back through future aid pledges. Implied in the idea was that dramatic reductions in vaccine preventable deaths today would free up future aid resources for other priorities. The first bonds issued in 2006 generated 1 billion USD in available capital, all of which flowed to GAVI for implementation. Of that, a 139 million USD grant was provided to the Measles Initiative through the United Nations Foundation. This was one of several critical finance injections that culminated in a reduction of measles death by 74 percent globally (and by 89 percent in Africa) between 2000 and 2007.[2]

- *Energy Future Coalition*. Energy policy has been (and remains) a politically divisive topic in the U.S. and the choices made domestically will have an undeniable impact globally. Founded in a non-partisan manner by Tim Wirth, C. Boyden Grey (Chief Counsel to President George H.W. Bush) and John Podesta (Chief of Staff to President Bill Clinton), the Energy Future Coalition brings together business, labor, government, academia, with environmental groups as a means to break the gridlock that has prevented substantive advances in energy policy in the U.S.. Their cross-sector work has been critical in promoting energy efficiency policy shifts and in the development of the Smart Grid concept within the U.S..[3]

- *Mobile Technology for Development Initiative*. Sponsored by the United Nations Foundation, Vodafone Group Foundation, and in close partnership with WHO and World Food Programme, this initiative connects the human and financial resources of the world's largest mobile phone provider with the UN and others to accelerate progress for health surveillance, data collection, and use of mobiles to improve emergency response. It has also spawned creation of a global "MHealth Alliance", which is fast becoming a central platform to bridge all sectors behind the application of mobile technologies to improve health and reduce deaths.[4]

- *The Sustainable Tourism Initiative* harnessed on-line travel company Expedia's power within the hotel and cruise "supply chain", with UNESCO and the UN Development Programme's policy setting and program development in the areas of World Heritage protection and eco-tourism economic development. Together during a three year period they aligned to form the World Heritage Alliance, a unique

2  *The International Finance Facility for Immunization* (IFFIM) [online], available from the World Wide Web: http://www.iff-immunisation.org

3  *Energy Future Coalition* [online], available from the World Wide Web: http://www. energyfuturecoalition.org

4  *Mobile Technology for Development Initiative* [online], available from the World Wide Web: http://www.unfoundation.org/global-issues/technology/mhealth-alliance.html, http://www.vodafone.com/start/foundation.html

cross-sector partnership that educates the traveling public through the Friends of World Heritage campaign and develops sustainable tourism best practices for investors and vendors that today include dozens such as Fairmont and the Mandarin Hotel Groups.[5]

- *The Global Water Challenge* was created to help foster improved knowledge sharing and collaboration between sectors around sustainable solutions for access to clean drinking water and sanitation. Incubated at the United Nations Foundation with the leadership of the Coca-Cola Company and UNICEF, the Global Water Challenge brought together leading sectors interested in water and sanitation together to build new partnerships, share best practices, and raise global visibility and support for the issue.[6]

- *(Product) RED* was launched in 2006 by Bono and Bobby Shriver. (RED), a for-profit company, licenses its brand to iconic companies, generates fees to support its business, and negotiates a percentage of profits from partner company (RED) product lines to be donated to the Global Fund to purchase antiretroviral drugs to treat AIDS in Africa. For some this model is controversial because companies are not merely donating money. I view it as a highly creative approach to sustained revenue for the Global Fund, in a manner core to the competency of the private sector. The nearly 140 million USD (RED) has generated (at no material cost to the Global Fund) in its three years of life is to me the best response to the critics.[7]

- *The Nike Foundation's commitment to adolescent girls* could have merely reflected its modest grant making budget and some public relations activities. Instead, the foundation's leadership quickly saw the power of blending Nike's brand and voice with the UN, partners and policy makers in the U.S. and across the world to launch the Coalition for Adolescent Girls. The Coalition has shown the importance of adolescent girls and mothers to development.[8]

There are myriad other examples, but these initiatives are diverse and representative of progress during this period. Leaders from all sectors began moving past the rhetoric of "whether", "how", "what's in it for whom" or credit, and just moved forward to establish workable – if often messy – operating models. Models that tapped the capacity and voice of the many, to achieve the scaled outcomes none could achieve alone. It is truly exciting

---

5 *The Sustainable Tourism Initiative* [online], available from the World Wide Web: http://www.worldheritagealliance.org

6 *The Global Water Challenge* [online], available from the World Wide Web: http://www.globalwaterchallenge.org

7 *(Product) RED* [online], available from the World Wide Web: http://www.joinred.com

8 *The Nike Foundation's commitment to adolescent girls* [online], available from the World Wide Web: http://nikefoundation.org

what can happen when the playing field changes from "those with the ideas pitching those with the money", to donors, implementers, and influencers on one side of a table, and the problem to be solved on the other. For global philanthropy and cross-sector partnerships, this was the period where "the pitch" began to give way to cataloguing resources, and then organizing those resources towards problem solving.

Buy (RED) save lives logo

Nevertheless, there is still a long way to go, especially within the philanthropic community itself, which lacks investment in partnering capacity between one another, let alone across sectors.

Ted Turner with Al Gore. Taken at the United Nations in New York
Photo: United Nations

## New catalysts

Also adding to momentum during this period were important new contributions of voice. President Bill Clinton created the Clinton Global Initiative (CGI) in 2005, I believe as a reflection of an increasing impatience with meetings that declare victory by bringing players to a forum. CGI's emphasis on participants making social and philanthropic commitments, and in most cases as part of collaborations with others, gave affirmation to the idea that it is worth the effort – that you get more done – when you align different resources to big problems. Philanthropy has routinely been at the center of many CGI commitments, and in fact, the above referenced Coalition for Adolescent Girls was born at the first CGI meeting.

During this period, President Clinton and his foundation were also prolific at sharpening their own sights – and his influence – to help launch major cross-sector partnerships. Some of the largest include the Clinton-Hunter Development Initiative and Clinton Climate Initiative. Clinton-Hunter, for example, was central to a groundbreaking deal with two pharmaceutical companies that drastically reduced the cost of second line antiretroviral drug prices in Africa. The philanthropy community was (and remains) a vital partner to the President, providing him and his ideas with seed resources, intellectual capital, and knowledge of "who to convene" on a given issue. I suspect many of the Clinton Foundation's largest accomplishments have quiet philanthropic partners in the middle of the fray.

## 2008-today

Today the landscape is rich with examples of important public-private partnerships. Across the sectors, there may be lingering skepticism about cross-sector partnerships, but largely the issue is less about whether they should exist but rather how to make them more efficient and available to a wider set of actors. Specific to the *philanthropic* sector, participation in cross-sector partnerships has grown dramatically, but remains inhibited by (at least) two factors:

- The lack of dedicated partnership capacity within foundations to foster cross-sector collaboration, as a systematic competency akin to program expertise; and
- The lack of sufficient structures within foundations, or via intermediary services, to make foundation knowledge, partnerships and investment opportunities widely available to individual philanthropists or other foundations (large and small) that would participate but for easier access to information and engagement opportunities.

On the former, during my years at the United Nations Foundation I knew of no other foundation that had a partnerships division paired with its program colleagues. Successful foundation participation in cross-sector global partnerships was (and largely remains) the result of the *ad hoc* and enterprising program officer, or because an issue is the personal priority of a foundation leader. As noted at the outset of this chapter, foundations have rhetorically (and often in practice) viewed grantees as partners. But, at a time when the role of foundations is – for those who wish it – increasing well beyond finance, and at a time such as now, when partnerships really are driving large scale progress, philanthropies would do well to formalize partnership capacity rather than rely on the hope that program officers will bring this totally different set of skills to the table.

In similar vein and to the second point, foundations (especially larger institutional philanthropies) committed to global issues have yet to formalize capabilities to share knowledge and proactively create doorways for others who, with the data, might join in. The current global recession only underscores the necessity for those of us working on global issues to increase the "size of the tent". Large foundations have yet to meaningfully make information (strategies, grants, partnerships, monitoring and evaluation information) available passively, let alone staff themselves to provide proactive and qualitative engagement with prospective philanthropic partners. Like our successful grantee "partners", until foundations are willing to proactively inform and encourage others, the field will remain fragmented and new investment in global issues will be slower than it needs to be.

At the Gates Foundation, within the Global Health program, I helped build a small program to make our activities more available to others who self-identify an interest in our work. It is a careful balance, but we have quickly learned that, for active or prospective donors to global issues around the world, from Argentina to Abu Dhabi, to any number of private banks or other philanthropy intermediaries, that merely by making ourselves available we are able to help others make investments or join partnerships they would not have otherwise. The Foundation will continue to nurture this area carefully.

## Conclusion

Bill and Melinda Gates refer to themselves as "impatient optimists". Ted Turner routinely tells a story of advice he received from Jacques Cousteau during a period when he was down about the state of the world – the summary of which is that *humanity has to keep trying*. Embracing partnerships proactively but also thoughtfully, where different competencies are truly aligned for big outcomes, is in reality the only way sustained progress at scale will ever come.

The philanthropic community has a unique luxury to direct itself – to paraphrase Warren Buffett, "...the challenge of philanthropy is that it doesn't face a market test". Partnerships certainly need not be for everyone and ultimately every donor has to decide what type of role and impact they wish to make. In the area of global philanthropy, as large and visible as some of the largest players are, the needs, simply put, dwarf them. Thus, the community of philanthropists today who are dedicated to global causes have a special responsibility to proactively encourage others, and to make it easier for others to enter the space by making knowledge and opportunities for partnership readily available.

My hope is that during the next ten years, global philanthropy will focus on institutionalizing the capacity to partner and share knowledge with one another and other sectors; and that we advance the trend in humility that positions foundations and their financial resources both as an equal "input" to what other sectors will do, and where a wider lens of foundation "resources" take full hold.

# 24 United States
## STORIES OF GIVING
## "ASKING, SAYING YES, SAYING NO"

*"Thank you for your good letter. It's not as hard as you may think. Of the three angles to money dealing, asking, saying yes, saying no; asking and saying no are terrible. Saying yes is a great pleasure, and I thank you for giving me the opportunity to do so."*

Carol Bernstein, 1972.

The following are stories from an engrossing and varied career as staff, executive, volunteer and/or board member in nonprofits and the giving which supports and encourages them. I focus on several foundations and comment on others. Each relationship has taught me something of value about the huge diversity in the field and the broad range of possibilities available to serious donors who have the commitment and vision to practice giving in an open and engaging society.

In this chapter, I welcome the opportunity to share this learning, just as I hope to gain in return from the experience of others. Three themes have been common threads among the projects and donors I've been working with. First, a commitment to social justice for the less resourced, for those subject to discrimination or exclusion, against violence, torture and the death penalty, second, for the conservation of the planet and its resources and third, for the most part, a determination to use resources during the life of the donor rather than storing up excess capital for others to distribute in the future.

Currently I am a Senior Advisor at The Atlantic Philanthropies, and a board member of The Overbrook Foundation, The Sister Fund and several other small family foundations and PATH, a Catalyst for Global Health. For the seventeen years from 1984 to 2002 I was Executive Director and Vice President at The Aaron Diamond Foundation and The Irene Diamond Fund. My start in philanthropy was at The DJB Foundation (DJB) in 1973, following work in the nonprofit world and with donors from the mid-1960s during the civil rights movement in the United States and while opposition to the Viet Nam War was growing.

As executive director of the six-thousand member Business Executives Move for Vietnam Peace (BEM) from 1969 to 1971, my job was to head their organization, based in Washington DC, to coordinate lobbying Congress and the federal administration and speaking and organizing programs across the country. The mission was to help end the Viet Nam War by adding the credibility and influence of business executives to the broader peace movement. A measure of BEM's limited success was the inclusion of its founder, executive director and many members in senior positions on President Nixon's "Enemies List", revealed during the Watergate investigations in 1973. Vice President Spiro Agnew dismissed BEM as "an effete corps of impudent snobs" just before he was forced to resign when deep corruption was uncovered in his prior position as Governor of the State of Maryland.

The broader peace and justice movement presumed incorrectly that BEM had a great deal of money, easily available. Projects often came to us to seek funding for anti-war work. Rather than turning them away it was possible on occasion for me to match up requests for help with one or another of the business executives who were willing to give money personally.

Several BEM members had foundations. Carol Bernstein, quoted above, was the widow of Daniel J. Bernstein, one of those executives. Carol, in 1973, hired me to help her, and her second husband, W.H. "Ping" Ferry with their personal giving.

It was civil rights and anti-Viet Nam War activity that brought me from Catholic seminary to college studies at night while working at a New York City law firm and to complete an undergraduate degree in 1967 at the University of Rochester while working during the day on the Eastman Kodak production line. The move to Rochester in the fall of 1964 came just as racial and class frustrations for blacks and other poor, non-white Americans had boiled over into riots in inner cities, including Rochester.

That fall also saw the U.S. presidential election which pitted pro-war conservative Barry Goldwater against Texan Democrat Lyndon B. Johnson, "the peace candidate" who astonished many including me as a first time voter, as he turned into a determined pro-war President. Work in the inner-city race struggles in Rochester and in the increased opposition to the war led me to protest the war loudly and to refuse cooperation with conscription for it.

My refusal resulted in prosecution and conviction for violation of the Selective Service Law and an appeal of that conviction to the Supreme Court of the United States. This took over four years and resulted in a two year prison sentence which began in July of 1971 after the Supreme Court ruled against me.

During the ten months and twenty-five days that I did serve at a minimum security federal prison I taught school to other inmates, had breakfast everyday with "ex" major politicians and high level mafia and mingled with a two-star general, small-level embezzlers and drug dealers, as well as other draft resisters and a group of Jehovah's Witnesses who refused conscription on non-political religious grounds. I was adopted as a "prisoner of conscience" by Amnesty International and later became active in its United States section, on the board and as chair in 1981 and 1982, visiting many other national sections in Europe and Asia.

All of this was a very rich experience which enabled me to look at life from a perspective that differed greatly from what I knew before and took for granted. I learned to avoid easy labels and preconceived notions and to try to meet people as they present themselves and to listen to them, learn their stories and earn their trust. Work on the Kodak production line and time in prison provided a graduate education in real life. It was important to discover the experience of others, and while attempting to be non-judgmental, to appreciate the struggles and hardship of individuals – and their families and communities – amidst the "opportunities" of post-World War Two American society.

Later, in the nonprofit and foundation worlds, I found that there were many similar "disconnects" between what is presumed about democratic opportunity and what may be achieved by hard work and the race, class and power components to which most of us do not pay enough attention.

The three pivotal "angles to money dealing" to which Carol Bernstein referred: "asking, saying no, and saying yes" define the emotional, intellectual, ethical and practical aspects of "philanthropy", whether it be giving from a foundation or from personal funds or in resources of volunteer time, expertise or sharing in family, community or broader contexts.

The average person of few resources probably shares a higher proportion of what they have with others in need – in the family, community and with strangers – than the affluent "generous".

Most of us on the donor side don't know from direct experience how hard it is to be asking all the time while having the responsibility to balance a budget, hire and retain staff and keep programs active and growing to meet needs. The work I have done and continue to do in organizations as staff, board or a volunteer give me a constantly challenging sense of what is involved in asking and being accountable. In real terms foundation representatives – donors, staff or board – spend most of our time saying "no"; perhaps graciously, sometimes peremptorily or indirectly and often after a long wait. It is much better to say "yes", but important to say "no" quickly, clearly and kindly – with a helpful suggestion or two if possible.

Giving away money and other resources effectively is not easy, but it can and should be a joy and satisfaction to share the burdens and possibilities of others, and so doing build a more just and equitable future.

The importance of focus was an early lesson: no donor can do everything. If you focus clearly about what you are willing to fund, grant seekers do not waste time and resources seeking your assistance. The introduction recently of GuideStar and other web-based avenues for information has eased this process, but it is still a fact of nonprofit life that requests for assistance often receive no answer and funding guidelines seem whimsical when compared to lists of programs which actually get funding.

I do not mean to suggest that there should not be exceptions to normal guidelines. But such exceptions merit explanation or at least classification as "out of program." This may be best done by including a category for non-program, community, discretionary, or "special" grants. Living donors have the opportunity to use their resources formally in a public program, but they may also make gifts anonymously, directly or through intermediaries.

## The DJB Foundation

The DJB Foundation was a modest foundation with a national and global program. It operated in tandem with the donor family's personal giving of deductible and non-deductible support for civil and human rights, efforts to reduce poverty among communities of color in the American South and West; for prison reform and, internationally, for work against apartheid and racial injustice in Southern Africa and for rapprochement with Cuba.

> Daniel J. Bernstein *"...wanted to be generous, but he did not know how to give away intelligently each year as much money as the tax laws encouraged – hence the Foundation, as a holding operation until he had sorted out in his mind what needed to be done. In the meantime, he was earning his living and that of his family in the stock market. When he died, in 1970, he had made a great deal of money, almost six million dollars of which came to the Foundation."*
>
> (Final Report of the DJB Foundation, 1974)

Dan and his wife, Carol, followed their heads and hearts and supported people and programs as they learned from travel and daily experience how often established society and governmental structures left large portions of people out – particularly minorities, newcomers, the rural and inner city poor, and those who raised their voices to protest and complain.

They followed the civil rights movement in the US South and were frustrated that many good ideas, even when turned into law, were not funded sufficiently or were blocked by local politicians who controlled spending. They worked to end segregated housing in their affluent area in Westchester County, where household workers, who could not afford housing even if racial barriers did not exist, had to be "counter commuters" from urban slums, passing their employers who took the train the same morning in the other direction – to Wall Street.

As the Viet Nam War developed and escalated, Dan and Carol saw the raw power of the United States being wasted in violence in a situation where investment in development and support for gradual change would have been preferable and productive. They saw that nationalism was stronger than the mighty forces of colonialism and communism. They listened to the growing opposition to the war on college campuses. Dan financed full page advertisements against the war in major newspapers carrying the message of student leaders. He also supported other efforts, both political and educational, to end the war and redirect resources into development and aid.

Daniel Bernstein died in 1970, forty-eight years old. He left the majority of the money he inherited and made in the stock market to the DJB Foundation and to his widow, Carol. He also left major gifts for continued work against the Viet Nam War and to the Institute for Policy Studies, a progressive Washington based "think tank".

After Dan's death Carol continued the giving they had been doing, both from the DJB Foundation and from personal accounts. But she stepped it up considerably. When we first met, in 1971, she showed me "the money machine" – a battered Remington typewriter and a pile of checks. Her daily activity, beyond caring for a son and daughter, was "unloading the loot" Dan had made so as to help people and ideas make a difference.

Becoming the staff of DJB I joined the "counter commuters" and took the train from home in Manhattan to Scarsdale and collected the mail from "Post Box 657", Scarsdale, New York 10583. Soon I would learn how important that address was to many small social justice, organizing, anti-poverty, anti-war groups across the United States and beyond.

I remember receiving a post card with the plea: "Dear Sir or Madam, Please tell us how to share in your generosity." It was from a newly organized group of wood cutters in the rural South. We advised them about a cooperative association and provided funding to help establish connections and assistance.

Our work day began around the kitchen table over a cup of coffee or tea. The mail would be divided among us three. Large manila envelopes had a part cut off, just enough so the top of the letterhead stuck out. Later, at lunch around the same table or at the dining room table if there was too much paper at hand, the notes we had put down on the envelopes while reading the letters and proposals would be discussed.

Decisions were made. If not of interest, a letter went out that day. If positive and either an immediate need or inappropriate for the foundation, a personal check would be prepared and sent. These personal gifts would range from several hundred to several thousand dollars. Always there would be a short and direct note of appreciation and encouragement; sometimes a suggestion or a mild disagreement, often a tip about another source of funds.

Carol and Ping made careful determinations about what projects fit in the tax-deductible categories set by the Internal Revenue Service. But they were equally content to spend non-deductible "hard money" to support what they believed in, and especially when they could make a personal gift to poorly paid workers or volunteers doing hard work in the trenches.

Grants for larger organizations recognized as "nonprofit and deductible" under the tax law were determined on a quarterly basis at meetings of the four member DJB Foundation board. I prepared and presented the grants "docket". The checks went out the next day.

Carol Bernstein Ferry and Ping, her second husband, felt very responsible about the funds at their disposal. They were determined to distribute them quickly and carefully and scoffed at any suggestion of generosity. "We have more than enough, our children are secure, the world is falling apart and we must do something about it!"

They thought that the DJB Foundation would last ten years, having made the decision not to say "no" because the grant budget exceeded annual income. In fact, the assets lasted only four years and DJB closed its mail box. Carol and Ping had boldly violated what they called "the eleventh commandment of the rich: 'Thou shall not invade principal.'" Over the remaining years of their lives they distributed each year all income and a portion of principal, saving enough to have a secure old age. Ping died in 1995. After Carol's death in 2001, her residuary estate was distributed through the still existing legal entity of the DJB Foundation. Its work over, DJB closed permanently in 2008.

## The Hunt Alternatives Fund (HAF) and The Sister Fund

In 1980 Swanee and Helen Hunt decided to learn philanthropy together. They were the youngest children of the legendary H.L. Hunt of Dallas, Texas. Mr. Hunt had made huge amounts in oil and was known to support very conservative causes. His youngest daughters began to take a different path after experiencing other people's pain, suffering and want through studies and travel beyond the family. They wanted to be seen as agents of compassion and change and they struggled to learn how.

They formed The Hunt Alternatives Fund in 1981 and hired me to assist. HAF was very small at the start but grew as the sisters received larger cash flow from family trusts. An initial focus on support for the chronically mentally ill expanded to broader social advocacy and support for abused women and families. At first HAF was active in Dallas, their home base, and New York City and Denver, Colorado, where the sisters lived. In 1993, the HAF split into two funds, Swanee keeping the original name and Helen creating The Sister Fund, with a focus on women and girls.

Gradually both sisters became advocates for women and their use of resources. Helen and Swanee helped initiate women's foundations: Swanee in Denver and then Colorado, and Helen in Dallas and New York City. They and the other women they worked with aimed to include those with major fortunes, inherited or earned or shared with a spouse, but most importantly, also working women, volunteers and home-makers.

The decisions in the women's foundations would be made by a cross-section of those involved and active, not only major donors. The opinions and work of all were essential. Learning from each other – listening to each other – made all the difference.

The early success of the work was instrumental in the development of women's foundations across the United States and internationally. Swanee Hunt's experience as a donor and advocate helped her as US Ambassador to Austria during the first Clinton Administration, to develop programs to raise women's voices in Central Europe and to get them to the table with men at all levels of the diplomatic and political worlds. She continued this work later at a center she initiated at Harvard's JFK School.

According to an article in the New York Times Magazine, August 23, 2009, Helen LaKelly and Swanee Hunt began an astonishing effort "Women Moving Millions" – which raised in three years 180 million United States dollars (USD) to add to work for women and girls. Helen said, "Women gave their heart, mind, body, intellect, will, blood, sweat, and tears, but not their dollars. Women didn't fund suffrage; now women are funding women. That's historic."

## The Aaron Diamond Foundation

An attorney involved in Aaron Diamond's real estate business introduced me to Mrs. Diamond in the fall of 1984, several months after Mr. Diamond had died suddenly of a heart attack. In the prior winter, the Diamonds, both in their mid-70s, made a plan to activate The Aaron Diamond Foundation (ADF) that they had founded in 1955 but used mainly as a modest "pass-through" for annual giving.

The Diamonds lived simply, compared to the wealth Aaron was building in his real estate business. They made modest gifts for political causes or the arts outside the foundation. But, early in 1984, Aaron decided that his business was just adding up numbers and he and Irene determined to begin returning those several hundred millions of dollars to institutions and people based in New York City where he made the money. The Diamonds chose three focus areas: medical research, minority education and culture. They also requested that the foundation distribute all of its assets within ten years of the death of either of them. As ADF ramped up its activities, Irene became more and more convinced that spending down was the right thing to do. She also made gifts from her own funds alongside ADF and she included in her will a similar provision for distributing her own wealth in a limited time after her death.

First as a consultant and then as Executive Director of ADF, I worked with Irene Diamond to put into action the plan they had sketched. From the start it was clear that AIDS was an area in which the foundation might have an impact. Irene Diamond had enough interest in and knowledge of science to recognize that AIDS was a virus spread by blood, by unsafe sexual practices and by dirty needles. She rejected the homophobic and anti-minority stereotypes which characterized the period and which had delayed medical and educational efforts to understand and protect against the disease. ADF had good advice from medical expert and essayist Dr. Lewis Thomas, former head of Memorial Sloan-Kettering Cancer Hospital, and Dr. Alfred Gellhorn, former Dean of the Medical School of the University of Pennsylvania and an advisor to the New York State Health Department.

We didn't have a preconceived notion that the foundation might play an important role but we hoped it would. We jump-started research – giving established researchers resources for their first work on the AIDS virus. Those efforts produced results that would qualify for federal funding in larger amounts and for longer terms than ADF could ever provide. The concept of a centralized AIDS research laboratory evolved from the observation that many institutions in and around New York City wanted to do AIDS work but did not have the protected lab space and other facilities required for this kind of retro-virus. To make a long story short, we quickly found space in a public lab building, and I devised a plan to have a private nonprofit corporation lease the space from the city.

Thus, the Aaron Diamond AIDS Research Center for the City of New York (ADARC) was incorporated. Early planning and research costs came from the foundation. The building renovation costs came from the foundation and from the city, which leased the space to us for twenty years at one USD per year. Good research results would bring long – term support from government sources and attract other private donors. If the work of ADARC was good it would not have to rely on The Diamond Foundation forever!

The fast track development of ADARC was possible only because of the "spend down" nature of ADF. We were able to use capital to back the plan, bargain with the City of New York, and avoid fundraising or other delays so as to get the work done as fast as the pandemic's pace demanded. ADF's strategy to build a critical mass of young scientists and get them to work paid off in ADARC's 1996 breakthrough in the development of the antiretroviral "cocktail" drug regimen which is helping to extend the lives of people throughout the world who are living with HIV/AIDS.

The foundation made its first AIDS research grants in 1985. The concept of ADARC developed in late 1987 was formalized in 1989, and the doors opened in April, 1991. The initial academic affiliation for the scientists was with New York University Medical School but eventually ADARC settled at the Rockefeller University and its renowned campus clinical hospital.

Mrs. Diamond was a quick study. She and I would meet daily. We were often joined by a scientist or a member of our staff. We had a small and excellent staff. Mrs. Diamond had been a script and talent scout in Hollywood – she worked with Hal Wallis for a number of years. (Her claim to fame was finding the script that became Casablanca!) In the foundation she saw herself as the boss and me as the technical expert. Maybe it had something to do with working through the problems associated with the settling of her husband's estate, but for various reasons we learned to trust each other. That doesn't mean we didn't have our differences; sometimes we argued like cats and dogs. But our scrapping would always end with a laugh, and we'd be back on track quickly.

ADF also had a high-powered board of directors, but one that did not micromanage our activities. In its formal meetings, held four times a year, the board would talk through new ideas, review what we had learned, and approve startup grants and various changes to the program. Remember, these were busy people, and to get them on the board in the first place and then to keep them focused on highly technical, changing fields required a lot of work.

Irene Diamond was not a fan of comprehensive and costly evaluations. First of all, we had a ten-year time-frame in which to accomplish something and we were learning as we went along. It wasn't unusual for us to make a small grant on trial basis and to increase support if the work bore fruit. As a matter of practice ADF granted general support in addition to project support, on the theory that people who were scrambling for the latter should not have to worry about how they were going to keep the lights on. In the case of some of the larger institutions we worked with, it wasn't unusual for us to fund as many as three different projects or programs in addition to providing general support.

Later, as we moved into the wind-down phase, we intensified our work with technical assistance and management groups, and by using our power to convene – usually by bringing people together in our conference room – we did our best to ensure that there were multiple funding streams for many of the projects and activities we supported and to move work into public budgets where possible. It turned out to be a very successful model.

While the Diamond Foundation is known specifically for its work in HIV/AIDS, we had interesting and productive results in other areas, especially in minority education. Aaron Diamond, the ninth child of a poor Jewish immigrant family in the U.S. South knew what it meant to be part of a minority. In addition, he and Irene recognized that the comforts and excitement they loved in New York City was made possible by the labor of minority immigrants of color – those who were often willing or had no choice but to do work the already settled avoided.

Early on, there was some feeling in the board to focus on increasing minority enrollment in prep schools and elite institutions of higher education. But Irene Diamond insisted that ADF attempt to influence the public systems of education to improve the possibilities for all children. We pioneered the "New Visions" schools, which others, including the Gates and Broad Foundations and the Carnegie Corporation and federal, state and local governments are putting hundreds of millions of dollars into around the country. This concept breaks up big and impersonal "factory" schools to create smaller learning modules, often with themes attractive to students. ADF also helped start minority recruitment programs for principals and teachers and collaborated with others to return the arts, which had been eliminated from most public schools during the city's fiscal crisis in the mid-70s, back into the curriculum.

For the culture category, ADF developed a focus on performing arts as a career vehicle for young people in music and dance. Because of Mrs. Diamond's long interest in free speech, personal liberties and human rights, we also developed programs in those areas. After all, how does a society have culture without human rights?

Irene Diamond also made large personal grants outside the foundation to expand minority presence in faculty and students at The Julliard School and she gave 30 million USD over fifteen years to Human Rights Watch.

At Julliard, this effort also included the development of education programs in middle and high schools so that talented younger students would have early training and practice essential to the qualifying exams for admission to the college and graduate work at Juilliard or other conservatories.

And though we initially set out to keep the foundation's AIDS work focused on medical research, we quickly became aware of the problem of AIDS in other settings – for example, children having parents with AIDS or being infected themselves and how people living with HIV/AIDS were discriminated against at school and in the community denied jobs, housing and health care. This HIV/AIDS stigma remains even today and it is not confined to faraway places. We discovered the importance of educating young people and teachers about HIV/AIDS, making possible programs in health education alongside pregnancy prevention. As a result, we quickly moved AIDS as a focus into the education and, later, human rights work. Mrs. Diamond was dubbed "Queen of Condoms" after ADF aided a program for AIDS education and condom availability in the public schools. In retort she said, "I'm a grandmother. We ought to be talking about this candidly. This is a disease that can be avoided, but people have to know how it's transmitted and they have to change their behavior based on the facts."

Mrs. Diamond was the central figure and decision-maker in all that the foundation did. But her role was balanced in that she and I and the staff worked well together and the board respected what we were doing. They understood that this was a ten-year program and that their participation was very important – being a sounding board, generating ideas, and setting policy. They knew they were stakeholders in the foundation's success, but also that they had a different kind of ownership in that success. Almost all of our board members had an active interest in a nonprofit organization as an active volunteer or a founder, but they resisted pitching their own projects to us, unless the projects clearly complemented work we were seeking to fund. That was crucial, and it made it easier for everyone; we were able to avoid the internecine power struggles that frequently develop whenever money, power, and influence are involved.

In the years we worked together Irene Diamond became a strong advocate for the wealthy to give while they were alive and active. She excoriated what she saw as foundation investment pools based in ever expensive offices and lavish travel and benefits. She often brought her own lunch and homemade sandwiches for her guests. She did not like or have the patience for process and long learning curves. She once said to me, "Look, you have youth and time to talk about process. I don't. I'm the fire engine driving your process down the street!!" That impatience was energizing, but at times it cut conversations shorter than they might have been. But you don't get to play the game over. We had an extraordinary effective run that was characterized by a low level of acrimony and a lot of joy and satisfaction.

At times both Mrs. Diamond and I criticized foundations and foundation culture for being insular, overly cautious, and arrogant. To avoid those pitfalls, we tried to listen, listen, listen and learn. We attempted to get into other people's shoes. We'd ask grant seekers to forget about what they thought we wanted to hear and tell us what they needed.

We had our focus and kept to it mostly, but made exceptions when the situation demanded it. We tried to keep things simple and straight forward. We made decisions quickly, especially when we had to say no, and we tried to give helpful suggestions when we did say no.

## The Overbrook Foundation

Returning from out of town one evening there was a message on my answering machine: "Vinny, this is Margaret. Please call my brother Arthur, say 'yes' and call me back."

Margaret Altschul Lang and her brother Arthur Altschul were the two second generation siblings active on the board of The Overbrook Foundation, which was founded by their parents Frank Altschul and Helen Lehman Altschul in 1948. Frank Altschul was an early partner in the U.S. branch of Lazard and went on to lead his own investment house. His wife Helen was a member of the Lehman investment family. Their son Arthur was a partner in Goldman Sachs and active in other investing business.

The Overbrook Foundation had functioned as a family giving instrument typical of its time. Annual grants were made to organizations that the family was involved with or concerned about: colleges, museums, a botanical garden, civil rights efforts, anti-poverty work. But by the mid-1990s assets had grown considerably, as had the third and fourth generations in the family. In addition, Arthur and Margaret were older and had less energy. We had met through mutual interests in human rights and civic affairs. They had sought my advice about funding from Overbrook for work in the HIV/AIDS field.

They asked me to join the Overbrook Foundation as its only non-family member and provide guidance in a transition of authority to the next generations. The ensuing process over several years was an extraordinary careful and open discussion, and learning curve for the family and me. The result was a new structure including the retirement of the second generation, sadly just before both of their deaths, and the election of twelve family directors, four from each of three branches and me as the one "independent" director.

Gradually, a professional staff was recruited and the program mission and focus established, striving, "to improve the lives of people by supporting projects that protect human and civil rights, advance the self sufficiency and well being of individuals and their communities and conserve the natural environment."

## The Atlantic Philanthropies

In 1984 Charles F., "Chuck", Feeney secretly gave his 40 percent share of the Duty Free Shoppers Group to an anonymous foundation he had established in Bermuda two years earlier. Feeney was emulating Andrew Carnegie, sharing the belief that surplus wealth should be given during life to those who will use it well for public benefit. Feeney's feeling is that problems do not wait and that "if I have ten dollars in my pocket, and I do something with it today, it's already producing ten dollars worth of good."

The 1999 the public sale of Duty Free revealed that Feeney was not the billionaire he was believed to be, but that his foundation, The Atlantic Philanthropies, was!

Secretly Atlantic had already distributed almost 2.5 billion USD to rebuild Irish higher education, to support Feeney's "alma mater" Cornell University and other US education programs and schools and to encourage the philanthropic sector. In addition, Feeney himself was playing a major role behind the scenes in promoting the peace process between the Republic of Ireland and Northern Ireland.

In 2002 Atlantic's Board determined to follow its founding chairman's "Giving while Living" philosophy to its logical conclusion and spend down its remaining assets of approximately four billion USD and close its doors by 2020. It would be the largest foundation to do so.

Today Atlantic's program areas are fourfold: ageing, children and youth, population health, and reconciliation and human rights. Its countries of interest are: the United States, the Republic of Ireland and Northern Ireland, South Africa, Viet Nam, Bermuda, Australia and Cuba. In 2008, under the new leadership of President and CEO Gara LaMarche, long time justice and human rights advocate, Atlantic's Board adopted an explicit social justice framework for all of the foundation's programs.

Atlantic attempts to work closely with other funders, especially governments, advocating integrated concepts and models for long-term public support. Atlantic champions such advocacy and broad civic participation as essential ways to bring lasting positive change into the lives of disadvantaged and underserved people.

Chuck Feeney's strong push in secret foundation grants in Ireland, for example, vastly changed the nature and scope of higher education, bringing huge new allocations of continuing public support to match Atlantic's building programs. The same model was used in Viet Nam for education and libraries and now to rebuild regional hospitals and local medical clinics which would then be staffed at higher and more comprehensive levels, long term, by national and local budgets. In South Africa major support has encouraged advocacy and legal action to make life prolonging antiretroviral medication publically available to those living with HIV/AIDS, to protect the rights and safety of gay, lesbian, bisexual and transgender persons, for the rights of rural landholders, especially women who formerly had no right to own land; to expand and upgrade health systems and human resources in health, particularly for nurses and doctors in rural settings.

In Australia Atlantic grants prompted the government to allocate substantial support to a significantly expanded and successful bio-medical educational and research industry, much of it which also benefits the Asian region beyond Australia itself. In the United States Atlantic's grants are the largest from private sources in improving the lives and health of ageing populations. Other programs advocate for improved health insurance legislation for children and the general population where millions have no insurance at all, for the rights of immigrants and to improve services to children in after school and health programs. Special grants disseminate the community public health model developed in Cuba as well as its programs of medical education which serve its own population and provide medical personnel throughout the underserved world, including many African countries.

As Atlantic faces its fast approaching final grant making years, increasing attention is being paid to efforts to attract long term government commitments and to assist its funded programs, fields and geographies to strengthen resource development, outreach and advocacy as well as to encourage new donors to follow the "Giving while Living" philosophy which guided Atlantic's own creation and practice.

## Stories of giving in process: Thinking, listening, doing....

As the foundation field has grown – in size, assets, and diversity – over the last decade or two – the culture of giving has changed in many ways but so has the culture around us. My critique of the power dynamic in foundations is similar to my critique of power in business and government, it's overly "top-down". Those people with the power do not take the time to listen and pay attention to the things people tell them. We rarely admit how little we know about reality for the less resourced. This is partly attributable to the shortness of attention span in our culture, "learning by sound bites". Also, people tell us what they think we in power want to hear.

It is not easy to give money and resources – advice and counsel – effectively. Many foundations and donors feel that adequate staffing is a luxury; doing research or hiring consultants or other professionals is a waste of money and time, AND that the donor and the board ALWAYS know best. Sometimes that is true but often it's not. I often ask business executives or lawyers who are on boards how they feel when those who do not have their expertise or training second guess their professional decisions. I ask them if they look to professionals and specialists when entering a new business or a new area of practice. I ask them if they trust those professionals and how they use them effectively, yet without sacrificing their ability to make the final decision and retain authority.

There is a significant infusion of new money into philanthropy, much of it from younger entrepreneurs who have had brilliant success in specific industries and think this experience will automatically translate into similar success in nonprofit work. Many quickly discover that lots of money and time can be wasted learning how not to do philanthropy. To do philanthropy well, you need patience, practice, humility – and you need to listen, listen, listen and learn new skills.

It is true also that those of us who work in foundations and nonprofits are sometimes overly cautious because we want to keep our jobs. We are careful not to rock the boat too much and do not speak as candidly as we might. While it is essential to speak candidly, timing and context are also important – to wait for the right opportunity and have the right research or the right information. Then candor can have results.

Foundations and nonprofits are very much in the public view and are often challenged. The bigger foundations and large nonprofits are using funding strategies and "metrics" to measure the outcomes and publicize them. That's fine. In fact, it's important, because good work and resources can be wasted if programs don't know how to budget or formulate strategies to plan for the future. However, there's a delicate balance between who funds the process and who is responsible for making the decisions.

Is the nonprofit doing something mostly because a donor or a foundation wants to fund it? Or not doing something because it might cause controversy or public scrutiny? Is it paying too much attention to a local legislator's complaints, to management consultants and advisory and foundation program staff who may not know as much about a subject area or the specifics of the nonprofit's work as they think they do?

It is very hard for nonprofits that need funding to say no to a donor, to push back with hard questions or to say, "That's too much your strategy, your idea of what we need – and that's too much money. That will ruin us." The danger is what I call "funder sponsored mission creep" and you will see it all the time – missions that keep changing to fit a funder's agenda, or the shifting sands of public opinion. It is something nonprofits and foundations need to think more about: if you were established for a specific purpose but are continually morphing into something else, you are probably not going to be as effective as you could or should be. It is also fine to go out of business when a mission is largely accomplished, or to merge forces with others with in a stronger or broader set of resources or goals.

Too much money often creates a higher risk of failure than having not enough. If things are working well, more funding can usually be found. But you cannot take money out of a project or organization that goes off the rails. I also think there is value for nonprofits in having to go out into the marketplace to look for money from donors and the community and the public sector. Doing so tests ideas in the marketplace. If you have more money than you need and are able to hire whomever and do whatever you want, things get taken for granted. You are also less likely to take advantage of a lot of the people and resources in a community that would benefit from participation in your project.

An essential responsibility of a nonprofit and foundation board is to oversee the finances and the budgeting. Too often boards are either not paying enough attention to detail or are not getting sufficient and timely information. It is important to plan with real numbers at hand and realistic expectations about fund raising and other income. Many nonprofits in service fields have contracts with government. These contracts usually "cost" the nonprofit because all expenses needed to complete the service are not included or unanticipated needs add to the budget. These essential "extras", as well as the operational and planning needs of the nonprofit must be carefully monitored by staff and board. General support grants from foundations and income from the public are essential to bridge gaps.

"Private" foundations are a public trust – funded with tax-exempt money which otherwise would have largely gone to the government. We need to be open and accountable as a field. We need to be less thin-skinned and more available to those who seek assistance. We need to test work that the public might fund later on.

But it has to be done carefully. I don't like situations where all of a sudden a foundation that has been active in a field decides it is not going to make grants for a year or two as it re-evaluates its program. That can be very destructive, both in terms of the foundation's responsibility to specific projects as well as in the broader field. In situations like that, it is much better, in my opinion, to phase out a program gradually in parallel with open discussion and lot of consultation and transparency. It is important in situations of change to listen and see what you learn, to pick the brains of the people you have come to know and trust. But don't take advantage of them. If you ask project people to do some serious thinking, give them adequate time and funding to do it well.

At the same time, it's important for foundations to stick with a focus for a reasonable period of time. Every field has a learning curve and it takes time to master the basics, to achieve something, and then have a wind-down that gives other funders or the public adequate time to pick up where you left off.

You are seeing more of that kind of thinking in the bigger foundations, where the foundation will commit a portion of its resources or grant making budget to a specific field or area over a fixed period of time. The idea is to see how it works and then, after ten years or so, to make a decision about sticking with it or moving on to something else. In either case, it is important to commit to a healthy investment of both time and money up front, as well as to the intellectual legwork that is part and parcel of any successful program, and to do everything humanly possible to make sure the lessons learned from the project are shared as widely as possible

It is also important for foundations to communicate their failures. We learn from successes and from failures. One of the first things I look at when considering a new proposal or project is the budget and the list of funders. My comfort level goes way up if I see foundations or individual donors whom I respect already giving support. If I have a contact, I'll pick up the phone and say, "I've just seen something from so and so, what do you think?" Or, "Why are you funding them – or why have you stopped funding them?" It saves you from having to reinvent the wheel. The same thing applies if you make a mistake. You have to ask, "Whose mistake was it? Did we really understand the proposal? Did we put in too much money? Were our expectations too high? Had we thought through our involvement going forward?" When something fails, you have to take the time to look for the positives and any lessons learned, and at least to consider how some amount of continued support can help the organization or the field to learn something from the experience.

In the last five to ten years, particularly since 9/11, the confidence of Americans in their government and other institutions has sunk to historic lows and the confidence of the world in us is also at a low. The mixed participation rate of Americans in the electoral process is just one illustration of the disillusionment and feeling of powerlessness experienced by many, many Americans. But how do people find the hope and optimism that would motivate them to participate? Foundations and nonprofits can do a lot about that. There is a growing appreciation, for example, of the importance of ethnic media and grassroots publications in minority and undeserved communities. In California, where more people get their news and commentary from ethnic media than from the mainstream media, 'New America Media' has become a model for raising minority voices across the country. Similarly, institutions of all kinds increasingly are perceived as being less responsive to the commonwealth and more likely to serve the interest of big business. That is not a sustainable trend. If allowed to continue, it will ultimately destroy the fabric of this country and turn our friends into enemies. Philanthropy can and should play a much bigger role in documenting the influences of and changes in the global economy, in informing the public about transnational issues, in funding research and scholarship on solutions to transnational problems, and in leading the way with bold new ideas. There is a lot more we can do to step up to the plate.

In the last decade, thanks to the Web, we have seen whole communities, regions, and even countries leapfrog a hundred years of expensive landline infrastructure and it has made a tremendous difference. At the same time, it has opened a Pandora's Box of hopes and expectations. Private philanthropy can do a great deal to anticipate and develop models and document ways that government can connect to this new global, digitally savvy generation.

Maybe it can even figure out a way to change the conversation about taxes and distribution of wealth? It's crazy to think we can pay less and less in taxes and still live in a fully functioning society, let alone remain a global power and leader. Philanthropy, unlike other sectors, can play a role in changing perceptions of our actions and motives without being inappropriately political; it has much more potential than it realizes to influence and speak from a position of authority.

New donors should be careful but not shy. One should get involved sooner rather than later and try to learn for the long run. Learn how to listen and do periodic hard-nosed appraisals of your own expertise, as well as your tolerance for change and experimentation. Try to be relaxed and open about what you are doing. A good sense of humor helps! Talk about what resources you have and what giving means with your spouse and your children and family. Be sure to tell them why you are interested in giving and try to involve them in your activities. Learn from the world around you and find partners and mentors. Don't allow yourself to believe you are the only one who can change the world, but work at change as if you are!

There is a great diversity possible in philanthropy and great freedom to learn and experience it. But it is hard work also and takes discipline. The results can be very satisfying and uplifting. The most effective and generous philanthropy happens in families and in communities. Those of us with access to larger resources have the opportunity and the challenge to make a difference. How well we handle that responsibility will bring new levels of hope and possibility for all.

JANE WALES

# 25 United States
## THE GLOBAL PHILANTHROPY FORUM: FINANCING SOCIAL CHANGE

The capacity of private actors to contribute to the public good is ever growing. Yet the path is not always clear.

That realization is what led to the birth of the Global Philanthropy Forum (GPF) and the learning community it now represents. As of this writing, it comprises over 750 principals of family foundations who are joined by more than forty senior executives of staffed private and corporate foundations. These grant-makers serve as an ongoing brain trust to one another as they develop their strategies for giving and social investing. Their commitment is to systemic change – to creating the conditions under which giving is no longer needed, so that they can apply their resources to helping to tackle another problem, and then another. They define philanthropy broadly to include all private means of financing social change – be it through giving, investing or partnership.

### The Global Philanthropy Forum: Origins and purpose

The Global Philanthropy Forum began in 2001 as an effort to increase international giving at a time when Silicon Valley's high technology sector was generating great wealth, but redistributing only a small portion of this gain.

The context was one of rapid and sometimes wrenching change, creating new dangers, empowering new actors and requiring a new imperative for collaboration among those who could advance the social good. I had written about and was motivated by the recognition that three unstoppable trends were changing relations within and among states and across sectors and disciplines.

The *first* trend was the communications revolution and the rapid diffusion of information, capital and ideas. While we could not know the full effects of this third industrial revolution, it was clear that it had decentralized decision-making and authority, and had given rise to networks of non-state actors. Their power to do harm had vastly expanded. So too had their power to do good.

The *second* related trend was the restructuring of the global economy – the redistribution of wealth, production and power. While the global economy had created great wealth, it had also created uncertainty and stunning reversals of fortune. Furthermore, the income gap between those with access to education and those without had widened. In just ten years, the income gap in the United States (US) had doubled between those with a high school education and those with a college degree. Similar effects globally threatened new divisions along educational lines.

Population surges at the bottom of the economic and educational ladder constituted the *third* trend. While population growth was leveling off, due in large measure to the education of women, we still anticipated a world population of about 9.4 billion by 2050. Roughly six billion would live in poverty and two billion would be experiencing a declining standard of living. Restless young men were already moving to cities in the developing world at a rate of about one million per week. No society could be fully prepared for the environmental and social instability that might result.

It was in response to globalization's effects that I co-founded the Global Philanthropy Forum, along with philanthropists who generously lent both their financial support and their sweat equity. Its initial members were Silicon Valley denizens, who were both the architects and the beneficiaries of the Information Revolution. That revolution had vastly accelerated the process of globalization, and they hoped to see its benefits more evenly shared.

It was in this context that we conceived of the Forum and the learning community it comprised.

While some argued for a one-time conference, that idea soon gave way to the recognition that a single event was unlikely to effect lasting change. We chose instead to consider the barriers to giving and develop a longer-term effort to overcome them. And we worked to demonstrate its efficacy and then offer a menu of strategies and a set of partners with whom to act.

And so, although its annual conference represents the public face of the GPF, I experience it day to day quite differently as I and the GPF team devise funding strategies for its members and match-make among donors, so that best practices and knowledge can be systematically shared among them. That continuous service helps to build and sustain the learning community that is GPF, while creating feedback loops about donor interests and discoveries – and the effectiveness of the GPF itself.

The Global Philanthropy Forum's more public launch was with our first conference in March of 2002, made possible by the financial support of the William and Flora Hewlett Foundation and John and Tasha Morgridge's TOSA Foundation, led by their daughter Kate. The initial support of these early partners went beyond finances to include the deep engagement of their leaders, and the volunteer help of many friends who shared a commitment to the mission.

I was persuaded that two misperceptions stood as barriers to giving by those who had made significant wealth at a young age. The first myth to debunk was that philanthropy was the preoccupation solely of an older generation, rather than those at the height of their careers. Participants were surprised to be surrounded by likeminded individuals in their thirties, forties and fifties. The second myth was that there was insufficient evidence that philanthropy produced meaningful social or economic outcomes. Our task therefore was to test the hypothesis that, were they offered that evidence, they would give – and give generously. What we did not pre-suppose was that there was any lack of commitment to social change; we saw entrepreneurs as change makers by nature. Furthermore, Silicon Valley was characterized by the combination of idealism and audacity – qualities that philanthropists share. Pair those qualities with a clear strategy, and impact results.

We set out to design the "un-conference" – a learning and networking opportunity that would build knowledge, friendships and partnerships among donors, and between donors and grantees. The goal was to establish relationships that would both inform and endure, embedding new philanthropists in a supportive learning community. We reached out to existing donors as well as to people of means who had not yet made that commitment, or whose giving was transactional rather than strategic. Within months of the first conference, there were 583 individual philanthropists in our orbit, almost half of whom were new to philanthropy.

Having grown so swiftly, it became clear that designing the Global Philanthropy Forum, organizing its conferences and recruiting its participants could not be a hobby that I ran from the basement of my San Francisco house in the wee hours of the morning. Instead, with support from Hewlett, TOSA, the Rockefeller Foundation, the Skoll Foundation, the Gordon and Betty Moore Foundation, the David and Lucile Packard Foundation, the United Nations Foundation, the Rockefeller Brothers Fund, the Ford Foundation, the Carnegie Corporation of New York, and, later, the Bill and Melinda Gates Foundation, Fundación AVINA, the

World Bank's International Finance Corporation, the John D. and Catherine T. MacArthur Foundation and several other supporters, we established a team of three within the World Affairs Council of Northern California, where I was, and am, chief executive officer (CEO).

My earliest memo on the Global Philanthropy Forum stated its aim "to build a learning community of donors and social investors committed to international causes – and to inform, enable and enhance the strategic nature of their giving and social investing." That mission remains unchanged.

## Strategy and theory of change

That first memo described a logic model, stating that "the GPF operates on the premise that when donors and social investors are brought together around a problem and armed with the information they need with respect to the nature of the problem, the strategy for addressing it, potential partners with whom to collaborate, and vehicles for giving, they are more likely to give and to give strategically to advance social change."

We were shortly proved right.

Through its annual conferences and other programs, the GPF strategy was and remains to connect individual donors to issues and actors; to fellow donors to share best practices; to foundation executives with well-honed strategies that could be shadowed; to leaders of re-granting organizations with which to partner; and to emblematic agents of change from around the world. By building and continually refreshing a lasting learning community, we hoped to expand the number of philanthropists who would be strategic in pursuit of international causes.

From the start, the GPF's audience was comprised of grant-makers and social investors, who were principals of family foundations. We felt these individual donors lacked the staff resources and the discretionary time to research issues and vet grantees and would therefore benefit most from a community of likeminded colleagues as well as the speakers we recruited. We soon learned that in addition, executives of private foundations also gained from the gathering. We had invited them to our first conference because they had a treasure trove of knowledge to share. However, it was Gordon Conway, then president of Rockefeller Foundation, who told me that the GPF represented a welcomed opportunity to see existing colleagues in a relaxed setting and to meet new colleagues with whom to partner.

In recent years, the Bill and Melinda Gates Foundation, Humanity United and others have put their program officers to the service of these family philanthropists, holding special sessions in which they have described their theory of change, the strategies they have adopted or rejected and their reasons why. In the process they have provided guidance to philanthropists seeking to enter the fields of public health or nutrition, in the case of the

Gates Foundation, and the fields of conflict resolution and post-conflict reconciliation and reconstruction in the case of Humanity United.

We often feature up to forty leaders of social enterprises and non-profit organizations who speak not as grant-seekers but as experts in the fields in which they work. This placement, combined with our insistence on a "no-fundraising zone," serve to suspend the granter-grantee relationship, create an environment of mutual respect, and often results in donors turning to these experts for counsel as they develop their strategies for impact.

We cap participation at five hundred philanthropists, so as to assure a high degree of interaction. While we struggled to attract 360 attendees at our first conference, all subsequent annual meetings have been sold out with waiting lists of donors from around the country, and now from around the world.

## Building a community

We rapidly saw results.

Wishing to practice what we preached, and to be strategic in our own approach we sought external evaluations of our work. In 2003, McKinsey conducted a review, followed by similar studies by independent contractors every three years. This independent research took advantage of annual surveys of a representative sampling of participants in the GPF network.

Most importantly, these surveys and strategic reviews revealed[1] that a learning community has been formed, with 81 percent reporting in 2008 that they have chosen to continually tap into the "brain trust" of GPF speakers and donor participants as they form their strategies for giving. We value this outcome most, as our method is to build a lasting learning community that will grow increasingly strategic. Furthermore, surveys revealed that:

- The GPF comprises over 750 individual donors (mostly with family foundations) who are regular participants;
- 41 percent have been giving for six years or less;
- 68 percent report devoting more than a quarter of their portfolio to international causes;
- 46 percent had made new grants as a direct result of their participation in the GPF;
- 31 percent had entered into co-funding arrangements as a result of GPF programming;
- Participants overwhelmingly reported (84 percent) that the GPF has a meaningful impact on their grant-making. In particular they noted that the GPF:
  - Connected them to substantive issues and strategies for addressing them;

---

1 The statistics in this section are based on the 2008 surveys.

- Connected them to fellow donors from whom to learn;
- Connected them to emblematic agents of change from overseas;
- Enabled them to explore new approaches to giving or social investing;
- Promoted interaction with emerging leaders in philanthropy;
- Provided networking opportunities relevant to their grant-making.

While we limit each conference to five hundred philanthropists, we also hold a third of those seats for newcomers, thus expanding the number of donors who take part in the community. A smaller, sister event to the GPF annual conference is its Summer Seminar, which offers twenty GPF members four days with peers in a retreat setting to explore the values that underlie their philanthropy and their means of giving those values philanthropic expression.

In addition, several times per year, GPF participants attend luncheon and dinner programs with leaders in philanthropy and economic development, or take part in conference calls with philanthropic leaders, experts, and agents of change, allowing them to connect to experts, regardless of time zone or locale.

## Serving new philanthropists

Finally, on an ongoing and individual basis, the Global Philanthropy Forum offers services to individuals and organizations that are seeking advice, partnerships and introductions to like-minded donors.

For new foundations and those at an inflexion point, I draft strategic plans designed to reflect the interests of the donors and the opportunities that exist for impact. These confidential services are provided to members, with a limit on the number each year.

For corporations wishing to encourage their employees to make a commitment to social change, the GPF team develops tailored programs that increase employee knowledge about and involvement in the philanthropic sector. For example, the GPF worked with Google.org and an independent contractor to design semester-long courses and select the accompanying readings. These seminars were held at the Google campus and offered hundreds of interested 'Googlers' in-depth learning about global poverty, global health and climate change.

The central feature of GPF, however, is still that of matchmaking and one-on-one introductions made throughout the year.

## Trends in philanthropy: Lessons learned from the GPF philanthropists

Just eight years after inception, the GPF has among its members individuals who are committed to the advancement and improvement of philanthropy – and who are helping to reshape and refresh this already vibrant sector. These "new philanthropists" reflect six broad trends in philanthropy.

The *first* trend is that foundations led by living benefactors have matched the size, scope and potential impact as those founded as the result of estates. The "new philanthropists" are strategic. They are engaged and global in outlook, and most are shaped by their private sector experience. Like traditional foundations, they seek results.

*Second*, these donors are willing to take on large problems and seek a comprehensive strategy for addressing them. Philanthropists see poverty as a system that needs to be replaced with a new system. While many newcomers to the field impatiently seek a silver bullet – most know that poverty is a package that needs to be unbundled and understood.

*Third*, their emphasis on sustainability and their desire to bring solutions to scale has led these philanthropists to focus on opportunities for leverage. They leverage one another through peer learning organizations like the Global Philanthropy Forum, which offer venues for pursuing co-funding opportunities. They also leverage the private sector by investing in companies that yield a social return, by supporting microfinance, social enterprises and by making social change part of their own companies' value chain.

Furthermore, they leverage the public sector through public-private partnerships. This path was forged by large private foundations such as the Rockefeller and Ford Foundations, which pursed the Green Revolution in this way, transforming India from a grain importer to a grain exporter. New philanthropists travel down that path with ease. Gates, Rockefeller, Hewlett, Packard, Skoll, the Case Foundation and many others regularly partner with the government to advance economic development goals.

The *fourth* trend is that in the process of pursuing partnerships, philanthropists have accelerated the convergence of the social and private sectors. Social actors are adopting private sector methods, mechanisms and measures of success, so as to attract grants, loans and investment dollars. They enter into agile partnerships to bring their solutions to scale. At the same time, the corporate sector has expanded its view of corporate social responsibility by ensuring that the achievement of social goals is intrinsic to the company's value chain. There has been a normative shift fueled as much by employee interest as by that of farsighted CEOs. A recent study of the Goldman Sach's "10,000 Women" program argued that it works in part because a business case can be made for it. Cisco would make the same argument when it comes to education.

*Fifth*, while this has led to the convergence of the private and social sectors, there is recognition that markets cannot solve all problems. Markets may provide for the rational distribution of wealth, but not its equitable distribution. That is the role for policy and philanthropy. Unregulated markets can exacerbate some of the world's most pressing problems, such as weapons proliferation or environmental degradation. Philanthropists know that sound policy is needed in both rich and poor countries to assure a rules-based system that allows market forces to work, provides equal access to opportunity, removes barriers, sets standards, and provides protections for individuals and groups. New philanthropists have been engaged in supporting those who advocate aid reform here in the United States or in their efforts to measure and advance aid effectiveness.

Furthermore, private foundations have joined philanthropists in supporting independent sources of analysis in the developing world, so that recipient countries can be held accountable by their own citizens. In this vein, the Hewlett Foundation launched a ten-year, 100 million United States dollar (USD) initiative to strengthen independent research centers in the developing world. The money will provide both long-term general operating support and technical assistance to support high-quality research by think tanks in developing countries that they can use to formulate more effective national policies. The Andrew W. Mellon Foundation undertook efforts toward the same goal in South Africa by providing more than 75 million USD in grants to develop the diversity of students able to participate in higher education, and also to support the development of national research networks and leadership forums.

The *sixth* and final trend is the recognition that philanthropy faces the task of informing and engaging the world's publics. Many of the problems we face – as well as their solutions – are the result of the aggregate effect of millions of individual choices, such as whether to use more water than needed, to cut down a forest, to take up arms, to engage in un-safe sex or to vote and demand that each vote be counted. Informing those choices is an essential task and the ultimate form of leverage. One day we may therefore conclude that a business decision taken by a company – Google – to translate the world's knowledge into the languages of the developing world is among the most important contributors to sustainable social change.

## Looking forward

In thinking on the future of the Global Philanthropy Forum, and philanthropy more generally, I continually return to the reasons for the GPF's creation. During those 2001 conversations in World Affairs Council meeting rooms, Stanford University class rooms and the Morgridge's living room, we spoke of spurring philanthropy where it was nascent, but in fact our goal grew larger. It became an effort to harness the spirit of innovation in Silicon Valley to effect positive and lasting change.

Reflecting on those original ideas, conversations and aspirations, I am struck by the success of our initial model, but hunger to do so much more. As we consider ways to move this community to the next level of efficacy, it is clear to me that the new philanthropists who comprise the GPF membership have become experts and thought leaders. They are willing to teach as well as to learn from their colleagues. It is this brain trust that is not only the signal of success, but also the vehicle for continued impact.

It is they who will help carry this work forward, wisely and energetically. It is a joy to work by their side.

As Fundación AVINA president Brizio Biondi-Mora told fellow GPF members, "We are living in a world where local occurrences and crises are shaped by global systems and synergies." In light of the global recession, it would be easy to feel that the challenges are too great and our own individual impact too small. But as Her Majesty Queen Rania Al Abdullah of Jordan told fellow GPF members this spring, "when the sky is darkest, that's when we see the stars." GPF advisory board member Muhammad Yunus urged participants at the GPF to think of the current financial crisis as an opportunity for positive change. We should be asking about new systems that will best serve humanity going forward. "We are free to imagine and free to set new goals."

We have. And we will.

# United States
## SUPPORTING OPEN SOCIETIES AROUND THE WORLD: THE STORY OF THE OPEN SOCIETY INSTITUTE

## The beginnings: The Open Society Institute and the fall of communism

Though many did not know it, Hungary was on the cusp of revolution when George Soros began his work there in 1984 with a simple philanthropic gesture: a shipment of state-of-the-art photocopiers to be distributed to Hungarian public libraries and universities. Until then, the Communist Party had maintained strict control over the country's few copiers in an effort to limit citizens' access to information. As intended, the influx of new machines helped open the floodgates of dissent, with dissident activists throughout Hungary using them to circulate underground literature calling for peaceful democratic change.

By the time of the fall of the Berlin Wall in 1989, Soros had established foundations in Poland, China, and the Soviet Union, in addition to the one in Hungary. Much of the early work of those first foundations was in the spirit of the photocopier project: innovative and practical, aimed at opening up avenues for debate and responding quickly and effectively to the needs of civil society on the ground. The Polish foundation created scholarships so members of the country's embattled Solidarity movement could spend time in London and Paris. The Russian foundation helped Soviet nuclear scientists find their place in the new system, stemming the dangers of nuclear proliferation when these experts were abandoned after the communist collapse. Such strategic interventions helped ensure the peaceful collapse of communist totalitarianism in Eastern Europe and set former Eastern bloc countries on the road to democracy.

Throughout the transition process, as the newly democratic nations overhauled their economies and political institutions, the Soros foundations network continued to expand its scope and reach. By 1993 there were foundations across the expanse of what had once been communist Europe and Central Asia. That same year, Soros created the Open Society Institute (OSI), an operating and grant-making foundation with central offices in both New York and Budapest, in an effort to provide support and cohesion to the growing foundation network. Since its creation, the Open Society Institute has served as the base for both regional directors, who help oversee the work of the national foundations and network programs, which operate through the foundations on a variety of issues, from education to public health, justice, and access to information.

While the unifying goal of the foundations has been to promote open society – a concept articulated by philosopher Karl Popper as a social and economic system based on diversity of opinion, flexibility, and a rejection of fixed dogma – the foundations were also created to be highly local, indigenous institutions. Each one has a board made up of national civil society activists that is empowered to determine foundation priorities, and give grants accordingly, in the effort to promote open society values. In the wake of wrenching change in Central and Eastern Europe, this emerging network of foundations was well-placed to help guide the region toward a peaceful transition and bolster the forces of humanism and democracy against the competing trends of nationalism and conflict.

And in cases where such a peaceful transition proved elusive, the foundations were also poised to respond. When violence marked the disintegration of the former Yugoslavia, the network marshaled its resources to carve out a space for open society in the face of humanitarian crisis. In 1993, with Sarajevo under daily attack by Serbian bombers and sniper fire, its electricity and water supply cut off, the network provided 50 million United States dollars (USD) to the besieged city. The money was intended both to provide much-needed humanitarian relief and to focus an international spotlight on the plight of Bosnian civilians. Most immediately – and most visibly – the money was used to restore drinking water to the city's residents and electricity to its hospitals. Braving snipers' bullets and artillery shells, workers laid wires and piping throughout the city so Sarajevo could regain some semblance of livability.

But the money also did more than that. In line with OSI's mission of creating and sustaining vibrant open societies, the money went to projects that addressed issues beyond basic physical survival. For example, the Open Society Institute helped keep alive Sarajevo's multiethnic daily newspaper, which, despite operating out of a bomb shelter, managed to turn out a paper every day except one during the two-year siege. It funded art exhibits and radio stations, films, and textbooks. It sought to make Sarajevo a real city again – a place filled with ideas and arts and culture, not just a war zone.

Since the collapse of Yugoslavia, OSI has been at the forefront of efforts to rebuild civil society in the region and ensure long-term stability by bringing the wars' perpetrators to justice in both international and local courts. A strong proponent of the International Criminal Tribunal for Yugoslavia, OSI has also applied lessons learned in the Balkans to the wider movement for international justice. In addition to promoting *ad hoc* war crimes tribunals and other forms of transitional justice, OSI has been steadfast in its support for the International Criminal Court and its efforts to establish a mechanism for holding lawless leaders accountable. Such a system holds the promise of deterring the most egregious atrocities – from genocide to crimes against humanity – and overturning the culture of impunity that all too often protects war criminals from punishment.

## OSI in South Africa

The Open Society Institute was also an early supporter of microfinance, which unlocks sources of capital to poor and low-income communities so that they can build their own homes and businesses. In one of its first major projects outside of Europe, OSI funded a massive housing development initiative in post-apartheid South Africa that made it possible for hundreds of thousands of families to own their own homes. Soros had inaugurated his career as a philanthropist in South Africa in 1979, when he created a scholarship program so that black students could attend the University of Cape Town. With the dismantling of apartheid a decade and a half later, Soros immediately returned to South Africa to establish an open society foundation in the newly democratic nation.

The foundation's work initially focused on the most urgent issues in a transitional society by funding reconciliation projects and helping to build a democratic infrastructure. But it soon became clear that homelessness and poverty would hamper any effort to bring about real integration and equality. After decades of state-sponsored racial oppression, which forced black South Africans to live in jerry-rigged shacks in segregated shantytowns, South Africa faced an acute housing crisis. To address the issue, OSI funded Nurcha, an organization dedicated to providing modest homes for the nation's poor through loan guarantees to developers. With OSI's help, Nurcha has been able to guarantee loans for the construction of some 250,000 homes, paving the way for a massive nationwide housing effort that is gradually eradicating some of the worst vestiges of apartheid. Where there had once been jumbles of dilapidated lean-tos made of scrap wood and cardboard, there are now neat rows of bright simple houses, made of brick and corrugated steel, many of them with small vegetable patches out back.

## OSI and human rights

Much of the work of OSI and the Soros foundations network is marked by a commitment to promoting social inclusion and the rights of minorities and other vulnerable communities. OSI has been one of the largest supporters of Europe's Roma minority, who have been largely denied the benefits of economic and democratic development in Central and Southeastern Europe. From the beginning, the foundations in Europe recognized that racism against Roma would be one of the biggest obstacles to lasting democratic progress in the region. Locked out of jobs, segregated into inferior schools, and driven into slums, the Roma live on the margins of society throughout Europe – a massive violation of human rights that undermines open society values and Europe's long-term progress. OSI has been at the forefront of efforts to bring Roma issues to the attention of policymakers and to overturn racist practices and attitudes in wider society.

Among other initiatives, OSI in 1996 founded the European Roma Rights Centre, which, through its work focusing on strategic litigation, has since been one of the most vocal advocates for the Roma cause. In one of its most notable achievements, in 2007 it argued successfully before the European Court of Human Rights that the shunting of Roma children into schools for the mentally disabled – a common form of *de facto* segregation throughout much of Central and Southeastern Europe – constitutes unlawful discrimination. OSI was also key in bringing about the Decade of Roma Inclusion. Launched in 2005, this is the first European-wide effort to secure a commitment from governments to create policies promoting Roma integration. Following an upsurge in anti-Roma violence this past year, OSI's efforts are now more critical than ever.

As with its support for the Roma, OSI often embraces causes and tackles issues that other donors overlook – whether for reasons of political caution or lack of resources. For example, since 1995 OSI has been one of the strongest supporters of harm reduction alternatives to address the social and public health effects of drug use. Recognizing that the burgeoning HIV epidemic in Eastern Europe was due in large part to the practice of sharing needles among drug users, OSI's Public Health Program was among the first major donors to fund needle exchange and other HIV prevention efforts in that region.

## OSI in the United States

Similarly, OSI has taken a powerful stance in the debate over criminal justice in the United States (US), where a fiercely punitive legal culture is one the biggest challenges to the values of an open society. From the beginning of its work in the US, OSI has been a leading force for justice system reform. After expanding the open society network throughout Europe and Central Asia, and establishing foundations in South Africa and Haiti, in 1996 OSI also began operating in the US. Following the fall of communism, the US was far from a perfect model of open society, and could no longer be defined solely by its opposition to authoritarianism. The 1980s and 1990s had seen a dramatic upsurge in incarceration rates alongside steep cuts to social services in the US – trends that threaten democracy and equality by contributing to an ever-widening income gap and fewer opportunities for disadvantaged communities.

Nearly alone among leading donors, OSI has backed its belief in the need for justice reform with aggressive philanthropy. Since 1996, OSI has spent more than one billion (USD) on a wide variety of justice projects, including efforts to improve legal aid services, advocate for sentencing reform, and combat racial profiling. Its support to groups fighting capital punishment, including the American Civil Liberties Union and the Innocence Project, has enabled advocates to mount successful challenges to execution protocols in more than a dozen states – at a time when even liberal politicians saw abolition as a hopeless cause. When states and the federal government began locking up children in adult prisons, OSI and its grantees mobilized a diverse coalition to oppose this inhumane practice. Reversing ill-conceived drug policies that have decimated whole urban neighborhoods in a frenzy of over-incarceration is another OSI priority. To that end, OSI has helped lead the fight to create sensible drug laws that emphasize treatment over imprisonment and the allocation of resources to building schools rather than jails.

Since founding its US Programs, OSI has also been engaged in a targeted philanthropic experiment in Baltimore, one of the poorest and most troubled cities in America. Soros and the US Programs Board were interested in finding a location where OSI could learn more about the dynamics at play in urban centers that result in persistent poverty and injustice – and then invest significant charitable funds to address their root causes. They looked at a number of cities and ultimately decided that Baltimore, a city with typical urban problems but the resolve to address them, had a unique set of attributes that would make it a good choice as a "laboratory", where a number of initiatives could be tested and evaluated. Just forty miles from the nation's capital, Baltimore has some of the highest rates of unemployment, school dropouts, HIV, crime, and drug use. But while Baltimore may be a particularly dramatic example of urban devastation, it is also exemplary of larger American trends and problems. Once a major industrial city, deindustrialization has left Baltimore with limited opportunities for high-wage labor, while federal defunding of cities has left municipal coffers with few resources.

To address the city's most pressing challenges, OSI-Baltimore decided to focus its work exclusively on three intertwined problems: untreated drug addiction, an overreliance on incarceration, and obstacles that impede youth in succeeding inside and outside the classroom. The Foundation also supports the Baltimore Community Fellows, a corps of social innovators who work directly to revitalize underserved communities. After more than a decade of philanthropy and expenditures of over 60 million USD, OSI–Baltimore has made a direct impact on the city: its educational initiatives have increased after-school programming, engaged thousands of students in debate training, and reduced school suspensions and expulsions; its work to reduce incarceration rates has led to parole reform and increased reentry and job training services for ex-prisoners; and its drug policy efforts have resulted in a 156 percent increase in city funding for drug treatment, which has in turn helped reduce crime and HIV infection.

OSI has also been one of the few major donors to support the rights of immigrants in the US, who, already vulnerable, have seen their troubles deepen since the launch of the so-called "War on Terror" in 2001. Under growing attack in the media and facing stricter regulations and increased scrutiny from state authorities, immigrants in the US have few advocates. OSI has helped provide legal assistance to documented immigrants and asylum seekers in the US, while its Democracy and Power Fund seeks to engage immigrants and other disadvantaged groups in political and community life. OSI grantees were also instrumental in securing the rights of Guantanamo detainees to file a writ of *habeas corpus* requesting release from unlawful detention.

While the Open Society Institute was focused on developing programs in the United States, it also extended its work to other parts of the Western Hemisphere, beginning with the establishment of a foundation in Haiti. Since its founding in 1995, the Fondation Connaissance et Liberté has sought innovative solutions to improve access to education and empower civil society in the face of entrenched poverty and political instability. One of its most notable initiatives has been an extensive nation-wide network of local community libraries, which give children and youth from poor communities access to information and new technologies. The flagship library is located in Port-au-Prince and serves as a popular hub for cultural and educational events. One of the foundation's most recent and ambitious projects is a joint effort with the Haitian government and the European Union to create a national park in Port-au-Prince that will provide social and cultural services. The park will serve as the anchor for a range of neighborhood projects addressing issues such as gang violence, sanitation and water treatment, education and professional training, and local business development. At seventeen acres, it will also be the single biggest green space in Port-au-Prince.

Soon after the establishment of the Haitian foundation, the open society network again broadened its scope within the Americas. Since its founding in 1997, the Fundación Soros Guatemala has been particularly concerned with rebuilding a society torn apart by a decades-long civil war. The projects it funds include cultural initiatives about memory and artistic representations of political violence, to projects aimed at creating a more tolerant, integrated nation in the aftermath of conflict. The foundation has been a key supporter of the rights of women and indigenous groups, seeking to increase their voice in politics, labor unions, and national culture. Recognizing that there can be no peace without justice, the foundation has also supported the investigation and documentation of war crimes.

## Global issues: Migration, statelessness, HIV/AIDS, and the resource curse

As the open society network has expanded its geographic reach, it has also focused its attention on challenges that are international in scope. Migration, for exam ple, has become a key open society issue in recent years. As globalization, wealth disparities, and climate change intensify – forcing more and more people to travel across borders in search of work and security – migration will increasingly raise questions around citizenship, human rights, and social equality. In an effort to challenge abuse and prevent conflict, the Open Society Institute has begun work to systematically address the often deplorable conditions and treatment migrants face, and the alarming increase in abuse and discrimination against them. Many of the national foundations have been at the forefront of these issues, particularly in the countries of the former Soviet Union, where a large number of laborers, unable to obtain work at home, travel to Russia in search of jobs. The foundations, together with OSI, have worked to mitigate the impact of labor migration in the region through programs that provide social and legal services to labor migrants and advocate for the promotion and protection of their rights.

Another key Open Society Institute priority, closely tied to issues around migration, is the growing crisis of statelessness throughout the world. As multinational states collapsed all over Eastern Europe and Central Asia after the fall of communism, large populations of ethnic minorities found themselves in newly independent countries that now viewed them as foreigners. In Africa, the legacy of colonialism coupled with state succession has created pockets of ethnic communities with no citizenship rights. In Asia and the Middle East, too, governments have increasingly used citizenship status to deprive women and unpopular ethnic minorities of political power. Stateless people, now estimated at more than ten million worldwide, wield no political power and are systematically deprived of public goods and services such as health care, education, and housing. Lack of documentation often prevents them from obtaining gainful employment, resulting in a cycle of poverty for generations. This situation is not only inhumane, but a recipe for conflict. The Open Society Justice Initiative is responding to the crisis of statelessness with a comprehensive approach, working at the national level to implement existing legal norms prohibiting discrimination and arbitrary deprivation of citizenship, and also at the international level to promote an effective global framework to guarantee the universal right to citizenship.

Migration and statelessness are just two of the issues that OSI is working on at the international level. Without losing sight of its commitment to grassroots change and reliance on local knowledge, OSI is increasingly focused on a host of worldwide problems that defy national and regional borders – and that require high-level advocacy and cooperation – such as HIV/AIDS. OSI has been a leading player in tackling the HIV/AIDS epidemic through initiatives that seek both to build broad international coalitions and draw on the experiences of those working on the ground. Its Public Health Program, for example, has been one of the most vocal advocates for the rights of sex workers, and has cooperated with both national and multilateral actors to promote policies that take into account the needs and opinions of this marginalized yet crucial group in the fight against HIV/AIDS. It has brought together sex worker activists from South Africa to Thailand to Brazil, ensuring that they are given a role in the debate over stopping the spread of the disease. Such efforts reflect a holistic, rights-based approach to public health – one that seeks to effect change by appealing to international norms and local expertise, finding pragmatic solutions to pressing problems.

The Open Society Institute has been a leader in promoting better natural resource management, an issue that is likewise both highly local and transnational in scope. For nearly a decade, it has been a major donor in a growing global movement to increase transparency and accountability in extractive industries. Efforts to overturn what has become known as the "resource curse" – which all too often dooms nations rich in oil, gas, or minerals to poverty and instability – are key to preventing conflict around the world. OSI in 2002 funded and helped launch Publish What You Pay, which has become a global civil society coalition helping citizens of resource-rich developing countries hold their governments accountable for the management of revenues from the oil, gas, and mining industries.

That same year, OSI launched Revenue Watch to monitor the use of resource revenues. While its work initially focused on Central Asia and the Caucasus region, it soon extended its efforts to Iraq, Africa, and East Asia.

Now an independent organization with significant funding from OSI, the Revenue Watch Institute seeks to improve democratic accountability in natural resource-rich countries by equipping citizens with the information, training, networks, and funding they need to become more effective monitors of government revenues and expenditures. In addition to working with civil society, the Revenue Watch Institute engages governments in both importing and exporting countries, international financial institutions, and the board members and managers of companies that pay governments to extract natural resources. These efforts are crucial to ensuring sustainable development and promoting good governance globally.

## The Open Society Institute in the twenty-first century

The Open Society Institute in the first decade of the twenty-first century was operating in a dramatically changed climate from when George Soros began his philanthropy. America and the waging of its War on Terror had discredited the US as a global leader in the eyes of much of the world. Whereas in 1993 being a US-based foundation had been a boon in many parts of the globe, the United States had lost much of its international stature as a paradigm of open society. Whereas a decade earlier Europe was preoccupied with how it would incorporate the newly democratic nations of the east, it had now become a model – albeit an imperfect one – of how to fashion a coalition of multiple states that is committed to human rights and democratic participation. Believing that Europe offered a powerful vision of an open society, George Soros established the European Council on Foreign Relations (ECFR) in an effort to help bolster Europe's leadership role in world affairs. The ECFR, conceived as a think-tank and advocacy organization, works to encourage the European Union to become more proactive in integrating its member states, so they can speak with a unified and authoritative voice on a wide range of international concerns, from climate change to extremist violence. The ECFR is committed to ensuring that Europe fulfills its promise as a global leader promoting open society.

Just as the open society network was reorienting its work in Europe away from operational programs and toward policy advocacy, however, OSI again found itself adjusting its priorities to meet an urgent crisis. The world financial disaster that exploded in 2008 threatened to undo much of what had been accomplished in advancing open society in Central and Eastern Europe and the former Soviet Union. In the spring of 2009, as countries throughout the region were reeling from the economic downturn, OSI pledged 100 million USD to help mitigate the impact of slashed state budgets and cuts in social services. A committee was set up to evaluate the severity of the crisis in each country and determine the projects most in need of funding, which could range from support to keep children in school, to grants protecting endangered cultural institutions to projects helping the hard-hit middle class in a bid to stem the rise of angry nationalism.

This massive emergency grant to Europe was announced around the same time as Soros made two similar one-time gifts to fight poverty in New York. As homelessness surged throughout the city and both governmental agencies and philanthropies grappled to cope with a growing social crisis, George Soros allocated 50 million USD to help people in New York City in need of basic services like food and shelter. The grant was given to the Robin Hood Foundation, which pledged to match it dollar for dollar, in an effort to inspire other philanthropists and institutions to step up their giving.

A few months later, George Soros announced another large-scale gift, this time to New York State families struggling to pay for school supplies. The 35 million USD donation unlocked 140 million USD in unused federal stimulus funds allocated to the state, allowing hundreds of thousands of low-income families across New York to receive a one-time benefit of 200 USD per child to purchase supplies for the upcoming school year. Together, the two gifts to New York, totaling 85 million USD, are among the largest private contributions ever made to satisfy basic necessities.

They also reflect the Open Society Institute's flexibility as a foundation and its open-minded approach to philanthropy. Over three decades and with expenditures of some 7 billion USD, the open society network has strived to foster long-term transformation and respond effectively to immediate on-the-ground needs. From supplying besieged Sarajevans with running water to leading a global movement to promote the just management of natural resources, OSI has demonstrated its commitment to a broad vision of open society that safeguards human rights and ensures equal opportunity for all. Indeed, such expansiveness goes to the very heart of the meaning of open society. As it enters its next decades, the Open Society Institute's mission inevitably will continue to evolve – embracing new challenges, new voices, and new ideas in the effort to ensure that open society remains a powerful force for peaceful, progressive change around the world.

*27* Canada

# BUILDING CAPACITY IN INTERNATIONAL AFFAIRS IN CANADA: THE BALSILLIE SCHOOL OF INTERNATIONAL AFFAIRS, THE CANADIAN INTERNATIONAL COUNCIL AND THE CENTRE FOR INTERNATIONAL GOVERNANCE INNOVATION

As an entrepreneur, I recognize that one must seize the moment and grasp the opportunity. Where there is a clear need, the chance exists to build a better product, find wider markets, and have a greater impact. As a philanthropist in Canada, I saw a need and took an opportunity. The times were changing quickly, and the governance structures (both legal and political) with which we governed ourselves fifty years ago were no longer adequate. As a contemporary chief executive of a global business, I believed that I must make informed decisions about change, innovation and risk. Moreover, as a citizen of a country with open borders which depends on export and globalization for its economic success, I was deeply and personally interested in ensuring Canadians are at the forefront of determining equitable and peaceful solutions for global problems

Why, I asked as the new century began, does Canada, a G-8 country with enormous international interests with one of the most diverse populations in the world, have weak private sector institutions to support Canada's role in the world? As the co-chief executive officer (CEO) of Research In Motion, I travelled the world to promote the BlackBerry. I often encountered substantial organizations beyond government which played a major role in the promotion of the national interest in international affairs. The contrast with Canada was striking. The Canadian Institute of International Affairs (CIIA) once had enormous influence in Ottawa and strong linkages with similar institutions internationally, but no more. Its small budget limited its activities to support of a few branches which did useful work in furthering discussion of Canadian international policy. However, the business community was not involved in the Institute, and the overall budget was less than one million Canadian dollars (CAD).

Canadians once claimed that they lived in a fireproof house, far from danger, but no longer. Canadians live today in a world that is replete with dangerous and intractable problems: from Iraq, Afghanistan, Palestine, Darfur and the Congo, to name only the bloodiest; to Al Qaeda, the Taliban and the Janjiweed, the most murderous; to HIV and AIDS, malaria, avian flu, climate change and the proliferation of nuclear weapons, the most insidious. A few years ago, scores of thousands of Canadians in Lebanon and Israel suddenly found themselves in a war zone, caught up in an unexpected conflict as cluster bombs and rockets rained down, needing rescue in what was to become the largest evacuation in Canadian history. The global economic crisis has impacted Canadian jobs, the housing market and the Canadian dollar. Canadians, therefore, are neither immune nor, in most cases, remote from the harm they can cause. Rarely has it been so important for us to understand the world and to engage it. Rarely has the need for international cooperation been so necessary.

Canadian capacity fell far short of Canadian need. There were some other, mostly academic, centres where the focus was international affairs. The Munk Centre at the University of Toronto brought together the outstanding researchers at that fine university as did the Liu Centre at the University of British Columbia. Other universities, such as Carleton with the Norman Paterson School, the University of Victoria with the Centre for Global Studies, and the Université de Montréal with its Centre d'études et de recherches internationals were important research and teaching centres. Private philanthropy did contribute to this work, notably at Toronto where Peter Munk gave generously to create the Munk Centre and at Calgary where Fred Mannix provided considerable funds. Yet Canadian private and public support fell far short of what was found elsewhere.

I soon learned that Americans and Europeans have invested far more into developing capacity in international affairs – most of the major journals on international affairs are published in either the United States (US) or the United Kingdom. The examples are striking

- The Brookings Institution in Washington had an operating budget of 60.7 million United States dollars (USD) in 2007.
- The Council on Foreign Relations in New York has a profound influence not only on public discussion but on policy choice.

- The Center for American Progress has an operating budget of 23 million USD.
- Chatham House, the Royal Institute of International Affairs, has an international range, leads the discussion on many important topics, and plays the role in British public life that the Canadian Institute of International Affairs (CIIA) once did in Canada. Ironically, the CIIA began as a branch of Chatham House.
- The South African Institute of International Affairs, also an offspring of Chatham House, has a staff of almost fifty, thriving branches, and an extensive research program.

These and many other national think tanks were incubators for the ideas politicians drew upon to guide national policy. Their role was central to the process of policy formation and, equally important, to public education.

There was, therefore, an opportunity where philanthropy could make a difference. With significant investment in building capacity in the area of international affairs, Canada could play a larger and more effective role on the world's stage and Canadians could understand that role much better. Waterloo, Ontario, Canada was the home of two major universities, Wilfrid Laurier University and the University of Waterloo. The former was principally an arts-oriented university with a thriving business school while the latter had an international reputation in the fields of mathematics, computer science and engineering. Despite many outstanding faculty members with international interests, neither university had an educational or concentrated research focus upon international affairs, although there were some smaller centres, such as the Centre on Foreign Policy and Federalism at Waterloo and Laurier's Centre on Military, Strategic, and Disarmament Studies, which held conferences, published books and papers, and mentored students. In short, there were seeds that could be nurtured.

As Research In Motion grew rapidly, my wife Heidi and I began to share some of the benefits which flowed to me with the broader community, including an art gallery in my home town of Peterborough, contribution to local charities, and a major donation to the library at Trinity College at the University of Toronto, my *alma mater*. In 1999, my Co-CEO Mike Lazaridis established in Waterloo the Perimeter Institute for Theoretical Physics, which will soon be the largest centre for the study of theoretical physics in the world. I donated 10 million CAD to assist its early growth. I told Mike that my own interest was in international affairs, and I began a process of studying how an institute in that field might be established in Waterloo.

# The Centre for International Governance Innovation (CIGI)

Although the proposed new centre had no staff, I had quietly approached the City of Waterloo about the possibility of acquiring the former Seagram Museum, a remarkable building which had won the Governor General's Prize for its architecture. It had closed in the mid-1990s, and a software firm headed by my good friend Rick Brock was the City's tenant. With that idea in mind, in February 2001 I asked a group of people to come to my cottage in Muskoka, a vacation district north of Toronto. They were diverse and represented educational and foreign policy expertise. At the end of the meeting on those clear winter days on Georgian Bay, I charged the meeting to come forward with a concrete plan for action. That fall I engaged University of Waterloo Professor John English to develop that plan in consultation with the local universities and the Government of Canada. The government was immediately curious, particularly Finance Minister Paul Martin whose experience in international financial circles led him to believe that substantial changes would occur in international institutions. He and Lawrence Summers of the United States had created the G-20 of finance ministers when the G-8 proved inadequate to meet the challenges of the Asian financial crisis. When I met with Mr. Martin, he expressed great interest in building a think tank that would study institutional change, and I made a proposition: I would match funds the government would give to create such a research centre.

In 2002 I made the original contribution of 20 million CAD to CIGI's endowment fund and Mike Lazaridis, President and Co-CEO of RIM, contributed 10 million CAD. These donations were matched by the Government of Canada with 30 million CAD. I subsequently gave additional funds, some for the endowment, others for programs. In 2007 I matched a 17 million CAD contribution from the Ontario government, and in 2009 I donated 50 million CAD to support the work of CIGI carried out in cooperation with the Balsillie School of International Affairs, which I will discuss below. Over the years I have made other additional donations in support of CIGI's work as have others including my former Research In Motion Colleagues Michael Barnstyn and Louise MacCallum and an anonymous donor who contributed a 10 million CAD gift in support of an "African Initiative," which is currently a major research program on the impact of climate change upon the continent most affected.

## The mandate of CIGI

CIGI has grown from three people in 2002, when it was founded, to a staff of 62 in 2009, with many other fellows throughout the world. It is an independent, non-partisan think tank that addresses international governance challenges. Led by a group of experienced practitioners and distinguished academics, CIGI supports research, forms networks, advances policy debate, builds capacity, and generates ideas for multilateral governance improvements. Conducting an active agenda of research, events and publications, CIGI's interdisciplinary work includes collaboration with policy, business and academic communities around the world. It has an operating board which includes representative of Canada's Department of Foreign Affairs and International Trade. I am the chair of that board. An International Board of Governors, the majority of whose members are non-Canadians, gives research advice and evaluates CIGI's programs.

In carrying out its work, CIGI has identified six major areas of Global Governance that need structured thought and dialogue:
- Shifting global economic power;
- Environment and resources, particularly the growing recourse to nuclear energy, energy efficiency and climate change;
- Health and social issues, especially the prevention and response to pandemic disease;
- Trade and finance, including investment issues;
- International law and institutional reform; and
- Global and human security, including the protection of the vulnerable and powerless.

CIGI approaches these issues of international governance by asking itself what is in the best interests of the planet, rather than what is in the best interests of a particular nation state.

## The Canadian International Council

As mentioned above, the Canadian Institute of International Affairs (CIIA) had a long and distinguished history. Founded by Canadian leaders in business, politics, and academia in 1928, the CIIA was fully the counterpart of Britain's Royal Institute of International Affairs and the United States' Council on Foreign Relations. Close to those in power, respected for its non-partisan stance, and the research leader in the area of foreign affairs, the CIIA played a major part in shaping the golden age of Canadian foreign policy after the war.

In the eighties, a decline began, caused in part by the rise of university centres on foreign policy, the luring of business support to the partisan Business Council on National Issues (later the Canadian Council of Chief Executives), and the decline of the department of external affairs as the central agency for Canadian engagement with the world. The research component of the CIIA, which dominated the field in the postwar years, disappeared by the 1990s. The organization remained with a weak central office and numerous branches which maintained the tradition of non-partisan public debate on international issues.

A member of the International Board of Governors of CIGI, Andres Rozental, and a member of its operational board, Ken Cork, were deeply influential in drawing my attention to the embarrassing weakness of Canada's premier institute. Ken had been a member of the CIIA board in its better days and Andres was the president of the Mexican Council on Foreign Relations. Andres told me that Canada could not participate in the international meetings of institutes of international affairs even though much smaller countries did. Ken reminded me of what the CIIA had been. At their suggestion, I gave 1 million CAD to reinvigorate the CIIA. But I soon learned it was not enough to build the solid organization with an emphasis on non-partisan, fact-based research. As a result, I began negotiations with the CIIA board to create a new institution that built upon its illustrious path while shaping a new organization appropriate to the networked, digital world of the present.

An internal evaluation of the CIIA recommended that a new name be chosen to mark the departure from the past and to signal the arrival of a new and powerful voice. We chose the Canadian International Council. It benefited from the remainder of my personal donation, but we also began in 2007 an annual fundraising dinner which honoured the "Globalist of the Year." The dinner has been highly successful, raising almost 3 million CAD the first year and almost 2 million CAD each succeeding year despite worse economic times. It has allowed the CIC to develop a solid research program and to express a clear mission, which is expressed in the following statement issued at its foundation.

- *The CIC is a non-partisan, nationwide research council established to strengthen Canada's foreign policy. It promotes research and dialogue on international affairs issues through a network that crosses academic disciplines, policy areas and economic sectors. The privately funded CIC research program features a number of dedicated working groups and promotes competitively selected research fellows who focus on Canada's most important foreign policy issues and work out of universities and research institutions across the country.*
- *The CIC's council activities offer Canadian corporate, academic, media, and policy communities the opportunity to participate in an important forum on international issues, operating on the premise that the application of expert and evidence-based research on complex international issues provides the cornerstone for effective policy making.*
- *The CIC is a unique, nation-wide foreign council that incorporates the voices and feedback of citizens across the country through its branch network, currently numbering fifteen from coast to*

*coast, that engage local communities with programs that involve
speakers, seminars, roundtable discussions and conferences as well
as study groups that generate citizen dialogue and involvement in
international affairs.*

At the CIC's inaugural dinner in 2007, I indicated how I believed that
the CIC built upon my earlier efforts to establish a world class think tank.

- *A partnership between CIGI, the Canadian Institute for International
  Affairs (CIIA) and the Canadian International Council will be housed
  at the University of Toronto.*
- *The creation of the CIC is a further, promising step down the
  path that started with the launch of the Centre for International
  Governance Innovation (CIGI) in Waterloo, in 2002.*
- *CIGI's global governance mandate will be a strong complement to
  the CIC.*
- *The CIC will provide a uniquely Canadian approach to the world.*
- *Canada can only be effective and coherent on the international
  stage if the decisions Canadians make – public policy and private
  enterprise – integrate evidence-based insights and understanding.*
- *Successful Canadian business leaders are worldly-wise, but few
  would describe themselves as foreign policy experts.*
- *At the same time, our experts sometimes lack clear, actionable goals.*
- *I would add that I suspect that significant research is often
  undertaken in Canada , but that it is not always effectively
  integrated into business decision-making or distributed to the proper
  government channels.*
- *As a comprehensive foreign policy research network devoted
  exclusively to Canadian interests and Canadian values, CIC can
  improve both public and private decision-making in Canada.*

The CIC's initial research program aimed to identify major foreign
policy issues and challenges and outline the best possible recommendations
to help build Canada's strategic foreign policy position on those issues.
Each research area was aimed to generate high-end, empirically valid
research and foreign policy advice grounded in scholarship.

- Arctic sovereignty and security
- Border issues
- Canada and the Americas
- Canada-India relations
- China and emerging large powers
- Energy
- International financial crisis
- Strategic studies

These issues framed the research in 2007 and 2008, and many research papers and briefing notes were produced. Our research in China, the area of focus in 2008, attracted wide national attention, and our research and our giving of the Globalist of the Year award to Chung Suewie, an eminent Chinese public figure, played a role in changing Canada's policy towards China.

In 2009 the CIC undertook a major project to establish a "Global Positioning System" for Canada for the next decade. Recognizing the fundamental shifts in the international system caused by the rise of emerging powers and the financial crisis, the CIC took the lead in an evaluation of those events upon Canada and Canadian foreign policy. Edward Greenspon, the former editor-in-chief of Canada' national newspaper, The Globe and Mail, is the director of the project. A panel of younger Canadians will guide him in his work. The report is due on the eve of the meetings of the G-8 and G-20 in Canada in June 2010.

This heightened activity has brought new members to the CIC and the establishment of new branches including one in Winnipeg, the site of one of the first branches of the CIIA, and Quebec City, which housed the francophone wing of the CIIA in earlier times. Finally, Canada is developing a voice to join the conversations among national institutes of international affairs.

## The Balsillie School of International Affairs

When CIGI was established, we took advantage of the proximity of the neighbouring universities and drew upon some of their faculty for leadership positions in the new think tank. The University of Waterloo and Wilfrid Laurier were enthusiastic participants in the creation of the new think tank. Although CIGI was independent, its early successes depended on the leverage that was available from the presence of two strong post-secondary institutions.

CIGI's leadership recognized that the universities were necessary partners for CIGI to build capacity. Initial talks began in 2005 about the possibility of establishing new chairs at the two universities. These discussions gave rise to the idea of a new school of international affairs, which would be a joint effort of the two universities. The result was the Balsillie School of International Affairs, a collaboration of Waterloo and Wilfrid Laurier in cooperation with CIGI. When the decision was made to establish the school, the City of Waterloo, after discussions with CIGI and the universities, agreed to lease the land beside the CIGI site for a new school.

In the summer of 2009, the construction of the new school began. Initially planned as a modest 25,000 square foot building, now planned as a structure of over 100,000 square feet. There are also plans for a LLM program and other initiatives in a second building on the site. I made a further donation which permitted an expansion of the initial six chairs. We expect there will be eighteen chairs at the new Balsillie School. Most have already been recruited, and the recruits include prominent international scholars. It is already the largest graduate school of international affairs in Canada, and its faculty ranks with the finest schools in the world. The students, many of them supported by Balsillie Fellowships in international affairs, are mainly international and have outstanding backgrounds. The school will complement CIGI in its work and will make Waterloo the "place to go" for informed opinion and lively discussion about foreign affairs in Canada.

The Balsillie School mission statement incorporates the principles which have guided my philanthropy:

> *The Balsillie School of International Affairs is an institution devoted to the study of international affairs and global governance. Home to a critical mass of extraordinary experts, the school provides students with an interdisciplinary learning environment in which they develop knowledge and expertise of international issues from the core disciplines of political science, economics, history, environmental studies and other related fields. Students will be prepared for careers in teaching and research in the field of international affairs, as well as for a growing range of careers within national governments, international organizations, the non-government sector, and the private sector.*

It's all about building capacity. Policy research and education are important and the Balsillie School will fill a major need. It is vitally important that we Canadians understand the world if we are to protect ourselves, and others, from its dangers and profit from its opportunities.

The Balsillie School will complement CIGI by attracting scholars and experts from across Canada and around the world, as the two universities build a world-class institution to understand world-scale problems and to educate generations of students to have a cosmopolitan appreciation of the world. The Centre for International Governance Innovation, working with the Balsillie School, in cooperation with the CIC will grow and mature as an international centre of excellence that generates evidence-based policy advice for the people of this city and province, for the Government of Canada and for the world at large.

So much has happened in so little time. But the need is urgent. My concern is not simply for Canada and its role in the world. I have turned so much of my energy and my funds to the creation of institutions and leaders prepared to face the overwhelming challenges of our time: climate change, inequality, militarism, terrorism, financial uncertainty, and international institutional weakness. With partners and friends, I have tried to create a Canadian voice in the world that is informed, articulate, generous, and powerful. The times are tough, the need is great, and my commitment is deep.

# About the Editors

# Norine MacDonald QC, President of the NEF-Mercator Fund

Norine MacDonald QC is President of the NEF-Mercator Fund, an initiative of the Network of European Foundations (NEF), which brings together twelve of Europe's leading philanthropic organisations. In 2008, Ms MacDonald co-edited *Philanthropy in Europe: A rich past, a promising future* (Alliance Publishing Trust, 2008) with Luc Tayart de Borms, Managing Director of the King Baudouin Foundation. She is also the President of the International Council on Security and Development, (ICOS), a project of the Network of European Foundations' Mercator Fund working on grassroots research and policy innovation at the intersections of security, development, counter-narcotics and public health. Ms MacDonald also leads the group's research work in conflict zones including Afghanistan, Iraq and Somalia. Her work has been featured in many international print, radio, and television media outlets. In February 2007, Norine MacDonald was awarded the First Class Medal of Merit of the Italian Red Cross for outstanding contribution to international humanitarian cooperation.

# Luc Tayart de Borms, Managing Director of the King Baudouin Foundation

Luc Tayart de Borms' experience in the foundation sector makes him one of today's influential players in the global philanthropic community. Author of *Foundations: Creating Impact in a Globalised World* (Wiley 2005), and co-editor of *Philanthropy in Europe: A rich past, a promising future* (Alliance Publishing Trust 2008), Mr Tayart has over twenty years experience in the foundation sector. In addition to his current role as Managing Director of the King Baudouin Foundation in Belgium, Mr Tayart is also the Treasurer of the Network of European Foundations, a member of the Advisory Council of the European Policy Centre, Trustee at the European Venture Philanthropy Association and Chair of Guidestar International. International recognition of Mr Tayart's contribution to the foundation sector has been demonstrated in his role as President (2000-2002) of the European Foundation Centre, member of the Board of Directors of the Council on Foundations (2002-2005), and his former position as President of The Hague Club, as well as many other senior foundation roles.

# About the Authors

# Olga Alexeeva

Olga Alexeeva is Head of Charities Aid Foundation Global Trustees (CAF GT), a division of Charities Aid Foundation (CAF) focussing on the development of private and family giving in the world. Prior to this, Olga Alexeeva worked for twelve years in the Russian office of CAF, serving as Director for seven years. Under Olga's leadership CAF Russia grew to become one of the largest and fastest-growing grant-making foundations in the country. Olga and her team provided advisory support in the creation of over 80 percent of Russian private foundations. She is author of four books on civil society and philanthropy in Russia: *Who helps children* (CAF, 1994), *Charities in Russian regions* (CAF, 1995), *Third Sector or Charity for Beginners* (BBC, 1997), *History of trust in distrustful times* (EKSMO Publishing, 2007), one of the authors of the publication *Working with the non profit sector in Russia* (Kluger Publishing, 1999), and the author of over one hundred articles and research publications.

# Jim Balsillie

Jim Balsillie has been Co-Chief Executive Officer of Research In Motion (RIM), since 1992. At RIM, Jim is responsible for driving corporate strategy, business development, marketing, sales, and finance. The success of RIM and its flagship BlackBerry® wireless solution has provided Jim with the opportunity to give back to his community and country. In 2002, he established the Centre for International Governance Innovation and in 2007 Jim founded the Balsillie School of International Affairs and the Canadian International Council. Additionally, Jim is a founding donor of the Perimeter Institute for Theoretical Physics and a patron of the Grand River Hospital. Jim received an honorary Doctor of Laws degree from Wilfrid Laurier University, University of Toronto and Dalhousie University, and was also elected a Fellow of the Institute of Chartered Accountants of Ontario.

# Namık Ceylanoğlu

Namık Ceylanoğlu studied at the Middle East Technical University and Ankara University. He worked as the investment expert of the General Directorate of Highways for several years before he joined the Koc Group of companies and worked under the logistics and investment areas. Later he served as the General Manager of the Turkish Education Foundation. Mr Ceylanoglu has been the General Secretary of TÜSEV (Third Sector Foundation of Turkey) since 1999. His experience with civil society organisations began thirty-five years ago and he has been involved in many local and international projects concerning the right to information, civic rights and institutionalising civil society organisations. He was also among the founders of the Turkish chapter of the Lions Clubs International District 118-U. Currently, he is involved in training and research projects on the Turkish NGO law in comparison to European Union legislation. Mr Ceylanoğlu is married and has two sons.

# Tariq H. Cheema

Dr Tariq H. Cheema is the founder of the World Congress of Muslim Philanthropists. He received his MD from the University of Istanbul in 1992, and earned a Certificate of Advanced Study in Philanthropy at Loyola University Chicago. Dr Cheema co-founded Doctors Worldwide, a medical and disaster relief agency; Indo-Pak Peace Network, a diaspora movement to promote goodwill among two rival nations; and Diversity Forums, a project to encourage dialogue and understanding across critical social divides. Dr Cheema is the recipient of several awards recognising his service. He is the Executive Director of the Association of Physicians of Pakistani-descent of North America and serves on the Boards of Chicago Global Donors Network and the HEED Foundation, Pakistan. Dr Cheema ranks among the five hundred most influential Muslims in the world according to a study released by Georgetown University in 2009.

# Peter Cleaves

Peter Cleaves is the CEO of the Emirates Foundation. He has been engaged in international development, philanthropy, research administration and the private sector for over thirty years. Mr Cleaves, a US citizen, has most recently been executive director of the AVINA Foundation, the largest private foreign foundation operating in Latin America, with a capital fund of over 1 billion USD. He was previously Director of the Institute of Latin American Studies and Director of the Center for the Study of Western Hemispheric Trade at the University of Texas. He earlier served with the Ford Foundation as representative for Mexico and Central America and for several years was a corporate banker at First Chicago. Peter Cleaves has authored or co-authored five books. He speaks – and lectures in – English, French, Spanish and Portuguese. He has a PhD in Political Science from the University of California, Berkeley, an MA from Vanderbilt University and a BA from Dartmouth College.

# Rayna Gavrilova

Rayna Gavrilova is the Executive Director of the Trust for Civil Society in Central and Eastern Europe. Rayna holds an MA and PhD in History from the University of Sofia, Bulgaria and teaches at the same university. She was a Fulbright fellow in Harvard University; research fellow at the Annenberg Institute in Philadelphia and at the Maison des Sciences de l'Homme in Paris; and visiting professor in Macalister College, Saint Paul, Minnesota. In 2000 Professor Gavrilova was appointed Deputy Minister of Culture in the Bulgarian government. In 2001 she became the Executive Director of the Open Society Institute, Sofia and in 2005 the Executive Director of the Trust for Civil Society in Central and Eastern Europe. Rayna Gavrilova is a member of the Capacity Building Committee of the European Foundation Centre and of the International Committee of the Council on Foundations.

# Jennifer Gill

Jennifer Gill is the Chief Executive Officer of the ASB Community Trust in Auckland, New Zealand. Her career in philanthropy began in 1985 when Sir Roy McKenzie appointed her as the Executive Officer of his personal foundation. Over the next two decades Jennifer was appointed as a Trustee of the J R McKenzie Trust, and a number of smaller family grant-making trusts. She has chaired the J R McKenzie Trust and the Wellington Regional Community Foundation. She was a founding Board member of both the Funding Information Service and of Philanthropy New Zealand where she has just completed a five year term as Chair. Jennifer has been a Board member of the Asia Pacific Philanthropy Consortium since 2007.

# Rui Hermenegildo Gonçalves

Mr Gonçalves has been deputy of the Office of the President at the Calouste Gulbenkian Foundation since 2003. He graduated in Law from Coimbra University in 1999, and is currently a PhD student at the New University of Lisbon, preparing a thesis on foundation law. He was a lecturer on the tax law of non-profit organisations at the Portuguese Catholic University between 1996 and 1997. Since 2002, he has been a member of the Portuguese Bar Association. His recent publications include a study on *Foundations and the European Union's Law* (2008), with Emílio Rui Vilar, and a compilation of legislation on the non-profit sector (2006), with Raquel Campos Franco. Mr Gonçalves held a Marshall Memorial Fellowship from the German Marshall Fund of the United States, in 2004. He held a solo exhibition of his photographic work at Trem Azul, Lisbon, in 2009.

# Trevor Gray

Trevor Gray is currently Manager of the Tindall Foundation, one of the largest family foundations in Australasia, a position he has held for the past seven years. Trevor comes from a diverse background including education, agriculture, management consultancy and community enterprise and development, primarily in the socially disadvantaged Far North of New Zealand. Trevor's main interests are community-led development, social entrepreneurship, climate change and sustainability. He and his wife Mary have four children and two grandchildren and now slave on a lifestyle block outside of Auckland.

# Shamsh Kassim-Lakha

Dr Shamsh Kassim-Lakha's wide and varied experience in the private sector and in public service have given him a deep understanding of the nature of the political, social and economic factors and cultural and religious sensitivities that influence policymaking in South and Central Asia, the Middle East and Sub-Saharan Africa. How these can be addressed in practical terms for improving the lives of people around the globe has been part of his life-time goal. He served as Founding President of the Aga Khan University for twenty-seven years. Later he served as Pakistan's Minister of Education. Dr Kassim-Lakha is the founder and current Chair of the Board of the Pakistan Centre for Philanthropy. He also sits on the Higher Education Commission of Pakistan and on the Board of International Baccalaureate Organization. He has received the degree of Doctor of Laws, *honoris causa* from McMaster University of Canada as well as awards from the Presidents of Pakistan and France.

# Steve Killelea

Steve Killelea, Chairman and founder of Integrated Research Ltd, has over thirty years experience in the information technology industry. Highly skilled in international marketing, business and product strategy, he has developed two highly profitable global companies with exceptional track records. He established his own private foundation (TCF) in 2000. The aim of TCF is to substantially change the lives of as many people as possible with special emphasis on targeting the poorest of the poor. TCF is one of the largest private charities in Australia focused on developing countries. Steve is also the founder of the Institute for Economics and Peace, a research institute focused on understanding the relationships between peace, economic development and business, and of the Global Peace Index, the first ever tool for measuring the peacefulness of countries and identifying the drivers of peace.

# Atallah Kuttab

Dr Kuttab holds a PhD in civil engineering from the University of London. He spent three years working in engineering consulting in the private sector and ten years in education in planning, teaching and research at Birzeit University in Palestine and at Heriot-Watt University in Scotland. Dr Kuttab was a GTZ technical consultant for informal sector employment in Zambia for three years, and served with Save the Children for eleven years, most recently as Middle East Regional Manager. His management specialty areas are in staff management, fundraising and in forging private sector/non-government sector relationships to further development efforts. He joined the Welfare Association as the Director General in August 2005 supporting Palestinians primarily in Palestine and Lebanon. He is a Founding Member of the Arab Human Rights Fund and of the Arab Foundations Forum. He also serves on the Editorial Board of Alliance Magazine and on the WINGS Coordination Committee.

# Sujin Kwon

Dr Sujin Kwon is a Program Officer who leads the Toyota Foundation's Asian Neighbours Program. The Asian Neighbours Program supports activities across Asia and the wider world, which bring broad and long-term benefits to society in various program areas, such as document translation and publication, indigenous document preservation and utilisation, and skill-training programs for young researchers. Raised in Kyeong-Ju, Korea, Dr Kwon moved to Japan to study Political Science in the University of Ritsumeikan. She has previously been a spokesperson of the Kyoto prefecture, providing information activities on Korean cultures and history to the public in Kyoto, and has volunteered at FM COCOLO, a multilingual radio station, as an announcer. She has administered a volunteer project called "Common Ground", which provides foreign students with an opportunity to interact with their local community through social activities.

# Michael Madnick

Since March 2010, Michael has been the Deputy Executive Director of the Global Alliance for Improved Nutrition, a Swiss foundation dedicated to ending malnutrition worldwide. During the writing of his chapter, Michael served as Deputy Director in the Global Health Policy and Advocacy division of the Bill and Melinda Gates Foundation. In this role, Michael oversaw external relations, furthering the Foundation's Global Health government, multilateral, and private sector relationships, as well as relations with emerging donors globally. He previously served as Senior Vice President of the United Nations Foundation, where he institutionalised an organisation-wide partnership strategy to generate additional financial and other support for UN causes. Michael, his wife Angela, and their daughter Tess reside in Washington, DC.

# Vincent McGee

Vincent McGee is a long-time foundation executive and donor advisor. He has been Senior Advisor at The Atlantic Philanthropies since 2007. He was Vice President of the Irene Diamond Fund (1991 - 2002), Executive Director and Secretary of the Aaron Diamond Foundation (1985 until 1996). He was on the Board of Amnesty International, United States, for over ten years and was its Chair for two years. He was Board Chair of The Overbrook Foundation (2008 and 2009), sits on a number of foundation Boards and that of PATH, A Catalyst for Global Health, and two committees of the European Foundation Centre, has been a member of Rockefeller University Council since 1988 and the Board of Overseers of Smolny College of the State University of St Petersburg, Russia, since 2008. He graduated from the University of Rochester and received an honorary Doctor of Law degree from the Graduate Center of the City University of New York in 2003. Mr McGee lives in New York City.

# Karen Menichelli

Karen Menichelli served for many years as Executive Vice President of the Benton Foundation, a private grant-making institution operating primarily in the field of communications, focusing on media policy and public service media. In 2006, she stepped down from her day-to-day leadership to focus on programmatic activity in the area of community media. She now serves as Program Liaison to the foundation's new community media re-granting program, New Routes to Community Health. Active in the philanthropic community for over twenty years, Karen was a founding Board member of the Washington Regional Association of Grantmakers, served on committees and task forces of the Council on Foundations, and was founding Board member and Treasurer of the Communications Network.

# Zeynep Meydanoğlu

Zeynep Meydanoğlu is currently Program Director at TÜSEV (Third Sector Foundation of Turkey) which aims to strengthen the legal, fiscal and operational infrastructure of the non-profit sector in Turkey. She is also an Executive Board member of KA-DER (Association for the Support and Preparation of Women in Politics). Zeynep has authored, co-authored and co-edited a number of articles and reports on civil society in Turkey. She has also participated in designing and implementing a number of civil society strengthening initiatives. Zeynep also had the privilege to be the first Turkish NGO representative to be awarded the European Citizen Action Service Scholarship. Born and raised in Istanbul, Turkey, Zeynep has a double Bachelor of Arts degree in Political Science and Cultural Studies from McGill University, Montreal, Canada.

# Bhekinkosi Moyo

Dr Moyo joined TrustAfrica in March 2007 as a Research Fellow and became Program Director in May 2009. Known for his expertise in philanthropy, civil society, and governance, he holds a doctorate in political science from the University of the Witwatersrand in South Africa. He previously worked at the Africa Institute of South Africa and at the Institute for Democracy in South Africa. He has written and published more than fifteen conference papers, journal articles, and book chapters and co-edited *What About the Children: The Silent Voices in Maintenance* (2004), which explores issues of poverty, abuse, and the social security system in South Africa in the twenty-first century. His latest collection of edited articles, *Africa in the Global Power Play: Debates, Challenges and Potential Reforms* (Adonis & Abbey, London, 2007), addresses the current position of Africa in international political and economic relations. He is fluent in English and working on his French.

# Tamzin Ractliffe

Tamzin Ractliffe worked both in South Africa and internationally in financial services, asset management and venture capital for more than a decade before returning to South Africa after the 1994 elections to address the need for services to facilitate more effective utilisation of social investment capital and development finance. She established Funding South Africa, a corporate social investment services consultancy, in 1997 and in 1999 created the first South African online development networking platform, which in 2004 became GreaterGood South Africa. For the past eighteen months, Tamzin has focused on establishing NeXii – a NeXus for Impact Investment worldwide, and GSIX - The Global Federation for Social Investment Exchanges. GSIX is an independent federation of national and regional social investment exchanges which provides members with support, standards and a public voice.

# Fernando Rossetti

Fernando Rossetti has been Secretary-General of GIFE (Group of Institutes, Foundations and Enterprises) since 2005 and is Chairman of WINGS (Worldwide Initiatives for Grantmaker Support). Having studied Social Sciences at Unicamp (State University of Campinas, Brazil), he worked from 1990 to 1999 for the main Brazilian daily newspaper, Folha de S. Paulo, as education reporter and correspondent in South Africa (1994-95). In 1997 he attended the Human Rights Advocates Training Program, at Columbia University, New York. He was one of the founders and, for four years, Executive Director of the NGO Aprendiz (www.aprendiz.org.br). He also acted as consultant for many national and international organisations, such as UNICEF, for whom he wrote the book *Media and School: Perspectives for Public Policies*. He has also been a commentator on education public policies at the Futura Chanel since 1997, and is a Senior Fellow of the Synergos Institute and AVINA Foundation.

# Gerry Salole

Gerry Salole has been Chief Executive of the European Foundation Centre, an association of over two hundred and thirty public-benefit foundations and corporate funders active in philanthropy in Europe and elsewhere, since 2005. He previously served as representative of the Ford Foundation's Southern Africa office and director of the Department of Programme Documentation and Communication of the Bernard van Leer Foundation. He has also worked for Save the Children Federation (USA) in Ethiopia and Zimbabwe, and Norwegian Save the Children, OXFAM UK, and UNHCR in Ethiopia. Mr Salole studied Social Anthropology and African History at the School of Oriental and African Studies, University of London. He holds an MA (Econ.) and PhD from the University of Manchester. He is the Chair of TrustAfrica, an independent private foundation set up in Senegal in 2006 to promote peace, economic prosperity, and social justice throughout the continent. He also serves on the Board of Alliance Publishing Trust in Foundation.

# Michael Seltzer

Michael Seltzer is a leading strategist and advisor on creative, innovative grant-making strategies. In a career that spans more than forty years, he has worked at the Ford Foundation, the New World Foundation, the American Freedom from Hunger Foundation, the Funding Exchange, and the Bread and Roses Community Fund. At the Ford Foundation, he was responsible for promoting organised philanthropy around the world. Most recently, he served as the president of the New York Regional Association of Grantmakers (now known as Philanthropy New York). He also is a well -known pioneer in the field of nonprofit management. He is the author of *Securing Your Organisation's Future* (The Foundation Center), writes regularly on Philantopic, the Foundation Center's blog, and has lectured widely around the world. He is a trustee of EMpower – The Emerging Markets Foundation, and a board member of the Forum of the Regional Associations of Grantmakers. He is in charge of philanthropic services at Rabin Strategic Partners, a global consulting firm.

# Maria Alice Setubal

Maria Alice Setubal earned a degree in sociology and an MA in the field of Political Sciences from the University of São Paulo. She received a doctorate in Educational Psychology at the Pontifical Catholic University of São Paulo. She is President of the Tide Setubal Foundation and the Centre for Studies and Research into Education, Culture and Community Action.

# Dina Sherif

Dina Sherif has been the Associate Director of the John D. Gerhart Center for Philanthropy and Civic Engagement since it was established in 2006 at the American University in Cairo. Further to that, she also frequently consults with companies based in the Arab region with regards to their corporate social responsibility efforts. Prior to her position at the John D. Gerhart Center, she was the Deputy Director of Projects at Financial Technical Consulting Services, a consultancy firm that specialises in rural development in sub-Saharan Africa. Ms Sherif also has wide-ranging experience in development at the local level in Egypt through her work at the Institute for Cultural Affairs in the Middle East and North Africa, and her work at Environmental Quality International. Ms Sherif is co–editor and contributing author of the book *From Charity to Social Change: Trends in Arab Philanthropy* (Volume I) (American University in Cairo Press, 2008) and is also a contributing author to Volume II of the same book, due to be published in 2010.

# Laura Silber

Laura Silber is Director of Public Affairs at the Open Society Institute, where she runs the Communications Department and plays a leading role in advocacy. Prior to joining OSI in 2000, Ms Silber was a contributing writer at Talk magazine and covered the United Nations for the Financial Times. From 1990 to 1997 she was the Financial Times Balkans correspondent. She was also an Independent Project Fellow at OSI and a visiting scholar at the Remarque Institute at New York University. From 1987-1989, she was a Fulbright Scholar in Yugoslavia. She is the co-author of the critically acclaimed *Yugoslavia: Death of a Nation* (Penguin, 1997), which was selected a New York Times notable book in 1996. She was series consultant to the accompanying television documentary series, "The Fall of Milosevic", which won the duPont Gold Baton and Peabody awards.

# Rory Francisco-Tolentino

Rory Francisco-Tolentino was, until August 2008, Chief Executive of the Asia Pacific Philanthropy Consortium (APPC). Most of her professional life has been spent in non-profit and philanthropy work. She is currently a consultant for philanthropies and non-profit organisations. Rory would like to acknowledge the valuable support of Alexie Ferreria-Mercado, APPC Program Officer and Tina Villadolid-Pavia, former APPC Program Officer.

The Asia Pacific Philanthropy Consortium is an independent association of grant-making philanthropic institutions and organisations that support the growth and development of philanthropy in the Asia Pacific region. Since 1994, APPC has built up an excellent and unique platform for leaders in the philanthropy sector to exchange ideas and share best practices. Its mission is to increase the quality and quantity of philanthropy for Asia by strengthening the institutional infrastructure and improving the operating environment for the philanthropy sector. To achieve this mission, APPC serves as catalyst, convener and network builder.

APPC

ASIA PACIFIC PHILANTHROPY CONSORTIUM

# Denis Tracey

Denis Tracey worked in the field of philanthropy and social investment for more than ten years. He has written books on family business *Family Business; the Volatile Mix of Money, Power and Love*, (Information Australia 2001) and on philanthropy *Giving it Away; in Praise of Philanthropy* (Scribe 2003) as well as many reports, conference papers, and media articles, on these and other topics. He has taught, researched and consulted in the field of philanthropy and fundraising at Swinburne University of Technology, Melbourne and the University of Sydney. He was founding CEO of Family Business Australia, of the Constitutional Centenary Foundation and of the Melbourne Community Foundation. He has been a professional musician, a barge captain in France and a delivery driver for Maserati cars.

# Emílio Rui Vilar

Since 2002, Emílio Rui Vilar has been President of the Board of Trustees of Calouste Gulbenkian Foundation, and Chairman of the Board of Directors of Partex Oil and Gas (Holdings) Corporation. He also serves as President of the Portuguese Foundation Centre; Chairman of the European Foundation Centre; and Co-Chairman of the Portuguese-Spanish Forum. From 1998 to 2005 he was Guest Professor at the School of Economics and Management, Portuguese Catholic University (1998-2005). He has had an extensive career in business and politics, and has served as Chairman of Banco de Portugal's Audit Commission since 1996. Between 1989 and 1996 he was Chairman and CEO of Caixa Geral de Depósitos (National Savings Bank). He previously served as General Commissioner Europalia Portugal (1989-1992), Director General, European Commission, (1986-1989), Deputy Governor of Banco de Portugal (1975-1984), Portuguese Minister of Transport and Communications (1976-1978), Minister of the Economy of Portugal (1974-1975), and Portuguese Secretary of State for External Trade and Tourism (1974). Mr Rui Vilar graduated in Law from Coimbra University in 1961.

# Jane Wales

Jane Wales is CEO of the World Affairs Council and the Global Philanthropy Forum and Vice President of the Aspen Institute. She is host of the National Public Radio show, "It's Your World". She served as Acting CEO of The Elders, chaired by Archbishop Desmond Tutu, and in 2008, chaired the Poverty Alleviation Track for the Clinton Global Initiative. She served in the Clinton Administration as Senior Director of the National Security Council and Associate Director of the White House Office of Science and Technology Policy. She chaired the international security programs at the Carnegie Corporation of New York and the W. Alton Jones Foundation, and directed the Project on World Security at the Rockefeller Brothers Fund.

# Ailing Zhuang

Dr Ailing Zhuang has committed herself for twenty years to philanthropy, having worked for both a Chinese NGO (the Amity Foundation) as Program Director and for INGOs (Orbis International and the Christian Blind Mission International). She founded the NPO Development Center in Shanghai in 2004, one of the very few pioneers committed to capacity building for non-profit organisations in mainland China. She has published many articles on third sector issues in books, magazines, newspapers, and websites. She is the first person from a Chinese non-profit organisation to speak at the World Bank headquarters and Harvard University. Due to her outstanding contribution to the development of philanthropy in China, she was presented with the "2008 China Philanthropy Award" by the National Government.

# Jane Francis, Alexander Jackson and Shivani Satija

Jane Francis and Alexander Jackson are Project Coordinators for the Network of European Foundations' Mercator Fund. Their input focuses on supporting and facilitating the work of the NEF-Mercator Fund in its endeavour to create spaces and opportunities to work on new, more effective approaches to security, development and counter-narcotics, and to bring together the global philanthropic community to take leadership on sensitive and chronically stalled issues. Shivani Satija worked with the NEF-Mercator Fund in India until October 2009, collaborating with the Sir Ratan Tata Trust on an innovative project on food security. Jane, Alexander and Shivani prepared the chapter on the Trust through conducting research and interviews with the Sir Ratan Tata Trust.

# The Network of European Foundations' Mercator Fund

The global philanthropic community has a vital role to play in promoting and implementing the work necessary to bring about social and political change. By developing projects on core global social issues, the objective of the NEF-Mercator Fund is to generate innovative ideas to respond to key global challenges.

Taking into account this goal, the NEF-Mercator Fund works on a series of projects to address policy issues of pressing global relevance, such as the International Council on Security and Development, the Rome Consensus for a Humanitarian Drug Policy and the Centre of Excellence on Public Security.

The NEF-Mercator Fund is also engaged in a series of projects which have the goal of supporting the core architecture of philanthropy, such as a series of books on the subject, its Ease of Global Giving project and the Raymond Georis Prize for Innovative Philanthropy in Europe.

www.mercatorfund.net

## Other NEF-Mercator Fund publications

*Foundations: Creating Impact in a Globalised World* (Wiley, 2005), Luc Tayart de Borms

*Philanthropy in Europe: A rich past, a promising future* (Alliance Publishing Trust 2008), Norine MacDonald QC and Luc Tayart de Borms

## Current projects of the NEF-Mercator Fund

**Ease of Global Giving**

Current laws and regulations are not sufficiently developed to allow the free flow of philanthropic funding across borders. It is vital to develop an enabling regulatory environment that supports global institutional philanthropic work. The NEF-Mercator Fund's Ease of Global Giving project aims to develop a Standard Global Protocol of general principles to guide the regulation of global giving.

**THE RAYMOND GEORIS PRIZE**

**for innovative Philanthropy in Europe**

The Raymond Georis Prize for Innovative Philanthropy in Europe was established by the NEF-Mercator Fund to reward an individual, organisation, foundation or project which has conceived and implemented an outstanding and innovative philanthropic programme in Europe.

www.mercatorfund.net/modules/awards

**ICⓄS** THE INTERNATIONAL COUNCIL
ON SECURITY AND DEVELOPMENT

The International Council on Security and Development is an international policy think tank working to combine grassroots research and policy innovation at the intersections of security, development, counter-narcotics and public health issues. Through a unique mix of field research, reports and project implementation, ICOS examines the root causes of current crises, and works to achieve measurable and direct policy results.

www.icosgroup.net

**ROME CONSENSUS**
FOR A HUMANITARIAN DRUG POLICY

Since 2005, the NEF-Mercator Fund has supported the Rome Consensus for a Humanitarian Drug policy, a framework for dialogue and cooperation that commits 121 National Societies of Red Cross and Red Crescent from Africa, Asia, the Americas and Europe to promote and implement humanitarian approaches to drug policy. The Rome Consensus aims at raising the profile of drug policy to the forefront of social concerns, focussing drug policy formulation and implementation on public health concerns.

www.romeconsensus.net

**CENTRE OF EXCELLENCE** ▬▬▬▬▬▬▬▬
▬▬▬▬▬▬▬▬**ON PUBLIC SECURITY**

Based in Rio de Janeiro, the Centre of Excellence on Public Security (CEPS) identifies global challenges for public security in the twenty-first century, and provides innovative research, advocacy and policy analysis to promote pragmatic responses. It supports states to solve public security crises and pave the way for social and economic development.

www.publicsecurity.icosgroup.net

## Global Food Security
## ▮▮▮▮ Initiative

The NEF-Mercator Fund, in collaboration with the Sir Ratan Tata Trust and CINI, is developing a new project examining the intersections between food security, development, and state security. The project currently has its focus on India and Brazil, as two countries that are widely affected by these issues. This tri-phased project – comprising a knowledge management portal, an international symposium, and comparative research - will draw attention to the issues and will help to develop a food security community of foundations.

# theglobalmediacentre

The Global Media Centre was created by the Network of European Foundations Mercator Fund to provide the specialised advocacy and media outreach work that the policy-making and philanthropic community needs. Its objective is to provide assistance in reconciling philanthropic, policy, academic, scientific, and social objectives with the need for a 'media friendly' story, developing and tailoring messages to resonate with key decision-makers.

www.theglobalmediacentre.com

# The Network of European Foundations (NEF)

The Network of European Foundations (NEF) is a compact and flexible not-for-profit international organisation located in Brussels.

Comprising twelve foundations, NEF acts as an operational platform for the development of joint initiatives by foundations and other types of organised philanthropy as well as other giving programmes related to Europe and the role of Europe on the global stage.

NEF was created to strengthen the potential for cooperation between foundations at European level. It provides its members with the ability to identify common goals and, as an open structure, to join forces with other foundations in Europe which may share similar concerns and objectives.

www.nefic.org

European Cultural Foundation

www. eurocult.org

Compagnia di San Paolo

www. compagniadisanpaolo.it

Charles Stewart Mott
Foundation

www. mott.org

Joseph Rowntree Charitable
Trust

www. jrct.org.uk

European Foundation Centre
(Observer)

www.efc.be

Fondation de France

www. fondationdefrance.org

FUNDAÇÃO
CALOUSTE
GULBENKIAN
Fundação Calouste Gulbenkian

www.gulbenkian.pt

King Baudouin Foundation

www.kbfus.org

Institusjonen Fritt Ord

www.fritt-ord.no

Fondation Gabriel

Robert Bosch Stiftung
Robert Bosch Stiftung

www.bosch-stiftung.de

Bernard van Leer  Foundation

Van Leer Group Foundation,

www.vanleergroupfoundation.nl

Erste Stiftung

www.erstestiftung.org